Skills for Success

Personal Development and Employability

3rd edition

Stella Cottrell

macmillan education   palgrave

Askham Bryan College

First edition 2003
Second edition 2010
Third edition published 2015 by
PALGRAVE

Palgrave in the UK is an imprint of Macmillan Publishers Limited, registered in England, company number 785998, of 4 Crinan Street, London N1 9XW.

Palgrave Macmillan in the US is a division of St Martin's Press LLC, 175 Fifth Avenue, New York, NY 10010.

Palgrave is a global imprint of the above companies and is represented throughout the world.

Palgrave® and Macmillan® are registered trademarks in the United States, the United Kingdom, Europe and other countries.

ISBN: 978-1-137-42652-9

This book is printed on paper suitable for recycling and made from fully managed and sustained forest sources. Logging, pulping and manufacturing processes are expected to conform to the environmental regulations of the country of origin.

A catalogue record for this book is available from the British Library.

A catalog record for this book is available from the Library of Congress.

Printed in China

Contents

Introduction   1

Getting started; Personal development planning (PDP); Making the right choices; Taking and making opportunities; How it fits together

Part 1 Self-management   25

Defining success; Personal influences, inspiration and values; Vision, goals and motivation; Personal investment; Ingredients of success; Congruence and goal inertia; Taking and making opportunities

Your life narrative; Your top forty successes; Your learning history; Responding to setbacks; The Expertise Metaphor; Using personal expertise

Your personal performance and learning SHAPE; Evaluating factors in personal performance; Your personal performance profile; Identifying your Personal Performance Formula; Task-specific performance factors

SWOT analysis; Personal resources; Time management; Attitudes; Responsibility, self-belief and solution-focused thinking; Emotional intelligence; Managing distress, change, confusion and uncertainty; The Eight Levels framework

Part 2 Managing people and tasks   129

Evaluating your skills; Developing rapport, listening skills and mutual trust; Team work; Action sets; Constructive criticism; Assertiveness; Dealing with difficult people; Negotiating; Leadership

Evaluating your skills; Basic approaches and key steps to task management; Problem-solving approaches and techniques; Goals, criteria, priorities, targets, action plans and time planning; Starting and completing tasks; Projects; Performance indicators and benchmarks; Competitiveness

Part 3 Extend your thinking   191

Evaluating your creative thinking skills; Using your brain; Creative problem-solving techniques; Working with raw material; Creativity and risk taking

Reflection in everyday life, in PDP and as a practitioner; What is 'reflection'? Evaluating your own skills in reflection; Basic steps for reflection; Types of structured reflection; Transferring skills; 'Critical events'; Using feedback; Models of reflection; Developing your own model for reflection; Presenting your reflection to others

List of abbreviations

CEO   Chief Executive Officer

CPD   continual professional development

CV   curriculum vitae

CVCP   Committee of Vice Chancellors and Principals

HE   Higher Education

HEI   Higher Education Institutions

IiP   Investors in People

PDP   personal development planning

PI   performance indicators

QAA   Quality Assurance Agency

Acknowledgements

For this edition, I offer especial thanks to the following for their contributions to Chapter 10: Femi Bola MBE, Director of Careers and Employability, University of East London; Joanne Beaumont, Head of Careers and Employability, University of Bradford; Dr Bob Gilworth, Director of College Careers Services, University of London Careers Group; and Mohammed Hussain, Academic Guidance Officer, University of Leeds.

The author and publishers would also like to thank the following who have kindly given permission for the use of copyright material:

Shell (p. 254); Juergen Maier, Chief Executive, *Siemens Industry UK* (p. 257), and Danella Bagnall, Vehicle Architecture Planning Director, *Jaguar Land Rover* (p. 259), in *The Guardian UK 300*; Donna Miller, European HR Director, *Enterprise Rent-A-Car*, in *Which? University*; *Travers Smith LLP* (p. 258); *Tesco PLC* (p. 262); *RDS*, a *KCA Deutag Company* (p. 263); and *Heinz Company* (p. 264).

Introduction: taking charge of your life, learning and career

Shaping your future

- What would 'success' look like for you – as a student, in life and in your future career?
- What skills, experience and personal qualities would you need in order to achieve such success?
- Why do personal development and forward planning matter for your career prospects?
- What is meant by 'employability'? What do employers look for?
- How can you improve your personal performance and profile so that you 'stand out from the crowd'?

This book helps you consider such matters so that you can start planning effectively towards your future – even if you don't know for sure quite what you want.

What kind of future?

Your time as a student is a major step in your professional career.

When you graduate, you will be competing with millions of other graduates from around the world. Like you, they will be looking to stand out in a graduate employment market that is now global. The time you spend now in gaining a good degree, in nurturing your talents and building a distinctive personal profile, can make the difference in how far you achieve the life you want.

Make it happen

1 **Aspire.** Be ambitious for yourself. Aim high, considering the portfolio of jobs you might have over many years.

2 **Investigate.** Be well informed about the range of career and life options open to you – and how to access these.

3 **Reflect.** Increase your self-awareness: develop good habits of introspection, self-evaluation and self-questioning. Become more attuned to what matters most to you.

4 **Decide.** Put time aside to think through the implications of potential choices – and then choose a direction. Make decisions, as this brings focus to your planning and studies.

5 **Plan.** Map out what to do to have a good chance of achieving the life, career and academic success you want.

6 **Personalise.** Adapt your strategies to suit your individual combination of skills, strengths, experiences, interests, needs, preferences and style.

7 **Achieve.** Follow through on your plans, adapting these to suit changes in your interests and ambitions.

Getting started: initial steps

Step in the process	Rationale
Read *Getting started: the foundations* (page 3)	This provides you with some general tips for getting the most from personal development planning (PDP) and from this book.
▼	▼
Find out what is meant by personal development planning (pages 4–6)	This looks at why personal development planning is considered so important in higher education, and its relevance to your own life.
▼	▼
Consider the challenges (pages 8–9)	PDP doesn't tend to happen spontaneously, as we can see from the students' experiences on pages 8–9. Give thought to where the challenges would lie for you – so you can address them.
▼	▼
Identify the benefits (pages 10–11)	Typically, we tend to put off PDP and need to motivate ourselves to give it the time it deserves. This can be helped by identifying the personal benefits.
▼	▼
Do I need personal development planning? (page 12)	Complete the self-evaluation on page 12 as a means of beginning to identify your development needs.
▼	▼
Identify your priorities (pages 13–15)	Complete the self-evaluation on pages 13–15, to tease out in more detail your PDP priorities.
▼	▼
Make use of opportunities (pages 16–17)	Give active consideration to what opportunities are available to you, which you can make use of, and what you could create for yourself.
▼	▼
Develop a sense of how it all fits together (pages 18–23)	Read pages 18–23 to develop your understanding of how the different aspects of personal development planning fit together, the skills you will need, and what you can gain from the different chapters in this book.
▼	▼
Select, reflect and list	Choose one or more key priorities for yourself. Decide what the first steps are for taking these forward. Make a detailed 'To do' list of these.
▼	▼
Plan into a diary	Use your diary, calendar or planner to map out when, exactly, you will undertake the first few actions.

Getting started: the foundations

1 Give it time

Be prepared to give yourself the time you need to investigate, reflect upon and evaluate yourself, your studies and your future.

2 Engage

Bring the right mindset: be prepared to think, plan and act now for outcomes that might be many years away. In practice this means such things as:

- Taking responsibility for your future: it is up to you to think things through and take action
- Engaging with the seven aspects of the process listed on page 1
- Finding out as much as you can about your options
- Making decisions to give a focus to your planning and actions
- Using the tools available, such as the self-evaluation questionnaires, reflections and other activities in this book
- Monitoring your progress and keeping yourself on track
- Keeping updated records to demonstrate your skills and experience.

3 Experiment

Bring thought and self-awareness to the process:

- Have a go at using resources, strategies, models and activities that are available in the book and through your college or workplace.
- Combine and adapt these to suit you.
- Find out what works best for your circumstances and ways of thinking.

4 Select and personalise

- Identify chapters and sections relevant to you.
- Use these in the order that best suits you.
- Notice whether you resist undertaking particular activities. Such resistance can be a good indicator that you need those most.

5 Reflect

Find a light notebook or set up a file or folder on a portable device, for use as a 'reflective journal'. If you prefer, use a diary, log, blog, 'ideas book' or portfolio, or use the e-resource bank that accompanies this text.

Use your reflective journal to:

- complete reflective activities from the book
- capture your insights and inspiration
- develop your initial thoughts in more detail
- consider your attitudes, feelings and behaviours, and the implications of these for you and others
- identify helpful and unhelpful responses to events
- look back over earlier entries and consider how your perspective changes over time
- generally think things through.

Giving attention to your experiences in such ways helps to clarify your thinking and understanding. Put time aside regularly to make entries in your journal and to look back over previous entries.

Thandi struggled under the weight of an active imagination, carefully noted on a daily basis

Personal development planning: what is it?

About you

Above all else, personal development planning (PDP) is about you. It is about your studies, your life, values, career and future. It is about thinking ahead so that you take the most appropriate steps now in order to give yourself the best range of choices in the future.

A reflective process

We change as we go through a course of study and gain new experiences, so reflection needs to be a continual process rather than a one-off event.

The Quality Assurance Agency (QAA) for higher education in Britain advocated that PDP be made available for all students at every level. It described PDP as:

> Structured and supported processes to develop the capacity of individuals to reflect upon their learning and achievement, and to plan for their own personal education and development. (QAA, 2000)

A creative process ...

PDP is a creative process, requiring time, curiosity, enquiry, toying with ideas, looking for inspiration, taking risks, learning new skills, building strengths, trial and error, discussion, false starts, rethinking, and even soul searching. The more you put in, the more you get out.

Developing self-awareness

Self-knowledge is invaluable. It may seem rather self-indulgent, and even unnecessary, to put time aside to think about ourselves. However, our happiness, contentment and sense of fulfilment is often dependent upon such introspection. To plan ahead effectively, it makes sense to give thought to some of the bigger questions that affect our lives, especially those that we might take for granted, such as:

- what kind of life we are leading now
- where we are heading
- how we became the person we are today – and how far that reflects the person we are becoming or would want to be.

Self-awareness can help us in myriad ways, such as making decisions about:

- study and work
- how to use our time now
- which opportunities to pursue
- finding ways of coping with stress or organising everyday life
- managing relationships in life and at work.

A journey of exploration and discovery

PDP involves finding out about ...

- yourself, your likes, dislikes, ambitions, goals, values, motivations and uncertainties
- what you thought you might want from life – and where your interests might be changing
- the range of jobs and life options open to you
- what these are really like and would entail
- what you need to do to achieve these opportunities
- what others have experienced and would advise.

It also involves:

- drawing useful lessons as you go along
- unexpected self-discoveries.

Personal development planning: what is it?

Being open to possibilities

- Recognising possibilities
- Seizing opportunities that arise
- Creating opportunities for yourself
- Trying out new things
- Taking the trouble to ask
- Thinking short, medium and longer term
- Being flexible, adaptable and resilient in the face of changing circumstances.

Decision-making and risk management

Engineer

Accountant

Artist

Journalist

Project Designer

Whatever decisions we make, day by day as well as longer term, have consequences. Ideally, we will be pleased with the decisions we make, but inevitably we will make mistakes, miss chances, make life harder than it need be. The full impact of our decisions won't be evident for many years.

Although we can't avoid mistakes completely, we can take steps to reduce these. That is a key function of the process of PDP. It gives us space to:

- pause to evaluate past choices and their outcomes
- use more structured approaches to thinking things through
- weigh up costs and benefits in the light of experience and valid criteria
- estimate the value of opportunities that arise, and choose between these
- manage the risks sensibly.

Mindfulness and just 'being'

Most of us spend the majority of our time distracted by such things as work, social life, entertainment and almost anything else apart from just sitting quietly with ourselves.

Whilst PDP involves an active process of reflection, it also benefits from quiet time where we don't chase after answers and information. Being still and quiet creates a space where different kinds of thoughts can emerge. These can give us unexpected insights into ourselves and our situation.

Taking charge of your own destiny

Nobody is going to be as interested in what happens to you as yourself. Ultimately, it is down to you to make things happen. That can seem daunting, so it is useful to have a process that helps you to think through the issues. PDP can help to:

- structure your thinking
- understand the terrain better
- generate information relevant to you, upon which you can draw to make decisions and take action
- help you find direction.

Personal development: what students say

My promotion – and my attitude!

I thought 'personal development planning' was a bit of a mouthful, so I just ignored it. That is a bit of a habit with me. Then, when I went for promotion at work, they asked me about my 'commitment' to my personal and professional development. I couldn't think of what to say. I even forgot to mention I was doing a qualification at university. I hadn't thought about how I was already using what I learnt at Uni in my job. My careers adviser has helped me to think about how to plan and prepare for promotion. He asked me whether my general attitude to things that sound complicated or difficult was helpful – which it obviously isn't ... so I'm working on it!

Start early – or miss the chance

My tutor said: 'It really is up to you. Plan now for your future.' I thought 'OK – soon' and did nothing about it. Now I am in my final year, applying for jobs like everyone else ... and I see why I should have started preparing earlier. I feel I have wasted a lot of time so I am trying to catch up quickly. The jobs I am most interested in are overseas. If I had realised this earlier, I would have started to learn another language. I could have done that using my electives for three years ...

On the right course?

I wasn't sure what 'PDP' was and it seemed a bit of a distraction from my study. Anyway, we had to do some careers sessions as part of a skills module in the first term. I went to talk to a careers adviser and found out that I was doing the wrong course for the jobs I want. So that was a bit of a wake-up call ... Luckily, I was able to negotiate a change of study units. It was hard work catching up but if I pass these units, I can transfer next year to the course I need. It was scary how close I came to wasting three years of study.

A return on my investment

I have a huge loan for my study so I want a good job, a well paid job ... I told my personal tutor and she told me to make sure my CV looks outstanding and to put in more study hours so I get a good degree – both count. Basically, you have to think how you will look well-rounded and interesting to employers many years from now. So, I have really gone for it, like it is a full time job. One thing is ... I do a lot of organising of events and entertainment for senior citizens, and fund-raising for it as well. It takes up a lot of time but actually is quite a lot of fun and you learn a lot about managing events, marketing, and persuading people to get involved – I found out so much I wouldn't have picked up just by studying. I am more confident about getting on with people. I have also changed a lot. I do think I will have a lot of good experience to talk about when I apply for jobs.

It's study first for me

To be honest, I only wanted a degree so I could get a better job. I picked up very quickly that you have to build your personal profile from day 1. I did this by getting involved with the student union. I became a course 'rep' and got a lot of training for this. I do rowing, I do 'Global Studies' so I can talk about more than just my course (psychology). I competed in an enterprise prize ... I helped a project on science for school kids ... I can pretty much tick every box. The career I want, it is hard to get in without a really good degree. I am not all that strong academically so I am trying to pick up as much as I can about good study skills so I get better grades.

Making the right choices: what graduates say

Least wanted, most valued

The last thing I ever really wanted to do was open the PDP file (which I had labelled 'Me'). I didn't want to think about my career or waste time 'navel gazing'. I didn't want to think about 'work'. I didn't want to 'reflect' either. If my tutors hadn't made this a compulsory part of the course so I couldn't escape it, I am sure I would never have bothered.

Looking back, I think this was because, even though I was studying a professional course in petrology, I didn't have any idea what I really wanted to do after Uni. But then one day (maybe I had been reflecting!) it struck me that it was ridiculous to feel it wasn't worth spending time thinking about myself and my life so I started to take it more seriously.

The careers and PDP sessions got me doing things to put into my CV, and just looking at life differently. They were probably the most useful part of the course because without them, I doubt I would have got a place on the graduate programme that led to my first job.

Rahan, Operations Manager, SME.

Gaining breadth of skills and knowledge

I was lucky because the year I started my engineering degree in the States, they gave us the option of combining this with business and professional studies. I took that option and it was the best decision. It was exactly what this company was looking for so it landed me my first job and then, eventually, this line of work. I think it's great when graduates can think beyond just one subject and can converse intelligently with colleagues from all fields.

Brett, Senior Recruitment Officer, large international company.

Checking out the 'dream' …

All the way through school, I thought I was going to do a medical degree. I had a rather exalted view of what I thought that meant. When I found out more about the job, I couldn't see me living that kind of life. I am not good without sleep; when I realised that I would have to live for many years on 100-hour working weeks and constantly interrupted sleep, that put me off. I could see myself as a consultant, but not as a junior doctor. I didn't know then what I would do – but I was glad I found out early in my degree and could change my career path. I didn't at that point think that the volunteering work I did as a student would lead to a good career in the Voluntary sector.

Henry, CEO, voluntary sector.

Challenge fixed career views

I already had a job working as a children's care assistant. I thought, as I was a mother, and knew about children and had experience in that line of work, that was my life planned out. That was why I didn't go to any careers sessions in the first two years – I was sure it would be pointless. Then we studied juvenile offending and I started to become interested in that, especially the legal aspects. I gradually became interested in being a lawyer. This spurred me to study harder so I could get onto a post-graduate course. Now that I am a lawyer, professional development is an essential part of my job.

Sofia, family lawyer.

The challenges of personal development planning

Focusing on your own development should be of evident value and interest, but it is all too easy to put it to one side and hope that it will take care of itself. There are lots of good reasons why that is the case, some of which are listed below. Take a look through the following approaches and decide which are true of you ✓.

☐ **1   I am not clear what it is**

Personal development planning, or PDP, can sound rather vague or abstract. Like many things, it gets easier with practice and familiarity. It is worth noting that for many job applications, you will be asked to demonstrate commitment to ongoing personal development. This also forms part of your annual appraisal in most jobs.

☐ **2   It's too early for me to think about it**

It can seem as if the end of college is a long way off, and that career planning can wait until your final year, or even until after you have finished your course. It may feel very difficult to imagine what you would want to do in several years' time. The more true this is of you, the more you are likely to benefit from a few visits to the Careers Service as soon as possible.

☐ **3   I am too busy**

There can be many demands on our time which appear more urgent to deal with right now. Even with good intentions, it is easy to keep putting off the moment for thinking about your future. If this is true of you, schedule time into your planner at least once a month where you focus just on you, and your future.

☐ **4   I don't' need it**

If you are already in a profession or on a particular career route, it may feel unnecessary to think about planning how to advance on your chosen career path, or to consider other possible careers. However, be wary of focusing too much on a single career route without investigating other options. You might find there is something that suits you much better.

The challenges of personal development planning

☐ 5 Why bother before I make my mind up?

If we don't have a clear direction, it can seem pointless, or even difficult, to think about the future. However, personal planning is about much more than simply heading down a single career path. It is more of a journey of discovery and about opening up possibilities for yourself. See page 4.

☐ 6 I can rush through it at some point

Personal planning can sound like the easy option that can be put aside whilst you focus on your 'real' work. However, personal planning is about making time to think about you and your likely journey through life. It merits time. The more that people put into the process, the more they tend to value it.

☐ 7 I don't know where to start – so I don't

It can feel hard to get started. Generally, people find that once they engage with the process, it gets easier. However, if you put off thinking about your future because you don't have an obvious starting point, rest assured that you are not alone. There doesn't have to be a 'right place' to start. Working through this chapter gives you some options.

Reflection: Attitude to personal planning

- How, if at all, do these scenarios match your own ways of thinking about personal planning?
- Where do the challenges lie for you in doing this well?

Personal development planning (PDP) as a student

More than just a degree

When students complete their qualification, they usually have a good understanding of their subject discipline and have developed skills associated with their course of academic study. This is good, but is only part of the story.

Being at university or college provides opportunities to mix with a wide range of people, to take part in new activities, to manage positions of responsibility and to broaden your outlook. Most of these opportunities lie outside of the taught curriculum although, increasingly, programmes are being designed to include personal and professional development. Students are being encouraged to adopt a broad-based approach to their time as a student and to use their time and the curriculum imaginatively.

Why is PDP actively encouraged for students?

The kinds of jobs that most graduates want to enter require a range of qualities and skills that take time, support and good planning to develop. These include people skills, problem-solving, project work and self-management. Such skills cannot be suddenly acquired in isolation or at the last minute. In the past, many graduates felt disappointed that they were not better prepared for when they left university. It has now been recognised that students need structured opportunities to think about, and plan towards, their future.

Can you really plan for the future?

Whist you can't control the future – the unexpected will happen – you can prepare for likely eventualities and plan for your own development. This enables you to be more in charge of your own life and to create opportunities.

Preparing for graduate jobs

Typically, students regard their degree and other qualifications as a passport to a better job – especially to a graduate job, for which a degree is essential. For some, this means obtaining the best possible salary or opportunities for a first job. For others, it means gaining promotions or other advancement in their current professions or workplace, even whilst they are still studying. Some students create their own jobs, setting up their own businesses.

Whichever route applies to you, PDP is about preparing now towards the employment you will want in the future. That covers a range of preparatory thinking, planning, decision-making, practice and record-keeping.

Achieving well academically

Usually, students want to gain the best possible academic outcomes for their time as a student. This is for their own satisfaction, and because employers often require a particular degree classification.

The process of personal development helps you to understand more about what hinders or enhances your performance. This is relevant to academic performance as well as to performance in the workplace or other spheres of life. Some of the benefits of PDP for academic study are listed opposite.

What kind of skills can you bring to Super Any-job Ltd?

I...um write a mean essay...wicked at exams...um, things like that...

The benefits of PDP

When undertaken in supported and structured ways, PDP gives you a much deeper understanding of your performance. You develop abilities in evaluating this for yourself. Instead of being locked into a routine learning cycle, you enter into an upwards learning spiral. PDP puts you in charge.

Read through the potential benefits of PDP listed below.
☑ Tick any of these that you consider would be of relevance to you.

1 Benefits of PDP to academic performance

The potential benefits of PDP for my studies are:

☐ a clearer focus for my academic work

☐ more control over personal motivation – and the ability to direct this to achieve my goals

☐ skills in self-management

☐ greater independence and confidence through gaining a better understanding of how to improve my performance

☐ more enjoyment and less stress from my academic studies as I become consciously skilled

☐ greater awareness of how to apply what I have learnt to new problems and contexts

☐ reflective, strategic, analytical and creative thinking skills that strengthen academic performance.

PDP can have a positive impact on your academic achievement, especially when combined with attention to study skills relevant to higher education. These are addressed in detail in companion volumes such as *The Study Skills Handbook,* 4th edn (2013) and *Critical Thinking Skills* (2011).

2 Benefits of PDP to professional life

The potential benefits of PDP for my career and professional life are:

☐ strategies for improving personal performance

☐ a better sense of the life and work I want

☐ more confidence in the choices I make

☐ confidence in the skills, qualities and attributes I bring to the career of my choice

☐ being in a better position to compete for jobs and to discuss my skills with employers

☐ the positive attitudes, creative thinking, and problem-solving approaches associated with successful professional life.

3 Benefits of PDP to personal life

The potential benefits of PDP for personal life are:

☐ gaining a better understanding of myself and how I 'tick'

☐ being in a better position to make appropriate choices to meet my aspirations

☐ gaining a better sense of myself as an individual

☐ greater awareness of my needs and how to meet these

☐ greater awareness of the unique contribution I can make

☐ developing a positive, forward-looking approach

☐ developing skills such as reflection, strategic thinking, self-direction and self-evaluation, useful in most life contexts.

Activity

- Browse through the benefits you ticked in the three lists above. Which of these are most important to you?
- Choose 3–5 of these and jot down in your own words what these mean for you.

What PDP do I want and need?

The activities on the following pages enable you to stand back and consider:

- what kind of personal development planning you might need
- your priorities for PDP.

Do I need personal development planning?

Self-evaluation

For each of the following statements, rate your responses as outlined below.
Note that *strongly agree* carries no score.

Rating: *4 = strongly agree   3 = agree   2 = sort of agree   1 = disagree   0 = strongly disagree*

		Rating
1	I am certain that I can keep myself motivated towards achieving my degree	0 1 2 3 4
2	I am very clear what my goals are for the next seven years	0 1 2 3 4
3	I am confident that I have planned sufficiently to enable me to achieve my goals	0 1 2 3 4
4	I am very clear how my degree fits into my life plans	0 1 2 3 4
5	I am clear what employers are looking for	0 1 2 3 4
6	I am confident that I can demonstrate the skills, values and behaviours that employers are looking for	0 1 2 3 4
7	I am very clear about the importance of reflective activity to professional life	0 1 2 3 4
8	I am confident in undertaking structured reflection without guidelines	0 1 2 3 4
9	I am confident that I can develop an effective strategy to meet most circumstances	0 1 2 3 4
10	I am confident that I can set well-formed targets	0 1 2 3 4
11	I have a clear understanding of how to evaluate my own performance	0 1 2 3 4
12	I am confident that I know how to improve my performance in most circumstances	0 1 2 3 4
13	I know how to apply and transfer my expertise from one area to a different field	0 1 2 3 4
14	I am confident that I can see myself as others see me	0 1 2 3 4
15	I am confident that I have effective listening skills	0 1 2 3 4
16	I am an assertive person	0 1 2 3 4
17	I am a good 'self-starter'	0 1 2 3 4
18	I am aware of the best roles for me to fill for team work	0 1 2 3 4
19	I am confident at problem-solving	0 1 2 3 4
20	I am confident that I know how to make best use of my mind	0 1 2 3 4
21	I am confident that I will take a creative approach to most problems	0 1 2 3 4
22	I am confident about making competence-based applications for jobs	0 1 2 3 4
23	I am always very clear about which skills I am developing	0 1 2 3 4
24	I can see clearly how my skills apply to a wide range of other situations	0 1 2 3 4
25	I know where my own 'developmental edge' lies	0 1 2 3 4
	Add up your score out of 100.	Total score _____

Although this is only a rough guide, you now have a personal development 'needs' score. If this is less than 100, then you would benefit from some personal development. The lower your score, the more likely it is that you need to undertake personal development. Even if you do not need any personal development today, this is likely to change within a few months or even weeks, as your circumstances change.

What are my PDP priorities?

- Identify in column A which aspects of personal development are important to you at present. Give a rating between 5 and 0, giving 5 for *very important* and 0 for *not important at all*.
- In column B, consider how essential it is that you develop this aspect soon. Give a rating between 5 and 0, giving 5 for *very essential* and 0 for *not essential at all*.
- By adding scores in columns A and B, you will gain an idea of where your priorities lie (column C).

Aspects I want to develop further I want to …	A How important is this to me? *Rate from 0 to 5*	B How essential to develop it now? *Rate from 0 to 5*	C Priority score *Add scores for columns A and B*	See chapter
1 Clarify my vision and goals for my life				1 and 2
2 Clarify my values				1 and 2
3 Identify a source of inspiration				1
4 Clarify what 'success' means to me				1
5 Clarify what I want to achieve from university				1
6 Strengthen my motivation				1 and 3
7 Understand what reflection is about				8
8 Identify ways of approaching reflection				8 and 11
9 Evaluate my learning goals				1
10 Develop a reflective journal				8 and wherever you see
11 Write about my personal development planning				8 and 11
12 Develop a strategy for improving performance				3 and 6
13 Make sense of my life story				2
14 Understand the effect of my personal choices				2
15 Gain a sense of my strengths and areas for improvement				2, 3, 4, 8 and 11
16 Make better use of my own expertise				2 and 8

What are my PDP priorities?

Aspects I want to develop further I want to …	A How important is this to me? *Rate from 0 to 5*	B How essential to develop it now? *Rate from 0 to 5*	C Priority score *Add scores for columns A and B*	See chapter
17 Understand my personal performance profile and preferences				3
18 Identify personal qualities				2 and 11
19 Know how to make a SWOT analysis				4
20 Improve my time management				4
21 Develop more constructive attitudes to achieve my goals				1 and 6
22 Develop my self-confidence				2, 3 and 4
23 Understand more about emotional intelligence				4
24 Manage change and uncertainty more effectively				4
25 Understand what prevents me from achieving my potential				2, 3, 4, 6 and 10
26 Complete tasks more effectively				6
27 Improve my problem-solving skills				6
28 Know how to set effective targets				6
29 Be better at getting down to tasks				6
30 Become a good 'self-starter'				6
31 Develop project-management skills				6
32 Identify my 'competitiveness' in task management				6
33 Develop my listening skills				5

What are my PDP priorities?

Aspects I want to develop further I want to …	A How important is this to me? *Rate from 0 to 5*	B How essential to develop it now? *Rate from 0 to 5*	C Priority score *Add scores for columns A and B*	See chapter
34 Develop team-work skills				5
35 Set up a support group (or action sets)				5
36 Be better at giving and receiving criticism				5
37 Be more assertive				5
38 Deal well with difficult people				5
39 Develop negotiating skills				5
40 Develop leadership skills				5
41 Develop creative thinking skills				7
42 Understand more about the brain and how to use it				7
43 Develop skills in applying for jobs				9, 10 and 11
44 Make use of personal records when applying for jobs				11 and Resource Bank
45 Understand more about what employers are looking for				9 and 10
46 Analyse how well my values and behaviours match what employers seek				9 and 10
47 Utilise my academic studies better in my workplace				9 and 10
48 Consider what it would mean to set up my own business				9

Development priorities
- Look back over the priorities table above.
- Identify the three aspects that you gave the highest scores. If there are more than three with the same score, select three.
- Write the three priorities in words that are meaningful to you.
- If you are ready to start on these, you may find it helpful to use the Action Plan on p. 119.

Taking and making opportunities

Whilst you are a student or recent graduate, there are more opportunities open to you than at any other time, usually at no cost. Many of these will be arranged on campus or via your college, university or student union.

Seize the chance

Employers will expect this

When you apply for jobs, employers will be aware that you have had great opportunities open to you and will be interested to see how you made use of these. This will tell them a lot about you.

Great for building your CV

- Develop new skills
- Learn new things
- Gain a range of experience
- Demonstrate social responsibility

Good for networking

- Mix with a wider range of people
- Consider new perspectives
- Develop awareness through exposure to more cultures, backgrounds, languages
- Enjoy a wider pool for making friends

Amaze yourself

- Try out things you wouldn't usually consider
- Test your limits
- Take a lead in organising activities and networks that interest you
- Discover a new side to yourself

Find out what is available

It is likely that there will be many avenues for finding out about the opportunities open to you. Good starting places are listed below. Check ✓ these off when you have looked to see what they have to offer you.

- ☐ Freshers' Fair (even if you are not a first year)
- ☐ Students Union
- ☐ Careers Service
- ☐ Student Services
- ☐ University or college website
- ☐ Citizens Advice Bureau
- ☐ Community centres and community groups
- ☐ Local colleges
- ☐ Job clubs and Job Centre
- ☐ Local newspaper

Identify the next opportunities ...

From the list below, check off ✓ those opportunities that are available to you. Highlight those you want to follow up.

Work-related opportunities

- ☐ Entrepreneurship courses or awards
- ☐ Being a course rep
- ☐ Roles within the student union or student clubs
- ☐ Contributing to a student magazine or radio
- ☐ Mentoring/coaching in local schools
- ☐ Setting up a club or support group
- ☐ Taking part in activities in the local community
- ☐ Projects for employers
- ☐ Voluntary work
- ☐ Employer talks and skills sessions
- ☐ Information about local part-time jobs
- ☐ Jobs available at the university/college
- ☐ Industrial or other work placements
- ☐ Work placements overseas
- ☐ Internships

Taking and making opportunities

Jamila's efforts at personal development knew no bounds.

Areas to improve
Snorkel control
Large fish avoidance
Note taking under water

Opportunities through the curriculum

- [ ] Credit-bearing PDP/career-planning modules
- [ ] Credit for work experience or work-based projects
- [ ] Credit for voluntary work
- [ ] Training and credit for mentoring others
- [ ] Skills development built into the curriculum
- [ ] 'Electives', 'discovery' or 'venture' modules outside of the main subject, to broaden outlook and experience
- [ ] Year/term studying or working abroad

Opportunities for advice and guidance

- [ ] Helpdesks and/or information zone
- [ ] Tutorials/personal tutor meetings
- [ ] Guidance about making academic choices
- [ ] Careers information, advice and guidance
- [ ] Support for study skills
- [ ] Facilities for learning new languages
- [ ] On-line personal development resources
- [ ] Web-based resources and tools
- [ ] Student Union

How it fits together: skills for success

Academic and career skills

Typically, universities and colleges identify specific sets of skills and attributes that they expect students to develop throughout their course. Employers also tend to provide lists of skills and attributes as part of their job descriptions and person specifications. Higher education institutions (HEIs) generally look for ways of building into their courses the means of developing skills that are relevant to employment as well as to study.

Once drawn together, the skills, qualities, attributes and experiences required of students and graduates can appear to be a long and rather daunting list. As different vocabulary is used on different lists, it can also be confusing.

The APT-S framework

Specialist and technical skills aside, skills can generally be conceptualised more simply and clearly into just four organising categories. The APT-S Framework (Cottrell, 2013) organises skills into 4 categories which are relatively easy to manage and remember:

Academic   People   Task   Self

Academic skills such as critical thinking and problem-solving and task management, skills such as undertaking research projects are more readily recognisable as necessary for students. However, in recent years, the people skills required for working with others have also become recognised as important to student success. It is increasingly recognised that skills in self-management are essential and underpin most other skills.

Together these four sets of skills enable you to manage the various complexities and challenges of:

● *the learning environment*, whether at college, university, the workplace or in other learning contexts
● *your past experience* and its impact on your current thinking and skills
● *your future aims*, and what this means for where you need to focus now.

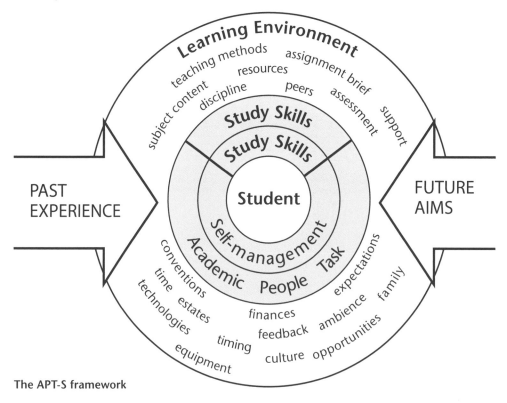

The APT-S framework

How it fits together: skills for success

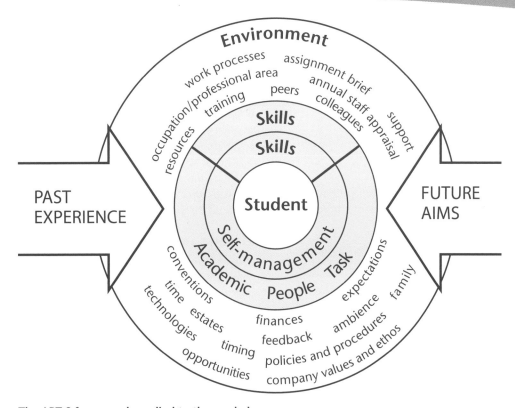

The APT-S framework applied to the workplace

The categories of skills used for the APT-S framework are also applicable to work and most other areas of life.

The four categories in the framework are those most relevant to the academic world of the student. If you have been a student, it is likely that you will continue to bring an academic dimension to the way you approach tasks and situations in the future.

Although the skills you use in the workplace may be very similar, the language used to describe these may vary outside of academia. For example, you could also come across the following terms:

- **Academic**: Intellectual; cognitive; metacognitive
- **People**: Interpersonal; social
- **Task**: Operational; organisational
- **Self**: Intrapersonal.

Most students will need skills in each of the four categories both as a student and in employment

– although the specific skills required for each category may vary depending on your chosen field of study or work. This means that:

- there is value in developing all four skills areas
- it is a good idea to find out more about the kinds of academic, people, task-management and self-management skills relevant to your field and intended career path.

Skills are mutually reinforcing

You will find that, in developing skills in any one category, you usually draw upon or develop skills in one or more of the other categories. It is important to note the range of skills that you are developing across the various activities that you undertake. Sometimes, it is less evident than at other times, just how many skills you are honing on a given task.

How it fits together: self-management skills

Overall structure

The book is divided into four main sections or Parts, with additional introductory and closing sections and a Resource Bank. Parts 1–3 organise material into the 4 skills areas identified within the APT-S framework.

- Self-management
- Managing People and Tasks
- Thinking skills (Academic skills).

The final section draws these skills together and applies them to the particular task of career planning.

Below, there is a synopsis of each section and chapter, to guide you through the book and to help you to select where to focus.

Self-management

We are the key to our own successes – and we are often our own greatest enemies. If we can take charge of our own mental processes, behaviours and emotions, we can accomplish a great deal. To do so, though, we usually need to become much more self-aware. That means drilling down to find out more about what really goes on in our own minds, why we hold the beliefs that we do, why we value certain things over others, why we sometimes sabotage our own goals. The first four chapters look at different aspects of self-management.

Understanding 'success'

Chapter 1 takes as its starting place the notion that all students want to experience success – even if they have different notions of what success might look like. Most make sacrifices to put themselves through college or university, and expect a better future as a result. However, many students are very vague about what they want and how to plan for the future. It is not the end of the world to leave university and still not know what you want from life. You may never answer that question fully.

However, it is useful to start to clarify your thinking so that you bring more control to the choices that you make, and keep a wide range of relevant opportunities open to you. Chapter 1 helps you consider questions such as:

- What does success mean to you?
- What motivates you?
- What are your ambitions, goals, values?
- Who or what inspires you?
- What kind of life do you want to find yourself living 10 or 20 years from now – and what would be your worst nightmare?

Making sense of experience

Chapter 2 encourages you to look in detail at you – and what helps you to achieve. Use Chapter 2 to gain different perspectives on:

- Your life story so far and the role you play in your own story
- How you may be perceived by others
- How you respond to opportunity and adversity
- The impact of your learning history on your current performance
- Where your expertise lies – and how that could be applied to new contexts.

I know people see me as intimidating but I am about more than pest control. My real strength is working with textiles.

How it fits together: managing people and tasks

Understanding personal performance

We are each distinct in what helps or hinders us to perform at our best. In Chapter 3, you have the opportunity to:

- analyse in depth the conditions that have most impact on your performance
- identify your 'personal performance formula'
- identify the optimum conditions for you when undertaking different kinds of task.

Taking charge

Success begins with knowing and managing yourself. Whilst the first three chapters focus on knowing yourself, Chapter 4 looks at successful 'self-management'. Use this chapter to increase chances of personal success by improving:

- your emotional self-management
- your time management
- your 'emotional intelligence'
- your attitudes
- how you manage change and uncertainty.

Managing people and tasks

Interpersonal and organisational skills can make study more interesting, more enjoyable, and less stressful. These skills are also very much in demand from employers – and they will be essential if you intend to take on a leadership and management role or to become an employer in your own right. The two chapters in Part 2 focus on these skills and provide tools for developing them.

People skills

How good are your 'people skills'? Good people skills mean that teams work better, and that individuals gain the consideration and support that they need. People skills create more effective and manageable work environments, which is why employers place such a high value upon them. Use Chapter 5 to consider ways of developing your people skills. It addresses such issues as:

- developing rapport
- listening skills
- team work
- assertiveness and negotiation skills
- leadership
- giving and receiving constructive criticism.

Managing tasks

Good problem-solving strategies will enable you to take on almost any task and will greatly increase personal confidence when you enter new situations. Use Chapter 6 to:

- organise time and tasks effectively
- learn basic problem-solving strategies
- select and apply problem-solving strategies to more complex tasks and problems
- develop planning skills, such as identifying priorities, setting targets and finding good solutions
- learn skills useful to project management
- gain familiarity with concepts such as performance indicators and benchmarking
- audit your personal 'competitiveness'.

How do I manage people? Usually my presence is enough but sometimes I roar and if all else fails ... I eat them.

How it fits together: thinking skills; employability

Extend your thinking

Part 3 looks at two sets of thinking skills, creative and reflective, that are becoming ever more valued both for academic study and for employment. These are also skills with which many students and employees struggle.

Creative thinking

Many people doubt their own creativity, thinking that this is just for artists and performers. Creativity is essential to problem-solving and task completion: it is the 'spark of creativity' that brings the right idea to mind at the right time. Chapter 7, 'Thinking outside of the box', looks at ways of nurturing creative thinking skills. Use Chapter 7 to:

- develop confidence in your creative abilities
- harness a basic knowledge of how the mind works so that you can develop your thinking skills further
- try out a range of activities to hone your creative thinking.

Reflection

Many professions now require their employees to adopt a reflective practitioner approach. Your course tutors may also require you to reflect upon your performance. But what is 'reflection'? How do you go about it? How do you write about it?

As you work through the book, you will find many opportunities for structured reflection. Chapter 8, 'The art of reflection', outlines different methods and approaches, along with guidance on the kinds of structured reflection typically required for marked assignments in higher education. Browse these and select those methods that suit you and your course.

Enhancing your career prospects

Surveys of students show that their main objectives for pursuing higher education are associated with finding a graduate job or improving their work prospects. This may include:

- enhancing their career through promotion at work
- gaining greater job satisfaction and expertise in their existing employment
- moving to a better job elsewhere
- embarking on their first substantial job – as a first step on the career ladder
- gaining more experience of employment through internships or a graduate scheme.

The skills developed throughout the book are those especially associated with graduate careers. The following chapters consider the issue of 'employability' from the perspective of both employers and students.

Employability

The process of gaining a job can seem rather mysterious. When there is a lot of competition for work, as is usually the case for good graduate jobs and placements, it can be hard to find a job without experience, and hard to find a job to gain such experience. Even if you have been in employment for some time, it is not always obvious how to go about getting a better job.

Chapter 9 looks at what is meant by 'employability' from the perspective of employers, and what they are looking for when they take on new employees. The chapter provides an introduction to the labour market and provides suggestions of activities that can help you to make sense of segments of the labour market relevant to you. It looks at differences between large employers and SMEs, and at changes in skills needs over time. It also looks at self-employment as a potential option.

But I am a really good swimmer!

How it fits together: getting that job!

Get that job!

Chapter 10 considers employability from the perspective of you as the potential employee going through the process of applying for jobs. It looks at such issues as:

- identifying what you want from your first, or next, job
- making good choices and finding the right job for you
- using the personal development planning process to enhance your career prospects
- making strong and successful job applications
- understanding the role of job descriptions, person specifications, competences, CVs, and assessment centres
- preparing well for interviews and assessment centres, so you can approach these with confidence
- using work placements or other employment opportunities to best effect, taking a structured, critical approach to observing and reflecting on what is going on around you, in order to develop your awareness and understanding of the world of work.

Maintain up-to-date personal records

Chapter 11 outlines the rationale for keeping personal records. It is linked to the Resource Bank referred to below. Together, these make it easy for you to reflect and record in a structured and purposeful way about:

- what you have learnt to date from your course and experiences, *and*
- how these are relevant to jobs that interest you.

Accurate record-keeping is essential for completing application forms for jobs. Building a bank of information about your experiences and skills provides you with an invaluable resource for making good applications and preparing for interviews. You are likely to draw upon it for many years to come.

Raise your game

In Chapter 12, you draw together what you have learnt so far and consider how you can build on this further. The chapter encourages you to:

- recognise personal change and to review your values and goals in the light of this
- build connections between your skills and expertise so that you can more easily transfer your skills from one context to another
- identify your next set of personal challenges and 'working edge' for personal development.

Resource Bank

A resource bank is provided at the end of the book for recording and collating key personal information, evaluations and reflections. You can use these resources to devise personal strategies, models, planning tools and prompts.

You can also use them more than once so as to compare how your responses change over time and with more experience. You can monitor your progress and see how you develop in your thinking and confidence. These can be photocopied for updating by hand or are available electronically, for your personal use, at www.palgrave.com/studyskills/pdp.

🅐 This symbol indicates that there is a mobile App that you can download to support your work on this area of the book. A full list of Apps can be found in the Appendix.

Closing comments

This introduction opened with seven sets of actions that run through the introduction and the book as a whole. Working through these will help you in planning towards success, whether academic or professional.

Aspire. Be prepared to be ambitious, setting yourself high goals towards which you can work over the longer term. Although you may be keen to complete your qualification or gain a better job, keep an eye on the distant future too. It is likely that you will have many jobs, each building on previous expertise. Avoid taking steps that narrow your options too early. Be flexible and open to a range of possibilities. Take opportunities that help you to build towards leadership roles should you wish to apply for them.

Investigate. Put in the time to find out as much as you can about the wide range of career and life options that could be open to you. Develop a clear understanding of what you would need to do in order to access these for yourself.

Reflect. Don't fool yourself – give thought to what you really want and why. Increase your self-awareness so that you understand the basis of your motivations and behaviours. Develop good habits of introspection, self-evaluation and self-questioning, so that you become, and remain, attuned to your changing interests, motivations and ambitions.

Decide. Decision-making is important, even if you don't know exactly what you want to do next. Making decisions gives your planning and development greater focus. Put time aside to think through what is likely to be really right for you – or at least the most likely best direction of travel for you. Think through, in depth, the potential implications of your choices, so that you don't close down your options, either through making the wrong choices – or through inaction.

Plan. Map out what you will do to put yourself in the best possible position to achieve the kind of life, career and academic success you want.

Personalise. Adapt your approaches and strategies to suit your personal skills, strengths, needs, interests, experiences, preferences and style. Be your own person and true to what is right for you.

Achieve. Follow through on your plans, adapting these to suit changes in circumstances and opportunities, as well as changes in your own interests and ambitions.

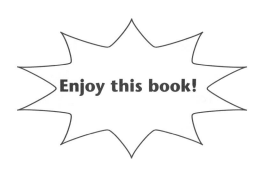

Enjoy this book!

Part 1
Self-management

Good self-management skills provide a solid foundation upon which to build all other skills, whether academic or professional or for managing life in general.

Knowing yourself

It is easier to adapt to the changing requirements of study, work, new contexts and new people if you are building on a solid base. This comes from gaining a deep understanding of yourself- not just the superficial, obvious things that strike you on a first consideration, but the more profound insights that come from recurrent and structured self-reflection, self-questioning and challenge.

Without such self-awareness, it is likely that, at some point, you will experience a disconnection between what you think matters to you and what does in reality. It is difficult to maintain high levels of motivation, energy, confidence, time on task and focus when there is such a disconnection.

Conversely, it is easier to be successful in working towards your goals when these really excite you, when they match your ambitions, values and interests, when you are being true to yourself.

Personal Performance

We are also more likely to succeed in our endeavours when we know what impacts on our performance. That puts us in a good position to identify ways to fine-tune the ways we work and study, removing potential barriers and distractions, so we can perform at our best. Sometimes, quite small alterations to the way we approach our work, study, tasks or situations can reduce negative feelings such as boredom, stress and anxiety, and incite greater interest, enjoyment and desire to engage.

This section provides a wide range of activities, reflections and resources to help you to:

● delve beneath the surface and examine what matters to you, what inspires you, what will get you through your course and help you achieve your longer term ambitions

● pinpoint key contextual factors that are most conducive to your performing well

● consider the skills, habits, attitudes, preferences, experiences and strategies that impact on your current learning and performance

● think through how you might adapt your approaches and study conditions to improve your future performance

● manage your time, resources and energies to best effect to achieve the kind of success that matters to you.

Chapters in this section
1   The Vision: What does 'success' mean to you?
2   Know yourself
3   Understanding your personal performance
4   Successful self-management

Chapter 1
The vision: what does success mean to you?

Learning outcomes

This chapter offers opportunities to:

- reflect upon the nature of success
- understand the importance of personal vision to successful outcomes
- formulate a personal definition of success
- gain insight into personal motivation, inspiration and values, and see how these assist current study
- refine your vision of the future and consider how current study contributes towards that vision.

Introduction

Everybody wants to be successful – but in their own way. We each have our own versions or definitions of what 'success' means, for ourselves and for others. The kinds of success characterised by Barack Obama, Angelina Jolie, Beyoncé, J. K. Rowling, Lionel Messi, Aung San Suu Kyi or Shah Rukh Khan, are all very different, but no less valuable to the people concerned.

Our concepts of success can be rather vague and open to change. This is especially the case for students – even if some objectives appear clear cut. Embarking on a programme in higher education is, typically, a time of transition – a time for leaving behind the worlds of school and family, or barriers to progression at work, or perceived gaps in knowledge. It is an exciting time, full of potential. As a student, you are exposed to new ideas, new perspectives on the world, new people and opportunities. It is likely that your horizons will be stretched, your values challenged, your ambitions changed. Anything might be possible, all kinds of paths may open up to you.

Students today expect their time in higher education to be a passport to many kinds of success apart from simply gaining a qualification:

to good grades, to the specialist skills and knowledge required for particular professional pathways, a graduate-level job, a rewarding career, leadership and management roles, financial security, new possibilities, a better lifestyle.

Competition for such opportunities is generally high – and a degree alone is unlikely to make you stand out. As a student, you will be making decisions that will have an impact on your future opportunities, such as in:

- the options you select
- the way you approach your studies
- the projects you undertake
- the way you apply your learning in work settings if you are already employed
- the skills and qualities you develop through activities you undertake outside the curriculum
- and the chances you don't use too.

The activities in this chapter aim to sharpen your thinking about your aims, ambitions and the versions of success you most value. That, in turn, should assist you in making sound decisions that affect your future as well as motivating you to do what is needed to achieve success.

Defining success

There are many ways of looking at 'success'. Some people define success in terms of objective material criteria. (How much money, how high a position in a company, how big a house?)

However, successful athletes may win world records, even fame, without earning a great deal of money. Successful artists may measure their success by how true they are to their artistic endeavour. Others judge success by the integrity they brought to a task: the confidence that they did their best in honest ways and can live with their conscience. It used to be a sign of success to still have your own teeth at an advanced age!

In other words, 'success' is a very subjective matter. It depends on what is meaningful to you and the people around you.

Activity ⟳ Successful people

- Jot down, as quickly as you can, the first ten people you think of as 'successful'.
- Do these have anything in common?
- What makes you think of them as 'successful'?
- How do you think your list might differ from somebody else's? You could compare your list with that of a friend.

Activity ⟳ Symbols of success

- Jot down quickly the first ten things (or symbols) you associate with success.
- How important is each of those symbols to you personally? Are these things that you want very much from life?
- How do you think your list would differ from somebody else's? Compare your list with a friend's.

Activity ⟳ Spectrums of success – or knowing what you want

Below are pairs of statements, each of which relates to different points on a spectrum of opinion about success. For each statement, mark on the spectrum where you would wish your own success to lie.

For example, _____ **✗** _____

Being immensely rich	Having enough to survive
Having high expectations	Being content with little
Being a world expert	Knowing enough to survive
Gaining higher degrees	Passing part of one degree
World fame	Recognition by colleagues and peers
Achieving high goals	Achieving something
Seizing big opportunities	Being aware of some opportunities
Winning on a world stage	Taking part in any activity
A very high profile job	Having some work, paid or unpaid
Being very popular	Having some good friends
Being a world leader	Living a quiet life
Being important on a world stage	Being recognised for personal achievements
Having a close family life	Escaping the family
Outstanding physical appearance and physique	Minimum interest in personal appearance
Material wealth	A strong spiritual life

- Is there another aspect of success which is more important to you than any of those listed above? If so, what is that?
- If you could be successful in only one area, what would that be? Why is this so important to you? What would it mean not to have this in your life?
- What do your responses tell you about your own concept of 'success'?

Reflection: Spending life your way

There is only one success – to be able to spend your life in your own way.

Christopher Morley

- What would it mean for you to 'live your life in your own way'? What would this involve?
- What, if anything, stops you from doing this?

Complete the sentence below. In doing so, consider what personal success would be in your own case. Don't worry if you find this much more difficult than you imagined. You will be asked to return to this statement later in the chapter, when you may wish to change or refine it.

For me, being successful means …

Personal influences

Some of the definitions of success that you use were probably adopted originally to please other people – or are those you have inherited, or picked up from peers and the media. This is not necessarily a bad thing: these may be influences that you respect or that matter to you. External influences can be very valuable and help us to form our sense of who we are.

However, sometimes, we live out ideas of success that we pick up from other people, without thinking through what they really mean for us. It can be easy to lose ourselves in the values and interests presented by others, especially if we are surrounded by these for much of the time. We can 'forget' that there may be alternatives that are better suited to our personal circumstances, character and beliefs.

Activity **Personal ambitions**

Sometimes we come up with different answers if we frame the question differently. This activity invites you to give some initial thought to your ambitions for different areas of your life. Later activities explore this in more detail.

My ambitions for my academic work are:

My ambitions for my professional life or career are:

My ambitions for my personal life are:

As so much personal investment is likely to be involved in working towards your concept of success, it is worth considering how your own view of success has been influenced by others – and how far you can say 'This is really me.'

Reflection: Personal influences

Who do you consider to be the greatest influence on your life? How far do your ideas of 'success' reflect the influences of that person or group?

- Look again at your responses to the above activities about success.
- What values and beliefs are associated with your responses?
- Are these influences still valuable to you or do you need to develop more independence?

Owning the influence

Your goals may have been strongly influenced by others but ultimately, when you decide to act upon them, you have made those goals your own. The important thing is to be clear that your action is a personal choice no matter who influenced it. This means recognising your own role in the action you take, rather than saying later, 'Well, I only did that because my parents/teacher/friend/children/boss, etc., wanted me to.'

Inspiration

Sometimes influences act as positive inspiration, moving us to achieve things we value. Many people have used a role model from their personal life, history or public life to inspire them.

Reflection: Inspiring people

Look back to the list of successful people you jotted down in activity 1. Do any of these inspire you? If you answered 'No', think of at least one person who does inspire you. If you answered 'Yes', which person from your list do you find most inspiring?

Consider the person that you selected as inspiring. What is it about them that most inspires you:

● What they achieved?
● Hurdles they overcame?
● Their level of skill or ability?
● Their personal qualities?
● Their effect on the lives of other people?
● Something very individual they bring to life?

In what way has that person already inspired you? In what other ways could you use that person as an inspiration towards achieving your goals?

Other sources of inspiration

Anything may be a source of inspiration. For some people, a piece of music, a rap, a poem, a painting, a postcard, a view of the sea, an episode in history, a personal event, can be inspiring. Alternatively, doing something for a cause or to bring about change can be a source of inspiration. Traditionally, artists and thinkers used to write, paint or compose for a 'muse' – a real or a mythological person to whom they dedicated their lives or their work.

Thinking about your sources of inspiration can be like receiving a burst of energy – it can boot you back into action when your spirits are flagging, and keep you focused. Inspiration, in other words, is another tool you can use to achieve your objectives.

Reflection: Sources of personal inspiration

Consider:

● Apart from people, what has inspired you most in life? This could be a book, music, etc. What was it about this that inspired you?
● What things inspire you to feel good about life?
● What things inspire you to go beyond yourself, to do more than you thought you were capable of?
● What else would you consider to be a source of inspiration to you?

Reflection: Inspiration to succeed on your course

● What, if anything, inspired you to come on this course or to return to study?
● What inspiration can you draw upon to increase your motivation to succeed?

Values

You will probably already have noticed that thinking about personal success raises questions about values, beliefs and ethics. It is not always easy to square our desires with our values and beliefs. It can also be hard to identify what we really value – sometimes this is not possible until we are faced with a life-or-death challenge. However, if we work against our values, we are likely to experience self-conflict, which can undermine our chances of success. The following activities aim to help you identify what things you hold important relative to other things.

Activity ⟳ The Zed box (1)

Imagine that you are given a 'smart' or magical box, known as the Zed box. If you open the Zed box, you may be given the thing that you want or value most in life. (The box cannot change the past.) You have five seconds to jot down the one thing you would most want the box to give you.

The thing I would want most is:

Layers of the onion

Knowing what we 'really' want is not easy. There are many layers to our 'wanting' and 'needing' and 'valuing', like skins on an onion. It is worth taking time to reflect on the things we value, asking why we value them, following each answer with 'And what is it about this that I value?' For example, do you value celebrity because you are excited by the lifestyle that it represents? What is it about that lifestyle that you value? Is it being in the public eye? In which case, how many other ways are there of being in the public eye? Is it about the money celebrities earn? If so, what other ways are there of earning that money? Is it because famous people seem to gain recognition? If so, are there other ways of gaining recognition that you would value as much or more? Is it really popularity that you are seeking? Keep going until you run out of questions.

Sometimes it is easier to aim for the surface of things (money, power, celebrity) rather than looking at what is creating a need for such things. Whether those things are good or bad in their own right is a value judgement – and may depend on the circumstances. It is worth remembering that we need very little in order to survive.

Activity ⟳ The Zed box (2)

However, the Zed box is 'smart' and magical: it can read your most secret wishes. It may give you what you wish in your heart, even if you are not aware yet that this is something you want. For example, you may think you want to be a football champion but deep down wish to be an artist, travel the world, or take up a caring role. The Zed box would know that and would give you that opportunity rather than making you a football star. The choice the Zed box makes may come as a shock to you. You have one minute to jot down an answer to the following questions:

1   **What would you most fear that the Zed box decided you really wanted?**

2   **What do you most fear the Zed box would take away from you, thinking it knew best?**

You may have found this activity difficult if you have not spent time thinking about what you feel you *ought* to do with your life as well as what you *want* to do with your life. You may find it useful to reflect upon this over some time or on a long walk. Consider:

● What do I want to do with my life?
● What do I feel I ought to do with my life?
● What are the key characteristics of the lives of people who inspire me?

Reflection: Core values

● What is at the 'core of the onion' for you? What is really driving you towards the things that you want?
● How far are your values being shaped by your wants and needs (for yourself, others or the world)?

What I most value is ...	Important to me ✓	What I most value is ...	Important to me ✓
1 A good car	☐	23 Leaving something for posterity	☐
2 Challenge	☐	24 Making a difference to the world	☐
3 Contributing to society	☐	25 Money	☐
4 Feeling I am in control of my life	☐	26 New experiences	☐
5 Creativity	☐	27 Personal qualities such as kindness	☐
6 Fairness	☐	28 Physical appearance	☐
7 Fame and celebrity	☐	29 Popularity	☐
8 Family and home life	☐	30 Good-quality possessions	☐
9 Friendship	☐	31 Power	☐
10 Having a good time	☐	32 Being needed	☐
11 Health	☐	33 Security	☐
12 Help received from others	☐	34 A feeling of self-worth	☐
13 Helping others	☐	35 Social Life	☐
14 Honesty	☐	36 Solitude	☐
15 A big house	☐	37 Spiritual life	☐
16 Independence	☐	38 Sporting ability	☐
17 Influence	☐	39 Being wanted	☐
18 Integrity	☐	40 Other things: (*state what*)	☐
19 Intellectual abilities	☐		
20 A good job or career	☐		
21 Justice	☐		
22 Leadership and authority	☐		

Select the ten items you value most and list these in order of importance, where 1 is the most important, 2 for the next in importance, and so on.

1		6	
2		7	
3		8	
4		9	
5		10	

Consider the top ten items that you valued. What themes can you identify? For example, do your choices suggest you place a high value on any of the following:

- personal qualities (character)
- control over something
- people
- material objects
- power and influence
- mind and body
- personal recognition.

Are you comfortable with your responses or do you feel you 'ought to' value other things? If so, what does this response tell you about yourself?

Reflection: Put to the test?

Identify a time when your values were put to the test. In your reflective journal, jot down:

- What happened?
- What did you find out about yourself on that occasion?
- What did you learn about your personal values from that occasion?

Life qualities

The following quotation refers to a number of qualities that one person, Gordon H. Taggart, wished to develop in his life.

> I wish I were honest enough to admit all my shortcomings:
>
> - brilliant enough to accept flattery without it making me arrogant
> - tall enough to tower above deceit
> - strong enough to reassure love
> - brave enough to welcome criticism
> - compassionate enough to understand human frailties
> - wise enough to recognise my mistakes
> - humble enough to appreciate greatness
> - staunch enough to stand by my friends
> - human enough to be thankful of my neighbour.
>
> Gordon H. Taggart

Reflection: Life qualities

- Which of the qualities identified by Taggart do you most value?
- Which do you make a conscious effort to develop?
- Which three of these qualities would be of most relevance in achieving your goals or vision?

Activity **Feeling Valued: Compliments**

Our values are also reflected in what we want others to think about us- such as the comments we do or don't want made about us and the compliments that we treasure.

What three compliments do you most want to hear from other people?

1
2
3

Reflection: Valued compliments

In your reflective journal, jot down:

- What do these suggest about what you value?
- What do you do to make it possible to receive such compliments?

Vision

It helps to get to the top of a mountain if we have seen the pinnacle and know where we are headed.

This does not necessarily mean that we should have very clear life goals, with every detail planned out. Successful people seem to be characterised by not having very rigid life plans (Taylor and Humphrey, 2002).

However, it is important to have a vision of the general direction in which we are going, the kind of life we want to lead, and the levels of personal investment we want to make in different kinds of activity. It is this vision that keeps us going when the inevitable unexpected setbacks occur. If we are assembling a bookcase or doing a jigsaw puzzle, it helps to have the picture before us of what we want to achieve, so that we can see the end goal as a realistic possibility. A vision of what we want to achieve is even more important when we are undertaking a project that lasts for several years, such as working towards a degree or a career.

Ambitions

An obvious starting place is to clarify your current sense of what your ambitions might be. Some people have very clearly formed ambitions and goals by the time they enter university. However, many students have given little thought to what they want after university. It is not necessary to have clearly defined goals, but it is useful to start clarifying personal ambitions, so that you can check both how important these really are to you – and how far you are working towards what matters to you.

The dream

Dream lofty dreams, and as you dream so shall you become. Your vision is the promise of what you shall at last unveil.

John Ruskin

When we are young, we are often told to stop day-dreaming. However, many great inventors and scientists attribute success to the combination of their analytical work with the inspiration that came through dreams or day-dreams.

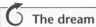

Activity — **The dream**

This activity is linked to the activity, 'The Long-Term Vision', page 35.

First, undertake an activity that uses up any surplus energy and leaves you alert and awake. Taking a walk or doing housework is ideal, but any moderately strenuous activity will do. This will get the blood flowing to your brain (so you think better) but work off excess adrenalin (so you are open to being creative rather than defensive).

Then, find a comfortable seat where you will not be disturbed. Read the quotation by Ruskin (above) a few times and let your mind wander over what this means for you.

- What dreams have other people had for you (if any)?
- What are the dreams and ambitions of people you know well?
- How are your dreams different from those of people around you?

Your 'dream' does not have to be the same as anyone else's, and it does not need to be well defined. It may be something as simple as 'happiness'.

Clarifying the dream

To gain a clearer view of the 'dream', come back to the 'Dream' activity and repeat it from the beginning once you have undertaken the 'Vision' exercise below.

You may find that the more analytical nature of the 'Vision' activity focuses the mind. Let go of particular details when you return to the 'Dream' activity.

Your mind will automatically play with the ideas you had and feed them back, either straight away or at some time in the future. However, as our relaxed brain likes to play with images and metaphors, it may return the ideas to you in a way that is hard to recognise at first.

Whatever images come to mind on this second occasion, however unexpected, hold them in mind for a few days, and see what emerges.

The long-term vision

For the activity on pp. 35–6, imagine yourself travelling forward into the future, to a time approximately 10 or 20 years from now. This activity is not about laying down a rigid plan for your future but, rather, is to help you form a general idea of what you would like to experience, as far as you can tell now. The aim is to gain a sense of the type of life you want, so that you can make the right kinds of choices to achieve it.

Activity ⟳ The Long-Term Vision

Ten years from now, I see myself …

Aspect	Write your own vision of this aspect below	How important is this aspect to me?
Living in which part of the world?		
Living in what kind of place (city, town, village, countryside, by the sea, etc.)?		
Considering the most important things in my life to be …		
Solitary? Or surrounded by people?		
Working with colleagues who are … artistic? intellectual? practical? caring? down-to-earth? active? thoughtful? kind?		
Working to stress levels which are … Pressurised? Reasonable? Very low level?		
Enjoying privacy? Public attention? Celebrity?		
Working 20, 30, 40, 50, 60, 80, 100 hours a week?		
Taking a lead? Being a good second in command? Happy to be part of a team? One of a large crowd?		
Wanting to 'get by' unnoticed? Gaining reasonable recognition for my work? Being top management? World-famous?		

Activity: The Long-Term Vision *(continued)*

Ten years from now, I see myself …

Aspect	Write your own vision of this aspect below	How important is this aspect to me?
Based mostly in an office? On the road? In the field?		
Working for myself? Working for a large company? Working for a small company?		
Doing work which is very varied? Very routine? Predictable?		
Likely to stay in the same job for years? Changing job occasionally?		
Living with a large/small/minimal family. With strong/weak/some family connections?		
Considering my work to be central/important/not very important in my life?		
My contribution to my community or society will be through …		
My time outside work will be spent doing …		
My friends will be the kinds of people who …		
I will be the kind of person who …		
My main achievements in life are likely to be …		
Other important aspects of my vision of the future are …		
The main influences, inspirations and values on this vision of my future derive from …		

Draw on your vision

Look again at the third column of the activity, *How important is this aspect to me?* (pp. 35–6). Consider what this tells you about the kind of lifestyle and career that you are likely to enjoy?

If you found it difficult to answer many of the questions on pages 35–6, this suggests either that you are very flexible or that you need to spend more time thinking through what sort of things you want from life. This will help you to make certain decisions about programme options, work experience, extracurricular activities and early job applications.

Rethinking the dream

- Be open to 'rethinking the dream' – you can change your mind!
- Create opportunities to reconsider your life journey in the light of your experience and reflections.

Return now to p. 34 and complete 'The Dream' again.

Reflection: Using the vision and the dream

- In what ways can you make use of the 'Vision' or 'Dream' that emerged through these activities to motivate you further?
- In what ways do your current study and extracurricular activities help take you forward towards your 'Vision'?

a Goals

The long-term vision gives us a sense of how well we know ourselves and a goal at which we can aim. To help identify the goals you wish to achieve from your time as a student, complete the table on page 38, 'What do I want to gain from my time at university/college?'

Deferred gratification

Some people are very good at 'deferring gratification': that is, at making personal sacrifices in order to achieve a goal many years down the line. They usually have a very clear vision of what they want to achieve.

However, it is not easy to 'defer gratification' unless there are lots of small successes along the route. It is difficult to put effort and energy into study, work, research or exercise if we do not have mini-goals, or milestones towards which we are working. Success at these spurs us on to greater triumphs. If we are not successful, this can also be valuable, providing time to take stock and re-evaluate how important something really is to us.

Create milestones

Smaller goals or targets enable us to experience success along the way and test us in the short term. For example, we can:

- perform in concerts whilst training to become a professional musician
- put on exhibitions if we wish to be an artist
- publish material if we want to be a writer
- make a speech at a wedding if we are likely to work in the public eye
- take on voluntary work to develop skills in preparation for paid employment.

Assessed coursework and exams offer the experience of 'being tested' and can develop a range of qualities that go with such 'testing'.

Set short-term goals

Once you have given thought to what you wish to gain from your studies, use the activity on page 39, 'Short-term goals', to set some interim milestones for yourself. These will help to provide a focus in the weeks and months ahead. They will also help you to monitor whether you are on track to achieve your longer-term goals.

On the table below, indicate with a ✓ if the item is something that you want to gain from your time at university. Put more than one tick if you feel this is very important. ✓✓✓

Go through the items you ticked and rate them in order of importance (1 for the most important, 2 for the next in importance, and so on).

From my time at university I want to:	Important to me?	Order of importance	From my time at university I want to:	Important to me?	Order of importance
'Get the piece of paper' (the qualification)			Develop technical skills		
Achieve a good classification of degree			Develop a wide range of skills		
Gain a deeper understanding of my specialist subject			Work with a wider range of people		
Enhance my thinking ability			Develop problem-solving skills		
Broaden my mind			Develop people skills		
Stretch myself intellectually			Try out new things		
Know myself better			Develop a broader set of interests		
Learn to believe in my own abilities			Gain work or volunteering experience		
Gain the confidence to speak in public			Make friends		
Experience student life			Make contacts for my career		
Enhance my career opportunities			Take on positions of responsibility		
Be able to get a well-paid job			Other things:		

Select the three items to which you gave the highest ratings (page 38). Consider what short-term goals you can set in order to give yourself an initial taste of success. You may need several short-term goals for each item you select. These goals are 'milestones' along the road to success. Copy this table and keep it where it will remind you to complete the goal. See p. 176 for an alternative action plan.

Item	Short-term goals	When I will do this	How will I know I have achieved this?
1	a		
	b		
	c		
2	a		
	b		
	c		
3	a		
	b		
	c		

Putting in the time

The most likely route to success is putting in the hours required to achieve it. There is a wealth of research that indicates that what separates high achievers from others is the amount of time they spend in becoming expert at what they do.

This is true even of apparent 'geniuses' or protégés; it has been claimed that the most successful, from Mozart to the Beatles, tend to devote around 10,000 hours to fine-tuning their craft. You may not have 10,000 hours as a student, but the general principle holds true. Even those who are successful at social and emotional skills tend to put in much more time in practising, reflecting upon and discussing these.

High achievers and time

High achievers tend to put more time into such activities as:

● *elaboration*: working out the precise nature of a problem, task or issue

● *preparation*: making sure that they are set up for the task, with suitable space, materials, mental preparation

● *perseverance*: sticking with difficult problems and going over them time and time again, looking for clues about where they are going wrong, until they find a way of resolving the issue

● *practice and rehearsal*, going over and over their work until they are fluent in the skills.

What if I don't have the time?

There are many demands on students' time so, inevitably, choices have to be made. That is why it is important to look at your decision-making in the round, weighing up the diverse aspects of your life, your values and aims, and how much time you can give, realistically, to each. It helps if you can be clear in your own mind about the reasons underpinning your choices, and then be able to make peace with the consequences of difficult decisions.

As well as the total amount of time spent, there is also the consideration of how well you spend your time. Chapters 4 and 6 can help you deploy time more effectively.

Maintaining motivation

Success is associated with high levels of motivation. For this reason, it is useful to be clear about what is likely to motivate you the most. Each of us is motivated by different things. Below are some techniques people use to keep themselves motivated.

Setting high expectations

Success is linked to high expectations. These may take the form of very specific things which you wish to achieve, or a more general vision or ambition. If you set low expectations, you will probably achieve very little. Once you set high expectations, you need to plan accordingly, making sure you create the right opportunities for yourself. If your expectations are low, you are likely to be unprepared for opportunities that arise.

Being realistic

Little is achieved without setbacks, effort and hard work, and even moments when you feel like giving up. Although positive thinking is an asset, unrealistic thinking sets you up for failure as you will be unprepared to meet hurdles that are set in your way. Think through what setbacks you may face and make plans to deal with these. Take them in your stride as part of the natural process, rather than as disasters which mean you will fail.

Setting realistic milestones

The section above, on goals, refers to the importance of setting milestones so that you can chart your progress. The more challenging the overall goal, or the longer it takes to achieve, the more important it is to set yourself intermediate targets to check you are moving in the right direction.

Rewarding achievement

Promise yourself a reward for reaching your intermediate targets – something you would really appreciate but which is appropriate to the size of the task – and then make sure you really do take that reward when you reach the target. You can set rewards such as a break, a coffee, a special meal, a phone call to a friend, for small targets on a single day.

Harnessing support

If you feel it will be difficult to keep yourself on track, ask a friend or mentor to check at set, regular intervals that you are keeping to plan. You may work better if you set up a support group to encourage you to keep going. These can work best if you set clear targets and your support team is given a specific date on which to check whether targets have been met.

Recording success

It is easier to monitor and reward your successes if you keep a record. This can be useful for the task in hand and also in retrospect when you reflect back upon what you achieved. A record of past successes can be very motivating for future enterprises.

Activity ⟳ **Sources of motivation**

When the going gets tough, I am most likely to be motivated by …
(*tick all that apply to you*)

- ☐ my long-term vision
- ☐ lots of short-term goals
- ☐ my values
- ☐ my belief system
- ☐ my will to win
- ☐ my sources of inspiration
- ☐ people who are close to me
- ☐ my desire to do good for others
- ☐ my desire to prove something
- ☐ achieving lots of small successes along the way
- ☐ giving myself a reward for completing a stage
- ☐ enjoyment of the activity
- ☐ finding something in the activity to interest me
- ☐ the support of other people
- ☐ having another person monitor my progress
- ☐ recording my successes

Hunting out the interest

It is much easier to succeed at a task if we find it engaging. We often react towards things we find difficult as if they were inherently boring. However, we can make something appear interesting even if, at first, we do not think it is. For example, we can make it a personal challenge to complete the task, or set up challenging time targets for each stage. Perhaps paradoxically, if we find out more than we need to know about something, we are more likely to find it interesting: feeling we have expertise can increase our interest.

The important thing is to know what kinds of motivational spurs work for you.

Personal investment: benefits, costs and commitments

> Put your heart, mind, intellect and soul into even your smallest acts. This is the secret of success.
> Swami Sivanandi

> The person who makes a success of living is the one who sees his goal steadily and aims for it unswervingly. That is dedication.   Cecil B. DeMille

> You can be an ordinary athlete by getting away with less than your best. But if you want to be great, you have to give it all you've got, your everything.
> Duke P. Kahanamoku

 Reflection: Commitment

- Do you agree with the comments quoted above?
- What, if anything, are you willing to commit to in such dedicated ways?
- What phrase would you find more motivating than those in the quotations?

For some people, success is measured by the achievement of a goal at any cost. For others, success is measured by overall outcomes. For example, the building of a new dam may be regarded as a successful outcome (it got built). On the other hand, some may view the event as a limited success or even a failure (it was built but at too great a cost financially, or to local inhabitants, or to the environment).

Identify one personal goal. Using the chart below, consider what a successful outcome would mean to you. What is it really worth to you? Write your responses in the boxes on the right.

Your goal	
Perceived personal benefits of achieving this goal?	
Perceived benefits to other people if the goal is achieved?	
What would you need to invest to achieve this goal (time, money, possible loss of self-confidence, friendship, etc.)?	
What level of such costs would you consider unacceptable?	
What costs would there be to others (time, money, possible loss of trust, etc.)?	
What level of such costs would you consider unacceptable?	
How would other people's opinion of you change if you were successful? Would this differ if the 'costs' were different?	
Would other people's opinion matter to you?	
How would your opinion of yourself change if you succeeded? Would this be different if the 'costs' were different?	
At what point would the benefits outweigh the costs for you? (Or at which point would the costs outweigh the benefits?)	

Success to some people (those who benefit from the dam) may be a loss to others. This is an extreme example, but it illustrates the point that each act is accompanied by benefits and loss. Each of us has to weigh up, for ourselves, what 'costs' we are willing to bear in order to achieve what kind of outcome. Often, we proceed without even considering the full picture – without considering what we already have, really want and value.

In planning for success, it helps to know certain things about yourself, such as:

- What you really want – 'no matter what!'
- Your assets: what you bring to the task in hand, that you are willing to 'invest' or risk. This includes such things as time, effort, money and material resources, friends and family, practice, endurance, willingness to wait or try again.
- Your limits: what sacrifices you are really prepared to make and where your limits lie. In this respect, the cost to others, the opinion of others, your values and your sense of self may all be relevant.

Ingredients of success

Taylor and Humphrey (2002) analysed interviews made with 80 UK and US business leaders, drawn from a wide range of businesses. They identified the skills and attributes which were most common amongst those who had been successful at chief executive level. Although most (91 per cent) had a degree and relevant technical skills, success was not closely linked to a level or type of knowledge: few had business degrees or outstanding technical ability.

Characteristics of successful chief executives

The Chief Executive Officers (CEOs) worked very long hours – but loved their work. They enjoyed leadership and recognition. They were noticeably self-confident, good at communicating with others and putting the interviewers at their ease. Their excellent inter-personal skills included patience and tolerance, often learned through the job itself. They were energetic, but took care to manage stress levels and stay healthy. Male directors were more sensitive to variations in their emotional lives and needed emotional stability in order to succeed. Most had a wide range of interests and part of what they brought to a company was 'breadth of vision developed from a wide range of

experience'. Most of these are self-management and people skills rather than unusual abilities or technical skills.

Attributes associated with success

The surprising outcome of Taylor and Humphrey's survey was that the range of personal skills and qualities associated with success were ones that most people could nurture. The researchers wrote: 'Board directors are not a race apart … we found ourselves in the presence of bright, hard-working people, but not creatures from another planet. They had a variety of IQs, expertise, and backgrounds. In other words, directors are just like the rest of us – and their positions are up for grabs.' The skills and attitudes of successful people can be developed by others.

The main skills valued by the CEOs included:

- self-knowledge and self-awareness – this was especially noticeable, and the directors were frank about their skills and their shortcomings
- inter-personal skills, especially the ability to work with, and lead, teams
- problem-solving ability, using creative approaches and positive attitudes
- a desire to win, especially on behalf of the company or team
- a willingness to work very long hours and to 'do what it takes'
- emotional intelligence, especially when relating to others
- the ability to manage stress and to take care of their health
- a love of change
- confidence
- a broad range of personal interests
- readiness to seize opportunities rather than making rigid personal plans.

Many of these skills have long been recognised as essential in the caring professions. It may be surprising to find this list associated with business success. However, similar skills are likely to be required across a very wide range of professions.

Increasingly, employers expect employees to be able to work in project teams on complex problems. This requires many of the other skills listed: good people skills, emotional intelligence, self-knowledge, a positive attitude, a willingness to put the team's interests first. Negative-thinking, selfish people who lack confidence, who get easily stressed, fear change or who are not aware of how they are coping with their own emotions, are unlikely to be a great asset to a team.

However, the qualities needed for different kinds of success may vary from the above list. Academic success requires a willingness to refine analytical thinking skills. Successful relationships may require a willingness not to work very long hours outside of the home, but are still likely to require a willingness to 'do what it takes' to

achieve a successful outcome for the relationship. High levels of success in any field tend to require long hours, hard work, practice, and a willingness to keep going towards achieving the goal even when you do not feel like it, or when you are tired or want to give up. There are few areas of life where an individual is unlikely to benefit from the characteristics associated with chief executives, as listed above.

Activity Self-evaluation of personal qualities associated with success

	Good	Wish to improve	Not relevant to me	See chapter
Self-knowledge and self-awareness	☐	☐	☐	1 and 2
Problem-solving ability	☐	☐	☐	6 and 7
A creative approach	☐	☐	☐	7
Positive attitude	☐	☐	☐	4
People skills	☐	☐	☐	5
Team working	☐	☐	☐	5
Leadership	☐	☐	☐	5
Negotiating skills	☐	☐	☐	5
A desire to succeed	☐	☐	☐	1
A willingness to 'do what it takes'	☐	☐	☐	4 and 6
Emotional intelligence	☐	☐	☐	4 and 5
The ability to manage personal stress	☐	☐	☐	4
The ability to cope with and/or promote change	☐	☐	☐	4
Self-confidence	☐	☐	☐	4 and 5
A broad range of personal interests	☐	☐	☐	1
Self-knowledge (reflection, self-analysis)	☐	☐	☐	1, 2 and 3
Risk management	☐	☐	☐	6
Ability to cope with uncertainty	☐	☐	☐	4

The goal or ambition analysed here is:

To achieve this goal or ambition, the following attributes will probably be needed:

Attribute	Highly relevant	May be relevant	Not relevant	Don't know
Self-knowledge and self-awareness	☐	☐	☐	☐
Problem-solving ability	☐	☐	☐	☐
A creative approach	☐	☐	☐	☐
Positive attitude	☐	☐	☐	☐
People skills	☐	☐	☐	☐
Team working	☐	☐	☐	☐
Leadership	☐	☐	☐	☐
Negotiating skills	☐	☐	☐	☐
A desire to succeed	☐	☐	☐	☐
A willingness to 'do what it takes'	☐	☐	☐	☐
Emotional intelligence	☐	☐	☐	☐
The ability to manage personal stress	☐	☐	☐	☐
The ability to cope with and/or promote change	☐	☐	☐	☐
Self-confidence	☐	☐	☐	☐
A broad range of personal interests	☐	☐	☐	☐
Good health	☐	☐	☐	☐
Self-knowledge (reflection, self-analysis)	☐	☐	☐	☐
Risk management	☐	☐	☐	☐
Ability to cope with uncertainty	☐	☐	☐	☐

Other skills needed to achieve this goal or ambition:

1

2

3

Personal qualities needed to achieve this goal or ambition:

1

2

3

Any other attributes needed to achieve this goal or ambition:

1

2

3

Where are you now? Self-evaluation of personal qualities associated with success

On the chart above (p. 45), identify whether each of the personal qualities associated with success are ones that you already possess, or wish to develop or are not relevant. The final column of the activity indicates where in the book you can find out more about this skill or aspect.

Skills and qualities needed to achieve your goals

It is worth comparing the list of the attributes associated with successful outcomes at chief executive level with the attributes you regard as necessary to achieving your goals and ambitions. You may find that your personal goals call for a very particular set of skills and qualities. However, it is important to think through all the kinds of situations and problems that you may have to address in order to achieve your goals. What qualities would help you in those circumstances?

Is there a good skills 'match'?

At this point, it is useful to compare the attributes that you identified as necessary for achieving a successful outcome of your goal (p. 44) with the attributes you ascribed yourself in the activity on p. 45. Is there a good match? If not, which skills and qualities will require further development? What will you do to develop these?

If you added further skills, goals and attributes to your list, which of these would benefit from being further developed whilst at university? What will you do to develop these?

Breadth of vision and experience

In the section on successful CEOs above, Taylor and Humphrey (2002) identified 'breadth of vision developed from a wide range of experience' as an important characteristic of successful people. It is easy to see why this would be the case. Experience gained from many different settings brings you into contact with a more diverse range of people. This provides opportunities for learning about people, developing inter-personal skills and net-working. Each context provides knowledge, skills, opportunities to develop personal qualities, as well as new perspectives and information.

Reflection: Extending experience

In your reflective journal, jot some thoughts on the following questions.

● In what ways do you already have a breadth of experience drawn from different contexts?

● In relation to your current goals and career aspirations, what opportunities are open to you for extending your breadth of experience? Consider, for example, your job, work experience, travel, taking on a position of responsibility, joining a student society, community or voluntary work, sporting activity, mentoring schemes, etc.

● What opportunities are offered through the curriculum for designing a personal programme that extends your range of skills and experience?

Congruence

'Congruence' refers to consistency in our thoughts, actions, behaviours and beliefs. It is about all our energies flowing in the same direction. It takes less effort to achieve goals if there is a high level of congruence between the different factors that influence, inspire and support those goals. If you are struggling to see the way towards success, it is worth checking whether there is a high level of congruence (or a 'good fit') amongst the following:

● your vision
● your motivation
● the 'influences' you value
● your sources of inspiration
● your short-term goals, targets or milestones
● your values and beliefs
● the attitudes of the people around you
● your means and resources
● your current situation.

In particular, it is worth checking that your 'vision' is still relevant to you. New experiences can change your vision, either reinforcing it, modifying it, or making it irrelevant.

Are your vision, ambitions, values and inspiration in alignment? Where might there be sources of internal conflict that could be undermining your efforts? On the chart below, jot down a response to the questions, using the space boxes.

Goal (e.g. what I want to achieve from my time at university)?	
What is my vision of success in relation to this goal? What would success look like?	
How does this goal fit into a bigger 'vision' for my life and my longer-term ambitions?	
What motivates me to pursue this goal – what do I want to gain from achieving this goal?	
What has influenced me, perhaps over many years, in forming this goal?	
What inspiration can I call upon to help me achieve this goal?	
What are my short-term goals? How do these support my main goal?	
How does this goal fit with my beliefs and values?	
How do the attitudes of people around me support me in working towards my current goal?	
What resources do I have, to support me towards my current goal?	
What else in my current situation supports or undermines me in working towards my goals?	
Conclusions	

'Goal inertia'

If you have 'vision inertia' or 'goal inertia', you continue to work towards a vision that may seem appealing but, in reality, no longer inspires or motivates you – there is no longer congruence between what you are doing and what you really want to do. This is especially true if your values change in the light of your experience. If this happens, tasks can seem to be more difficult or tiring. You may feel it more of a struggle to complete tasks, that you are looking for excuses to put tasks off, or even that you don't want to do anything at all. If you experience goal inertia it is time to recoup, to reconnect with your initial ambitions in at least some way, or else to change direction.

The preceding activity, 'Does it all add up?' can help identify the congruence of your own position.

Opportunities

Forks in the road

If you know what you want, either generally or in fine detail, are you taking and making opportunities that advance your aims? Are you somebody who looks for the opportunities in whatever comes your way or are you more likely to wait, hoping for the perfect moment to arrive? In every moment of the day, we make decisions that create a 'fork' in the path of our life. By acting one way or another, or by not acting at all, we make a choice to move in one direction and not another.

In the example shown on the flowchart below, at 15, Paulette decided to leave her part-time job at a local shop and work part-time in an electronics company. At the time, she just wanted a 'change of scene' that allowed her more flexible hours. From that decision, she met new people, overcame a fear of 'technical things', and travelled to China. These changes affected her choice of subject and friends at university.

What if I ... ?

What ideas emerge if you keep asking yourself the same question and have to give a different answer each time? The obvious answers tend to get used up after a while so that you draw more on your imagination to find new responses. Some of your responses may become rather far-fetched. However, sometimes, unexpected and useful responses can emerge. For the 'What if I …?' activity on p. 49, let your mind range broadly. Avoid censoring your thoughts, even if an idea seems unlikely. Be imaginative. See what emerges.

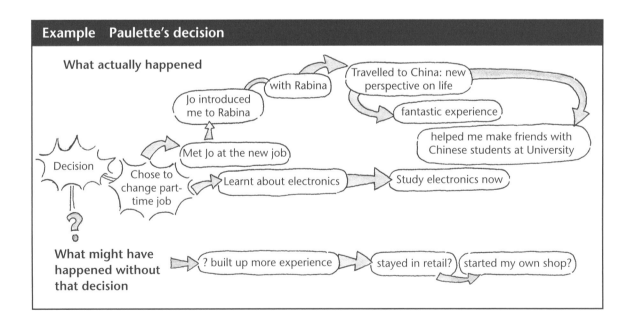

Example   Paulette's decision

What actually happened

Decision → Chose to change part-time job → Met Jo at the new job → Jo introduced me to Rabina → with Rabina → Travelled to China: new perspective on life → fantastic experience → helped me make friends with Chinese students at University

Learnt about electronics → Study electronics now

What might have happened without that decision → ? built up more experience → stayed in retail? → started my own shop?

The road walked

Take approximately three minutes to jot down choices you have made that you look back on and feel good about. This may include significant friendships, work, how you dealt with difficult situations, saying or doing the right thing, presents given, offers that you accepted or turned down, your dedication to your learning or to resolving a problem, the benefits from learning a new skill, acts of kindness, and good decisions you made. Focus on your role – what you did or did not do – rather than on what others did to you.

Read through your list and select your best use of an opportunity. It may appear small, such as giving somebody a card and seeing their face light up, or it may have been a major event such as saving a life.

Take a piece of paper and write the example at the top of the paper, as in the example above under 'Paulette's decision'. Spend a few minutes jotting down the various impacts of that one occasion on other aspects of your life. What opportunities, large or small, arose for you from seizing that first opportunity?

Activity The road unwalked

Now take approximately five minutes to brainstorm all the decisions you look back on and feel less good about. This may include opportunities that were present that you did not recognise at the time. For example, as well as the items on the above list, you may consider the things you did not do, say or learn. Focus on your role – what you did or did not do – rather than on what others did to you.

Read through your list and select the one opportunity that you feel you missed that has had the greatest impact upon your life.

Take a piece of paper and write down this decision as in the example above under 'Paulette's decision' (see p. 48). Spend a few minutes brainstorming all the ways that that one occasion has had an impact upon your life since. What other choices could you have made then? What might have been the consequences of making each of those other choices?

Activity What if I … ?
(from p. 48)

In your reflective journal, jot down at least thirty times:

'What if I … ?'
'What if I … ?'
'What if I … ?'   etc.

Take about five minutes to write responses to the whole set of 'What if I … ?' statements. For example:

'What if I … spoke Japanese?' (I'd apply for a job in Japan)
'What if I invented a toy?' (I could set up a business)
'What if I rode a pogo stick?' (I would be fitter)

Make rapid replies so that you do not have time to check how sensible your responses are.

Look through your responses.

● Which ones surprise you?
● Which ones provide useful information?
● Which one would be the most interesting to put into action?
● Consider what the answer to some of these questions might be? Where does that line of thinking take you?

Take three minutes to jot down all the alternative paths you could have chosen today.

● What did you not do today that you could have done?
● What might the impact of some of those decisions be?

Closing comments

When engaged upon a long-term project such as gaining a degree or developing a career path, it is important to stay focused on what you want to achieve. This may be very different for each person. It is for you to decide what 'success' means for you, what you would consider to be an 'achievement', and what you want to gain from the experience. For some, the 'travelling' is as important as arriving: the journey may be the goal.

This chapter has encouraged you to think deeply about the future and the things that influence, motivate, inspire and guide you. Long-term goals such as gaining a degree and working towards a career require commitment. Though it would be lovely if everything ran smoothly, this is unlikely always to be the case over a period of several years. When things feel difficult, it is quite common to feel like giving up. It is then important to find ways to keep going until the path gets easier and to keep yourself motivated. Motivation is the key to success. It provides the energy and the drive. That is why the goal or 'vision' must contain something within it that really motivates you.

It is also important that you are true to what you really believe. The obvious reasons for personal goals are not always those that motivate us the most. This chapter has encouraged you to look more deeply below the surface and examine what is really important to you. You should now have a much clearer idea of your visions for your life, your goals, your targets, values, motivation and skills.

In the next chapter, you will have a chance to look more closely at further aspects of what makes you unique. Chapter 2 provides an opportunity to look back over your life journey and the events that have most significance for who you are now and how you make decisions. It will also enable you to consider how you construct your personal narrative and perception of yourself, and the impact this may have on the choices you make. By identifying expertise you may have hidden in your repertoire, you can consider how you do things now – and how you might do things differently in the future.

Further reading

Cottrell, S. M. (2012) *The Exam Skills Handbook: Achieving Peak Performance*, 2nd edn (Basingstoke: Palgrave Macmillan).

Cottrell, S. M. (2013) *The Study Skills Handbook*, 4th edn (Basingstoke: Palgrave Macmillan).

Covey, S. R. (2004) *The Seven Habits of Highly Effective People: Powerful Lessons in Personal Change*, 15th Anniversary edn (London: Free Press).

Taylor, R. and Humphrey, J. (2002) *Fast Track to the Top: Skills for Career Success* (London: Kogan Page).

Chapter 2
Know yourself

Learning outcomes

This chapter gives you the opportunity to:

- consider the impact of your own life story upon your current life and performance
- analyse how you construct your personal narrative and perceptions of yourself
- analyse your learning journey and the impact of this upon your current approaches to study
- identify areas of personal expertise that can be applied to new tasks and areas of learning
- make use of your experience.

Introduction

This chapter focuses on how your life story so far, and the narratives that you construct to make sense of your experience, contribute to your uniqueness. It encourages you to investigate how your personal history, attitudes and beliefs about your ability might be influencing the way you do things now and your current achievement.

If you undertake the activities in this chapter with different goals in mind, you are likely to gain different sets of responses. If you find that a particular type of task is proving especially difficult for you, go through some of these activities again but with only that task in mind. You may uncover unexpected hindrances that you can then address.

Your life narrative

Personal narrative is used more and more in professional fields as a way of helping practitioners to understand the way they operate in the workplace. It is one of a number of tools that help individuals, by gaining a deeper understanding of themselves, to:

- make sense of their current reactions and responses in specific contexts
- understand why their responses might be different from those of colleagues
- reconnect with the feelings of significant events, so as to enable greater empathy with others

- value their own experiences and those of others
- identify where issues from the past might be having a negative effect now, so that these can be addressed.

It does take time to work on personal narratives, but the experience can be rewarding.

The 'true story'?

Each time you review your life story, it changes. The events may be the same, but different aspects become significant. If you write out your story every few years and look back at past versions, you may be surprised at how much your attitudes, responses and the themes of your story change over time.

In this chapter, you can consider your life story from different angles so as to gain different perspectives on yourself – rather than assuming there is one fixed version or interpretation.

The life metaphor

Before you launch into your story, it is helpful to stand back from it and take a snapshot of how you view it overall. One way of doing this is to consider the metaphors that you use – that is, the ways you describe your life, or events within it, in relation to other things. Some people regard life as a journey, or as a mission or a battle. Others think of it as a burden, a gift, an adventure, a lesson to be learnt, a trial, a treasure trove, a bottomless pit, a walk in the dark. These are their personal metaphors for their own lives.

Maybe you catch yourself using expressions such as: 'My life is a disaster waiting to happen ...' or 'it's all part of life's rich tapestry ...'. If so, these may indicate your metaphor for your life. By identifying and analysing the metaphors you use currently, you can gain insights that you might not have noticed before about how you view life – and how this might come across to other people.

Activity **Life metaphor**

- What is your personal metaphor for your life? You may need to give some thought to this. If you do not think there is *one* metaphor, just select one for this exercise.

- What words do you use, if any, to express that metaphor in daily life?

- How does it help you to make sense of your life?

- In what ways, if any, does this metaphor offer a constructive way of approaching your life?

Activity **A new life metaphor**

After the previous activity, you may feel that you would like to create a new metaphor for your life, to inspire you for the future. If so:

- Choose an item that inspires a positive reaction in you.

- Jot down the words: *My life is a ...* (or *My life is like a ...*).

- List as many points of comparison as you can between the item and your life.

- Continue with different items until you find one that is satisfying. Pin this up for a while as a reminder.

Significant components in the plot

To produce the narrative for your life story, the first step is to work out key components of the plot. Use the list opposite to identify key events and people in your story.

Activity **Components in the plot**

Take five minutes to make a list of the people and events that you regard as most significant in your life. For example:

The most significant events

- 'first times' you did something
- successes
- crises
- challenges
- opportunities that arose
- important events in the family that were significant in their impact upon you
- happy memories
- school memories
- holidays that were important in some way
- friendships and relationships
- work experience
- other things (*state which*).

People who had the most influence or impact

- parents, carers, guardians, relatives
- siblings and cousins
- teachers, school staff, pupils, students
- friends
- romances
- people you met on holiday, at social events, etc.
- professionals such as nurses, doctors and dentists
- neighbours; people who lived locally
- employers or work colleagues
- people who acted kindly or unkindly
- chance encounters who made a difference
- someone you didn't know well but who said, did or experienced something that affected you.

Your lists will be used for further activities in this chapter.

Life Chart: Plotting the journey

Now that you have identified the main components of your story, the next stage is to lay these out in such a way that you can work with them, plot out your life journey and draw connections between events. The visual and motor/kinaesthetic aspects of this task are important.

Activity **Life Chart: Plotting the journey**

Using the items on your lists for 'Components in the plot' (p. 52):

- Use a large sheet of paper or card.
- Separate out each event and person on your list (such as by cutting up the list).
- Organise these into the order in which they occurred.

Arrange these so that you can 'see' the events in the order they occurred, leaving space to write and draw around them. Alternatively, work directly onto the card.

- Fix these lightly so you can change them round later or add new material if you choose.
- Add in the people where they played most significant roles.
- Build the visual aspect, using drawings, photographs or symbols to represent an occasion (such as a symbol of an ice-cream for a holiday, a dark cloud for a significant argument, etc.).

Find the links

Once you have plotted out the key events and players in your story, the next stage is to draw out the connections between these. You may already have had to do this at a superficial level in order to work out the sequence in the plot.

Now, consider more deeply, if someone was significant in your life, what was their influence? How did that influence affect particular events? This may generate new material to add to your chart. Which events involved you meeting or losing someone who was significant in your life? In effect, you are looking for broad areas of 'cause and effect'.

Activity **Find the links**

On the chart you made for 'Life Chart: Plotting the journey':

- Give the date of each event (an approximate date will suffice).
- Using different colours, indicate whether each event or person was, overall, positive, negative or neutral for you.
- Write a brief commentary next to each item: a few details of each event and person, what you felt about them then, and what you feel now.
- Use arrows or other signs to draw connections between the events, and between people and events. Who or what influenced later stages in your journey?
- Circle just a few people and events that have the most significant impact on your life and performance now.

Create the narrative

You have gathered and ordered the raw material of your story. Now all you have to do is to write it out – or tell your story aloud and record it. It is tempting to cut out this step – but it is important to let the narrative develop. This will not only draw together your thinking, it will develop it.

Moved to house by river ⇨ Fell in river– Saved by postman ⇨ Sent to swimming lessons ⬇

Decide to study sports sciences ⇦ Won swimming championship ⇦

Activity Create the narrative

Write out your story. Make sure you include how you feel about your experiences. Be honest. This copy is just for you – so you don't need to worry about writing a good introduction or about your writing style. Just tell it.

Once you have completed your story, leave it for a few days and then go on to the next activity.

Themes in the tale

We noted above that each telling of a story, and especially our personal narrative, is likely to be different in some respects. There may be differences in terms of detail, the links made between events, interpretations, emphasis, and so forth. To this extent, our story is always a construction. By analysing what we choose to include and exclude, what we emphasise or brush over, the themes that run through our story of events, and changes in our interpretations from one telling to another, we can gain clues about ourselves that we might otherwise miss.

Reflection: Themes in the tale

Read through your 'narrative' or 'story' considering the following points:

- Have you included more positive or more negative experiences and events for your story? Could you have included more positive items? Are you avoiding negative or difficult issues that throw light on your experiences?

- What themes or patterns emerge from the story? For example, is the story full of adventures? Disasters? Effort and reward? Disappointment? Seizing and creating opportunities? Meeting and losing people? Solitary achievement or collaboration with others?

- What is the general tone of your story? Is it a sad or a happy story? Does it contain either much praise or much blame?

- What do the themes in your narrative tell you about the way you view your life? Is this the most helpful view you can take? Does this view further the 'vision' you identified in Chapter 1?

Activity The Hero

Consider the roles you have given yourself in your narrative: what part do you play in the plot? Are you active, taking the lead, and making things happen? Do you sit back and wait for things to happen? Are you the passive recipient of other people's actions? Maybe you sound like you are forever in battle, holding your ground? Overall, have you written the narrative so that you sound mainly like:

- the Warrior stepping into battle and fighting your own or others' wars
- the Saint who is always doing good and in the right
- the Martyr who has to suffer so others can benefit
- the Adventurer, looking for new experiences
- the Scapegoat, carrying the blame for others
- the Ruler, commanding the troops or the people
- the Sportsperson, playing a good game
- the Villain, who has been lucky or clever enough not to be caught
- the Wounded Soldier, who needs time to heal
- the Conjuror, pulling unexpected rabbits out of hats
- the Dragon, the Knight, or the Maiden awaiting rescue
- a different kind of hero? (*Identify what type*)

Yourself as Hero

You are the key player in your story, its 'hero'. One way to make sense of your life is to analyse the role you give yourself within your life story. This can give you insights not only into your character, but also into how other people may perceive you. For this to be helpful, you need to be honest with yourself and about what kind of character comes across.

Reflection: You as 'hero'

- Do you feel comfortable about the kind of hero that comes across in your story?
- How far does the hero you have chosen represent the way you really think, feel and act?
- What does this choice tell you about the way you view your life or yourself as an active agent in your own story?
- Do you play very different roles depending on who you are with, where you are or what you are doing?

Caricature

Self-recognition is notoriously difficult to achieve. However, one way of gaining perspective on the self is through use of a 'caricature' technique.

A good caricaturist helps us to recognise a character by exaggerating particular features. These are often the characteristics that make the person more individual and distinctive. By exaggerating our own personality traits, behaviours, speech patterns, or events that seem to recur in our lives, we can stand back and take a look at these with a fresh eye. This may bring home certain aspects of ourselves more clearly. We gain a great deal from such insights – although self-recognition can involve a certain degree of embarrassment or discomfort.

The activity below allows you to stand back for a moment from your main narrative and work with some emerging themes. This is intended as a light-hearted activity that can, nonetheless, enable useful personal insights to emerge.

Activity **Create a personal caricature**

If you feel you are up to the task, jot down your narrative again – or selected sections from it. This time, deviate from your memory of actual events in order to exaggerate certain key themes. Select personal traits, mannerisms, behaviours, speech, and/or themes in your life that you think are typical of you. If you are not sure about what these might be, ask a friend. For example:

- If the first draft of your story (or your life in general) contains many examples of 'beginning' and 'starting' activities, exaggerate this theme, adding in many more things that you 'started' (real or imaginary).
- If it contains many examples of meeting people, then flood your next draft with meetings, inventing meetings that never happened.
- If there are a number of accidents or disasters in your story, invent a whole lot more.
- If you think a particular comment is very typical of you, write it out seven times each time you introduce it:

I was just about to do that.
I was just about to do that.
I was just about to do that.
I was just about to do that.
I was just about to do that.
I was just about to do that.
I was just about to do that.
I was just about to do that.

Next:

- Read through your story, aloud. What does it tell you about yourself?
- Are you comfortable with your personal caricature – or do you want to change it?
- Were you able to laugh at your caricature?
- What do you think is the value of using this 'caricature' or 'exaggeration' technique for personal development?

Choices

Sometimes, it can feel that other people, events, history or 'destiny' rule the plot of our lives. Whilst it is true that we are all only part of a much bigger story, and that there are many influences on our lives over which we do not exercise control, it is also the case that we are agents in our own tale. There are choices that we make every day, some of which turn out to be more significant than others.

Activity **The choices made**

Look again at your life chart and mark in all the occasions when you made a choice that had an impact upon your life. You may need to add new material to your chart as as result. Then consider,

- What kinds of choices have you faced?

- What opportunities have you taken or not taken?

- What were the effects of the choices you made on later events?

Visualise at least two different scenarios of how your life might be different now if you had made different choices. If possible, select one choice that you consider to have been a bad choice, and one that is a good choice.

 Reflection: Re-evaluating choices

- In retrospect, were all the outcomes of the 'choice' good ones you would still welcome?

- In what ways did the 'bad choice' provide different opportunities for you that, in retrospect, could be regarded as positive in some way? The examples on p. 49 ('The road unwalked') may serve as a useful prompt.

- What do you think characterises a 'good choice'?

Evaluating the opportunities

All experiences offer opportunities to learn and to develop strengths – no matter how wonderful or awful they may have been. Your story will contain examples of where there were experiences, welcome or not, that have given you opportunities to develop as a person. The way in which you responded to these may have had a significant impact on your personality and the way you view the world now. This may be apparent from your personal narrative.

Activity **Evaluating opportunities**

Look again at your story.

- What things happened to you that would not be typical of everyone's experience? Identify at least one way that these provided some advantage (such as the people you can communicate with easily as a result, the realism they bring to your life, the different range of skills they developed, etc.).

- What were the most difficult things you had to face? What lessons did you learn from those events that can be of advantage to you either in completing your current programme or in achieving the 'vision' you identified in Chapter 1?

- How easy or difficult do you find it to regard experiences and challenges as 'opportunities'?

The 'next chapter'

Having written the narrative of your story to date and analysed it from various perspectives, it is time now to think about what the next chapter in your story might be.

Activity **The 'next chapter'**

Consider now:

- How do you want the plot of your life to unravel over the next 10–20 years? What kind of story do you want to be telling in 20 years' time?

- What kind of role do you wish to play in this next chapter of your life?

- What would need to change in your life now in order for you to play that role successfully?

Your top forty

Look again at your life story. Count how many examples of personal success you included. Was there at least one for every year of your life? If not, consider writing in some more.

Our personal success is rather like breathing: we rarely notice it on an everyday basis. However, it is hard to ignore 'hiccups' – the things that go wrong. Beaver (1998) argues that we do not spend enough time thinking of all the things we *can* do and spend too long focusing on what we cannot do. She encourages us to draw up very long lists of what we can do – and much shorter ones of things we cannot!

Activity ↻ Top forty strong points

Make a list of your strong points, successes, qualities, attitudes and attributes. List at least forty things. If that sounds like too many, you are underestimating yourself. Draw stars by the ten that are your greatest assets. Draw circles around the seven of which you are most proud.

№		№	
1		21	
2		22	
3		23	
4		24	
5		25	
6		26	
7		27	
8		28	
9		29	
10		30	
11		31	
12		32	
13		33	
14		34	
15		35	
16		36	
17		37	
18		38	
19		39	
20		40	

Reflection: Value your strengths

In your reflective journal, jot down your thoughts on the following questions.

- What is the ONE thing that you do best?
- What is it like to recognise so many strong points in yourself now? How often do you stop to value them?
- Are these strengths appreciated by the people around you? If not, how do you account for this? Is it, for example, because you are embarrassed about showing your strengths?
- Do you surround yourself with people who do not appreciate you? If you want to gain realistic recognition for your attributes, it is up to you to make that happen. What could you do to change the situation?

Activity **Seven areas for improvement**

List a maximum of seven areas for improvement in your life.

1	
2	
3	
4	
5	
6	
7	

- What is it like to recognise these weaker areas?
- What do you do to cope with them or to work around them on a day-to-day basis? Do you hide them, develop strategies, blame other people or find help and support?
- Who or what can help you to manage better in these areas?

Your learning history

In writing out your life story, you may already have included some events that had an impact upon the way you approach learning. Our early learning experiences are amongst the most profound influences upon our attainment and current levels of performance. They shape our approaches to learning itself, shaping our belief in ourselves and our ability to see opportunities for improving our performance.

This aspect of our story is a particularly important one, and this section provides a focus for considering its impact on you.

Activity **Learning history**

- List the incidents that have had the most significant **positive** impact on the way you now approach study and learn new things. This may be anything from times you were happy at school, unexpected success in a subject, support provided over a long period of time, or even just a few words that appeared insignificant at the time but left a lasting impression on you.
- List the incidents that have had a significant **negative** impact on the way you now approach study and learn new things. In what ways do these affect you now? Now you have identified these, what could you do to reduce their effect on you?

Activity **Positive learning experiences**

Think back to your time at school. Call to mind occasions when your learning seemed to flow, when it was fun, when you enjoyed learning and felt a sense of accomplishment. Make a list, now, before reading on, of all the conditions that gave rise to such positive learning experiences for you.

If you find this hard, keep returning to the sentences:

'My best learning experiences were when …'

or

'I got most out of learning when …'

Common responses

Below is a list of common responses to the activity above. The list is typical of responses drawn from diverse groups of people within educational contexts. Check your list against it. You can add items to your own list if you think they are true of your experience.

My best learning experiences were when … ☑

Nature of the task

☐ I felt the task set was interesting, worthwhile or of value to myself or others

☐ the learning was relevant to the real world or had practical uses

☐ the work was going to be seen and appreciated by somebody other than a teacher

☐ it was clear what was expected from me

☐ I could move around or there was movement built into the activities

☐ there was a creative aspect to the task

☐ there was personal choice in some aspects of the task

☐ there was a 'teaser', mystery or puzzle to be solved

With whom

☐ I could work with my friends

☐ we did small group work or worked in pairs

☐ we taught each other

The teacher

☐ the teacher was fair

☐ the teacher thought of interesting ways of introducing new material

☐ the teacher worked beside us and inspired rather than preached at us

Feelings and emotions

☐ there was praise and appreciation which came across as genuine

☐ I was treated like I mattered or my opinions and ideas counted

Timing

☐ I had time to finish what I was doing without rushing

☐ I had time to take it in

☐ there were lots of breaks so I didn't feel overloaded

Mastery

☐ I felt I understood one thing before moving onto another

☐ the tasks set were manageable but challenging so that there was a sense of both competence and achievement

Assessment

☐ I felt the way it was marked was fair

☐ I felt I had a fair chance of handing in what was expected

☐ my hard work was recognised

☐ I knew I couldn't get away with not doing my best

Special features

☐ we went on field trips or visits

☐ we had guest speakers or celebrity visits

☐ we showed our work to parents or visitors

Reflection: How typical are your experiences

In your reflective journal, jot down responses to the following questions.

- Is the list you completed about positive learning experiences, on p. 58, similar to or very different from the general trend outlined on this page? If your list is considerably different from that given here, what reasons might there be for that?
- At school, you may have been dependent upon other people to create the right conditions for your learning. Which of the items on this list could you put in place for yourself now, to enhance your current learning experience as far as possible?

　　　　　　　　　　　　　　　　　　Know yourself 59

The impact of educational experience upon performance

Reflection: The impact of your educational experiences

In your reflective journal, jot down responses to the following questions.

- In what ways do you consider your educational experiences have had an impact upon your performance generally?
- What positive things did the educational experience give you that you carry through life (this may not be classroom learning)?
- Look again at the items you identified as beneficial to your learning in the activity 'Positive learning experiences' (p. 58). Which of these could you bring into other situations, such as work or personal life, in order to enhance your performance, enjoyment or sense of satisfaction there?

Responding to setbacks

In your narrative (page 54) and in your consideration of your learning journey, you may have identified certain setbacks on your path. Setbacks can produce feelings of disappointment, discouragement or even 'denial' – a pretence that nothing went wrong. Whilst we would all rather that everything flowed well and without problems, when that doesn't happen, there are still benefits to be gained even from disastrous experiences – though such benefits may require some rooting out or take time to become apparent.

Setbacks and difficulties contain the seeds of our future success. As they hold the secret to 'what went wrong', they also contain valuable information about what could be done differently. Indeed, successful people often claim that they learnt more from their failures than from their successes, or that they are 'better people' because of them.

Apparent failure often brings us face to face with realities that we otherwise try to avoid. Setbacks can make us stop and take stock, follow new paths, meet new people, learn new skills, try things out that we wouldn't have done. In particular, they

tend to build personal qualities such as resilience, coping skills and empathy.

Turn it to advantage

Many people ascribe their success, relative or actual, to the way they responded to bad news or to adversity. We can make the decision to use our experience:

- as an excuse for not doing something
- to 'prove' something
- to keep going as before
- to learn and move forward.

Reflection: The 'best failure'

In your reflective journal, jot down responses to at least five of the following questions:

- What, on the surface of it, was the best 'mistake' of your life?
- What happened? What was your role in the event?
- What characterised this event as a failure?
- What bad choices did you make?
- When did you first realise you had made a mistake? How did you find out?
- What lessons did you learn?
- What benefits resulted from learning those lessons?
- What opportunities arose out of this event?
- How did the event spur you to action that you might not otherwise have taken?
- What does this event tell you about the nature of success and failure?

It is noticeable that the stories of many successful people include a critical experience when they were dismissed, belittled, ignored, suffered discrimination, or suffered a serious setback. Paradoxically, dealing with such events, whether at the time or later in life, can become the driving force that leads to unexpected successes.

This is very noticeable amongst students who face the most extreme difficulties or complex circumstances. Students with serious disabilities or mature students with multiple responsibilities find ways of completing their degrees and developing careers when those with fewer difficulties turned back at lesser hurdles. Typically, they learn to use the apparent disadvantage as an advantage – developing skills in managing time, applying technologies, negotiating, multi-tasking or prioritising. Anybody can make use of difficulty in order to emerge stronger – but not everybody does.

Reflection: Make setbacks work for your goals

In your reflective journal, consider:

- What are the potential setbacks that you are likely to face in achieving your current goals?
- What things might make it difficult for you to achieve these goals?
- What kinds of things might be preventing you from achieving the 'vision' you identified in Chapter 1?

- Consider how you can turn these setbacks 'on their heads', so that they become sources of strength, inventiveness, motivation or contact with others.

Copy this and attach it where you are likely to see it on a regular basis.

Expertise metaphor

When confronted with new tasks, people often say things such as:

- *I don't know where to start.*
- *I can't cope with this.*
- *I am no good at things like this.*
- *I am not good enough.*

Sometimes, the gap between previous experience and the current task can make the task difficult to achieve. Sufficient time and support may make it more achievable.

However, we can take on challenges more easily if we can recognise, value and draw upon an area of personal expertise. This can happen even if the area of expertise seems to bear little relation to the task in hand, as the examples below illustrate. Conversely, failing to recognise the similarity between problems with which we are faced and those that we can solve already, is a key obstacle to performance.

Read through the examples below, looking at the ways that each of these three students made effective use of their current expertise in addressing apparently very different problems they had had with their studies. As you read, consider how you might draw on their general approach in order to make use of your own expertise.

Examples of expertise transfer

Victor and car maintenance

Victor's challenge was in producing academic writing. He had little writing experience because he entered university from a foundation programme that did not use formal written assignments. He was very reluctant to write and was convinced that he lacked the logical, sequential skills needed for continuous prose. On the other hand, Victor identified a strong interest and practical experience in car engines – which he used as his 'expertise metaphor'.

Victor listed all the processes and skills he used when working with car engines, and those he used to write an essay. He then looked for significant points of comparison between the two sets of lists. He analysed the ways car mechanics use skills in:

- finding out information (about the engine)
- sequencing the order of tasks
- planning time to meet deadlines
- weighing up options
- forming a theory about what is wrong
- testing out ideas (about how to fix it)
- selecting between options using the appropriate methods for the job
- prioritising tasks
- testing out results
- re-evaluating the work done
- reflecting on performance.

Victor found that the most helpful approach for him was to compare the factors that make an engine run with those needed for writing an essay. He wrote these out as a list of key points which he could look at whenever he found academic writing difficult. His list is reproduced below.

This may not be how other people view an essay: the important point is that the metaphor worked for Victor. It released his potential, not simply to write essays, but to write *good* essays. This was because the process of writing now made sense in terms of things he really knew about.

Victor – My Engine

When I first started university, I had not worked at the academic level required by university before. When I visited the learning development unit … [it was] suggested that I treat an essay like a car engine. When I broke the metaphor (analogy) down, this is what I came up with:

1 Fuel – this supplies the necessary stored kinetic energy to power the engine – research at the library, lectures, seminars.

2 Battery – this stores the electrical energy – research notes, essay outline.

3 Oil – this lets the engine run smoothly – spelling and grammar.

4 The alternator – supplies electrical energy necessary for the engine to run – the essay question, unit guide, using aims etc.

5 Engine ignition system – supplies the spark to ignite the fuel, and the sequence in which the cylinders fire. Paragraphs.

6 Introduction – where this essay is going.

7 Main body – critical discussion of main points.

8 Conclusion – insights gained and mileage from essay, i.e.: 'What I have learned'.

9 Tool box – this is where the necessary tools are bought, borrowed or acquired, and stored – dyslexia workshops, English workshops, Accelerated Learning seminars, etc.

This can be broken down even more … When all the elements of the essay are integrated successfully then it should flow like a smoothly running engine.

Victor B.

Roger and aircraft assembly

Roger consistently failed to produce written work. He wrote well but was too much of a perfectionist. He evolved his ideas well during the process of writing and this also meant that, in practice, he would need to produce more than one draft. However, he always approached each draft as if it were the last, starting the whole of his work 'in neat' and editing beautifully as if this were the draft he would hand in. This meant he never reached the end; for all his hard work, he never had anything to hand in. In effect he was fine-tuning his work too early in the process.

Roger's area of expertise was assembling light aircraft that arrived from overseas as 'flatpacks'. He analysed the process of assembling a plane and how this might be similar to or different from assembling an essay. At this point, he recognised that if he tried to build a plane as he did an essay, it would also be impossible. If he tightened all the nuts and bolts, sanded it down, painted it and so forth on one part of the plane before going

on to the next part, it would be impossible to manoeuvre the pieces into place. Nuts and bolts should be tightened, and the final touches added, only when the whole plane is in place. Roger could easily see the comparison with fine-tuning an essay too early.

Once he had drawn the initial parallel, Roger saw many comparisons between aircraft assembly and academic problems. He used his previous expertise to address these. When introduced to new information, for example, he felt he should play around with it, like pieces of the flat pack, observing roughly how to structure these: '*As you bring them closer together, you are working quite globally – with an eye on how it all fits together. Then you can home in and complete sections.*' Similarly, he could see how good planning and structure was like 'glue' that held writing together: '*Keep an eye on how the sections will link. Aircraft glue is like a linking sentence, or a logical sequence that dovetails into the next item.*'

Luzia and dressmaking

Luzia also had difficulties with essay writing. She had extremely low self-esteem and was very reluctant to identify any area of expertise. Finally, she settled on dressmaking skills. She brainstormed all the processes that go into dressmaking, and drew parallels between these and essay writing.

For example, she saw that both dressmaking and essay writing required a clear vision of the final product. She couldn't set about choosing a pattern or buying materials until she had a sense of what she was trying to achieve. She compared this to interpreting the assignment title and having a strong argument: *'Your vision is your interest in it – without this, you just wouldn't get it done.'*

Similarly, both newly made clothes and essays need structure. Before she began to make a new item, she would decide whether it was to have a collar, cuffs or pleats and use this to guide her choice of pattern and material. For Luzia, laying out a pattern was like drawing up an essay plan: *'the pieces of a dressmaking pattern have to be laid out in a precise way so that the cloth falls properly'*. Similarly, in a well planned essay, all the pieces of the argument fall logically into place.

She made further comparisons between tacking a dress together before the final sewing and writing drafts before a final write-up. Trying a dress on to check for 'final flaws' was compared to proofreading. For Luzia, the most important element of dressmaking was having 'equal seams'. She compared this to treating different schools of thought equally when writing an essay: *'you must ask the same questions of each'*. The dressmaking analogy enabled Luzia to make sense of essay writing, calling upon her own expertise.

Make it 'make sense'

Just as Donaldson (1978) showed that young children are capable of performing tasks well above their supposed developmental level if the task is presented in a way that 'makes sense' to them, so Victor, Roger and Luzia were able to demonstrate that this is also true of adult expertise. They were able to use their own areas of relative expertise to address tasks that they had previously considered too difficult for them. They used extended metaphors – or an analogical thinking process – to accomplish this. If they can do this, so can anybody else.

It is very common for students to resist the idea that they are an 'expert' in anything. The first task, therefore, is to identify an area of expertise. This won't make you 'arrogant', as some people fear. Rather, it will provide you with a useful problem-solving tool. There will be one, or many, things that have several different stages or aspects to them and that you:

- perform with relative ease
- can complete without supervision
- feel comfortable doing – and may even enjoy.

Applying the Expertise Metaphor

Important aspects of working with the Expertise Metaphor are:

- Don't worry too much about the apparent difference between your area of expertise and the problem you are addressing.
- You don't need to be Olympic standard to consider yourself an 'expert' for this exercise.
- Expertise in everyday or mundane tasks can also work.
- Find out whether it works better for you to use features or component parts (as Victor did), processes (like Roger) or skills (Luzia).
- Where possible, aim to find points of similarity in the underlying structure of the tasks in which you are expert and those you are learning.
- Don't rush this – the obvious links can emerge if you allow yourself time to mull over the points of similarity.
- If the match in the points of comparison isn't exact, but still helps you understand what you need to do, that is the most important thing. This is a personal problem-solving approach not a literary exercise!

Activity ⟳ Identifying personal expertise

Select *one* task that you feel you can complete in the way described above (with ease, without supervision, etc.). This may be an item identified in the 'top forty' activity (see p. 57). It could be making a cake, dancing, playing pool, swimming, painting a picture, fixing a computer, etc. Consider this to be your area of expertise.

● Use the table below to list key components, processes and/or skills that go into completing typical activities in your area of expertise, as in the examples of Victor, Roger and Luzia above. Include the way you 'visualise' the task at the start. Pay special attention to the way you elaborate the problem at the beginning, working out what needs to be done.

● List all the skills and qualities that are needed to complete typical activities in your area of expertise.

(a) Area of personal expertise (state which):

Components (parts or features – see Victor), p. 61	Processes (the way things are done: see Roger), p. 62	Skills used in this area of expertise (see Luzia), p. 63

Analyse the Task

Use the table below to list key components, processes and/or skills for a task or problem that you need to address and which is proving tricky.

(b) Task or problem to address (state which):

Components (parts or features – see Victor), p. 61	Processes (the way things are done: see Roger), p. 62	Skills needed for this task (see Luzia), p. 63

Activity: Identifying personal expertise *(continued)*

Apply your expertise

Now, use the table below to draw parallels between your area of expertise and the area for improvement. Extend the metaphor as far as you can, so that you are really using your area of chosen expertise to assist you in the area for improvement. Think of all the ways that the second activity can be compared with the first.

For example, if your area of expertise was 'playing computer games' and your area for improvement was 'speaking in public', keep completing the following sentence: '*Speaking in public is like playing computer games because …*'. When you run out of ideas, take a break to do something different. Then come back and complete the sentence a few more times.

(c) Applying expertise

List below all the points of comparison between your area of expertise and the task you want to address

Area of expertise (component, process or skills)	Task (component, process or skills)

Select the best
- Read back over your responses.
- Highlight the points of comparison that you think will be most helpful.

Closing comments

This chapter has provided structured opportunities to reflect upon the way your experiences contribute to who you are now, the way you respond to challenge, and your approach to learning. It invited you to engage in a wide range of activities to explore personal experiences, choices, strengths and expertise. In this chapter, you commenced with a broad metaphor of your life and the sweep of your personal history.

You then analysed aspects of that narrative, and looked more specifically at your learning history. Finally, you narrowed your focus to an area of personal expertise and considered how you could use this, and your approach to adversity, to enhance future performance. Chapter 3 looks in more detail at the theme of managing personal performance.

When we write and explain our life story with integrity, it may seem as though there could only be one possible way to tell it and that we have been true to the 'facts'. However, if you work through activities that explore your experiences from diverse angles and at different times, you are very likely to find that your responses change. The main events may remain similar, but the way you write about them, the details you choose to emphasise, the way you interpret them over time, will change as your experience, attitudes and perspectives change.

It is because our personal narratives and their interpretation are open to change that we can take our story at any one time and look to see what it tells us about our approach to life. Some people have very extreme sets of life experiences, yet when they tell their stories, they emphasise the unexpected benefits or the people they met or the characteristics they developed as a result. Another person may have less challenging experiences and yet respond as if one of these has the power to control their life for ever.

We are the writers of our own story, we shape its narrative, we provide the interpretations. The interpretations we make can be a source of energy and motivation that carries us towards our vision of success.

Further reading

Beaver, D. (1998) *NLP for Lazy Learning* (Shaftesbury, Dorset, and Boston, MA: Element).

Cottrell, S. M. (2013) *The Study Skills Handbook*, 4th edn (Basingstoke: Palgrave Macmillan).

Chapter 3
Understanding your personal performance

Learning outcomes

This chapter gives you opportunities to:

- identify how your learning and performance are affected by your current skills, habits, attitudes, performance, experience and strategies (SHAPES)
- identify conditions that most suit your learning and performance
- gain an understanding of personalised approaches to learning and performance
- identify your personal formula for easier and more successful performance
- apply your personal performance formula to different contexts.

Introduction

In the previous chapter you considered your own life journey and how you characterised yourself within this by using metaphors such as 'the hero' or by exaggerating elements of your story to form caricatures.

This chapter is about deepening your understanding of what you need in order to 'get things done' – that is, to perform at all, to perform well and in ways that best suit you. It encourages you to take a personalised approach to learning and performance and provides a toolbox of resources to help you identify your personal preferences.

The activities enable you to consider the key factors that help and hinder you in achieving your best. From these, you will be able to derive your own personal formula for success and put this to the test. Activities also encourage you to consider how to work with your preferences – or, if necessary, how to work around them.

Learning or performance?

Anything we do depends partly on what we have learnt and partly on how we put that learning into action. Broadly speaking:

1 *Learning* is about finding out 'how to ...' – whether through accident, experience, instruction, developing theoretical instruction, practice, or other means.
2 *Performance* includes learning, but involves putting learning, knowledge, skills, personal qualities and experience into practice.

We may be better at one of these than the other, at either learning or performance. We may, for example, have learnt a speech well but not be able to deliver it in a public setting, or find it hard to learn a speech yet be good at public speaking once the pressure is on. In general, people judge us by how well we perform – not by what we think we have learnt. This means that it is well worth considering the conditions that enable us to perform at our best.

Types of learner

In recent decades, there has been much consideration of types of learner and styles of doing things – such as *visual* or *auditory* or *kinaesthetic* learning styles. There is a chance to have a go at this for yourself later in the chapter.

As performance includes learning, the information gained from such exercises is relevant to understanding your overall personal performance. You will probably find that what you discover about your performance preferences can also inform your approach to study.

Unique individuals

Although there are trends in preferences, which suggest 'types' of person or learner, this book takes the position that we are each unique in the particulars of:

● how we learn
● what we bring to our learning
● how we respond to new tasks, circumstances, people and challenge
● what we need in order to perform at our best.

Those particular details can be what really counts – if not all the time, then at least for specific activities or for significant tasks and occasions.

We all have preferences in the way we work and study. One of countless things may have a profound effect upon your performance. Dunn and Dunn, for example, isolated 21 different factors that affect learning. They found that some people are very sensitive to particular conditions, and they can under-achieve if these are not in place. Sometimes, changing something as small as your seating position, the light, or the way you study can have a dramatic effect (Dunn et al., 1995).

This chapter enables you to study your own learning preferences in detail.

Achieving peak performance

More than just getting by

Much of the time, we can 'get by' doing things in broadly the same way as other people or using strategies that have worked in the past. However, if we wish, we can take action that enables us to achieve more than just doing 'OK'.

We can benefit from considering what really works for us as individuals, from gaining an in-depth knowledge of ourselves and the conditions that enable us to perform well with maximum ease. The importance of attention to detail, even details that appear to be superficial, is recognised by those for whom success is important.

The example of top athletes

Top athletes look at how making fine adjustments to their training, equipment, and technique can give them an advantage, sometimes even of just a fraction of a second or point. They and the teams that support them look at every angle – the weather, features in the physical environment, diet, clothing, and so forth, both during training (whilst learning) and for the day of the competition. What is needed for training may be different from what is needed for competing.

This approach to shaping your mindset and behaviours in order to achieve 'peak performance' can be adapted and applied to academic and work performance too. The various activities in this chapter are designed to support you in considering the details of your performance.

Select the occasion

We do not need to pay minute attention to each aspect of every activity we undertake unless the stakes are very high. However, it is useful to be aware of what impacts upon our performance so that we can call on that self-knowledge on those occasions when we want to do well, have a competitive edge or conserve time and energy.

Personal performance and learning SHAPES

SHAPES stands for Skills, Habits, Attitudes, Preferences, Experience and Strategies. Combined, these make us distinctive in how we learn and perform. Understanding our own SHAPES for diverse activities can assist us in achieving our 'peak', or optimal, performance.

Skills

Skills, here, refers to abilities and techniques that help you to perform effectively at study or work – such as: Academic, People, Task and Self-management skills, mentioned on pages 18–23.

- In what ways is your own performance affected by your current skills?

🅰 Habits

When one set of actions or behaviours has served us well in the past, it is tempting just to repeat them in new situations – even if they don't work well any more. It is generally easier to do what is familiar rather than risk trying out new ways of doing things. Sometimes our habits were not very helpful in the first place. Consider:

- Are you attached to any study habits or patterns of behaviour that are not really helping your current study/work? If so, what needs to change?

Attitudes

Whether we are conscious of it or not, our learning and performance are affected by the attitudes and beliefs that we bring to them. These have a powerful effect on our behaviours and emotions, as well as on how others perceive us and react to us. That is true of academic contexts just as in everyday life.

- Do you bring a constructive, 'can-do', self-motivating attitude to your study?
- Do you feel comfortable about academic success? If not, do you let yourself underperform?
- How could you flex your attitude to your studies to help improve your overall performance?

Preferences

We all have preferred ways of doing things. Some believe there are inherent, immutable 'learning styles'; others consider such 'styles' to be deeply seated preferences that simply indicate our 'comfort zones'. Either way, it is useful to be aware of our styles or preferences, so that we can evaluate how well these are working for us.

Following our preferences can make tasks more enjoyable, less of an effort, more intuitive, and make it easier to stay on task for longer. However, we can become over-attached to one set of approaches: what worked last year or last week for a different assignment or with different people is not working effectively for us any more. It is useful to be able to recognise when that happens. Be ready to experiment afresh. If you find you are becoming bored or disengaged, try something new.

- How well do you draw upon your learning styles or preferences to shape your approach to study (or work)?
- Which, if any, have downsides that prevent you achieving at your best? What needs to change?

Experience

Our past experience shapes our readiness and confidence to take on new tasks, and the way we make sense of what is required. Pages 58–60 looked at the impact of experiences upon your learning.

- How are your past experiences shaping the way you approach your current study?

Strategies

If you have a good understanding of what has an impact on your performance, you are in a good position to devise strategies that help you perform at your best.

- Do you put time aside to devise study strategies that take account of the diverse factors that affect your performance?
- Do you reconsider and adapt your study strategies from time to time to meet changing circumstances and fit new study tasks?

Changing SHAPES

As with other kinds of critical self-evaluation, SHAPES can help you make sense of personal performance at a given moment and over time. You can capture your evaluation visually and see at a glance how your judgements change over time.

This is illustrated below for two students, Noleen and Idris. Their self-ratings changed a great deal in the first eight weeks of their course, as they gained more experience both of study and in making balanced self-evaluations. The criteria they used are available on pages 72–5 for you to use yourself.

Noleen's SHAPES

Self-evaluation of strengths and weaknesses (week 8)

Weaker areas					SHAPES	Strengths				
Non-existent	Very weak	Weak	Quite weak	A little weak		OK	Quite good	Good	Very good	Excellent
		☆			Skills					
		★			Habits					
					Attitudes					★
					Preferences				☆	
					Experience	★				
					Strategies		★			

Noleen

In week 1, Noleen gave herself the lowest ratings for almost everything. By week 8, she has both a more balanced appreciation of herself and more experience of study.

Noleen had had very little recent experience of study, so that, even in week 8, her study skills and habits are still relatively weak. On the other hand, she recognises that, in life and at work, she is self-motivating, well used to dealing with challenges constructively and sticking with difficult tasks until they are completed. These are useful attributes to bring to her studies. Her preferred ways of approaching tasks serve her well at work so she is monitoring them to see whether they prove effective for study too. This is reflected in her improved ratings for attitude, preferences and experience.

SHAPES Profile: Noleen

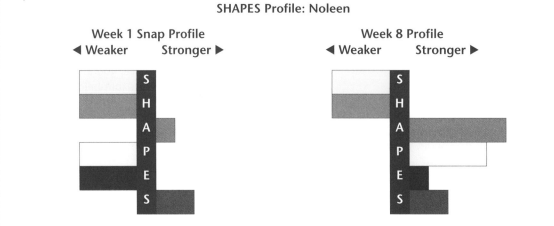

Week 1 Snap Profile
◄ Weaker   Stronger ►

Week 8 Profile
◄ Weaker   Stronger ►

Changing SHAPES

Idris's SHAPES
Self-evaluation of strengths and weaknesses (week 8)

Weaker areas					SHAPES	Strengths				
Non-existent	Very weak	Weak	Quite weak	A little weak		OK	Quite good	Good	Very good	Excellent
					Skills					☆
					Habits	★				
	★				**Attitudes**					
					Preferences		☆			
					Experience	★				
			★		**Strategies**					

Idris

Idris did very well at school and expected to find university easy. In week 1, all of his self-ratings were high.

By week 8, he finds study harder than expected and his SHAPES evaluation is more realistic – and looks very different.

Idris is aware that he has become over-distracted by his social life and doesn't put in the study hours that he should. He thinks his grades are likely to suffer as a result, and is starting to feel discouraged and demotivated.

Although school prepared Idris well for many aspects of his course, he didn't learn how to cope when things don't go well. He realises this, so his rating for 'Experience' has dropped. He still rates 'Skills' highly, but feedback from his tutors and friends has persuaded him that his study habits are not as good as he thought and that his attitude is holding him back.

Idris is honest in admitting that he tends to study in ways that suit his preferences for socialising rather than what might work best for his grades. He recognises that he needs to change his study strategy in order to achieve well on his course.

SHAPES Profile: Idris

Week 1 Snap Profile	Week 8 Profile
◀ Weaker Stronger ▶	◀ Weaker Stronger ▶

Find your SHAPES: Rate yourself for academic study

(a) First, use the 'snap' SHAPES profile, below, to make a quick judgement of your academic study 'SHAPES'

(b) Then complete the self-ratings below and on pages 73–5. For each, carry across your total scores to the 'Draw your ratings together' table on page 75. Then map your scores onto the chart on page 76, according to the directions that follow.

'Snap' SHAPES Profile										
Weaker areas					**SHAPES**	**Strengths**				
Non-existent	Very weak	Weak	Quite weak	A little weak		OK	Quite good	Good	Very good	Excellent
					Skills					
					Habits					
					Attitudes					
					Preferences					
					Experience					
					Strategies					

Rate yourself for skills

For each of the following sets of statements, rate yourself on a scale of 0–5, where 0 is a low rating for how true this is of you at present, and 5 is the highest rating. Then add up your total scores.

Skills		
1	I am aware of the academic skills relevant to this level of study on my course	☹ 0 1 2 3 4 5 ☺
2	I have well developed academic skills for this level of study on my course	☹ 0 1 2 3 4 5 ☺
3	I am aware of the 'people skills' relevant to this level of study on my course	☹ 0 1 2 3 4 5 ☺
4	I have well developed people skills for this level of study on my course	☹ 0 1 2 3 4 5 ☺
5	I am aware of the task management skills relevant to this level of study	☹ 0 1 2 3 4 5 ☺
6	I have well developed task management skills for this level of study	☹ 0 1 2 3 4 5 ☺
7	I have a good understanding of the kinds of self-management skills relevant to this level of study on my course	☹ 0 1 2 3 4 5 ☺
8	I have well developed self-management skills for this level of study	☹ 0 1 2 3 4 5 ☺
9	I regularly review the skills I have developed already and which could be developed further	☹ 0 1 2 3 4 5 ☺
10	I am proactive in developing a broad range of relevant skills	☹ 0 1 2 3 4 5 ☺
	Total score	

Rate yourself for habits and attitudes

Habits		
1	I have developed a good routine for daily study	☹ 0 1 2 3 4 5 ☺
2	I have developed a good system for settling down quickly to study	☹ 0 1 2 3 4 5 ☺
3	I understand the conditions I need in order to study most effectively	☹ 0 1 2 3 4 5 ☺
4	I am good at putting those conditions into place	☹ 0 1 2 3 4 5 ☺
5	I study at times of day (or night) when I can think best	☹ 0 1 2 3 4 5 ☺
6	I plan my time carefully to make sure I have enough time for study	☹ 0 1 2 3 4 5 ☺
7	I use all of my planned study time effectively	☹ 0 1 2 3 4 5 ☺
8	I am aware of things I do that make my study less effective	☹ 0 1 2 3 4 5 ☺
9	I am good at addressing poor study habits	☹ 0 1 2 3 4 5 ☺
10	I am good at managing potential distractions	☹ 0 1 2 3 4 5 ☺
	Total score	

Attitudes		
1	I am strongly motivated to achieve well generally	☹ 0 1 2 3 4 5 ☺
2	I am strongly motivated to study	☹ 0 1 2 3 4 5 ☺
3	I look for the enjoyment in what I study	☹ 0 1 2 3 4 5 ☺
4	I look for ways of making study interesting	☹ 0 1 2 3 4 5 ☺
5	I believe that if I put in the time and energy, I have every chance of doing well	☹ 0 1 2 3 4 5 ☺
6	Even when I don't feel like it, I find ways of settling down to work	☹ 0 1 2 3 4 5 ☺
7	I use tutor feedback constructively to improve my work	☹ 0 1 2 3 4 5 ☺
8	I welcome academic challenges	☹ 0 1 2 3 4 5 ☺
9	If things don't go well, that spurs me to do better next time	☹ 0 1 2 3 4 5 ☺
10	I always 'go the extra mile' to make my work as good as possible	☹ 0 1 2 3 4 5 ☺
	Total score	

Rate yourself for preferences and experience

Preferences		
1	I have given a lot of thought to how I learn best	☹ 0 1 2 3 4 5 ☺
2	I know whether I learn most effectively when listening, or looking, or 'doing'	☹ 0 1 2 3 4 5 ☺
3	I know whether I achieve better when working alone or with others	☹ 0 1 2 3 4 5 ☺
4	I know whether I work best in concentrated bursts or with many breaks	☹ 0 1 2 3 4 5 ☺
5	I know whether I work best working with the 'big picture' first – or the details	☹ 0 1 2 3 4 5 ☺
6	I know what kind of learning environment leads to the best outcomes for me	☹ 0 1 2 3 4 5 ☺
7	I am able to work to my preferences for 'structure' when studying	☹ 0 1 2 3 4 5 ☺
8	I make effective use of my learning styles and preferences to develop good learning strategies	☹ 0 1 2 3 4 5 ☺
9	I am aware of when my learning preferences are not the most effective way for me to get things done	☹ 0 1 2 3 4 5 ☺
10	I take care not to indulge my preferences at the expense of doing things well	☹ 0 1 2 3 4 5 ☺
	Total score	

You can undertake a more detailed analysis of your preferences using the tools on pages 78–86.

Experience		
1	I have recent experience of being in formal education	☹ 0 1 2 3 4 5 ☺
2	I have previous experience of work and/or study relevant to the course	☹ 0 1 2 3 4 5 ☺
3	My previous experiences of learning have been positive	☹ 0 1 2 3 4 5 ☺
4	My previous study experiences prepared me well for this course	☹ 0 1 2 3 4 5 ☺
5	The content of this course builds on material familiar to me	☹ 0 1 2 3 4 5 ☺
6	I have experience of the teaching methods used on this course	☹ 0 1 2 3 4 5 ☺
7	I have experience of the assessment methods used on the course	☹ 0 1 2 3 4 5 ☺
8	I had experienced success in my previous studies	☹ 0 1 2 3 4 5 ☺
9	I have a lot of experience of keeping myself motivated	☹ 0 1 2 3 4 5 ☺
10	I am proactive in reflecting on how I can learn from, and make use of, my experience	☹ 0 1 2 3 4 5 ☺
	Total score	

Rate yourself for strategies

Strategies									
1	I recognise that the approach I take to my studies can have a major impact on how well I perform	☹	0	1	2	3	4	5	☺
2	I put time aside to reflect upon my approach to my study, considering whether it is really effective or not, and how I can improve it	☹	0	1	2	3	4	5	☺
3	I use structured self-evaluation and/or reflections to help me understand how I study best in different kinds of circumstances, and why	☹	0	1	2	3	4	5	☺
4	I draw effectively on my understanding of my learning SHAPES to devise a suitable study regime for myself	☹	0	1	2	3	4	5	☺
5	I look out for tips, techniques and guidance on how to improve my study	☹	0	1	2	3	4	5	☺
6	When I find out about different ways of approaching study, I make a point of trying these out for myself	☹	0	1	2	3	4	5	☺
7	I make sure I continue to develop my study skills to match the greater levels of difficulty and complexity for each level of study	☹	0	1	2	3	4	5	☺
8	I have a system for monitoring whether I am slipping into study practices that are relatively ineffective for me	☹	0	1	2	3	4	5	☺
9	I am able to recognise when I am becoming bored or demotivated and adapt my strategy in order to keep my mind engaged	☹	0	1	2	3	4	5	☺
10	I adapt my strategies to keep study interesting and enjoyable	☹	0	1	2	3	4	5	☺
	Total score								

Draw your ratings together

Bring together your ratings from your total scores on pages 72–5.

	Skills		Habits		Attitudes		Preferences		Experience		Strategies

Map these ratings onto the charts on the following page.

Reflection: Personal SHAPES

Which SHAPES factors have the greatest impact upon your current learning and performance?

Map your SHAPES profile

- As in the examples of Noleen and Idris, on pages 70–1, use a star * to indicate where your ratings lie, using chart A below. Use the ratings that you have drawn together on page 75.

- Then, shade the boxes outwards from the central spine ◄ ► to those boxes with your star. You may find your SHAPES more interesting to consider if you use a different colour for each row.

SHAPES Profile											
Weaker areas					**SHAPES**	**Strengths**					
0–5	5–10	11–15	16–20	21–25		26–30	31–35	36–40	41–45	46–50	
Non-existent	Very weak	Weak	Quite weak	A little weak		OK	Quite good	Good	Very good	Excellent	
					Skills						
					Habits						
					Attitudes						
					Preferences						
					Experience						
					Strategies						

To make your SHAPES profile stand out more clearly, map your results onto the chart below.

Skills Habits Attitudes Preferences Experiences Strategies										
Date or week:										
			◄ Weaker			Stronger ►				
					S					
					H					
					A					
					P					
					E					
					S					

Using your SHAPES profile

Once you have derived your SHAPES profile, how can you make use of this to help you achieve success? Below are some suggestions.

1 'Honesty' Check

Look back over your self-ratings. Consider whether you might have made an inaccurate rating for whatever reason. Be frank and honest with yourself.

Amend your ratings if necessary so that they are a true reflection that you can rely upon if you want to compare your self-ratings at a later date.

2 Validity Check

Share your SHAPES profile with a friend, mentor, peer or tutor whose opinion you trust. Ask them whether it appears to them to be an accurate reflection of what they know of you as a student or colleague.

Although you do not need to agree with what they say, be open to their feedback. Consider what this tells you about yourself. If relevant, amend your SHAPES profile accordingly.

3 Evaluate your 'Snap' SHAPES profile

Compare the snap SHAPES profile you made initially with the one based on your detailed self-ratings. Reflect on the accuracy of your snap judgement. Where were you most, or least, accurate? How might that be significant for you in understanding your attitudes towards your learning and performance?

4 Provide your analysis

Look again at the brief analyses of Noreen's and Idris's SHAPES on pp. 70–1. Provide a similar brief analysis of your own SHAPES profile. In doing so, consider the interaction of the different factors with each other.

You may be able to identify where improvements or changes in one or two factors could lead to improvements across several others aspects of your profile and performance.

Personal performance factors

The activities on pages 78–88 are designed to help you analyse the impact of different influences and conditions upon your personal performance. For those activities that use scored ratings, a high score in one area does not necessarily mean that you are a certain 'type' of learner or person; it suggests that you have habits, styles or preferences that may influence successful performance.

5 Use your performance preferences

Our preferences for approaching a task can exert a strong influence over our ability to perform well. When studying and working independently, as is typical in higher education, we have much leeway to work in accordance with our own preferences. We can choose which preferences to use, adapt, or work around. In doing this, the following steps can help.

1   **Identify your options.** Think through the myriad options open to you for adapting the conditions under which you study or work. (See pages 77–8.)

2   **Identify your preferences.** Identify, in a systematic way, the options you prefer. Do this for your preferences generally and/or for your preferences for a particular type of task or assignment.

3   **Identify the strengths of such preferences.** Consider which of your preferences if any appear to exert a profound effect on your performance. These are likely to be those items with high self-evaluation ratings.

4   **Consider impact.** For such strong preferences (or aversions), consider when and how these affect the way you approach your study (or other tasks, if relevant).

5   **Take action.** Think of ways that you can adapt your study to take on board your preferences, to enhance your learning experience and achievement.

Use the following pages to identify and adapt your Personal Performance Formula.

Personal Performance Factors

1 Structure

The following activity looks at how far you prefer to work in structured or unstructured ways. Rate each pair of statements only once. **Rating**: select from a scale where 3 = 'very strong preference' and 0 would mean 'no preference'.

Less structure		More structure
1 I enjoy creative chaos	3 2 1 0 1 2 3	I enjoy being very organised
2 My desk/workspace is a mess	3 2 1 0 1 2 3	My desk is always neat
3 I never plan my work	3 2 1 0 1 2 3	I always plan my work in detail
4 I remember things in my head	3 2 1 0 1 2 3	I write lots of lists
5 I never use bookmarks	3 2 1 0 1 2 3	I always use bookmarks
6 I leave my papers out overnight	3 2 1 0 1 2 3	I tidy my papers away at night
7 I work whenever I find the time	3 2 1 0 1 2 3	I work to a strict routine
8 I study what interests me that day	3 2 1 0 1 2 3	I work to a strict timetable
9 I have a relaxed approach to time	3 2 1 0 1 2 3	I always meet deadlines
10 I am happy to 'go with the flow'	3 2 1 0 1 2 3	I need a clear sense of the end goal

Score for less structure _____   Score for more structure _____

Total score: [   ]

Interpreting your score

- Total score: **0–10** suggests you are flexible for this factor.
- Total score: **20–30** suggests you have very strong preferences, though these may not form a particular pattern.
- A score of **20–30** for the 'Less structure' column suggests you have a strong preference for working or studying in your own way at your own time. This can be a very creative and independent way of working. It is worth considering whether a more organised and structured approach would help. Danger points to watch for are missing deadlines and not fulfilling the requirements for an assignment.

- A score of **20–30** for the 'More structure' column suggests you have a strong preference for working or studying in an organised and systematic way. This can be a very productive way of working, and you are likely to be someone who gets things done and in an organised and timely fashion. It is worth considering whether more flexibility and openness to new ideas would benefit your performance. Danger points to watch for are over-rigid ways of thinking and working.
- Scores of **10–20** for either column suggest moderate over-dependence on your personal preferences. It may be useful to experiment with features of the opposite column.

2 External direction

The following set of questions looks at how far you prefer to work with or without external direction. Rate each pair of statements only once. **Rating**: select from a scale where 3 = 'very strong preference' and 0 would mean 'no preference'.

Less external direction		More external direction
I prefer …		
1 lectures to be unpredictable	3 2 1 0 1 2 3	to know what to expect in lectures
2 a lecture just to unfold	3 2 1 0 1 2 3	an outline or agenda at the beginning of lectures
3 to develop my own projects	3 2 1 0 1 2 3	to be given set assignments
4 to invent my own assignment titles	3 2 1 0 1 2 3	tutors to set assignment titles
5 to explore topics for myself	3 2 1 0 1 2 3	tutors to guide my thinking
6 to develop my own reading list	3 2 1 0 1 2 3	tutors to give the reading list
7 to do things my own way	3 2 1 0 1 2 3	to be told exactly what I have to do
8 to pick up how to use computer software as I go along	3 2 1 0 1 2 3	to go on a course to learn new software
9 to just get on with study for myself	3 2 1 0 1 2 3	the lecturer to give an early overview of the subject
10 to work out how to solve new new problems	3 2 1 0 1 2 3	clear guidance on how to approach new problems

Score for less external direction _____   *Score for more external direction* _____

Total score: [   ]

Interpreting your score

- Total score: **0–10** suggests you are flexible for this factor.

- Total score: **20–30** suggests you have very strong preferences, though these may not form a particular pattern.

- A score of **20–30** for the 'Less external direction' column suggests you have a strong preference for taking control over how you work. This can be very useful in developing as an independent, autonomous learner, capable of taking on new projects and setting targets for yourself. It is worth considering whether you need to be more open to ideas from others. Danger points to watch for are possible weaknesses in team working and not fulfilling the requirements for an assignment.

- A score of **20–30** for the 'More external direction' column suggests you are very open to direction and leadership from others. This can be useful in ensuring that you are going in the right direction, for using time economically and for team working. It is worth considering whether you need to take more control over your own learning and be more open to exploration and risk-taking. Danger points to watch for are reliance on others to do your thinking and planning, and underdeveloped personal independence and leadership.

- Scores of **10–20** for either column suggest moderate over-dependence on your personal preferences for study. It may be useful to experiment with features of the opposite column.

3 Working with others

The following set of questions looks at how far you prefer to work with or without other people. Rate each pair of statements only once. **Rating:** select from a scale where 3 = 'very strong preference' and 0 would mean 'no preference'.

Preference for working with others		Preference for working alone
1 I prefer group work	3 2 1 0 1 2 3	I prefer to work on my own
2 In a library, I prefer to sit near others	3 2 1 0 1 2 3	In a library, I prefer to sit on my own
3 I like to go through lecture notes with a friend	3 2 1 0 1 2 3	I prefer to keep my lecture notes private
4 I value hearing other people's ideas	3 2 1 0 1 2 3	I prefer to develop my own ideas
5 I enjoy the interaction in group work	3 2 1 0 1 2 3	I enjoy thinking through an idea in quiet reflection
6 I learn more through discussion than reading	3 2 1 0 1 2 3	I learn more from reading than discussion
7 I find groups come up with more ideas	3 2 1 0 1 2 3	I come up with more ideas on my own
8 For me, team working is really useful	3 2 1 0 1 2 3	For me, team working is a waste of time
9 I like to discuss study assignments with others	3 2 1 0 1 2 3	I prefer working alone on study assignments
10 I would find a study support group helpful	3 2 1 0 1 2 3	I work best if left to myself

Score for working with others _____   Score for working alone _____

Total score:

Interpreting your score

- Total score: **0–10** suggests you are flexible for this factor.
- Total score: **20–30** suggests you have very strong preferences, though these may not form a particular pattern.
- A score of **20–30** for the 'working with others' column suggests a strong social preference when working or studying. This can be very useful for gaining a wide set of perspectives and ideas, for developing social skills, for team working and for developing mutual support. It is worth considering how far you would benefit from more time studying independently. Danger points are possible over-reliance on others and not developing your own ideas in an independent way.

- A score of **20–30** for the 'working alone' column suggests a strong preference for solitary working. This can be useful for avoiding distractions, for achieving goals, and developing independence. It is worth considering in more depth what can be gained from working with others and the skills that emerge from reconciling different sets of opinions and personalities. You may lose out by not gaining access to a wide set of perspectives, especially in real-life or 'applied' settings. Danger points may be failure to appreciate the work of others and under-developed inter-personal skills.
- Scores of **10–20** for either column suggest moderate over-dependence on your personal preferences. It may be useful to experiment with features of the opposite column.

4 Level of physical stimulus

The following set of questions looks at how far physical factors may affect the way you work. Rate each pair of statements only once. **Rating:** select from a scale where 3 = 'very strong preference' and 0 would mean 'no preference'.

High stimulus		Low stimulus
1 I need to work in a very bright room	3 2 1 0 1 2 3	I need to work in a very dim light
2 I need music or TV in the background	3 2 1 0 1 2 3	I need absolute quiet to work
3 I work well when there is a lot going on in the background	3 2 1 0 1 2 3	My attention is very easily distracted
4 I always eat when I am studying	3 2 1 0 1 2 3	I can't think about food when I am studying
5 I need to drink a lot when studying	3 2 1 0 1 2 3	I never drink whilst studying
6 I work best when it is either very hot or cold	3 2 1 0 1 2 3	I prefer a moderate room temperature
7 I tend to fiddle with things as I work	3 2 1 0 1 2 3	I am quite still when I settle down to work
8 It helps me to think if I walk about	3 2 1 0 1 2 3	I can't think if I am moving about
9 Doodling helps me to listen in meetings and lectures	3 2 1 0 1 2 3	I focus on listening and making notes in meetings and lectures
10 I prefer to work on several things at once	3 2 1 0 1 2 3	I need to finish one thing before starting another

Score for working with others _____   *Score for working alone* _____

Total score: _____

Interpreting your score

- Total score: **0–10** suggests you have a high tolerance for working in most conditions.
- Total score: **20–30** suggests you have very strong preferences, though these may not form a particular pattern.
- Scores of **0–1** for any item suggests that you have a reasonable tolerance for working without that stimulus being present.
- Scores of **2** for any item suggests that your performance might be affected if that stimulus is not present.
- Scores of **3** for any item suggests your performance might be seriously affected if that stimulus is not present. You may need to think

creatively about how you can make it possible to provide that stimulus for most study contexts (for example, if you are light sensitive, by using bright lamps to increase the lighting or by wearing hats or sunglasses to dim light).

- A score of **20–30** for either column suggests a very strong overall preference for working either with or without stimulus. Given this preference, it is possible that if these stimuli were not present when you were being taught in childhood, learning may have felt difficult for you. High scores may also indicate a high level of stress. It may be helpful to speak to a counsellor or adviser about this.

Experiment

It is worth experimenting with studying with different kinds of stimuli present or absent. Monitor how far these do affect your performance. For example, many people have been surprised at how far they follow a pattern set down when they were at school as if that were the only 'right' way to study or work when alone. You will find that you learn more easily if you find the stimulus combination that suits you best.

5 Global or serialist

The following set of questions looks at how far your learning responds to 'global or 'serialist' approaches. Rate each pair of statements only once. **Rating:** select from a scale where 3 = very strong preference' and 0 would mean 'no preference'.

Which of the statements in each pair is more true of you? How does this affect the way you study?

Global styles		Serialist styles
When studying or working on a project, I prefer to …		
1 start off by gaining a broad overview	3 2 1 0 1 2 3	start off from interesting details
2 have the whole subject mapped out in a diagram or description	3 2 1 0 1 2 3	find the logical sequence
3 work from fully rounded examples	3 2 1 0 1 2 3	work from a clear list
4 use mind maps, 'picture' notes or a recorded discussion	3 2 1 0 1 2 3	use headings and bullet points or a recorded list of key points
5 launch in at the deep end	3 2 1 0 1 2 3	plan things out carefully first
6 use my intuition	3 2 1 0 1 2 3	adhere strictly to the facts
7 use my imagination	3 2 1 0 1 2 3	reason things out
8 search for connections between things	3 2 1 0 1 2 3	classify and categorise information
9 search for similarities	3 2 1 0 1 2 3	search for differences
10 draw things together	3 2 1 0 1 2 3	analyse the detail

Score for global styles _____   *Score for serialist styles* _____

Total score: [   ]

Interpreting your score

- Total score: **0–10** suggests you are flexible for this factor.
- Total score: **20–30** suggests you have very strong preferences, though these may not form a particular pattern.
- A score of **20–30** for the 'Global style' column suggests you have a strong preference for taking a holistic approach to work or study. This can be very useful for synthesising information, and making creative links. It is worth considering whether you need to bring more order and system to your activities. Look for possible weaknesses in managing clarity, detail, order and sequence in your work or writing.
- A score of **20–30** for the 'Serialist styles' column suggests you take a logical, analytical approach to study. This can be very useful in ensuring clarity and structure in your work. It is worth considering whether you need to create opportunities for developing your imagination and intuition. It may help to experiment with searching out links and connections between ideas. Possible weaknesses may be in drawing together your ideas into a strong whole and in making connections between what you are studying and the bigger picture.
- Scores of **10–20** for either column suggest moderate strengths for that style of working. It may be useful to experiment with features of the opposite column.

6 Pressure

The following set of questions looks at how far you prefer to work with or without pressure. Rate each pair of statements only once. **Rating:** select from a scale where 3 = 'very strong preference' and 0 would mean 'no preference'.

Which of the statements in each pair is more true of you? How does this affect the way you study?

Prefer high pressure		Prefer low pressure
1 I complete tasks in one go	3 2 1 0 1 2 3	I break tasks into manageable sections
2 I get everything done	3 2 1 0 1 2 3	I select certain things to do
3 I want to please everyone	3 2 1 0 1 2 3	I know I can't please everyone
4 I adapt well to the time available	3 2 1 0 1 2 3	I need plenty of time to do things properly
5 I work best when multi-tasking	3 2 1 0 1 2 3	I work best if I do one thing at a time
6 I work best with tight deadlines	3 2 1 0 1 2 3	I work best if there is no deadline
7 I need to feel a sense of urgency	3 2 1 0 1 2 3	I need to feel very relaxed when working
8 I work best without support from others	3 2 1 0 1 2 3	I work best with support from others
9 I catch meals when I can	3 2 1 0 1 2 3	I always take a break for meals
10 I need the final result to be perfect	3 2 1 0 1 2 3	I am happy if the final result is 'good enough'

Score for high pressure _____   *Score for low pressure* _____

Total score: [   ]

Interpreting your score

- Total score: **0–10** suggests you are flexible for this factor.

- Total score: **20–30** suggests you have very strong preferences, though these may not form a particular pattern.

- Scores of **20–30** for 'high pressure' suggest that you are likely to respond well to exams, competition and targets. You need to take care to manage stress levels and check carefully that they are not adversely affecting performance, behaviour and health without your realising. You may need to set your own targets for activities that you find boring or of low importance.

- Scores of **20–30** for 'low pressure' suggest that you may be good at protecting your health and well-being, and at producing good work even when there isn't external pressure to do so. You need to beware of over-sensitivity to stress and to external requirements and conditions.

- Scores of **10–20** for either high or low pressure suggest moderate preferences for that way of working. It may be helpful to experiment with features of the opposite column.

7 Method

When you have something completely new to learn, how do you set about learning it?
Tick the boxes that are true of you. ☑

I find it easier to learn through ...	
☐ listening	☐ reading
☐ personalising the material	☐ asking questions
☐ watching others	☐ adapting the task to suit myself
☐ picturing it in my head	☐ writing it out
☐ writing about it	☐ making a chart
☐ turning it into a picture	☐ colour-coding it
☐ turning it into headings	☐ talking it through with others
☐ categorising and labelling it	☐ linking it to what I know already
☐ day-dreaming about it	☐ describing or explaining it to others
☐ recording myself talking about it	☐ thinking about it whilst I do housework or similar tasks

- Which of the above methods are you not using at present that might be of use to you?
- Are there other methods you could use that you are not using currently?
- Highlight the methods that you feel are the most important in helping you to achieve well.

8 Honey and Mumford learning styles

Honey and Mumford (1992) developed a questionnaire that divided people into four main types. A broad outline of their learning types is given below. Which of the following are generally true of you (there may be more than one)? Which is the most true?

☐ **'Activist' learning style.** I prefer to work in intuitive, flexible and spontaneous ways, generating ideas and trying out new things. I usually have a lot to say and contribute. I like to learn from experience, such as through problem-solving, group work, workshops, discussion, or team work.

☐ **'Reflector' learning style.** I like to watch and reflect, gathering data and taking time to consider all options and alternatives before making a decision. Lectures, project work and working alone suit me.

☐ **'Theorist' learning style.** I like to learn by going through things thoroughly and logically, step by step, with clear guidelines, and to feel I have learnt solidly before I have to apply what I know. I prefer to learn from books, problem-solving and discussion.

☐ **'Pragmatist' learning style.** I like to learn by 'trying things out' to see if they work, just getting on with it, getting to the point. I like to be practical and realistic. I prefer to learn on work-based projects and practical applications.

- Do you think you might benefit from choosing certain types of study module or programme in order to ensure the teaching and assessment match your preferred learning type?
- Could you organise your study or your work to suit your learning type?
- Do you think it is helpful to see yourself as a 'type' of learner? How does this impact upon your performance in different circumstances? What might be the disadvantages of identifying too closely with one method or style of learning?

9 Visual, auditory and kinaesthetic learning styles

Rate each of the following statements, depending on how true you think it is of you, by drawing a ring round the number.

Rating: *4 = yes, this is very true of me   3 = yes, it is true of me   2 = sort of true/don't know*
1 = hardly ever true   0 = not true of me at all

1	When I'm reading, I picture the scene in my head	4 3 2 1 0
2	I have a good memory for conversation	4 3 2 1 0
3	I will remember something better if I have seen it written down	4 3 2 1 0
4	I remember things best if I get up and move about	4 3 2 1 0
5	I use my hands a lot when I'm speaking	4 3 2 1 0
6	I like to picture what I am learning	4 3 2 1 0
7	I remember phone numbers by the movement I make to dial to them	4 3 2 1 0
8	I repeat things out loud or over and over in my head to remember them	4 3 2 1 0
9	I doodle whilst I am listening	4 3 2 1 0
10	I add up numbers out loud	4 3 2 1 0
11	I can't add up unless I can see the numbers written down	4 3 2 1 0
12	I'm good at remembering the words to songs	4 3 2 1 0
13	I prefer to watch something being done before I try it myself	4 3 2 1 0
14	I like to ask a lot of questions in class	4 3 2 1 0
15	I find it easy to remember where I last saw something	4 3 2 1 0
16	I write out words to see if the spelling feels right	4 3 2 1 0
17	I have a good eye for colour	4 3 2 1 0
18	I'm good at sport	4 3 2 1 0
19	I am able to learn things off by heart quite easily	4 3 2 1 0
20	I have a good ear for music	4 3 2 1 0
21	I'm good at practical things	4 3 2 1 0
22	If somebody tells me a set of instructions, I can remember them quite easily	4 3 2 1 0
23	I tend to move around a lot on my chair when working	4 3 2 1 0
24	I tend to fiddle and play about with my hands a lot	4 3 2 1 0
25	I prefer to have instructions written down so I can see them	4 3 2 1 0
26	I like to learn by doing	4 3 2 1 0
27	I visualise a spelling to see if I have got it right	4 3 2 1 0
28	I run a film in my head of what I have to learn	4 3 2 1 0
29	I prefer to learn through discussion	4 3 2 1 0
30	I like to hear exactly what I have to do	4 3 2 1 0
31	I like to 'just try it out' rather than following instructions	4 3 2 1 0
32	I like to learn by doing practical things	4 3 2 1 0
33	I remember a phone number by the way it sounds	4 3 2 1 0
34	I like to learn from slides and pictures	4 3 2 1 0
35	I sing and hum a lot	4 3 2 1 0
36	I like the tutor to use slides and/or write on the board	4 3 2 1 0

Scoring

Each statement that you rated above indicates a preference for either a visual, auditory or kinaesthetic way of learning and performing.

- Visual learners find it easier to learn if information is presented so they can see it, and where they use their eyes or visual imagination to learn.
- Auditory learners learn best by hearing and recalling sound cues.
- Kinaesthetic learners tend to learn best where there is a physical sensation, such as movement, touch or a feeling.

Write down your scores for each statement and then add up your totals.

Visual scores		Auditory scores		Kinaesthetic scores	
Statement 1:		Statement 2:		Statement 4:	
Statement 3:		Statement 8:		Statement 5:	
Statement 6:		Statement 10:		Statement 7:	
Statement 11:		Statement 12:		Statement 9:	
Statement 13:		Statement 14:		Statement 16:	
Statement 15:		Statement 19:		Statement 18:	
Statement 17:		Statement 20:		Statement 21:	
Statement 25:		Statement 22:		Statement 23:	
Statement 27:		Statement 29:		Statement 24:	
Statement 28:		Statement 30:		Statement 26:	
Statement 34:		Statement 33:		Statement 31:	
Statement 36:		Statement 35:		Statement 32:	
Total					

Interpreting your score

No strong preference: If your scores for all three areas are similar, then you may not have a strong sensory preference for learning. If your scores are high (40–48 for each area), then you use all of your senses well to assist your learning. If scores are low (between 0 and 24), you may need to use your senses more consciously to assist your learning and experiment more with your learning.

A strong preference: The more marked the preference for one sense, the more you may need to ensure that you find ways of making good use of it, in order to make learning easier. Consider how you could incorporate into your study all the items listed above for that sense. Be creative. You might also like to consider whether you would gain from using the other senses more.

Personal Performance Profile

If you have worked through some or all of the activities in this and the previous chapter, it is likely that you have generated a great deal of information about what you need in order to get things done. The following activities enable you to pare that down to find the key factors in your performance profile.

Personal Profile: Chart

The chart below enables you to draw together your scores and ratings for the activities on pages (78–86) so that your preferences for each aspect stand out clearly.

If you notice that you feel energised when it comes to writing out some items, that already provides a clue as to your performance needs. However, if you feel your energy wanes when it comes to writing out certain items, this could indicate EITHER items you can omit as not significant to your performance OR items you know you should include as they work or are 'good for you' but which you don't actually like. If you need it, include it.

Personal Performance Profile Chart		
Aspect	**Score**	**Level and direction of preference**
Example: Structure (page 78)	*9*	*Very strong preference for 'more structure'*
Example: External direction	*27*	*No preference either way on 'external direction'*
Structure (page 78)		
External direction (page 79)		
Working with others (page 80)		
Physical stimulus (page 81)		
Global/serialist (page 82)		
Pressure (page 83)		
Visual, auditory, kinaesthetic (page 86)		

Reflection: Personal Performance Profile Chart

Use your responses on the Personal Performance Profile Chart above to analyse your profile. Consider what this tells you about your preferences. In particular:

- Note the aspect for which you gave the highest rating(s).
- Note the aspect for which you gave the lowest rating(s).
- Note whether you tend to have all high, or all low, or all moderate ratings, or whether you have no preferences at all.

What do these trends suggest to you about what you need in order to perform at your best?

Select key factors

The Personal Performance Profile Chart above enabled you to gain one perspective on your performance profile.

However, you may have noticed that you have strong preferences for particular factors listed in the activities on pages 78–86 but not for every factor as a whole. For example, you may have a strong preference for one or two items listed for 'Less Structure' (page 78) but all your other preferences might have been for 'More structure'. You may have had an even number of strong preferences on each list so that this balanced out as no overall pattern of preference.

The profiling activity below enables you to draw together specific information from each activity, so that you can see your key information more clearly. Look back over your responses to the activities on pages (78–86). Consider what each tells you about your preferences for getting things done. Select those items that you feel stand out strongly for you and list these below. An example of how you might approach this is given in italics on the chart below.

Activity Ò **Personal Performance Profile**	
Previous activity	**Personal preference factors identified through previous activities**
Example: *Structure (page 78)*	*I generally need a lot of structure and to structure things for myself. I need to personalise my workspace; I use lists a lot; I work to a strict routine and timetable.*
Structure (page 78)	
External direction (page 79)	
Working with others (page 80)	
Physical stimulus (Page 81)	
Global/serialist (page 82)	
Pressure (page 83)	
Methods (page 84)	
Honey and Mumford Styles (page 84)	
Visual, auditory, kinaesthetic (page 85)	
Learning history (pages 58–9)	
Expertise metaphor (pages 61–5)	
Other factors?	

Personal Performance Formula

The two previous activities enabled you to summarise a wide range of information about your personal performance. In the next activity, you can distil this information further in order to identify your Personal Performance Formula (PPF). This isn't a 'scientific' formula – it is your personal formula as identified through your own structured reflection, your analysis of how you do things, and your own selection of factors that are important to you.

Activity ↻ Personal Performance Factors

From the factors you identified in the two previous activities (pages 87–8), select and list up to 10 that are the most significant for you. It is up to you how many you list, where you select these factors from, and how you word them so that they are meaningful to you.

1	
2	
3	
4	
5	
6	
7	
8	
9	
10	

Name it!

It is likely that you have identified a unique combination of factors – which is why this is referred to as your *Personal Performance Formula* (PPF). As such, that unique combination, or formula, won't yet have a name. It is a good idea to give it one.

Naming your performance formula helps:

- to summarise the list of relevant performance factors
- to make the formula your own
- to remember it when needed.

That name will, of course, be personal to you – so the more individual it is, the better. It can:

- be as long or as short as you like
- summon up a sound, image or feeling that means something to you
- rhyme if you want it too
- include your name – or not
- hint at your performance preferences
- be based around a famous person or fictitious character
- be humorous – or not
- something entirely different!

Activity **Name your PPF**

- Read through the factors you listed for your Personal Performance Formula (PPF).
- Decide on a name that you feel sums up your personal performance preferences.
- Write it below – in a style that suits you!

Task-specific performance factors

When does the PPF work?

So far, you have identified a generalised performance formula. For some people, one broad set of factors, their Personal Performance Formula (PPF), is applicable to almost everything they do; for others, factors that influence performance vary greatly from one task to another. Indeed, one reason why people underachieve is that they cling to factors that were successful in the past or to a specific context, and apply them to tasks or contexts where they do not have the same effect.

Now that you have identified your Personal Performance Formula, it is worth considering when and how this applies in practice, using the following activities.

Activity **Test your PPF on different tasks**

Test out your *Personal Performance Formula* (PPF) for constancy.

- Select two distinct tasks or activities that vary in scale, character, or both. Write brief details of these in the two tables provided below (pages 91–2).
- On the tables below, write out the list of up to 10 factors that you identified for your PPF (page 89). If you wrote down many details against each factor, then just summarise the information you gave.
- Jot down *how* each factor applies to the task or activity you identified.
- Decide whether, overall, the PPF does apply to the task or activity (circle YES or NO).

Don't worry! Hold out your hand to it. Cats like to sniff you first to make sure you're friendly

© Stella Cottrell (2003, 2010, 2015), *Skills for Success*, Palgrave

Task specific performance formula (1)

Test your Personal Performance Formula (PPF): Task 1		
Task (*short description of the task*)		
Your PPF factors (from your list on page 89)	**How the PPF applies to Task 1**	**Applies?**
1		YES/NO
2		YES/NO
3		YES/NO
4		YES/NO
5		YES/NO
6		YES/NO
7		YES/NO
8		YES/NO
9		YES/NO
10		YES/NO
	Total number of 'Yes'	
Other factors or conditions that would enable me to perform best at this task:		

Task specific performance formula (2)

Test your Personal Performance Formula (PPF): Task 2		
Task (*short description of the task*)		

Your PPF factors (from your list on page 89)	How the PPF applies to Task 2	Applies?
1		YES/NO
2		YES/NO
3		YES/NO
4		YES/NO
5		YES/NO
6		YES/NO
7		YES/NO
8		YES/NO
9		YES/NO
10		YES/NO
	Total number of 'Yes'	

Other factors or conditions that would enable me to perform best at this task:

Did it apply?

If at least half of your PPF factors applied to both tasks, then you have identified a PPF with general applicability. The higher the number of factors that applied to each task, the stronger your formula is likely to be. This makes life relatively easy! It is worth noting your PPF and considering how you can apply it to tasks where you feel it will be helpful.

Could you have a stronger task-specific PPF?

Even though you have identified a personal performance formula that will work for you for different tasks, it is still worth checking whether a different formula might be even more successful for specific kinds of task.

You can do this by:

- evaluating the relative significance of each factor for particular tasks or contexts
- considering whether other factors could make a difference for specific tasks or contexts.

If you do note such differences, then you have identified a task-specific PPF which may serve you better. Note it down. Consider a way of ensuring that you will recall this when it would be helpful, such as by giving it a name of its own.

If the PPF didn't apply

It is not unusual for people to identify different sets of factors that impact upon their performance in distinct tasks. For example, the factors that apply to successful study when working on a piece of coursework are very likely to be different from those that apply in the exam room or a work-based project.

If few of the factors you had identified applied to the tasks you selected for testing the PPF, then you haven't identified a generally applicable Personal Performance Formula; you have identified that your PPF would be specific to certain types of activity.

Donna reckoned she performed best in a party atmosphere.

You are also likely to be more sensitive to context. Success for you may depend on how well you think through your performance needs in relation to particular tasks and situations. If you are not achieving the outcomes you want, then it is especially important for you to plan significant tasks carefully, identifying what you need and how you will put that into place so as to maximise your chances of success.

You may benefit from identifying a Personal Performance Formula for each type of significant task or context. If you think this is so:

- list the key factors (in summary)
- devise a name for each PPF
- consider a way of ensuring that you will recall this PPF when you need it – and the kinds of task or activity to which it applies.

Applying your Personal Performance Formula

Playing to your strengths

In the activities above, you identified how you *prefer* to do things and the conditions under which you prefer to take action. There is a lot of sense in working to your preferences as you are likely to be operating in ways that are most comfortable and familiar for you. If you are feeling at ease and happy with your conditions then, in general, you are more likely to:

- be 'playing to your strengths'
- be willing to engage with the task
- be able to focus on the task in hand
- avoid needless pressure and stress
- avoid emotional states that detract from your performance
- be less distracted by your surroundings.

If you have identified a PPF, then it makes sense to use it.

Making it work

Your performance preferences will sometimes be easy to accommodate where you work or study. Inevitably, on other occasions, there will not be an exact match between the way you want to work and study and the way that others teach or manage, or in terms of what is expected in the particular circumstances.

It is up to you to identify:

- what factors are essential to enable you to perform at your best
- whether there is some way that these could be accommodated
- how you can adapt either your needs or the task in order to work to your preferences
- how you will work around the 'gaps' if your PPF cannot be accommodated.

In the next chapters, you will find further ideas and resources that can help you to manage your performance.

Finding a way

Although there will be times when you have to work in conditions that are not ideal, consider whether you could negotiate with your employer or tutor for more flexibility so you can better apply your Personal Performance Formula. It might be possible, for example, to:

- complete part of a task at home where you can adapt the conditions to suit you
- work in a quieter room for tasks where you need to concentrate
- defer the task until a time that suits your ways of working
- have longer to perform one task if you can take less time on another
- work with a colleague on parts of the task that play to mutual strengths
- negotiate the deadlines on an aspect of the task
- swap that task for another.

Reflection: Find a way

Consider one task that you are finding difficult at the moment. Which aspects of the task or your work/study conditions could you negotiate in order to be able to work on this more easily in line with your personal performance formula?

'What I like' versus 'what actually works?'

Check whether your preferences are helping or hindering! Although it can be beneficial to work to your preferences, it may be that you have selected a range of factors that:

- narrow your overall range of choices
- make life more comfortable but offer too little challenge
- reduce pressure but don't get the job done
- reduce your chances of gaining something that matters to you
- put too much pressure on other people to accommodate your needs.

This requires you to be very frank with yourself. You are likely to know whether you are fooling yourself that your preferences are working if they are not. If your work, marks or feedback from others are not improving, then it is likely that you need to reconsider – and identify the formula that really will work!

Closing comments

In this chapter, you have analysed in depth many features of your own learning and performance. You had a chance to evaluate the relative impact of your skills, habits, attitudes, preferences, experience and strategies on your current performance. Your SHAPES profile can be used to reflect upon changes that you recognise in your approach to your studies over time. You may find it instructive to compare your own judgements with those made of you by friends or your tutors.

The activities enabled you to take stock of the conditions that you consider to be important if you are to perform at your best. You have been able to apply this self-knowledge in order to identify your own personal performance formula (PPF) and then considered how that formula might need to be adapted for specific tasks and situations.

Whilst you are encouraged to use your preferences and to identify ways of making these work to your advantage, you also need to be honest with yourself in identifying where personal preferences might be a hindrance.

As adult learners, we can adapt conditions to suit our personal needs. We can find ways of making effective use of our physical senses in order to better absorb and remember information. We can give thought to the assumptions we make about our learning and the restrictions we place upon ourselves. Whilst we cannot control all the circumstances that affect us, we do have the power to shape our thinking so that we learn more from our experiences. We can choose to have more power over our minds and to take control over our learning and performance.

Attention to the fine details of learning and performance in this way is akin to the work of athletes in attending to the multiple variables that enable them to achieve 'peak performance'. Applying such knowledge at the right time may give you the edge you need to achieve well in your studies or, indeed, in other contexts. If you find this approach interesting, you may also be interested in its application to tests and exams in Cottrell (2012).

Further reading

Cottrell, S.M. (2012) *The Exam Skills Handbook: Achieving peak performance*, 2nd edn (Basingstoke: Palgrave Macmillan).

Dunn, R., Griggs, S., Olson, J., Beasley, M. and Gorman, B. (1995) 'A Meta-analytic Validation of the Dunn and Dunn Model of Learning Style Preferences', *Journal of Educational Research*, 88 (6), 353–62.

Honey, P. and Mumford, A. (1992) *The Manual of Learning Styles Questionnaire* (Maidenhead, Berks: Peter Honey Publications).

Lawrence, G. (1993) *People Types and Tiger Stripes*, 3rd edn (Gainesville, FL: Centre for Applications of Psychological Type).

Chapter 4
Successful self-management

Learning outcomes

This chapter offers opportunities to:

- identify tools and resources for successful self-management
- understand the importance of constructive attitudes to success in any field
- evaluate and develop your emotional intelligence
- identify factors that prevent you from achieving excellence.

Introduction

Self-management encompasses a very broad range of skills, qualities, attitudes and experience. It can include some or all of the following:

- being able to analyse your situation, identifying strengths, weaknesses, opportunities and threats (SWOT analysis)
- identifying resources and sources of support
- managing your time
- adopting attitudes that support your aims
- taking a solution-focused approach to managing problems
- managing your own emotions
- coping when in distress
- managing change, uncertainty and confusion.

These are usually demanded of students whilst at university or in their first jobs, and are addressed in this chapter. There are associated skills and strategies covered in other chapters. For example:

- being a self-starter (Chapter 6)
- being able to motivate yourself to finish what you start (Chapter 6)
- taking steps to improve your own performance (all chapters)
- being assertive (Chapter 5).

Intra-personal skills

'*Intra*-personal' refers to your own inner world, in contrast to '*inter*-personal', which refers to how you relate to other people. Intra-personal skills help us to manage our feelings, responses and actions, so that we are able to function at our best. Some branches of psychology have long recognised the importance of our emotional well-being to our capacity to perform well. You may have noticed this on occasions such as exams, if anxiety or personal matters prevented you from concentrating or remembering.

The world of emotions

The 'intra-personal' world has the most profound effect upon our responses, our thinking, our behaviour, our views of ourselves, our feelings and our achievement. It touches upon what is closest to our hearts and being. It is, especially, the arena of the emotions. When we work with emotions, we can expect to feel emotional at times. Most of us can find this quite challenging, and so there is a temptation to shy away from developing intra-personal skills. If we try to avoid any issue where emotions may be involved, it can mean we do not get to the heart of the issue, and so do not achieve all we could. On the other hand, when we understand more about ourselves, know our own triggers, and develop our emotional intelligence, we are more able to manage every situation we enter.

This chapter forms a brief introduction to a very wide-ranging subject. It does not go into detail about sensitive subjects but, given the differences in our life stories, it is to be expected that some activities may be emotionally sensitive for individuals.

If you feel you need to talk something through as a result of any activities, it is worth noting that student counselling services were set up to deal with all kinds of matters, small issues as well as major ones. You do not need to be in a crisis to see them. Services are confidential and they may also be able to find support for you away from the university if you prefer.

Activity Focus

For this chapter, identify a personal goal or a situation that you wish to think about more deeply, in order to give focus to your responses.

SWOT analysis

A SWOT analysis is a useful, quick tool for taking stock of your situation. It is a simple way of analysing your level of readiness for a new task. It can take you to the core of an issue very quickly. SWOT stands for Strengths, Weaknesses, Opportunities, Threats.

Activity SWOT Analysis

- For the focus you selected in the previous activity, use the resource sheet on p. 99 to jot down as many examples of strengths and weaknesses as you can under each heading. Include personal qualities, skills, experiences, knowledge, resources and support.
- Under 'Opportunities', jot down any opportunities that could arise from achieving this goal. Include short- and long-term benefits.
- Under 'Threats', jot down the things that seem threatening, worrying, very challenging, or which are causing you some anxiety.

The Activities in this book, and especially those in this chapter, should help you to manage some of the 'threats'.

Emily prided herself on her emotional detachment.

SWOT Analysis Resource Sheet

Goal:

Strengths	Weaknesses

Opportunities	Threats

Personal resources

Very few of us have the ideal resources, but none of us is without any. This is especially true for students. A wide range of services is offered through the university, college or community, and listed in various leaflets, books and directories.

Activity ↻ **Finding information**

- Make a list of all the sources of support available through the Student Union and Student Services that are likely to be useful to you.
- Follow this up by making appointments – put these in your diary. Before appointments, read the literature provided so as to check the documentation or details you need to bring. Always take your student identity card or number.

Activity ↻ **Sources of support**

In the boxes below, list the sources of support available to you for each item. Put a tick in the box by those that you need to pursue in the next few weeks.

Academic advice and guidance ☐	Finding somewhere to live ☐
Financial ☐	Emotional questions, needs and support ☐
Careers/finding a job ☐	Health issues ☐
Meeting people ☐	Other resource needs:

Time management

Your time is one of your most valuable resources. How well do you use your time at present? Which of the following characteristics are typical of you?

Activity ↻ **Evaluating time management**

For each item, identify which one response is most true for you, indicating this with a tick ☑.

Characteristic	Yes, a lot	Yes, sometimes	No	I don't know
I recognise the following characteristics as true of me:				
Being late	☐	☐	☐	☐
Not knowing where I am supposed to be	☐	☐	☐	☐
Delays because I can't remember where I put things	☐	☐	☐	☐
Missing appointments	☐	☐	☐	☐
Rushing at the end of a task	☐	☐	☐	☐
Missing deadlines	☐	☐	☐	☐
Not being clear what I need to do next	☐	☐	☐	☐
Taking too late a bus or train	☐	☐	☐	☐
Getting caught up in interesting diversions	☐	☐	☐	☐
Finding it hard to get started	☐	☐	☐	☐
Taking too long to complete a task	☐	☐	☐	☐
Running out of time	☐	☐	☐	☐
Not knowing how long it takes me to complete a task	☐	☐	☐	☐
Dashing around all day	☐	☐	☐	☐
Forgetting what I have to do	☐	☐	☐	☐

- If your response to all of the above was 'NO' you seem to have very good time management. Is it perfect, or are there areas where you could improve further?
- If your response to some items was: 'I don't know', then you would seem to lack awareness about your time management. Speak to people who know you well and find out what they think about your time management.
- If your response to any of the above was 'Yes', the following activities and guidance may help.

For each item, identify which one response is most true for you, indicating this with a tick ☑.

Characteristic	Very true	Sometimes true	Never true
1 I use small pockets of time in the day to sort out minor tasks	☐	☐	☐
2 I get down to work quickly; I am well motivated to start	☐	☐	☐
3 I have timed myself completing the different aspects of larger tasks	☐	☐	☐
4 I know when I have done enough rather than aiming at perfection	☐	☐	☐
5 I say 'NO' when I lack time	☐	☐	☐
6 I delegate work to others when I can	☐	☐	☐
7 I ask for help where possible	☐	☐	☐
8 I have a go rather than worrying too much about getting things wrong	☐	☐	☐
9 I have strategies for starting a task rather than wondering where to begin	☐	☐	☐
10 I keep a diary and use it effectively	☐	☐	☐
11 I am well-organised so as not to waste time	☐	☐	☐
12 I plan my activities in a logical order	☐	☐	☐

Activity ⟳ Identify solutions

If you answered 'sometimes true' or 'never true' to any of the above time management factors, identify at least three you could improve.

- Some strategies for managing these time factors are given below. Which could you use to improve your time management?
- In your reflective journal, re-write these as positive 'I will…' statements. For example, 'I will keep an effective diary'
- Add specific details that make it more likely you will take action. For example, *'I will buy a diary today at the Student Shop after my Design lecture. I will carry it in my blue bag. I will check it every evening after dinner so that I can plan ahead for the next day.'*

ⓐ *Managing time effectively*

For each of the time management statements in the activity 'Factors in time management' (above), there are suggestions below about how to address that aspect.

1 Use small pockets of time in the day to sort out minor tasks

This is a key strategy for effective time management. Use time waiting in queues, on a bus or even waiting for the kettle to boil to recap on your learning, formulate lists, work out a problem, etc.

Keep a pencil and small notebook with detachable pages nearby to jot down your ideas. Make a mental note of the times in the day when you could multi-task in this way. This strategy also reduces the stress associated with queuing and tedious tasks.

2 Motivation to 'get going'

We saw in Chapter 1 how important motivation is to success. If you do not feel motivated, then be active in finding a source of motivation or inspiration. Focus on your long-term goals: check these are still important to you. Remind yourself of the benefits you expect. Write these where you can see them. Set short-term targets that you can manage, so that you get frequent tastes of success.

3 Time tasks

Time management requires you to know how long something takes. This is easier if you break a larger project down into smaller tasks. Often, one or two of these will take longer than you expect. It may be aspects of starting and finishing tasks that take longer than expected. Plan for all stages, and find out how much time you need to allocate for each stage.

4 Cost your time

Work out whether the amount of time you spend on each aspect of a task is 'cost-effective'. Usually the return (such as extra marks) decreases after a certain point. Academic work is hard to get perfect, as there isn't usually a single right answer. If you gain satisfaction from the additional study time, that is fine, as long as you have calculated what you are giving up in exchange.

5 Say 'no'

Identify what lies behind your difficulty in saying 'no'. It may be your beliefs, such as that 'a nice person' always helps out. If so, think what it means to be kind to yourself. Also, what are the negative consequences of always saying 'yes'? For example, does this give other people a chance to be kind or to take full responsibility? Alternatively, this might be a question of assertiveness or negotiation (see Chapter 5). There may be very long-standing or domestic issues which contribute to your difficulty in saying 'no'. If so, you should speak to a student counsellor.

6 Delegate to others

Identify what lies beneath a reluctance to delegate. For example, do you distrust others to do the job well? If so, what are the effects of this on your own time management, stress levels and personal efficiency? What would be the benefits to you and to others if you delegated more? How will others learn to do a job well if you do not delegate? Could you find a compromise where you share some tasks in the shorter term?

7 Ask for help

Recognise your own limits. Support services are set up because it is expected that people will need help. This is especially true for students. Asking friends and colleagues for help can contribute to their own personal development too. It can build their self-esteem and problem-solving skills. It gives them an opportunity to be helpful, which they may value.

8 and 9 Starting strategies

Use a basic starting strategy such as brainstorming or writing a list. Start with what you can do – and work from there. Often, a problem arises when we focus too much on what the end product should be rather than building from what we already know. Start small. Branch out. The ideas will come. If not, look for ideas in Chapters 6, 7 or 8.

10 and 11 Use a diary

A diary is an essential life tool. Some people prefer electronic organisers. Choose one that is light enough to carry around at all times. Check it at least three times a day. Develop the habit of writing everything in it to avoid double-booking. Enter all targets. Enter deadlines on the date of the deadline *and* the day you want to start work on that assignment.

Of all the donkeys, Geoffrey found it the hardest to say 'No'.

Student Day Planner

Early morning (to do before I leave home)				
Time	**Task**	**Place/Room**	**With**	**Bring/Say/Do**
8:00–9:00				
9:00–10:00				
10:00–11:00				
11:00–12:00				
12:00–1:00				
1:00–2:00				
2:00–3:00				
3:00–4:00				
4:00–5:00				
5:00–6:00				
Early evening				
Night				
Preparation for tomorrow (must do)				

12 Plan activities out in a logical order

Write a list of all the tasks you need to undertake during the day. Re-write the list, grouping the activities by place. Allow sufficient time to move from one place to another. Write the locations in your diary.

Student Day Planner

The Student Day Planner (shown on p. 104) divides time into sections most commonly used by students. Block in all your lectures, seminars, tutorials, workshops, lab-sessions, and assignment deadlines for each term or semester and then copy it. This saves writing it out several times. Indicate the room, the lecturer, and any materials you have to bring with you, so the information is easy to find.

Things that get forgotten

- The time it takes to travel between appointments – mark that in.
- The time when work for a deadline should begin – rather than just the deadline itself.
- New locations. These may be hard to find. Plan to leave time for getting lost.
- Queuing time.
- Transport delays. These are not usually accepted as excuses unless they are very rare with unusual circumstances.
- Information technology going wrong; waiting to use a shared printer, etc.

Time management for academic work is covered in more detail in *The Study Skills Handbook* (Cottrell, (2013).

Attitudes

Up to a point, every man is what he thinks he is.
F. H. Bradley

What's in a thought?

No two people respond in the same way to the same event. One person may be angry and determined to take action if something goes wrong; a second may shrug and forget it; a third may feel it is 'yet another example of why there is no point trying'. Our thinking about an event influences our response to it and the outcome. Our thoughts shape our experience, affecting what we feel physically and emotionally, how we interpret events, how we respond in a crisis and how we direct our lives.

Taking responsibility

One of the first steps in managing a situation is taking responsibility for oneself as an active, thinking, creative agent within the process. It may well be the case that 'someone' should have acted better, or may even be to blame for what happened. Taking responsibility does not mean excusing or taking the blame for somebody else's actions. It means moving beyond the 'blame' to find the most constructive outcome possible. The responsibility here is to yourself.

Often, the internal story that we create around events focuses on what went wrong and whose fault it was rather than on finding the best outcome. We run 'pre-recorded messages' about 'they' or 'it ', such as:

The Big Bad 'they'
- they make me …
- they should take the first step …
- they shouldn't put me in this position …
- they shouldn't set these deadlines …
- they should help me more …
- they started it …
- they design these so badly …

The Big Bad 'it'
- it is too difficult …
- it is too soon …
- it is too complex …
- it overwhelms me …
- 'it's doing my head in' …
- it won't work …
- it's a waste of time …
- it keeps doing this wrong …

Reflection: The pre-recorded message

- Which 'it' do you tend to blame (if any)?
- Which 'they' do you tend to blame (if any)?
- What other responses do you make when things go wrong that avoid taking personal responsibility for a constructive outcome?

Constructive messages

We can create alternative messages that lead to more productive outcomes. For example:

- I can do this …
- It's OK. There is a way of dealing with this.
- We can find a solution.
- In the circumstances, the best step is …
- The first step is …
- I take responsibility for my part in this.
- I'll have a go.

If we repeat these often enough, these become new 'pre-recorded messages' that will kick in automatically.

Activity **Change the message**

- Write down five constructive responses you could use when things go wrong.
- Check that these enable you to take responsibility for yourself.
- Choose the *one* you like the most and write it where you will see it this week. Try it out and record what happens.

Self-belief

Belief in oneself and one's own capabilities is essential. Low self-esteem creates stress, which makes the brain less efficient. It is also more likely to encourage a sense of defeat and a belief that there is 'no point'.

Self-confidence, a belief that one has the right to be and think and do what one wants, subject to reasonable limits and concern for others, enhances performance. It motivates and drives you forward.

Reflection: Self-belief critical incident

In your reflective journal, jot down a list of things you have done, no matter how small, that you are pleased about or proud of. Then, choose one to think about in more detail. Jot down:

- What happened? What did you do or say?
- What were the consequences? How did you or others benefit from this situation?
- What personal characteristics are demonstrated in this incident?
- What can you find in this incident that should ma ke you feel good about yourself?

- Brainstorm a list of 30 things that you like about yourself.

1. tall
2. handsome
3. flexible
4. manages change well…

- Go through your list, and underline all those that contain a positive description: 'I'm a reliable person', 'I am kind', 'I am helpful', etc.
- If there are fewer than 30 such positive phrases, add more to your list until there are 30. Don't underestimate yourself. If any phrases contain the words 'I try to …' or 'I am quite …', reword these so they are more definite and positive.

Which three descriptions of yourself do you like the best? What reasons have you for believing that these descriptions are accurate?

It is also attractive to other people. This can bring more interest, resources and support, increasing the likelihood of success.

Self-permission

Sometimes, we are unable to move forward because we refuse to give ourselves 'permission'. It is as if we hear a pre-recorded message saying:

- 'I'm not allowed'
- 'I'm not good enough'
- 'I'm not worthy of the risk'
- 'I'm not deserving of the consequences'
- 'I'm not made for this sort of thing'
- 'I'm not strong enough to cope with failure'
- 'It's not me'.

This can be true of anybody, but it is especially the case if there were strong messages at school or in the family that encouraged low expectations.

Activity Permission

Take three minutes each to complete the following two lists. Write quickly, without analysing your responses as you write.

List 1
I am allowed to …
(write as many things as you can think of).

List 2
I am not allowed to …
(write as many things as you can think of).

Check back over your two lists and see if you can spot any themes.

- What sorts of things are you 'allowed' to do?
- What sorts of things are you 'not allowed' to do?
- Which list is longer? What might be the reason for that?
- Who says 'you are not allowed to …'? Is it really true that you do not have permission to achieve in these areas?

Consider whether you could give yourself more permission to try out some of these things.

From this activity, you may recognise messages from a long time ago that are still echoing in the present. Many of the 'permissions' we refuse ourselves today began a long time ago. These do not have to remain as barriers to achievement. Take a look at your list and identify those on the 'I am not allowed' list that you could transfer to the 'I am allowed' list. Write these down.

Taking a solution-focused approach

*Whenever you are asked if you can do a job, tell 'em,
Certainly I can! – and get busy and find out how to do it.*

Theodore Roosevelt

Solution-focused versus difficulty-focused thinking

Difficulty-focused thinking
Focusing on the difficulty usually produces negative responses: the problem can seem insoluble. It depletes your own and other people's emotional and physical energy, creating a sense of weariness, hopelessness or helplessness. The dominant message is that the problem is difficult, it will be hard work to find a solution, and solutions are unlikely. The difficulty-focused approach uses words and phrases such as:

- 'but …'
- 'I can't see how …'
- 'oh no!', 'not again!'
- 'it's hard to believe …'
- 'that won't work'
- 'I doubt it'.

At worst, difficulty-focused people tend to pick fault with every proposal, draw attention to flaws in the best possible solution, and discourage others from believing that there could be a sensible solution.

A solution-focused approach

A solution-focused approach describes the situation, identifies the points of difficulty, and moves quickly to a search for the best possible resolution. It uses words and phrases such as:

- 'yes, and we could also …'
- 'what if we …?'
- 'are there other ways of looking at this?'
- 'let's brainstorm ideas …'
- 'let's look again at our options …'
- 'let's see if we have missed any options …'
- 'let's check whether we can make this work …'
- 'what could we adapt?'
- 'who else would know about this … ?'

The dominant message is that a solution of one kind or another will have to be found eventually, even if it is an interim one, so it is better to focus energies on finding the solution sooner rather than later. A solution-focused approach is often expected of those in managerial roles. As most graduates enter jobs with managerial responsibilities, it is worth developing this approach. If you have been surrounded by people who take a difficulty-focused approach, you might find this a useful challenge.

Reflection: Solution focus

- Do you tend to use the words and phrases associated with a 'difficulty-focused' approach or a 'solution-focused' approach?
- Which words and phrases are typical of you when faced with a complex situation?
- Do you tend to employ a solution-focused approach?
- What could you do to develop a more solution-focused attitude?

Ways of addressing a new challenge

Lazarus (1999) identifies two main strategies for approaching a difficulty: 'problem-focused coping' and 'emotion-focused' coping:

- problem-focused: looking outwards to the external, concrete problem and its circumstances
- emotion-focused: looking inwards at personal attitudes and emotions that impact upon your individual reaction to the situation.

A solution-focused approach can use either approach, adopting a constructive and positive attitude for either. The solution-focused approach takes the position that there is a solution to every problem and that we have that solution within us. Sometimes, we arrive at the solution more easily if we talk to others or use a particular strategy. The 'solution' is the best constructive outcome that can be found for the situation in the circumstances. This may not be everything that we would like, but it directs energy in a positive way so that the best outcome possible is achieved.

A solution-focused approach requires very little, beyond an attitude of mind.

Changing your environment

A negative, blaming, 'can't be bothered' environment is not inspiring. A few people with such approaches can spread negativity very easily. They can even create a culture which is self-defeating. You can probably think of the people around you who create an aura of negativity. (Maybe you are that person?)

As adults, we can monitor the impact of our environment on our responses, taking note of what leaves us feeling encouraged and what does not. We can take action to create an environment around us that supports what we want to achieve.

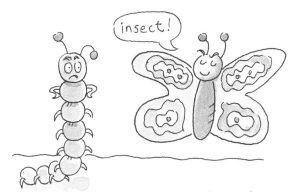

It wasn't what Cuthbert said as much as the way he said it.

Identify positive inputs

- Identify the people around you who leave you feeling positive about your goals, direction or programme of study.
- What is it about them that seems to increase positive responses?

- What other things in the environment support your goal? Competition and constructive criticism can be included as positive inputs.

Jot down these factors, starting with 'I ...', and identifying how you could increase the positive aspects of your environment. For example:

I appreciate the way Busola makes a point of saying she enjoys good seminars. I could identify the things I find positive about each seminar.

I find it useful that the library is open until 8:00 p.m. I could use it more in the evening.

Identify negative inputs
- Which people leave you feeling dejected, anxious, tired, despondent?

- What do you feel or do when you are in the presence of negative attitudes?
- What factors in your current environment could undermine or sabotage your goals?
- What can you do to reduce the impact of such factors upon you?

Emotional intelligence

Evaluating your emotional intelligence

The following activity enables you to evaluate your emotional intelligence. This is not a scientific test: emotions do not lend themselves easily to such testing. However, it gives you an opportunity to reflect upon your emotional life through a structured activity.

Activity ⟳ **Evaluating your emotional intelligence**

1 Emotional management (self)

For each item, identify which one response is most true for you, indicating this with a tick. ☑

Item	Always true	Usually true	Occasionally true	Not true	Don't know
1 I know which emotions I am experiencing	☐	☐	☐	☐	☐
2 I am aware of my emotions	☐	☐	☐	☐	☐
3 I allow myself to feel emotional	☐	☐	☐	☐	☐
4 I take notice of my emotions	☐	☐	☐	☐	☐
5 I can name the emotions I am feeling	☐	☐	☐	☐	☐
6 I tell other people what I am feeling	☐	☐	☐	☐	☐
7 I take responsibility for my own feelings	☐	☐	☐	☐	☐
8 I know what triggers different kinds of emotion in me	☐	☐	☐	☐	☐
9 I can respond without being overwhelmed by emotion	☐	☐	☐	☐	☐
10 I can express the right amount of feeling for the circumstances	☐	☐	☐	☐	☐
11 I can be assertive rather than aggressive or passive whilst feeling emotional	☐	☐	☐	☐	☐
12 I know when my feelings are not being expressed	☐	☐	☐	☐	☐
13 I make opportunities to express my feelings after an event, if needed	☐	☐	☐	☐	☐

Item	Always true	Usually true	Occasionally true	Not true	Don't know
14 I know the ways that my feelings affect my performance	☐	☐	☐	☐	☐
15 I regularly talk about my feelings to somebody I trust	☐	☐	☐	☐	☐
16 I reflect upon my feelings	☐	☐	☐	☐	☐
17 I allow myself to feel 'small' or vulnerable at times	☐	☐	☐	☐	☐
18 I cry if I need to	☐	☐	☐	☐	☐
19 I will allow myself to withdraw from a situation in order to experience my feelings, where feasible	☐	☐	☐	☐	☐
20 I am aware of how my feelings are affected by the people around me	☐	☐	☐	☐	☐

2 Emotional management (others)

For each item, identify which one response is most true for you, indicating this with a tick. ☑

Item	Always true	Usually true	Occasionally true	Not true	Don't know
1 I know which emotions other people are experiencing	☐	☐	☐	☐	☐
2 I am aware of other people's feelings	☐	☐	☐	☐	☐
3 I allow other people to feel their emotions	☐	☐	☐	☐	☐
4 I take notice of other people's emotions	☐	☐	☐	☐	☐
5 I can name the emotions other people are feeling	☐	☐	☐	☐	☐
6 I speak to other people about their feelings	☐	☐	☐	☐	☐
7 I take responsibility for my own feelings when other people are feeling emotional	☐	☐	☐	☐	☐
8 I know what triggers emotional responses in people I see regularly	☐	☐	☐	☐	☐
9 I am aware of my own responses to other people's emotions	☐	☐	☐	☐	☐
10 I allow others to express what they feel is right for the circumstances	☐	☐	☐	☐	☐

Activity: Evaluating your emotional intelligence *(continued)*

Item	Always true	Usually true	Occasionally true	Not true	Don't know
11 I can be assertive when other people are being aggressive, passive or emotional	☐	☐	☐	☐	☐
12 I am aware when other people are not expressing their feelings	☐	☐	☐	☐	☐
13 I make opportunities to enable other people to express their feelings	☐	☐	☐	☐	☐
14 I am aware of how I let other people's feelings affect my performance	☐	☐	☐	☐	☐
15 I regularly listen to someone I know well talking about their feelings	☐	☐	☐	☐	☐
16 I reflect upon the way feelings are experienced and expressed in groups	☐	☐	☐	☐	☐
17 I allow other people to feel 'small' or vulnerable if they need to	☐	☐	☐	☐	☐
18 I am comfortable when others cry if they need to	☐	☐	☐	☐	☐
19 I understand when other people withdraw from a situation in order to experience their feelings	☐	☐	☐	☐	☐
20 I am aware of how my feelings affect the people around me	☐	☐	☐	☐	☐

3 Emotions in action

For each item, identify which one response is most true for you, indicating this with a tick. ☑

Item	Always true	Usually true	Occasionally true	Not true	Don't know
1 I feel comfortable even when people disagree with me	☐	☐	☐	☐	☐
2 I can allow other people their own opinions	☐	☐	☐	☐	☐
3 I can feel angry without taking it out on others	☐	☐	☐	☐	☐
4 I can accept criticism without getting angry	☐	☐	☐	☐	☐
5 I can voice my own opinions	☐	☐	☐	☐	☐
6 I am able to remain positive even when the situation looks gloomy	☐	☐	☐	☐	☐

Activity: Evaluating your emotional intelligence *(continued)*

Item	Always true	Usually true	Occasionally true	Not true	Don't know
7 I can allow myself to be sad – and to experience the sadness without pushing it away	☐	☐	☐	☐	☐
8 I can make decisions and act upon them	☐	☐	☐	☐	☐
9 I can stop and assess a situation before I act or speak	☐	☐	☐	☐	☐
10 I feel comfortable working with people from very different backgrounds to mine	☐	☐	☐	☐	☐
11 I can enjoy diversity in the people around me	☐	☐	☐	☐	☐
12 I will speak out for what I believe is right	☐	☐	☐	☐	☐
13 I ask for help when I need it	☐	☐	☐	☐	☐
14 I can let myself feel emotions without taking a drink, cigarette, drug, or comfort eating	☐	☐	☐	☐	☐
15 I am calm in a crisis	☐	☐	☐	☐	☐
16 I can identify when my behaviour is unreasonable – and stop it	☐	☐	☐	☐	☐
17 I can manage uncertainty without having to have an answer straight away	☐	☐	☐	☐	☐
18 I can manage my emotions under pressure	☐	☐	☐	☐	☐
19 I take responsibility for my own part in events	☐	☐	☐	☐	☐
20 I can admit a mistake and apologise	☐	☐	☐	☐	☐

Scoring your responses

For each item on the above sets of questions, allocate to yourself the following scores: Always true (4); Usually true (3);   Occasionally true (2);   Not true (1);   Don't know (0).

1   Emotional management (self):   Score [　　　]

2   Emotional management (others):   Score [　　　]

3   Emotions in action: Score [　　　]

Total score: [　　　]

Activity: Evaluating your emotional intelligence *(continued)*

Interpreting your scores

150–200 If your answers are accurate, this suggests that you have a sophisticated approach to emotional life. You seem capable of managing your own emotions as well as coping with the emotions of other people. You seem able to make the kinds of responses that accompany emotional intelligence. Your emotional intelligence should provide you with an asset in almost any situation.

100–149 This is a good score. If your evaluations are accurate, you have a very good foundation for developing your emotional intelligence further. Emotional intelligence is an asset in most situations so this is very much worth nurturing. Look at the responses which have high scores: what do these tell you about your strengths? Are there any themes evident in the questions that received lower scores? It is worth noting whether one of the three sections had a lower score than the others. Identify which of these is your priority for further self-development.

50–99 This is a reasonable score, especially if you entered university straight from school. However, it suggests that you have lots of room to develop your emotional management skills. If your evaluation is accurate, you would benefit from making emotional self-management a priority area. Identify which areas are your strengths. These are the assets you take into most situations. Look for themes in the lower scores. Which types of issues are most relevant to the achievement of your goals? Identify which of these is your priority for further self-development.

0–49 If your evaluation is accurate, you may have a real challenge on your hands. Remember that this is not a scientific test. There may be many areas of emotional intelligence in which you excel that are not covered by this activity. For example, some people are exceptional in crises – but there is only one question related to managing a crisis above. Other people are emotionally sophisticated with particular types of people, such as children, the elderly, sick people, etc. In addition, your evaluation may have been harsh. On the other hand, you may really feel that the emotional world is rather a tricky one. You may feel that people misunderstand you or your motives much of the time. You are not alone if you feel that. However, it is not necessarily a very comfortable position to be in. The good news is that emotional intelligence is an asset that can be developed. The student counselling service at the university will probably be able to give you confidential advice if you are at all concerned.

What is emotional intelligence?

'Emotional intelligence' is a term made current by Goleman (1995). It is slowly becoming recognised that it isn't simply what we do and what we think that affects our ability to cope, manage and succeed, but also how we manage our feelings.

Emotional intelligence involves:

- knowing the appropriate feelings for the circumstances
- experiencing the appropriate feelings for the circumstances
- expressing feelings appropriate to the circumstances
- making opportunities to express feelings that cannot be expressed fully in the original circumstances.

This may sound easy. However, your reflections above may have indicated to you that emotions often get in the way of a rational interpretation of a situation. They tend to prevent us from working towards the best or most constructive solution to the issues. In general, people tend to over-express their feelings (excessive anger, passivity, distress and so forth) or to bottle up their feelings in order to cope. Different circumstances permit a different level of expression. We need to consider such matters as:

- What response will lead to the most constructive outcome?
- How will other people respond?
- What are other people's needs?

ASKHAM BRYAN
COLLEGE
LEARNING RESOURCES

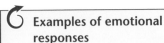

Activity: Examples of emotional responses

Think of three situations where you had a strong emotional response. Choose three different types of communication (in a group, individually, face to face, telephone, email) or three types of situation (work, study, with friends, with strangers). For each situation, jot down thoughts in your reflective journal in response to the following questions.

- What happened?
- What did you feel?
- Which feelings did you express?
- What did you do at the time?
- What were the consequences?
- What did you do or feel within the next 48 hours?
- Did your responses enable you to gain the most constructive outcome possible from the situations?

Consider whether your responses seem to be different depending on the circumstances or people involved.

Where do the unexpressed feelings go?

Whilst it is important to know what we feel and to acknowledge our feelings, there are times when it is not appropriate to express all of what we feel. In the activity above, you will probably have identified some feelings you did not express at the time. Often, such feelings go unexpressed for a long time. Unfortunately, they do not usually just disappear. Where do they go?

There are numerous ways that unexpressed emotions make themselves felt. A few of these are given here. As you read through them, identify which responses seem to be most typical of your own. You would be a very remarkable person if you made none of the following responses.

Displacement

The emotion is ignored and sneaks out when not expected, usually when you experience a similar emotion later. For example, you say nothing when you are irritated several times during a morning, and then snap or shout at somebody for something very minor later on in the day. Many

people are not aware of what they are feeling, yet their feelings may be all too evident to the people around them.

Ida knew for certain she had her anger under control.

Disproportion

This often goes hand in hand with displacement. When you express an emotion it should be proportionate to the situation. Disproportionate responses are noticeable when quite small things that do not seem to affect other people provoke a strong reaction in you. A small event may lead to tears, shouting, anger, violence, insults, or extreme distress.

If something has been building, unexpressed, for a long time, it is usually advisable to speak to a counsellor. They can help you release the emotion in a manageable way.

Reflection: Displacing emotions

Think of a situation when your emotional reaction was very strong for the situation.

- What happened? What did you do or say?
- Which emotion was being displaced?
- What had originally provoked the emotion – was it something recent? Was it the result of a long build-up of emotion?
- What could you have done to prevent displacing the emotion onto the later situation?

Distorted thinking

Unexpressed emotions can eat away at people, leading to distorted thinking such as:

- Believing there is no solution or way out of a problem.
- Exaggerating how bad things are.
- Over-generalising: judging everything from one or few examples. For example: 'My first essay was bad so I know I shouldn't be at university.'
- Exaggerating one's own role in events, so as to see oneself as very incompetent, bad, unkind or completely to blame for everything that went wrong. This is often a way of refusing to admit one's actual role (as it invites people to reassure you that you are not wholly to blame).
- 'All or nothing' thinking: 'If I can't have this then I don't want anything.'
- 'Magical thinking': believing that one is jinxed, doomed, specially chosen, fated.
- Mistaking feelings for facts: 'I feel it is all terrible, so it must be.'
- Focusing on the negatives: seeing only what went wrong, and judging a situation only by what was not perfect.
- Rationalising: finding a reason for doing what you want to do or for not doing what needs to be done.

Reflection: Distorted thinking

We are all capable of distorted thinking from time to time.

- Which of the above methods do you use when you are not feeling good about yourself or your work?
- What kinds of situations prompt you to distorted thinking?
- What benefit does the distorted thinking give you in the short term? Bear in mind that if you didn't feel it was giving you something, you wouldn't do it.
- How does the distorted thinking stand in the way of achieving your goals? (It does!)

Managing personal distress

The ABC model for dealing with distress

Ellis (1994) and Dryden and Gordon (1993) outline the 'ABC model' for managing situations that cause distress. The ABC model helps to analyse the source of the distress. It separates the core of the issue from the beliefs and attitudes that then amplify the problem. This makes it easier to find a solution or way of coping, keeping the core issues in perspective. ABC stands for:

A = **Activating event**: What happened that led to the emotional distress?

B = **Beliefs**: What beliefs contribute to the emotional distress?

C = **Consequences**: e.g. anger, illness, inability to work, difficulty getting down to work or concentrating

The example below (p. 116) also adds a 'D':

D = **Dealing with it**: What action will you take to manage the situation?

Activity — Would the 'ABC model' work for you?

- Read through the ABC model outline above and the worked example on the next page. Consider whether this is one that could be helpful to you.
- If possible, identify either a current or a past situation which created undue stress, pressure or distress to you or someone you know.
- Work through each of the stages of the model, applying them to the situation you identified.
- If doing this generated any ideas about dealing with such a situation, consider when and how you might apply these in the future.
- If this model wasn't useful, how would you adapt it so that it worked better for you?

ABC model for dealing with distress

A *Activating event*   The 'activating event' might be that a student, Gareth, has not read the course handbook. As a result, he did not realise that two essay deadlines fell on the same day. He asked for an extension, but was refused as it was not possible in the circumstances. Gareth must complete both essays in five days. If not, he will need to retake a module. The situation is not easy.

B *Beliefs*   Gareth can make a decision to work flat out to produce two essays, possibly accepting lower marks, or he can defer one of the modules and increase the possibility of higher marks for both in the long term. This would take a few months longer, but is feasible. However, Gareth argues that he is 'totally stupid' to have got into this situation and that this is typical of the mess he makes of his 'whole life'. He links the current problem with difficulties he experiences elsewhere so that the issue is no longer a missed deadline (which can be managed) but everything about his life. He does not believe he can write the essays as he has convinced himself that nothing he does will work.

C *Consequences*   The consequences are that Gareth's beliefs lock him into inaction. All of his energies are diverted into self-blame and hopelessness. He feels very small and is too embarrassed to talk to his friends. Instead of using his time to write the essays, he wastes time worrying or drinking, trying to push the problem away. Because he is stressed, he finds it difficult to concentrate. He can't study or make sense of what he reads. He misses his shift for his part-time job, making his overall situation even worse – convincing him further that his 'life' is a problem.

D *Dealing with it*   What could you do if you found yourself in a similar situation? In this case, it is beliefs that are fuelling the distress and leading to unhelpful consequences. You could either focus on the problem so as to divert yourself from the beliefs, or change the beliefs.

If you focus on the problem, you can:

- Describe the activating event, reducing it to the basics. Acknowledge what went wrong and what has been learnt. Yes, Gareth should have read the handbook. However, he is unlikely to make this mistake again, and this could be a critical lesson from which he learns and gains in the longer term. He is far from being the only student to get into such a position.
- Consider what has to be done. List all your options. Find out what these are and write them down. Write the advantages of each option. Then consider the feasibility and consequences of each.
- Move as quickly as possible into 'problem-solving mode', using a problem-solving strategy (see Chapter 6). Brainstorm options for solving the core problem. Evaluate these and choose one.
- Make a decision – and then stick to it and accept the consequences. The consequences might not be ideal, but they can be the 'best possible' for the situation. They are not life-threatening or catastrophic in the larger picture.
- Develop an action plan and follow it.

To challenge unhelpful beliefs:

- Write down words that motivate you, such as: 'there is a solution' or 'I can do this'.
- List your negative thoughts (beliefs). Go through the list, undertaking a 'reality check'. Ask 'Is this belief going to help me find a solution?'
- Challenge all beliefs that start with 'I should have …' or 'I always …'.
- Challenge all beliefs that refer to any other situation except the current problem.
- Cross out, with a thick line, all beliefs that do not help achieve a solution to the current situation.
- Brainstorm constructive phrases or messages until you find at least one that seems both helpful and true to you. Underline that belief or idea three times. Put a line through all the others.
- Speak to a friend or counsellor to put the situation into perspective.

Managing change, confusion and uncertainty

Activity ↻ **Approaches to change**

For each item, identify which one response is most true for you, indicating this with a tick.

Item	Always true	Usually true	Occasionally true	Not true	Don't know
1　I enjoy change	☐	☐	☐	☐	☐
2　I look for the opportunities in new situations and circumstances	☐	☐	☐	☐	☐
3　I feel comfortable meeting new people	☐	☐	☐	☐	☐
4　I am confident about coping in new surroundings	☐	☐	☐	☐	☐
5　I welcome new perspectives on an issue or problem	☐	☐	☐	☐	☐
6　I ask people for feedback	☐	☐	☐	☐	☐
7　I can change my plans at the last minute without feeling stressed	☐	☐	☐	☐	☐
8　I can study reasonably well in a wide range of circumstances	☐	☐	☐	☐	☐
9　I enjoy starting new subjects or projects	☐	☐	☐	☐	☐
10　I will work early or late at short notice	☐	☐	☐	☐	☐

Scoring your responses

For each item, allocate to yourself the following scores:

Always true (3)　Usually true (2)　Occasionally true (1)　Not true (0)

Score ☐

Reflecting on your score

24–30 This suggests you have a very strong and positive approach to change. What beneficial characteristics does this enable you to bring to study? How would this be of benefit in a work context? Do you look for change at the expense of continuity?

16–23 This suggests you have a positive approach to change. What beneficial characteristics does this enable you to bring to study? How would this be of benefit in a work context?

8–15 This suggests that you have an ambivalent approach to change. You can be positive about change. What benefits could you gain from developing a more positive approach?

0–7 Your score suggests a strong preference for continuity. You may need to be creative to find work and circumstances that enable you to maintain this level of continuity. It may be helpful to talk through your resistance to change with a counsellor. What disadvantages does your resistance to change bring you? Is there one area where you could develop greater flexibility?

The changing context

Technology and changes in the workplace have revolutionised the way we work and study. For most of history, people knew from childhood what kind of job they would have, their station in life, their relative income, the tools they would use. Lives were mapped out often before a person was born, depending on their family circumstances.

Today, things move quickly and change is the dominant pattern. More people have a chance to study for a degree and opt for almost any profession, at any age and, increasingly, anywhere. It is expected that we will continue training in new skills throughout our lives and it is likely that most of us will have several jobs, probably in diverse locations. The technical skills learnt today will become out of date very quickly; even factual information has a short shelf life.

Change inevitably brings uncertainty and, depending on what else is going on in our lives, we each manage this differently. There may be some kinds of change that you always welcome, and others that cause distress.

Reflection: Coping with change

- What kinds of change do you find easiest to accept and to cope with?
- What kinds of change do you find difficult to cope with?
- What actions do you take to help you manage change so that you are better able to cope with those difficulties ? You may find it helpful to consider the ABC model in dealing with this issue (pages 115–16).

Dealing with uncertainty

The 'right answer'

University life and study can be very challenging to our way of seeing the world. Many would argue that it should be, and that a university education should stretch students and make them re-evaluate their core beliefs and ways of thinking. The challenge can be difficult to manage at first.

In the 1970s, Perry undertook research with students at Harvard and Ratcliffe in the USA. He found that even outstanding students often expected to be given, or led towards, the 'right answers' by their tutors. How far is this true of you? Check your own responses using the following activity.

 Activity **Is there a right answer?**

This activity is likely to take at least half an hour and maybe much longer. There are three parts.

Part 1   Issues

On a piece of paper, jot down quickly your ideas about *three* of the following issues:

(a) It is ethical to clone human life.

(b) Students should be trained to develop their thinking skills as part of every programme.

(c) All adults should be required to contribute 50 hours a year to community or environmental work.

(d) To protect the environment, each person should have a restricted number of travel miles for holidays over their lifetime.

(e) Emotional intelligence should be part of the school curriculum.

(f) There should be a curfew on all people with a criminal record.

(g) Science requires creative thinking rather than logic.

(continued)

Part 2   Approaches

Below is a list of approaches that students take when considering new problems or challenging issues (adapted from Perry, 1970). For each of the issues you chose to consider, decide which of the following positions best describes where you stand on the issue.

1   Absolute answer

I think this is a question of right and wrong or that the right answer to this issue is obvious. I know where I stand, I know my own opinion, and I don't think an alternative answer is acceptable. Recognised authorities such as my tutor, a book, the law or a professional body will be able to tell me what the right answer is on this.

2   Temporary unacceptable uncertainty

The right answer hasn't been found yet but needs to be. Professionals, academics or other authorities need to clarify what the right answer is in order to avoid confusion.

3   Acceptable uncertainty

Everyone has a right to his or her own opinion. All answers are equally acceptable. My answer is as good as anyone else's. Lecturers and experts do not have all the answers.

4   Relativism

It's all relative. The 'right answer' would depend upon the circumstances. Another person may think differently from me and still be right, if their situation and experiences are different. There are no right answers. There is no real way of deciding what is right for all situations.

5   Commitment to a considered viewpoint, taking responsibility for the decision

I understand and can appreciate other viewpoints on this issue, but I believe some answers or perspectives are better than others and that I need to make a personal decision on where I stand amongst conflicting opinions.
I realise that making this choice of an answer may carry responsibilities and have implications for how I think, speak, and the choices I make.

6   On-going development

I am committed to this viewpoint, appreciate other viewpoints and realise that my decision carries personal responsibility. However, I also feel that this is something that I need to keep returning to, even if it means some uncertainty. The answer I have committed to is of great importance to who I am, to my values, and the kind of person I want to be.

Part 3   Interpreting your position

Perry explained the thinking that underlies each position. He ordered them into a hierarchy of responses (given below).

- Which position on his hierarchy is occupied by your answers? Are your answers generally in position 1, 2 or 3?
- In general, which of the nine stages described below do you think is most true of you?

Position 1: 'Right-answer positions' (Approaches 1 and 2 on the above activity)
1   Absolutist stage: there are right answers available. Things are either right or wrong. It is the teacher's job to provide the right answers.
2   Bad authority versus good authority: there are right answers but uncertainty is created unnecessarily by poor teachers or leaders. It is acceptable for right answers to be withheld when teachers want students to find the 'right' answer themselves.
3   Temporary uncertainty: there are right answers but it isn't clear what these are yet.

(continued)

Activity: Is there a right answer? *(continued)*

Position 2: Relativism stages (Approaches 3 and 4 on the activity above)

4   Acceptable uncertainty: 'Everyone has a right to their own opinion', despite what teachers or leaders might think. For assignments, it is important to find out the lecturers' opinions.

5   'All knowledge and value are contextual and relative.' For assignments, students should enquire: 'What is required of me in this context?'

Position 3: Commitment stages (Approaches 5 and 6 on the activity above)

6   Personal orientation: you feel it is necessary to make a commitment to certain viewpoints (out of a range of possibilities) with an understanding of, and tolerance for, other viewpoints.

7   You have made a commitment to certain viewpoints.

8   The implications of your commitment have been experienced and you realise the responsibilities this brings.

9   You regard your commitment to your views as 'an on-going, unfolding activity' through which your lifestyle and identity are expressed.

Reflection: Managing uncertainty

- What are your expectations of your lecturers? Do you expect them to provide, or lead you towards, a 'right answer'?
- How comfortable do you feel with the idea that there may not be 'right answers' to questions that are important to you?
- How open are you to hearing opinions that contradict your own?

If this subject interests you, ask your tutors for literature that discusses the nature of 'truth' or 'fact' or 'right answers' in your subject area.

Changing position

Perry found that it can take years for students to feel comfortable at stages 7–9 of this hierarchy. You may find you are in very different positions on the hierarchy depending on the issue.

You do not have to agree that Perry's hierarchy applies to every question. However, the hierarchy can be a useful tool for evaluating the nature of your own responses to issues, and your readiness to accept uncertainty on an issue. You will know how comfortable or uncomfortable you feel about applying any particular stage to your own ideas. You may need a greater knowledge of all the issues and the consequences of taking a particular position in a wide range of circumstances in order to change position on the hierarchy.

It can be hard to feel comfortable at levels 4–9 on some issues unless your sense of self, your beliefs

or your values also change. There isn't a 'quick fix' to changing the way we think. However, being aware of how we are thinking and responding can help the process of development.

You can also use Perry's hierarchy to help you understand where other people are in their thinking. It is important to be sensitive to where people are situated: you cannot force people into a different set of beliefs.

Transitional learning and 'disequilibrium'

Issues discussed in higher education may not have 'right' answers. There may be several answers or it may depend on how particular evidence is assessed, or there may be insufficient evidence to come to a firm conclusion. Some issues discussed at this level will directly challenge what you have learnt before, or seem to contradict views that you or people close to you hold as valuable. This can be unsettling or confusing.

Reflection: Confusion

- Do you feel that you are finding it harder to learn since starting university level study?
- Do you ever feel that you are more confused about what an issue involves when you find out more about it?
- Do you feel you are going backwards the more you learn?
- How does this make you feel? Do you think you are really 'going backwards'?

'Equilibration'

Saven-Baden (2000) uses the term 'transitional learning' to refer to 'shifts' that occur when students' frames of reference, or 'life world' are challenged by their learning, especially as the result of critical reflection. You may feel this at certain times when you move onto a higher level of learning. Saven-Baden describes this state as: 'characterised by frustration and confusion, and a loss of sense of self'.

This suggests that we can interpret some confusion as a healthy sign. It indicates that we are pushing ourselves, our learning, our knowledge, our skills beyond their former level. In other words, we are not stagnating. Piaget (1975) regarded this process of 'equilibration' as essential to our development. Equilibration occurs in three stages:

1 Equilibrium: first there is a state of satisfaction with our current ways of thinking and doing.

2 Disequilibrium: then we gain a sense of growing dissatisfaction and an awareness of the limitations of our existing ways of thinking and doing. This is the stage where confusion and worry can set in.

3 A more stable equilibrium: finally, if we persist in our enquiries, we can move to a more sophisticated way of thinking that overcomes the limitations of our previous thinking and performance.

Siegler (1991) cites the example of a child who thinks that only animals are living things. When she hears plants referred to as being 'alive', she becomes uncertain of what 'alive' means. This uncertainty, although temporarily uncomfortable, is a necessary stage in opening up to a new understanding of the world. Dissatisfaction begins an internal questioning which then opens us up to exploring new options.

For students to progress to more sophisticated ways of thinking, they need to be receptive to disequilibrium and to be able to manage or 'contain' short-term confusion. Otherwise, they may cling to the 'security' of their former equilibrium.

Reflection: Coping with disequilibrium

- Think back to a time when you felt you would never learn something – but did. What was it that was difficult to learn?
- How did you manage to work through the 'confusion' or disheartened stage to the stage where you had achieved your goal?
- What was it like to be successful in the end?
- How well do you feel you can manage the 'disequilibrium stage' as a student? What kind of support would help?

Holding the uncertainty

When we feel uncertain or confused, we lose our sense of equilibrium. Naturally, this makes us want to find our 'balance' again. The temptation is to act too quickly, rushing in to find a solution so that we feel better. Often, this leads to hasty action which limits our possibilities.

Although it may feel uncomfortable, it is important to learn to experience the feelings of discomfort and to 'sit with them' for a while, whilst we find out more about the situation. We need to:

- acknowledge the feeling of discomfort or anxiety
- allow ourselves to wait before rushing into action
- find help and support if we need it – talking to somebody can help

- find out more about the idea or situation that challenges us
- aim to understand what it is that we find so challenging – and look for potential opportunities
- consider our options, preferably within a problem-solving strategy
- act when we have weighed up the options.

Not everyone appreciated Gary's capacity to sit with uncertainty until he had weighed up all options carefully.

Reflection: Managing uncertainty

In your reflective journal, jot down your responses to the following questions.

- What kinds of uncertainty have you been faced with recently?
- What was your response?
- In retrospect, do you think you could have managed this uncertainty differently or more constructively?
- Did you look for any support in managing this uncertainty? If not, what stopped you?
- What could you do to improve the way you manage uncertainty?

Using motivators and inhibitors to manage personal performance

We are all subject to influences that either enhance our performance, or else inhibit our progress. You have already had the chance to identify a number of such factors in Chapter 3, 'Understanding your personal performance'. Here, you have an opportunity to build upon that understanding by applying a framework for analysing a broader set of influences. This can provide further insights that you can use to help manage aspects of personal performance.

Dilts et al. (1990) offered a six-level framework for exploring factors that can inhibit or promote learning. The framework below adapts Dilts's model, using eight levels to analyse performance.

The 'Eight Levels' framework

The Eight Levels framework enables us to look at performance from different perspectives. Items nearer to the core, such as 'higher purpose' and 'identity', are considered to have greatest impact and are referred to as 'higher level'. If positively engaged, these higher level motivators can go a long way towards overriding negative impacts, or 'inhibitors', at lower levels. It is as though the 'core' has a greater gravitational pull on our energies.

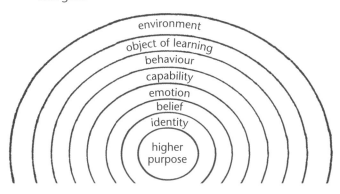

By analysing your experience in this way, you can identify for any task (or in general):

- at which level you feel the 'inhibitors' lie for you
- at which level the 'motivators' lie for you
- ways of managing inhibitors so as that your experience is better and/or personal performance improved.

1 Environmental (where? when? with whom?)

As we saw in Chapter 3, 'Understanding your personal performance', the context in which we learn and take action can have a profound effect. 'Environment' *here* can refer to the wider social, cultural or ideological context or the immediate physical environment such as the lighting or background distractions.

If you are strongly motivated or inhibited on a task at the environmental level, this may be evident in what you emphasise when speaking (as in the italics below):

> 'I love doing this/I can't do it *in this room*, with *this light, with people like these, at an institution like this.*''

Managing performance at the environmental level

If this sounds like you, consider what you can do to change the environment to suit your needs. Your responses to the activities in Chapter 3 may be useful in considering this issue. Environmental sensitivity can be caused by past trauma or current stress, so investigating those issues could also help.

Reflection: Environmental motivators and inhibitors

- How relevant do you think environmental factors are to your own performance in a particular area, either in motivating you or in preventing excellent performance?
- In what ways do these affect your performance?
- How can you better manage any negative impact or make more use of positive impacts?

2 The 'nature of the task' or 'content' (what?)

If you find you can usually perform in a given environment, but that you don't seem able to learn a particular subject or perform a specific task there, the difficulty would appear to lie with the content of what you are learning or the nature of the task rather than at the environmental level. If so, this is likely to be evident in comments such as:

> 'I can't learn *that'*; 'what's *this* supposed to be about?'; '*this* is what I call nonsense'.

Managing performance at the 'task' level

If you aren't able to change the overall task or subject, look for ways to change the way it is framed or worded. For example:

- look for a different way of thinking about the task
- break the task into manageable sections
- rephrase instructions
- put things into your own words
- imagine you are explaining the issue to someone much younger
- look for real-life examples that are similar
- sketch the problem as a chart, diagram or picture.

Reflection: Task-related motivators and inhibitors

- How relevant do you think the nature of the task is in the way it affects your performance in a particular area, either in motivating you or preventing excellent performance?
- Is it a motivator or inhibitor for your own performance?
- In what ways does it affect your performance?
- How can you better manage any negative impact?

3 Behaviours (what do we do?)

You may feel you want one thing, but behave as if you want something else. For example, students usually want good grades for their work but may not study in ways that develop their knowledge and understanding sufficiently. These behaviours may be the result of peer pressure, unhelpful habits, poor induction into a job or programme, lack of awareness of what is expected, etc.

There can be all kinds of reasons for counter-productive behaviours but if you are motivated by behavioural change, that is the focus for action. If, for you, the issue is primarily behavioural, this is likely to be expressed in speech that emphasises verbs ('doing words'):

'I can't *learn* or *do* that'; '*writing* essays is too difficult'; 'it takes me too long *to do* that'.

If you are motivated at this level, you may notice that typical responses from you include phrases such as:

'I'll *do it*'; 'I'll *have a go*'; 'I want *to get on with it*'.

Managing performance at the behavioural level

Managing behaviour at the performance level means that you address the behaviours directly, looking for ways of changing how you act or respond, rather than using an analysis of why the behaviour occurs to find a way forward. It can feel motivating if you feel you have the power to adapt your responses in ways that produce the outcomes you want. Some actions you can take are:

- Become aware of contradictory behaviours – ask a blunt friend, partner or sibling!
- Identify the trigger points – something you do that indicates to you or others that the unwanted behaviour or habit is about to kick in.
- Decide what you will do differently at that trigger point so as to initiate a different set of behaviours.
- Decide on appropriate rewards for particular changes in your actions.
- Ask a friend to prompt you if you don't spot the trigger.
- Make sure you do reward your successes in changing behaviour.

Counter-productive behaviours could indicate a lack of motivation for attaining the end goal. If a behavioural approach doesn't work, it is worth looking for solutions at one of the other levels. For example, it could be that the key inhibitor is at the environment level; tackling that directly might lead to a change in behaviour. Alternatively, the solution might lie in increased attention to one of the higher levels as outlined below.

Reflection: Behaviour as a motivator or inhibitor

- How relevant do you think your behaviour is in the way it affects your performance in a particular area, either in motivating you or preventing excellent performance?
- In what ways does if affect your performance?
- How could you change your behaviours in order to improve your performance?

4 Capability (how can I?)

If your prime difficulty in accomplishing a task lies at the capability level, you are likely to put the emphasis on words and phrases expressing ability:

'I'm *not able* to learn that'; 'I *don't know how* to learn that'; '*How can I* do that!'

If you are motivated at the capability level, you are likely to place emphasis on your ability to do something- or at least to have a go.

'I *can*!' 'I'm *able* to do all sorts of things!' '*Let me*!' 'I've *done this before* ...'

Managing performance at the capability level

If you feel you are having difficulties because of lack of knowledge, ability, skills or experience, consider why you are not able to do what you wish:

- it could be lack of practice
- it could be because you have not spent long enough building up a good foundation of knowledge and appropriate thinking skills: see Chapter 7 on the way the brain develops to support new learning
- you may need to improve study skills
- you may benefit from the section on 'Attitudes' above (pp. 105–9)
- you may be in the 'transitional stage' referred to above (p. 121)

- you may work better at a different pace: many people find university programmes are very rushed
- you may benefit from additional support and guidance.

Give yourself time to approach each task. Break bigger tasks into smaller, manageable targets. Find or set up a support group or action set (see Chapter 5).

Reflection: Capability as a motivator or inhibitor

- How relevant is 'capability' in the way it affects your performance in a particular area, either in motivating you or preventing excellent performance?
- In what ways does it affect your performance?
- What could you do to improve your capability in that aspect of your performance?

5 Emotional (how do I feel about ...?)

If the primary difficulty lies at an emotional level, you may emphasise words that refer to emotions:

'I *feel* I'll never learn this.' 'This *irritates, angers, upsets* me.' 'I *don't feel good* about this situation'; '*I'm getting annoyed* by this essay!'

Alternatively, you may express emotions through tears or your behaviour. The emotion may be related simply to difficulties with current study. However, there is very often a link to earlier learning which was distressing in some way.

On the other hand, positive emotions can have a beneficial effect upon learning. Positive feelings about oneself, the learning context, the course, and potential outcomes can produce much higher motivation and make learning easier.

Managing performance at the level of emotions

Key factors in managing emotions are being able to recognise that your emotions are engaged in a negative way and that you need to address these. Pretending that they don't matter probably won't help much, unless action at other levels results in a change in those feelings. Examining your emotional intelligence as outlined above (pp. 109–12) can help. If you do feel your feelings are getting in the way of you performing at your best, some basic steps you can take are:

- Don't push the emotions away; notice them, sit with them for a while; see if they change if you give them some attention.
- Consider whether there are some ways of approaching the task that would make you feel better.
- Query whether your emotions are in proportion: is this something that you can just 'shake off'?
- Consider whether you are displacing emotions (see p. 114). If so, what might the real emotional issue be?
- Consider using the ABC model to address these (p. pp. 115–16).
- If the emotions persist, talk to someone about them.

Reflection: Emotion as a motivator or inhibitor

- How relevant do you think your emotional responses are as key factors in particular areas of your own performance, either in motivating you or in preventing excellent performance?
- In what ways do they affect your performance?
- What could you do in order to manage your emotions better so as to improve your performance?

6 Beliefs and values (why?)

Our belief systems exercise a strong hold over our learning. We use beliefs as a basis for action. Beliefs about self-worth and individual potential are especially powerful: some students have a deeply held belief that they 'not supposed to be' at university. Have you ever felt that you are 'not good enough', or 'people like me cannot do well at university level study'? Do you believe the subject you are studying is really worthwhile?

If your primary difficulty lies at the belief level, this may be apparent in speech such as:

- 'I'm not likely to star at this subject'
- 'This is a soft option: I need to focus my attention on the other modules'
- 'It's only a discussion group so I don't need to turn up.'

There may also be a conflict between values and behaviours: 'Music is what is important to me, that's what I'd like to study, but I need a job at the end of this so, here I am, taking Business Studies.'

Managing performance at the level of beliefs and values

- Check whether you can reconnect with any initial belief in the value of the task that might then help you through.
- Identify a source of motivation that makes sense in terms of your values and motivation (pp. 30–6; p. 40).
- Check whether there is consistency between your values, beliefs and actions (see *Congruence* pp. 46–7).
- Challenge negative thinking (p. 106).
- Speak to someone who can give you useful and constructive advice about how to achieve your aims.
- Bear in mind that it can take time to change something as fundamental as our beliefs.

Reflection: Emotion as a motivator or inhibitor

- How relevant do you think your emotional responses are as key factors in particular areas of your own performance, either in motivating you or in preventing excellent performance?
- In what ways do they affect your performance?
- What could you do in order to manage your emotions better so as to improve your performance?

7 Identity (who am I?)

Some students, when they encounter difficulties, experience this at the identity level. They decide that they are 'the kind of person' who can't learn or doesn't perform well. They emphasise the 'I' in descriptions of their difficulties: '*I* can't learn it …' or even 'People *like me* can't …'.

Our sense of identity is very powerful, so if the primary difficulty is at the identity level, it is a good idea to address this as a priority.

Managing performance at the identity level

- Consider the positive aspects of your identity: what makes you who you are?
- How can you harness those positive aspects of your identity to help you accomplish the particular task or goal? What is it about you, or 'within you', that can make success possible?
- Do you identify with being:
  - *a 'bad student'*
  - *a 'lost cause'*
  - *'mediocre' or 'average'*
  - *'the clown in the group'*
  - *'the one who sits at the back'*
  - *'not a scientist'*
  - *a similar kind of negative identity?*

  If so, where did this sense of who you are come from? What can you do now to challenge that way of thinking about yourself?

If you are unsure of what your 'identity' is, it may help to work through selected aspects of Chapters 1 and 2, such as your vision for your life, your values, your life narrative and the kind of 'hero' you are in your own story (see pages 53–4). Don't get too tied down in the philosophical aspects of identity at this point.

Reflection: Identity as a motivator or inhibitor

- How relevant is your sense of your identity as a key factor in motivating you or preventing excellent performance?
- In what ways does if affect your performance?
- How could you make better use of your sense of who you are in order to better manage your performance?

8 Higher purpose or mission

'Higher purpose' and 'mission' refer to the overall direction and motivation that drive a person. This might be the good that you hope will stem from completing your degree, such as providing better for your family, being a role model, gaining more independence, entering a profession that matters to you, etc. As the term suggests, higher purpose is typically associated with ambition for something greater than self-centred desire – that is, it is 'higher than ourselves', such as:

- 'doing good'
- helping others
- 'making your life count'
- making a difference to your community, family, institution, country, sport, etc.
- creativity and artistic endeavour
- spirituality and/or religion.

Managing performance through 'higher purpose'

If you can find a relevant and meaningful connection between what you are doing and what really matters to you in terms of 'higher purpose', you are more likely to be well-motivated and to persevere through difficulties. Conversely, if there is never any space in your day to engage with what matters to you – or even to consider what that might be – then you lack an essential source of motivation and may eventually feel that life is frustrating or dull.

- What does 'really matter' to you? What would drive you to accomplish the most difficult of tasks if you really needed to?
- How or when do you provide space for that higher purpose in your life now?
- How or when could you enable more time to be given to what really matters to you?
- For tasks that you are finding problematic now, list some ways that you could change the way you think about these, or the way you perform them, so that they help you to connect with what really matters to you.

Reflection: 'Higher purpose' as a motivator or inhibitor

- How relevant is a sense of 'higher purpose' or mission in motivating you or preventing excellent performance?
- In what ways does this affect your performance?
- How could connecting to a sense of a higher purpose help to improve your performance?

Reflection: Identify your primary level for improvement

- Which of the previous levels do you think is most significant in its effects upon your learning and performance?
- Which levels have positive effects upon your studies or performance?
- To which levels do you most need to pay attention?

Closing comments

This chapter covers a great deal of ground. As with any issues that relate to intra-personal matters, it is not a chapter to race through and feel you have 'got it'.

Many of the exercises in this chapter can be repeated with specific issues or questions in mind. You will also find that the responses you give on a day when you wake up feeling confident and happy are very different from those you give on days when you feel more vulnerable. This is to be expected. The issues covered in this chapter provide useful material for further exploration through your reflective journal.

This chapter offered a basic introduction to some of the issues associated with personal self-management. The activities and strategies here may be all you will need for the issues that face you as a student and in your first graduate jobs. The chapter offers tools for analysing a situation quickly, for identifying resources, for managing your time, and for exploring your own mind-set. It offers strategies for developing a solution-focused, positive thinking style that can be applied in any circumstance, and not simply for study. It also offers you tools for beginning to analyse and understand emotional intelligence.

As a student, you are especially likely to experience times of uncertainty. A stimulating, higher-level education should be challenging. You should feel stretched. You should feel that occasionally the ground is moving beneath your feet. Confusion and uncertainty are characteristics of moving from 'novice' to more expert or sophisticated levels of thinking. If you know this, then you should be able to cope with that uncertainty without feeling something is very wrong.

Your intra-personal life is a rich source of information for you. It is one of the most important and valuable subjects you can ever study: you cannot know enough about the 'inner life' of your mind. The knowledge you gain about yourself and how you can best manage your own attitudes and thought processes will enable you to optimise your performance in any walk of life.

Further reading

Cottrell, S.M. (2013) *The Study Skills Handbook*, 4th edn (Basingstoke: Palgrave Macmillan).

Cottrell, S.M. (2015; new edition annually) *The Palgrave Student Planner* (London: Palgrave).

Covey, S. R. (2004) *The Seven Habits of Highly Effective People: Powerful Lessons in Personal Change*, 15th Anniversary edn (London: Free Press).

Fennell, M. (2009) *Overcoming Low Self-esteem: A Self-Help Guide Using Cognitive Behavioural Techniques* (London: Robinson).

Goleman, D. (1995) *Emotional Intelligence* (London: Bloomsbury).

Heron, J. (1992) *Feeling and Personhood* (London: Sage Publications).

Neenan, M. and Dryden, W. (2002) *Life Coaching: A Cognitive–Behavioural Approach* (New York: Brunner-Routledge).

Part 2

People and task management skills

Inter-personal skills

Although your work as a student is usually graded on individual effort, people skills are still very important. Indeed, on most courses, these skills are essential.

Many class-based and on-line sessions are designed to be collaborative. You may be asked to take part in joint presentations for seminars and workshops, peer-based support, peer-criticism, group work, on-line discussions boards, producing class journals, collaborative research projects within your institution or with students or colleagues from other organisations. Your course may require you to work with research participants, technicians, administrators, and supervisors.

These are just some ways in which you may be called upon to exercise people skills. In addition, you will have the chance to meet and interact with a wide range of people through your course, your institution, and through the opportunities open to you as a student.

It is likely, therefore, that during your time as a student, you will:

- develop your inter-personal skills naturally to a greater or lesser extent, through the experiences you encounter, adding to the portfolio of skills that you can carry with you into graduate roles, and
- benefit whilst still a student from developing such people skills as these, which can make study easier and more enjoyable.

Problem-solving and task management

Good task management skills help you to get things done more easily and efficiently, with minimum stress, leaving you more time and energy for other things. In completing tasks successfully, it helps to draw on a broad range of skills: intellectual, intra-personal and inter-personal, and operational. In particular, if you have a range of problem-solving approaches upon which you can call, this then helps you to feel confident in taking a solution-focused approach to new tasks and challenges.

Task management skills also oil the wheels in your dealing with other people. For example, you can build a great deal of good will, confidence and trust if people can depend on you to be organised, punctual, and likely to complete tasks on schedule. For collaborative tasks, whether as part of your study or at work, people are more likely to want you on their team if you are good at managing projects, systematic in your approach, and able to resolve problems that arise.

If you can combine good people skills with good task management skills, then you also have strong employability skills that should enable you to succeed in most work roles.

This section helps you to understand more what is meant by such skills and the various behaviours and attitudes that help you to put them into practice.

Chapters in this section
5   People skills
6   Successful problem-solving and task management

Chapter 5
People skills

Learning outcomes

This chapter offers you opportunities to develop skills in:

- building a good rapport with others
- being a better team member
- setting up an 'action set'
- giving and receiving constructive criticism
- assertiveness
- dealing with difficult people
- negotiation
- leadership.

Introduction

'People skills' are a combination of good inter-personal skills (being able to work well with others) and intra-personal skills (being able to manage one's own attitudes and emotions). 'People skills' are now critical to success in a wide range of careers. They are as important to the modern economy as are knowledge, information and technical skills.

This has been a much neglected part of the curriculum in the past, perhaps because there was less demand for subtle understandings of inter-personal relationships. However, changes in the kind of work we do, in technology, in tele-communications, in social structure, and the global economy have altered the way we interact. There are now much higher expectations for good inter-personal and communication skills.

In particular, compared with previous generations, we are more likely to meet and work with an extremely diverse range of people, often in global contexts. In the past, most people grew up and worked within a very confined world, with a narrow set of social rules. It was clear what

behaviour was expected of you down to the finest detail of your personal life. People knew almost from birth what they should say, to whom and when. They tended to meet people from a very small geographical area, often only their own village or part of town. Horizons were very narrow.

Today, most of the old social codes are disappearing. The context is infinitely more varied than in the past, the range of options in any one situation is much greater. This requires much higher levels of sophistication in our attitudes to others, in how we manage our personal beliefs and values in social settings, and how we respond to diversity. We have much more personal responsibility for developing good social relations, making relationships work and forming judgements about the appropriate behaviour in any setting. We all, too, have greater individual legal responsibility for our decisions and actions.

'People skills' is a vast and rapidly developing area. This chapter looks at some key aspects of developing people skills from the perspective of a student or new graduate.

Make two copies of this table. Complete one now and one later in your programme. Rate each of the following statements as follows:

Rating: *Strongly agree = 3   Agree = 2   Sort of agree = 1   Disagree/don't know/no opportunities = 0*

		Score
1	I have worked with a wide range of people of different ages and backgrounds	
2	I am told that I am very good at working with others	
3	I feel very confident about talking to people I do not know well	
4	I am comfortable about leaving silences whilst other people gather their thoughts	
5	I can start a conversation easily	
6	I find people extremely interesting	
7	I am aware of my body language and its effects upon others	
8	I can be very helpful and polite to people I hate or despise	
9	I can see the good points in most of the people I meet during a week	
10	I can listen well without interrupting somebody who talks a lot	
11	I am very good at developing trust between myself and others	
12	When I am in a group, I can easily tell the strengths of each person	
13	When I am in a team, I can tell easily who will be the best for each job	
14	I work very well as a member of a team	
15	I am clear about the particular strengths I bring to the group or team	
16	I am able to be very supportive of other people	
17	I am very good at resolving difficulties that arise in group or team work	
18	I know what support I need from others	
19	I am able to ask for what I need	
20	I am assertive	
21	I can deal well with difficult people	
22	I am able to accept, publicly, responsibility for my own part in interactions that go wrong	
23	I am skilled at offering constructive criticism to others	
24	I am able to take negative criticism well	
25	I am able to accept praise well	
26	I negotiate well with other people	
27	I know how to arrive at a good compromise	
28	I am clear what direction I need from people in leadership roles	
29	I feel very comfortable about taking the lead in activities	
30	I am very aware of what other people need	
Add up your score	**Total**	

Interpreting your score

70–90 This is an excellent score. If your ratings were accurate, you are able to manage very well your relationships with other people. This suggests an invaluable set of people skills. Consider how you could develop these further. How can you use these skills in the career areas that interest you?

40–69 This is a good score. If your ratings were accurate, this suggests your people skills are already well developed. Look for themes in the statements to which you gave lower ratings. Which areas could be further improved?

20–39 If your ratings were accurate, this suggests you have developed some people skills as well as an awareness of where you lack strengths currently. Look for themes in the statements to which you gave lower ratings. Taking your programme needs and career interests into consideration, which is your next priority for development?

0–19 If your ratings were accurate, this suggests that you have identified that people skills are not currently a strength for you. Check with people who know you well whether you have rated yourself too harshly. It is also important that you identify which people skills are most critical for meeting the requirements of your programme and career interests. Consider speaking to the Careers Service or your tutors to identify areas of priority for future development. This score also suggests that you might have difficulties in relationships generally. That can be stressful. If so, student counselling services can offer useful ideas about how to make your interactions with others run more smoothly.

Reflection: People skill needs

Which people skills are needed for:

- the careers areas that interest you?
- meeting the requirements of your programme?
- your personal needs and interests?

If you are unsure, speak to the Careers Service at the university and to your tutors.

- What are your priorities for developing your people skills?

Developing rapport

Forming a good rapport is the cornerstone of relationships with other people. Rapport requires such behaviours as:

- 'making a connection'
- taking a genuine interest in the other person
- skilful listening
- developing mutual trust and cooperation.

Making a connection

Making a connection requires only a little effort. From this, the basis of good trust or even life-long friendships can develop. The minimum required are a few very basic gestures that show good will:

- making eye contact
- giving a genuine smile
- being helpful when asked
- giving a friendly greeting
- showing basic consideration for the other person
- using a friendly, polite manner
- making a comment or asking a question that shows interest without being intrusive
- being consistent in either friendly or distant behaviour.

These may seem small and obvious. However, think about the contact you have with people you find difficult. Which of the above gestures were missing either at your first encounter or on a regular basis? Which of these gestures do you value? A forced smile, an abrupt response, an unpleasant tone of voice, and such small details can put relationships on a wrong footing – making hard work of any future connections.

Taking a genuine interest

Generally, we appreciate people with similar values and beliefs to our own, who do not challenge our own view of the world or our material interests. 'Difference' can be unsettling. It suggests there might be more than one way of doing or being. Our survival mechanisms do not like this idea: it suggests someone else might be 'right' and our way 'wrong'. We are not usually comfortable with such ideas. Our minds tend to throw us lifelines such as 'that's boring', 'he's a fool', 'that's rubbish!' very early, before we are even aware it is happening, so that we do not have to really consider what we are feeling.

As we develop people skills, we are better able to accept a wider range of differences in other people. We learn to find the point of interest in difference and the value of diversity. We cease to see the world in terms of 'right' and 'wrong', but as a rich spectrum.

The benefits of finding the point of interest in other people are that:

- we find the world around us to be more interesting
- boredom disappears and our life experience is richer
- we feel more comfortable, emotionally, when with strangers
- people are able to feel more comfortable around us
- we have a better understanding of the world around us and of the motivations of others
- we are better able to manage any situation that involves other people.

Activity **Balloon game**

In your journal or a notebook, give one page to each of the following (ten pages in all).

The characters
First, write the name of one person on the top of each page, so that you have the names of:

- two people that you really know, like and admire
- two people that you know vaguely and have no strong feelings about
- two people that you think are just not like you at all and that you do not like much
- two that you know well and really dislike or despise
- two people that you do not know at all (you may invent names for them if you do not know them).

The motivation
Now, imagine you are in a television challenge. You are aloft in a balloon with these ten people. You will receive a prize of your choice (up to £5 million) if you can bring all ten people back to earth. Otherwise, you will be fined your income for a year. If you fail, they get a prize instead.

The challenge
However, you are only allowed to transport back any person if you can convince the audience that each person is really worth saving. You will need to show that you know about the person and can say things about them that bring out their best features.

For each person, use their name page to brainstorm responses to the following:

- what I like, value, admire, find interesting already about this person
- what I dislike about this person at present
- what this person contributes to the world that is different or valuable
- questions I could ask, to find out more
- anything I could do to develop a better understanding of this person.

Reflection: Balloon game

In your journal or a notebook, note:

- Which things you were less willing to do in this exercise? What was difficult and why?

- In general, what kinds of people are you more likely to dismiss as 'not your type of person'? Who do you overlook? What kinds of things might you be missing out on because of that way of thinking? Are there ways that your current behaviour may come back to haunt you in the future?

- What effect might your behaviour be having upon other people?

Skilful listening

Good listening skills are invaluable to forming a rapport with others. Most people react very strongly to feeling they are 'not heard' or that 'someone really listened'. This is especially true where people feel vulnerable (if they are new to a group, distressed, angry, have received bad news, etc.).

Reflection: Being heard

In your reflective journal, jot down some thoughts on the following.

Think of a recent situation when you felt that you were trying to communicate your point of view and could not make yourself heard.

- What was the situation: what happened?
- How did you feel?
- What did you do?
- What could the 'listener' or 'listeners' have done differently to help you feel you had been listened to?
- What benefits would there have been for that person if they had listened more skilfully? For example, how did their poor listening skills affect your attitude or responses to the person or people involved?

'Listening' is something we take for granted. However, skilful listening is about more than 'hearing the words'. It involves understanding the message, the situation and other people.

Good listening skills enable other people to feel at ease, to trust the listener, and to express more easily what they really wish to communicate.

There is an art to being able to discover what another person is trying to communicate, and this can take many years to perfect. However, the following are good starting places.

Body language
Demonstrate clearly that you are listening, using appropriate body language. Usually this means slightly exaggerating what you would normally do anyway. For example, ensure you make eye contact, without staring.

Use body language that shows you are listening: lean forward a little, tilt your head slightly to the side, nod occasionally to show you are taking in what is being said. Many people do this naturally when they are really listening but some do not.

Let them finish
Let people complete the point they are making without interruption. Wait for a pause or an intake of breath before you start to respond. Make any necessary interruptions with consideration for the other person – even if you feel they have not been considering your needs. If you really must interrupt, because of time constraints, for example, apologise for interrupting. State the reason for the interruption politely. Make some reference, however brief, to what has been said, before you change the subject or rush away.

Listen for the underlying message
The 'underlying message' may be different from the actual words used. What does the person really mean? What do they really want you to hear or to know? Are they saying one thing but communicating something different? For example, they may say 'I'm fine!' but look or sound very angry or distressed. Just note these differences. If it feels right to say so, you may point out the message that you are receiving: 'You sound very upset' or 'You look very angry.'

Check for meaning

People may not be skilled at communicating what they want you to hear. Alternatively, you may mishear or misread the situation. The only way to be sure of the message being communicated is to feed it back to the person and check their response. Summarise what you think you have heard. Usually, this is best in brief phrases, prompts or questions when the other person is pausing for breath. Do this in ways that suggest you are trying to understand:

- 'They said you have to fill in the form today?'
- 'And that wasn't what you wanted?'
- 'So you don't want to go ahead any more?'

Clarify details

- Ask questions to clarify points and show your interest.
- If something isn't clear, point out that you haven't quite understood. Ask the other person to explain it again or in a different way.
- Be specific about the exact points you do not understand. Your confusion may arise because the other person is not fully clear about the issue either. Your questions may help them to clarify their thinking.

Leave silences

Some people find silence awkward and it can be tempting to keep talking in order to avoid silences. However, silence fulfils important functions:

- it gives a clear signal that you have finished speaking
- it gives opportunities for other people to contribute
- it allows time for reflection
- it gives people time to develop their ideas
- it allows people time to manage their feelings and emotions
- it can enable non-verbal communication to take place, which is often more powerful than speaking.

Reflection: Listening skills

- In your reflective journal, note down which of these listening skills you find easiest.
- Which do you find most difficult?
- Which could you develop further?
- Can you think of recent examples where you used any of these skills?

Developing mutual trust

Reflection: Developing trust

- Who do you really trust with your secrets?
- Who do you really trust with your money?
- Who do you trust to tell you the truth about themselves?
- Who do you trust to tell you the truth about yourself?
- In each case, what created that trust?

Your responses to the above activity probably elicited an awareness that trust develops out of acquaintance. It also takes time. It can be easily broken. It can take time to repair once broken. You cannot force trust onto people; the harder you try, the more suspicious people may become. You really do 'earn it' through the proof of your actions.

It is difficult to establish good working relationships if these are not founded on trust. Co-operation with others, sharing ideas, revealing personal information, negotiating compromises, commissioning work, offering contracts, and numerous other everyday activities are all facilitated by the development of mutual trust.

Reflection: Losing trust in others

In your reflective journal, think of an occasion when you lost your trust in somebody.

- What happened?
- What did this feel like?
- What were the consequences?
- How has this affected your behaviour towards that person?
- What would that person have to do to regain your trust?
- Which kinds of behaviour break trust?

Reflection: Losing trust in other people

In your reflective journal,

- Think of an occasion when you did something to undermine other people's trust in you.
- What happened?
- What did this feel like?
- What were the consequences?
- How has this affected the relationship between you and that person?
- What was (or is) needed to restore that person's trust in you?
- What did you learn about trust from this experience ?
- Which kinds of behaviour break trust?

Brainstorm:

- What kinds of behaviour develop people's trust?
- What kinds of things could you do to develop your abilities in gaining other people's trust in you?

You can build trust if you:

Are clear what you can and cannot do

Do what you say you will do

Avoid making promises you can't keep

Keep confidential information confidential

Are consistent in your behaviour from one day to the next

Are dependable and fulfil your responsibilities; turn up on time

Team work

Learning in groups reaps greater benefits than attending formal lectures or presentations. It gives students more scope to express themselves, to establish effective relationships with tutors and others in the group, and to develop a range of skills such as team working.

Skills and Enterprise Network, 2001

'Finding and keeping a good team' is amongst chief executives' most highly rated ingredients of success (Taylor and Humphrey, 2002). Despite the importance of team work to working life, few people have developed outstanding team skills. Team players are usually well-appreciated by both employers and colleagues. On the other hand, our natural self-interest in our own needs, moods, beliefs, wants and feelings can make it very easy for us to sabotage the teams or groups that we find ourselves in.

Sabotaging the team

You may have come up with a long list of items. Typical responses include:

- not bothering to get to know some of the team members
- dominating the group
- not contributing enough
- leaving one or two people to do all the work
- speaking badly about some team members
- trying to split the team into 'goodies' and 'baddies'
- not taking responsibility for tasks that need to be done
- being late or not turning up at all
- putting your own needs before those of the team
- not listening to other people's ideas
- not using the strengths and qualities of each person to best effect
- messing about
- not caring what happens to others on the team
- not being able to take criticism.

Activity Sabotaging a team

In your reflective journal, take two pages.

- On the first page, brainstorm a list of things people could do to sabotage a group. How could they make the group an unpleasant, unproductive, irritating experience? When you have finished, compare it with the list given above.
- On the second page, make a list of what people can do to make groups work. Compare your list with the one under 'Creating a good team' below.
- Which of those behaviours do you demonstrate? Be honest. What could you do to improve your own contribution to groups and teams?

Creating a good team

A good team will show the following characteristics:

Works as one

- It has a shared vision. It knows what it wants to achieve
- puts the desired team outcome first: individual interests take a secondary place
- is clear about targets and priorities – and agrees these together
- shares information
- can make decisions.

Works to strengths

- It has members with different qualities, who can make different contributions
- takes time to discover the experience, skills and interests of all and how it can make best use of these
- shares expertise. A team that is together for some time is strengthened if individuals share their knowledge and skills.

Includes everyone

- It makes efforts to ensure that nobody feels left out or undervalued
- gives room to individuals. Team work does not mean that everybody has to be and think the same. On the contrary, variety and difference can be a source of strength. There are different ways of being a good team player.

Respects its members

- It respects everyone's time by: being punctual for meetings, completing individual targets on time, being aware of how one person's own work affects other people's achievements, monitoring personal contributions to meetings so that time is not wasted in long anecdotes and tangents
- respects the opinions of the team and uses strategies to enable all team members to give their views: feeding in at the beginning of meetings, giving each member equal time to speak on an issue, inviting people who have not spoken yet to contribute their views.

What I can contribute to the team?

The skills and qualities you contribute to a team will develop through experience. However, if you are not used to team work, you will feel more confident at the beginning if you think of what you are already able to contribute. The following activity helps you identify some things you could contribute to team work at present.

For each way of contributing to teams (listed below) tick as many boxes as apply to you.

Contribution	Willing to do	Have experience of	An area of strength	Want to develop
Hearing other people's views, ideas and opinions				
Listening to others				
Weighing up options				
Making decisions, based on the facts				
Finding ways of working effectively				
Looking for solutions				
Administrative skills				
Working out priorities				
Speaking my mind				
Specialist skills that can be useful				
Seeing when the discussion has gone off track, and pulling it back on target				
Working hard				
Keeping going when it gets tough				
Seeing when people are left out				
Drawing in other people				
Logical thinking				
Numbers and statistics				
Charts and drawings				
Researching information				
Writing up findings				
Organising events				
Networking				
Time-keeping				
Other things:				
(1)				
(2)				
(3)				
(4)				

Activity ⟳ Weaknesses in team performance

How well do you perform in teams at present? Use the following statements to evaluate your performance and to guide your reflection.

Tick as relevant ✓

☐ I talk too much

☐ I turn up late

☐ I interrupt others

☐ I take up too much of the discussion space

☐ I let other people carry the team

☐ I always think I am in the right

☐ I act as if I were the team leader

☐ I like everything to stick exactly to the agenda

☐ I keep going off at tangents

☐ I get caught up in the details and lose the big picture

☐ I have lots of ideas, but many of them are not relevant

☐ I get too emotional

☐ I don't keep to the deadlines

☐ Other things:

☐ (1)

☐ (2)

☐ (3)

☐ (4)

☐ (5)

☐ (6)

☐ (7)

☐ (8)

☐ (9)

☐ (10)

Activity ⟳ Turn short-comings into strengths

- How realistic is the above view of yourself?
- Would you have the confidence to discuss this with someone else and be able to cope with their responses?
- What targets can you set yourself to improve your performance for one of those areas?
- What, if any, are the positive aspects to your 'short-comings'? What do these suggest about your potential strengths (such as flexibility, caring for others, willingness to accept responsibility, confidence in speaking your mind) that could be adapted to the benefit of the team?
- Take at least one short-coming and look for the way this could be adapted or converted into a strength. For example, if you are poor at attendance, how could you make up for non-attendance in other ways?

Belbin team types

Belbin and the Cambridge Industrial Training Research Unit made a dramatic discovery about teams. In an experiment that was repeated many times with different participants, it was found that teams made up entirely of the best business brains were far less successful than those with very mixed memberships. Belbin (1996) went on to outline different kinds of roles that people could occupy in a team, depending on their personal characteristics. The activity on p. 141 summarises some of the characteristics associated with each Belbin type.

- With which types do you identify?
- With which one type do you identify the most?
- Which three other types would you most appreciate having in your team?

140 **People and task management skills**

© Stella Cottrell (2003, 2010, 2015), *Skills for Success*, Palgrave

Belbin type	Positive characteristics	Potential short-comings	Tick all that apply to you. Mark *** by the most typical	The three 'types' I would most want on my team ✓
Implementer	Steady, reliable, sensible, gets things done. Well- disciplined, organised approach.	May not welcome change and new ideas. Expects too much from others.		
Co-ordinator	Focused, looks for consensus, tries to involve everyone. Delegates work; chairs meetings well. Can accept and reject the ideas of others.	Doesn't shine intellectually; may be seen as manipulative. Passes their own work onto others.		
Shaper	Outgoing, high-energy, no- nonsense, blunt; speaks their mind; ready to overcome obstacles; gets things moving.	Impatient, irritable, insensitive to others' feelings; may say the wrong thing at the wrong time.		
Plant	Creative, lateral thinker, generates ideas, enjoys looking for solutions, inventive. Good at holding the 'big picture'.	Inflated sense of their own 'genius'; ignores targets and details; in their own dream-world; does not communicate ideas well to others.		
Resource investigator	Curious, interested, outgoing. Likes exploration, information, meeting new people, challenge, trying out new gadgets.	Short interest or attention span; invests and then moves on to something else; may pilfer other people's ideas.		
Monitor–evaluator	Considers all angles; unemotional; takes on many perspectives; good at weighing up the evidence and making a judgement; good at decision making.	Rigid in ideas and in their love of 'logic'; not open to creative or lateral thinking; over-critical. Not good at generating novel ideas.		
Team-worker	Observant; listens and responds well; smooths over conflict; diplomatic; good social skills; sensitive to others; puts the team first.	Can be swayed by all views; easily influenced; prevaricates; finds it hard to come to a decision.		

Activity: Identify your team personality *(continued)*

Belbin type	Positive characteristics	Potential short-comings	Tick all that apply to you. Mark *** by the most typical	The three 'types' I would most want on my team ☑
Completer-finisher	Good attention to detail; conscientious; responsible; reliable; delivers to target; fine-tunes their final effort.	Bad at delegating and trusting others; picks fault; over-perfectionist.		
Specialist	Single-minded, dedicated, offers skills that are hard to find; gets on with the task; self-motivating.	Not interested in the big picture; doesn't mix with the team; narrow horizons.		

The best mix?

Belbin found some combinations work well. In particular, a group seems to work well if there is:

- a co-ordinator type – to chair the group
- a good 'plant' – an imaginative person with the right kind of creative skills for the project
- a monitor–evaluator who can spot and weigh up good and bad ideas
- a spread of other types. In particular, an implementer or completer-finisher is useful. A balance of types is valuable: extrovert and introvert, those who generate ideas and those who can assess them, those who bring in change and those who maintain some continuity.

What kind of balance is there in the team of four (including yourself) that you selected in the activity above.

What strengths would a team like that demonstrate? What would its weaknesses be?

If you wish to complete a full Belbin self-perception inventory, ask for a copy at your University Careers Service.

Action sets

'Action sets' (McGill and Beaty, 2001) are a particular kind of team. They are semi-formal groups which offer opportunities to gain input and alternatives from others and receive structured support.

Action sets, as the name suggests, focus on getting things done. Unlike most groups, however, the aim is to help each person to find a solution to a problem or difficulty of their own choice. The group brainstorms ideas and discusses solutions within a tight time-frame, and at the next meeting checks to see what action was undertaken. The group itself does not carry out the action: it merely proposes and monitors action, at the invitation of each member.

Advantages of action sets

The advantages of action sets are:

- the rules are easy to follow
- all members are equal
- they provide supportive contexts: usually, you choose to be in an action set
- you have a place where you can take a difficult issue and work it through
- they are very focused
- they offer a range of perspectives on a problem you choose to bring
- they generate ideas and solutions
- they require rapid decision making, and so assist decision-making skills for all members
- they give practice in arriving at a solution in a very short time
- they offer an additional source of motivation: reporting back to the group at the next meeting encourages you to take action
- members get to know each other well and know what works for each member.

You may find it useful to select an action set according to Belbin types. If so, bear in mind the aims of the group. What types of person are likely to work best together for the kinds of problems that arise from your programme? Would it help to include someone who is not on the programme?

The limits of action sets

Action sets are not usually:

- emotional support groups
- discussion groups: talk is very circumscribed
- social groups
- project groups: they do not 'do' the work needed to solve an individual's problem outside of the meeting.

Guidelines for the meeting of an action set

Ideally, leave at least 15 minutes for each member. If you have only an hour a week for such meetings, a set of four people is probably best. If you have 2 hours, a group of six is probably the optimum size. An even number will work best. The timing below assumes six people in a 2-hour slot. With a 15-minute break, that gives each person 17 minutes each.

For each person:

Stage 1 (3 minutes)

- Each person has a set time to discuss the area they wish to improve. Time is limited so each person needs to get to the point quickly.
- While that person is speaking, the group listens without interrupting.
- One person keeps the time.
- Once the time is up, the person must stop speaking immediately.

Stage 2 (2 minutes)

The group may ask one or two questions, briefly, to clarify the situation.

Stage 3 (3 minutes)

The person whose issue is being considered listens without speaking whilst the rest of the group brainstorms possible solutions and ways of thinking about the problem. Again, a limited time is allowed.

Stage 4 (4 minutes)

The person and the group have a set time to clarify and discuss options together briefly.

Stage 5 (2 minutes)

The person whose issue is being discussed has a set time to state which actions they will undertake before the next meeting. All members write down what has been agreed, and monitor this at the next meeting.

Stage 6 (3 minutes)

In the following session, each person reports back on actions they have taken. The group encourages successes and improvements. If the person has not followed through on what was agreed, this may be used as their focus for the session. Feedback must be timetabled into the time allocated to each person.

Running the action set

Ideally, action sets are meetings of peers where everybody takes equal responsibility. Tasks are rotated or allocated to individual strengths:

- organising the room
- phoning members to remind them of the next meeting and of agreed actions
- time-keeping in meetings
- keeping the group strictly to the right stage and item under discussion
- maintaining a supportive atmosphere
- ensuring everyone contributes
- ensuring everybody gets equal time
- ensuring different people go first or last each time.

Roles

You may find action sets work better if you allocate roles to the team. Useful roles to include are:

- A Co-ordinator or Implementer: to ensure the group sticks to task, keeps to time, and that everyone gets equal time. Each stage must be very strictly timed.
- A Plant or a Shaper or Resource Investigator: who may bring a different way of looking at things.
- A Team-worker: to enhance the social skills of the group.
- A Monitor–evaluator or Completer–finisher: to assist the group to move on and to choose between options.

Constructive criticism

Reflection: Constructive criticism

In your reflective journal, jot down some ideas about what you think is meant by 'constructive criticism'.

Criticism does not mean pointing out 'what is wrong'. Technically, criticism draws out what is good, bad and satisfactory. Constructive criticism goes further: it offers a clear and practicable 'next step forward' and is expressed in a positive way. It leads towards improvement. For constructive criticism to be effective, it has to be expressed in a way that is easy to 'hear' and understand.

Making constructive criticism and giving feedback

The aim of feedback is to help other people to see how they could improve their performance or gain a new perspective on their work. The focus of criticism is the other person, their needs or the requirements of the task. It is not about showing how clever you are at 'picking holes' in what other people do or say.

Constructive criticism is phrased so that it offers truthful but skilful feedback with ideas on how to improve or to progress. It is very easy to hurt people's feelings through unskilful feedback, and nothing is gained by this.

Good feedback involves:
- waiting until invited for your opinion
- recognising effort
- being well informed: ensure you know the circumstances, intentions and requirements before offering feedback
- being clear and truthful but not blunt or hurtful
- indicating what the other person has got right – so they continue to do this in the future
- indicating what has already improved
- indicating a small number of achievable goals for improvement
- giving concrete examples of what is required:
  'I think this would look even better if …'
  'I like this. Have you thought about …'
  'The first half was good. The second half would benefit from …'

It should:
- be formulated positively – as something which can be done to improve performance, rather than what is wrong
- take the person forward – it is not simply a vague directive to do something differently
- be realistic – the suggestion can actually be put into practice by the recipient
- be selective – it addresses priorities rather than every aspect of performance
- be offered kindly – delivered in a voice and manner that make it easier to accept.

Poor feedback includes:
- too much comment and criticism. This is off-putting. People stop listening and may get distressed
- negative feedback. People ignore this if they feel their efforts are not recognised
- vague feedback such as 'Unclear' or 'More detail needed'. State exactly what is unclear or which details are needed
- demoralising comments such as 'this is nonsense'; 'gobbledegook!'; 'could do better'
- illegible feedback. People usually do not bother to decipher illegible writing unless they think it says something very positive about them.

Reflection: Offering constructive criticism

Think of a recent occasion when you offered feedback to someone about their work or study. Jot down:
- What were the circumstances?
- What did you do or say?
- Which of the above constructive characteristics did you include or omit?
- What else could you have said or done to improve your feedback?

Constructive questions and responses

Use constructive questions to discover why the person made the choices or took the steps they did – and to explore their next step forward. For example:
- 'What did you think worked well?'
- 'Is there anything you would do differently next time?'

- 'What was your inspiration for this?'
- 'Did you find this worked?'
- 'That is an unusual approach. I am interested in why you did it this way?'
- 'Have you had any ideas about where we could apply this?'

Jane was starting to realise that her helpful advice was not universally appreciated.

Receiving criticism

Accept criticism gracefully, however it is given. Not everybody is skilled at giving criticism.

- Consider all criticism carefully, even if it sounds unacceptable.
- Look for the elements of truth in what is said. This is sometimes easier after you have had some time to reflect.
- Hear both the positive and the negative aspects. Many people hear only negative feedback.
- Check you have understood what is being said. It is easy to mishear, especially if it didn't sound positive.
- Acknowledge the feedback. It was probably not easy for the other person to give it.
- Say thank-you.
- Reflect upon the meaning of what you have heard. What steps could you take to improve your performance?

Reflection: Receiving criticism

Think of a recent occasion when somebody offered you feedback or criticism about your work or performance.

In your reflective journal, jot down:

- What were the circumstances?
- What did they do or say?
- How did you respond? What else could you have done to make best use of the criticism?
- What does this experience tell you about giving and receiving criticism well?

Being assertive

What is assertiveness?

Assertiveness means standing up for yourself without demonstrating anger. Assertive people look for solutions that suit both parties, respecting the rights of both.

Reflection: Characteristics of assertive people

What picture comes to mind when you think of an assertive person? Jot down your thoughts in your reflective journal.

Assertiveness is about:

- respecting your own and other people's rights
- respecting your own and others' needs
- being clear and straightforward with other people
- taking more control over your own life and taking responsibility for changing what you do not like.

Rights

Palmer and Dryden (1995) offer a list of rights associated with assertiveness. These include the right to:

- say 'no'
- make mistakes
- consider your needs important
- express your feelings in an appropriate way without violating anybody else's rights
- take responsibility for your actions
- respect yourself
- set your own priorities
- be assertive without feeling guilty.

You could include others, such as the right to:

- do well in life

- ask for what you need to know
- be taken into consideration in decisions that affect you
- fairness and justice
- personal safety
- love
- think
- be free of insult and discriminatory behaviour on the grounds of race, colour, nationality, sex, sexual orientation, disability, parentage, work history or personal beliefs
- your opinions.

Respecting your own and others' rights and needs

'Rights' are not universal nor equally applied. They are not all 'human rights' by international agreement and may not apply in all countries or conditions. People in prison cannot set all their own priorities, for example. Some rights are protected by law; others are commonly held beliefs about human rights. You may have to decide what rights are reasonable or legal for your own circumstances.

Activity **Your rights**

What other rights are important to you that you would like to add to the above list?

1	
2	
3	

- Which rights are most important to you?
- Do you know what your rights are in the circumstances which you usually encounter?
- Which of your rights do you find you need to defend the most often?
- Which do you find hardest to claim?

An individual's interests have to be weighed against the rights of other people and the nature of the circumstances. We are not generally comfortable with the idea that a surgeon might

have 'the right to make mistakes' on a regular basis. Having the right to an opinion means you have the right to hold the opinion, but not necessarily to subject other people to insult or harm as a result.

Assertiveness is not about insisting on your own interests, irrespective of the consequences to yourself and others or without consideration of the circumstances. When you are assertive, you ensure that:

- you look at the whole picture, but you put yourself in that picture
- you know your own opinions
- you are able to identify your own needs and interests
- you weigh up, realistically, whether it is appropriate to stand up for your rights and interests in the situation. Sometimes it is too dangerous or risky to assert our rights unless we can ensure safety and support.

Being clear and straightforward with other people

When we state our needs in a calm, clear, straightforward manner, then we are showing respect both to ourselves and to others. When other people know where you stand, they can then choose to respond in an appropriate way. You gain a clearer picture of their position.

Assertiveness is not:

- *Being aggressive* Assertiveness does not include: rage, shouting, forcing other people to do what you want, physical force or threats of force, aggressive body language, intimidating others. You have the right to feel angry, or to shout in private, but not to express these to others in ways that might make them feel coerced into doing what you want.

- *Being manipulative* Assertiveness does not include: using psychological games to manoeuvre people into doing what you want. For example, it does not involve shaming people, trying to make them feel guilty or anxious, reminding them of debts, playing upon people's doubts and fears.

- *Being passive* Assertiveness does not include: being silent about your own needs and interests; being a 'martyr'; letting other people have what they want whilst you go without; staying quiet when you want to speak out; effacing yourself so that you are not seen, heard or considered. This behaviour can be very irritating to others – and means they have to take responsibility for your needs.

- *Being passive aggressive*   Assertiveness does not include: appearing to be passive whilst being clear that you are angry. Passive aggressive behaviour is very distressing to other people, and confuses situations so they are harder to resolve. It includes behaviour such as saying 'I don't mind', 'do what you want', 'whatever!' whilst using angry facial expressions, body language or tone of voice. Angry silences, walking out of the room, making a noise to block out what another person is saying, not turning up to appointments and generally not co-operating, are ways of expressing passive aggression.

Reflection: Evaluating personal assertiveness

It is rare for anybody to go through life in an assertive and completely fair, reasonable, manner. Most of us tend to use at least one or two of the above approaches (aggressive, manipulative, passive aggressive, or passive) for some or all of the time in order to get our own way or to avoid an unpleasant situation. In your reflective journal, consider:

- Which approach do you use most often to get your way or to avoid unpleasant situations?
- Do people who know you well agree that this is the approach you use?

Taking control over your life

When we use assertiveness techniques, we take responsibility for our actions in order to increase our control over an aspect of our life.

Reflection: A recurring siuation

Select one situation where you feel you deserve to have your opinions, needs or interests taken into consideration and respected – and where you feel this does not happen at present. Select an event that recurs, which you will have to face soon.

- What usually happens?
- What do you do?
- What do you say?
- What rights are at issue in this situation?
- What are the rights of others in this situation?
- What kind of behaviour do you demonstrate when you feel you are unlikely to get your way (aggression, passive aggression, manipulation or passivity)?
- What do you gain by this behaviour?
- What are the effects of this upon others?

Assertiveness techniques

Activity **Assertive techniques**

Consider the assertiveness techniques below in relation to your 'recurring situation'.

1 Identify blocks to assertiveness
What has been preventing you from using assertive techniques up to now?

- ☐ Not being aware of the differences between aggression, passivity, manipulation and assertiveness
- ☐ It wasn't part of my family or cultural background
- ☐ Fear of other people's responses
- ☐ Fear of failure
- ☐ Blaming myself for the situation
- ☐ Not wanting to hurt other people's feelings
- ☐ I wanted a quiet life
- ☐ My current methods may not be fair but I get what I want

2 Put yourself in the picture
This means that you:

- look at the 'big picture': identify all the interests of all the parties, including your own
- ensure you are in the picture: if you are more likely to respond in a passive way, you may not feel you have a right to be considered

Put yourself in the picture.

consider whether you really should be at the centre, near the centre or on the periphery of the picture. Passive people can believe it is polite or kind or good manners to put themselves on the margins. If this happens all the time, it is likely to be irritating to others, as they will always be put into the position of being the more selfish, greedy, inconsiderate person, which is not pleasant. Aggressive people may always find reasons to be at the centre.

3 Make 'I' statements

People who find it hard to be assertive can find it difficult to make 'I' statements such as:

- 'I want …'
- 'I need …'
- 'I am responsible for …'

Sometimes this is very noticeable because they refer to their own needs in very general terms:

- 'Everybody needs …'
- 'We all need …'
- 'It is important to …'
- 'You have to …'
- 'One has to …'

Activity **Making 'I' statements**

Make 'I' statements for the 'recurring situation' you selected on p. 147.

Aspect	'I' Statement
What do you want?	I want …
What do you need?	I need …
How do you feel?	I feel …
What rights are involved?	I have the right to …
What are your responsibilities?	I am responsible for
My behaviours	I will (do). …

In your reflective journal, jot down your responses to the following:

- How easy was this activity for you?
- What kind of speech do you use in order to avoid using 'I' statements?
- Which statement was the most difficult to make?
- When will you use these 'I' statements?

---

4 Choose the moment

Ensure that:

- *The time is right.* This does not mean waiting for a perfect moment that may never arrive. It means choosing the best time available. Make an agreed time with the person or ensure that, at a meeting, time is put aside to discuss the matter. Be clear how long you need.
- *You have the person's full attention.* Ask for this if necessary. Choose a moment when they are able to give you attention. Avoid competing with television, radio or loud music.

5 State the issue and the desired change

Take responsibility for letting the person know what you find unacceptable or difficult about their behaviour. Do so in a manner that is calm, and does not sound blaming. Describe behaviours rather than the person. Say what the behaviour is, and acknowledge responsibility for your own part in the event and for your own feelings and responses. Make it clear what you want.

Example 1

'I feel hurt when you do not respond when I speak to you in the mornings. I would like you to say "hello".'

Rather than:

'You are so rude in the mornings. You make me feel ignored and angry and it affects my whole day.'

Example 2

'I need the price lists by 4:00 p.m. If you send them after 4:00, it is difficult to get our updates in the post.'

Rather than:

'You know the post goes out at 4:00. I don't know how you expect us all to get everything done when you can't be bothered to get the lists to us in time. It's your fault I was so upset last night – you really stress us out.'

6 Use positive language structures

When you make 'I' statements, use positive language structures. Positive language structures avoid the use of 'no', or 'not'. They are also clear, to the point and say exactly what you will do. Avoid words such as 'try', which suggests hard work or failure. Avoid modifiers such as 'some', 'maybe', 'sort of', 'quite'.

Positive language structure	Avoid
● I will ask for a lift.	I'll try and see if I can get a lift.
● I am entitled to this money.	I really think I should have what is due to me.
● I want these comments to stop.	I think it would be better if there were a little less of these comments.
● I will complete the race.	I intend to make a good shot at completing the race.
● Can I have help lifting this, please?	I can't lift this on my own! You could help!
● I need to say something.	I'm never given a chance to say what I need.
● I feel angry and upset.	I am trying not to get angry here!

7 Ask the other person's opinion

When you have stated what the issue is for you, check whether there could be a different interpretation. Ask the person how they see the situation and what they think about it. Show that you have a genuine interest in hearing their point of view. Let them give their interpretation without interrupting them.

8 Acknowledge the feelings

It is very common to see people arguing, even hissing through gritted teeth, 'I am not angry! I am not angry!' when it is clear to others that they are. This can make a situation difficult to resolve because the truth isn't being acknowledged.

It isn't always pleasant or easy to talk about feelings, but it is usually useful. Even if you do not voice your feelings, make sure that you at least know what they are. Otherwise, other people will know more about you than you do yourself.

- Check what you are feeling.
- Acknowledge to yourself how you are feeling.
- Make an 'I' statement about this: 'I feel …'
- Take care not to spill out the emotion on the people around you. You have a right to feel angry, for example, but not to coerce others with your feelings.
- Be prepared to hear how other people feel and consider what that means. You might not like hearing what they say, but they have the right to express how they feel too.

9 Suggest and invite solutions

Being assertive means looking for a solution that suits both sides as far as possible. Make constructive suggestions for a way forward. Point out the advantages to both parties. Ask the person for their suggestions and be prepared to negotiate (see p. 153).

10 Clarify what has been agreed

Check you both agree the details of what is agreed. This will avoid disputes later. Writing down the agreement strengthens the commitment. Read what the other person has written and check you agree with the details. Keep a copy.

If you are not used to being assertive, it will take time to change your habits and thinking. You can build your confidence by using some 'practice runs', either with a trusted friend or with a student counsellor. Keep a record of times when you are assertive so that you can monitor your progress.

Reflection: Assertiveness

In your reflective journal, jot down your responses to the following questions:

- What could you gain by being more assertive?
- What difficulties are there for you in putting assertiveness techniques into action?
- How will you address these?
- Which of the above techniques could you use?

Dealing with difficult people

On becoming a monster

Any of us can be a difficult person some of the time. Most of us have 'pet hates': situations and people that we do not manage skilfully and which seem to make us unreasonable. When we are confronted by a 'difficult person', empathy can be a useful starting place. It is worth considering that this person might, like us, be very reasonable if the circumstances were different.

Reflection: Being difficult

In your reflective journal jot down one occasion when you acted unreasonably or 'out of character' – when you found yourself shouting at somebody, complaining unnecessarily, making a difficult situation worse, or blowing something out of proportion.

- What was it about the circumstances that led you to behave like that?
- What can you learn from your own experience that might help you to understand when other people seem to be unnecessarily difficult?
- Jot down a list of all the circumstances that can turn you into a 'monster'. Are these things that might be typical of the day of a 'difficult person' you know?

Is it just me?

If you experience the same person as difficult on several occasions, you might conclude that the person is just plain awkward. That may be the case, but there may be ways that you can ease your own relations with that person, so that your day runs more smoothly. Consider:

- Do other people find this person difficult?
- Who seems to manage situations with this person best? What do they do?
- What is it about the difficult person that provokes a response in you?
- What is it about the person that makes you find it difficult to give calm and measured responses?
- What do you do that contributes to making the situation more difficult than it need be? What could you do to improve the situation?

Reflection: Dealing with difficult people

Think of one occasion with a 'difficult person' that you consider had a significant impact upon you. Jot down a brief outline of what happened.

- How did you feel at the time?
- How were you affected afterwards? For example, was it hard to settle down to work, enjoy your evening, sleep, feel calm?
- How many times did you narrate the episode to others? How much time did this take up? What would you have done with that time otherwise?
- In retrospect, how might you have responded differently, either during the event or afterwards, so the experience affected you less?
- What do you have to gain by changing the interaction you have with this person?

The effect on me?

Difficult people can have a profound effect upon the people around them. They can become the source of constant conversation and a good source of gossip. Dealing with them, talking about them, going back over what happened, planning what you will say or do on the next occasion, all take up time and energy. That time could have been spent more fruitfully. Although it may be important to plan how to cope with a difficult person, it is just as important to ensure that the person does not become an excuse for time wasting, and for diverting energies from other problems.

Whatever the difficult person may have done, you have a personal responsibility to yourself to manage the effects upon yourself.

Managing the situation

Identify the behaviour

The golden rule for interacting with people is to separate the behaviour from the person. This is easy to say but much more difficult in practice. When thinking about the person, make a conscious effort to focus on their actions. For example: '*That* irritates me' rather than '*She* irritates me'. This distinction will then come more easily to you when you are with the person.

Isolate the source of irritation

For the 'difficult person' you identified above, jot down all their behaviours that really irritate or concern you. For example, do they:

- interrupt you all the time?
- refuse to let you express your point of view?
- interrupt your study or work?
- arrive late for each seminar or meeting?
- take up all the discussion time with their opinions?
- other things?

Look for positive interpretations of their behaviour

Look for characteristics about the person that you can genuinely appreciate. Look for a positive aspect to their unwanted behaviour, such as a desire to please, a willingness to contribute, a sense of humour.

Consider their needs

Usually behaviour has an intention – even if it is inappropriate to the context. Sometimes people simply go about getting what they need in a misguided way. The people you find difficult will be acting the way they do in order to achieve something. This might be to:

- gain attention
- be noticed
- be respected
- feel that people think they are clever
- be heard
- draw attention away from something else
- make friends.

Consider how you (or the group) could give that person some of what they need. This may make them less demanding, and easier to cope with.

Acknowledge the other person

People behave unreasonably when their needs are not met. Listen to what they are communicating, and let them know you have heard. For example:

Their situation	Your response
• They are distressed	'I can see/hear that you are upset.'
• They are angry	'I can see/hear you are angry.'
• They want attention	'That is a good idea.' 'That's an interesting point.'

Identify what they want

- Ask the person what they want.
- Repeat this back to them so they know you have listened and heard them correctly.
- Consider whether the request is feasible.
- Let them know what is feasible.
- Stay calm and repeat this if the offer is refused.

Acknowledge your own feelings

- Identify your own feelings. This will give you more control over your own responses. Are you angry? distressed? unhappy? raging? guilty? irritated?
- Check how well you are managing your emotions? Do you need to calm down?
- State your feelings clearly and simply so that the other person knows how you feel.

State indisputable facts

Rather than get into an entangled argument, focus on statements of fact:

- 'They are closing the doors. We have to go now.'
- 'This is a seminar. The issue cannot be resolved now.'
- 'We haven't got the receipts here. We can look at this again once we have them.'

Keep it clear and simple

- Keep it simple. Unless it is really necessary, avoid arguing about points of detail.
- State what needs to be done.
- Keep to the present situation: avoid going over past events.

State what you want

Consider what would be a reasonable outcome for you from the situation. State this calmly, simply and clearly. Avoid unnecessary details or commentary. You may need to repeat what you want several times if the person is shouting or in full flow.

- 'I want to leave this until we all feel calmer.'
- 'I want you to stop ringing me after 9 p.m.'
- 'I want to have more time for group discussion.'
- 'I want to hear what other people have to say.'
- 'I want a refund.'

Offer positive solutions

- Maintain a positive focus. Look for an acceptable solution.
- Offer a way out of a stalemate.
- State the advantages of the proposed solution.
- Be prepared to negotiate a reasonable compromise or to find a 'bridge' – even if you feel the other person should be taking the initiative.
- Invite all parties to write down the agreed solution so that it is clear and on record.

Clarify tasks

If people are difficult team members, they may not be clear or happy about what is expected of them.

- Involve them in key decisions.
- Negotiate and clarify targets.
- Ensure their role offers sufficient challenge and interest.

Look for the 'bottled up' emotions

Even if somebody is being difficult, they probably think they are very reasonable. At that stage, there is probably very little you can say to change their mind. When we are emotional, we are not open to logical reasoning. Be prepared to let your perspective wait until the person is calmer.

The probability is that the person has built up emotions such as anger, frustration, rage or fear over a very long time. If this has not been acknowledged, they may be 'dumping' this emotion on other people without realising it. This will be evident in disproportionate responses to small things.

If the emotions are dumped on you: this is not fair, and you should not put up with it.

The angry person probably cannot see what they are doing. It is unlikely to be helpful to discuss this at the time unless:

- you know the person very well
- you have a relationship which permits discussing personal matters (as the source of the emotion may be very personal)
- you have agreed to set time aside for this
- you are both very calm.

Don't 'pass the parcel'

It is very tempting to respond to emotional 'dumping' by unloading all your own emotions. This may even feel good at the time. However, it is not a skilful way of dealing with the person or the situation, and makes it even harder to resolve differences over the longer term. To avoid unloading your emotions on others:

- Check which emotions you are most likely to unload onto others.
- What are the triggers for this response?
- What kinds of 'emotional dumping' do you seem to invite most from other people (their anger? guilt? shame? anxiety? fear?)?
- Plan a coping strategy so that you are not drawn into this sort of interaction.

Negotiating

Negotiation covers a wide spectrum. It can cover everyday situations, such as how much of the food budget goes on beer, chocolate or vegetables. It is an important part of group work, and most types of work include at least an element of negotiation with customers, clients or third parties.

Good negotiators exercise a broad and very subtle set of skills and qualities. These include:

- decision making
- reading the situation and the 'opposition'
- persuasiveness and communication skills
- assertiveness
- dealing with difficult people.

Decision making

When negotiating, you may have to make decisions very quickly. It is important to be well prepared before you arrive, and to have thought through the issues and the questions you will face so that you are clear about your own position.

The stakes

What is really at stake? What is the ultimate aim? This should inform the negotiation process. The ultimate aim may not be achievable now: world peace, a harmonious group atmosphere, or a successful group project will not be established by solving a single argument or making a single deal. However, the negotiation should aim to take you closer to the ultimate aim. If it takes you a small way forward, then something has been achieved. If it takes you a long way forward, then you have less to do in future negotiations.

The ideal outcome

Consider the ideal outcome for you. What would this look like? What would be the benefits? Form a clear picture of this so that it motivates you to negotiate strongly.

The bottom line

Consider your 'bottom line': what is the minimum you will accept? This is usually less than we really want. Negotiation usually involves two sides with competing interests. Each side will have to concede something if an agreement is to be reached. Be clear what you want from the situation. Consider:

The ideal solution What would be your ideal solution? A clear vision can strengthen your bargaining position.

 A good acceptable outcome What would this look like? What would be the benefits of this for you? What parts of your 'ideal outcome' are you prepared to relinquish?

The next best option This may mean giving up more of the 'dream option'.

 The likely outcome Be realistic. What is likely to happen? Is this acceptable? You may gain a better deal, but if you do not, how will you come to terms with the likely outcome?

The minimum offer What is your bottom line? What aspects are you prepared to negotiate, and what are your upper or lower limits for these? Practise saying these in a calm, clear way so that you sound firm and convincing when you come to argue your case. Write these down and take them with you so you do not concede on essentials.

Know when to concede

It is not always easy to strike the perfect balance between holding out for the best possible option, and knowing when to concede in order to gain something from the negotiation. You will need to weigh up:

- *Deadlines* How much time you have in order to hold out for the best option.
- *Costs* What might you lose if you take a long time to come to an agreement? How long can you hold out for what you want?
- *Risks* What will happen if you hold out and do not get what you want? Will you still be able to manage the situation (or your life)?
- *Competition* Is anybody else likely to make a better offer and put you out of the bargaining?
- *The history* In similar situations, or with this person or team, what usually tends to happen? What is likely to be agreed? What are the points that they are unlikely to concede?

All too late, George realised he hadn't included negotiation skills in his personal development plan.

Flexibility

From what has been described above, it should be evident that negotiation requires you to weigh up many possibilities, to assess the situation, and be able to accept one of a number of outcomes, depending upon the circumstances. One option is to be inflexible, and to insist on the best possible option. You may be successful, but you are more likely to leave with nothing. This usually means you have to start again on a new set of negotiations, so you need to weigh up the costs of a 'Nothing' option very carefully.

Reading the situation and the 'opposition'

Investigate the background

Find out as much as you can about the other person or team and their needs, interests and motivations. This puts you in a stronger position to negotiate.

Clarify mutual positions

Invite both sides to discuss their objectives and the possible options. This will enable you to see where there is room for manoeuvre. There will be a range of items that are not negotiable. It can take a lot of energy to try to alter the 'non-negotiables'. Ensure you are clear what the other side will or will not accept. If you can live with these requirements, then leave them out of the discussion, and focus on what can be negotiated.

Body language

The Institute of Management draws attention to the significance of body language as a means of communication – and the importance of understanding its impact in the workplace. Ribbens and Thompson (2002) argue that up to 90 per cent of communication may be non-verbal. Look for signs that suggest the other party is feeling defensive. People are less likely to negotiate to your advantage if they feel they need to 'defend' their own position. Look for:

- signs of distress (fidgeting; agitated movements; rocking; eyes looking downwards; moving hands over the face; pacing)
- a closed stance (arms and legs crossed; pursed lips; hands tightly clasped, the body leaning forward in a defensive position)
- obstructiveness (avoiding eye contact; shaking the head; refusal to engage in communication)
- anxiety about speaking (moving hands across the mouth; biting the lips)

• unwillingness to listen (sitting forward with hands moving over the ears; moving to interrupt; drumming fingers on the table).

Persuasiveness and good communication skills

Create an open relaxed atmosphere

If people look, sound or feel defensive, as described above, it helps to put them more at their ease so that they open up to your ideas. You can improve the situation if you:

• avoid 'hard sell' approaches
• focus on their agenda for a while, as this is familiar terrain for them
• ask for a break so you can interact more informally for a few minutes
• mirror their body language for a few minutes and gradually introduce more relaxed postures (arms in relaxed positions, legs uncrossed, sitting back in the chair, using calm movements of the head or hands)
• smile
• think through the situation from their point of view: you are more likely to act in a way they can accept if you are genuinely thinking about their position.

Speak to their vision

Let them know you have been listening to what they said. Keep referring to their objectives and interests, identifying how your proposal goes some way towards achieving these. Spell out the advantages. It is important that the other parties see that their goals can be met through the solution you propose. If not, they are unlikely to agree.

Show willingness to compromise

Let the other party know that you are willing to make concessions. Do not identify your own 'bottom line' straight away, as you will have no room to negotiate. Be clear about your 'ideal' scenario, so they can see clearly where you are prepared to negotiate: people do not like to feel that they are the only ones making concessions. Watch their response to your offer to see whether it is one they look comfortable with, or whether more persuasion is needed.

Keep the lines of communication open

Stay calm, even if you are not getting what you want. Do not 'burn your bridges' by walking out or giving ultimatums. Leave possibilities for further dialogue. If necessary, brainstorm more options together, take breaks and reconsider your options, start again from the beginning, or look for different combinations of options.

Activity ⟳ Changing a recurring situation

For this activity, identify a recurring situation where you could apply skills in assertiveness and negotiation. This may be the same situation that you used for other activities in the chapter. Write your responses in the boxes.

The situation. Give brief details of the context and what usually happens.	
What do you do? What kind of behaviour do you use?	
What are the effects of this behaviour?	
How do you feel about the situation? 'I feel …'	

Activity: Changing a recurring situation *(continued)*

A constructive way of thinking about this situation is …	
Identify your goal. 'The change I want to bring about is …'	
What are your rights? 'I am entitled to …'	
What are the rights of the other party or other people in this situation? 'They are entitled to …'	
What are your responsibilities in this situation? 'It is my responsibility to …'	
What are the responsibilities of other people? 'They are responsible for …'	
What will be the right time and place? How will you ensure you have their full attention?	
What other 'I' statements could you make?	
Your recommendations for a solution are …	
The minimum you will accept is …	
What support can you get from others (such as practice runs, somebody to encourage you)?	
Other comments	

Situation	What I did (include details of how you applied an assertiveness technique)	Positive outcomes for myself	The effect upon other people	Further action needed
1				
2				
3				
4				
5				

Activity: Monitoring effectiveness in negotiating skills and assertiveness *(continued)*

Situation	What I did (include details of how you applied an assertiveness technique)	Positive outcomes for myself	The effect upon other people	Further action needed
6				
7				
8				
9				
10				

What I notice about my negotiating skills and assertiveness through monitoring them:

Leadership

The role of leader

Leaders provide the vision. They motivate others. Leaders need to have a clear internal model of their role. This is likely to be strongly influenced by other roles that they fill in life, by their values, and by the sources of inspiration that they call upon. You will have an internal model in your head, now, of what you think a leader is or should be. For example, some people might describe a leader by using one or more of the following metaphors. A leader is:

- a conductor leading an orchestra
- an architect, designing and constructing a project
- a sales-manager, selling a vision
- a social worker, intervening to improve the lot of others
- a general, commanding an army
- an actor, playing to an audience
- a diplomat, pouring oil on troubled waters
- an artist, with a particular vision.

Leadership from the position of the led

Reflection: Leadership

- What metaphor of your own best describes your view of a good leader? What does this metaphor tell you about your feelings towards leaders and leadership?
- Does your view of leaders and leadership encourage you to be a leader or to avoid this? What metaphor would inspire and encourage you more to be a leader? Does that metaphor apply to any roles that you already fill?
- How do you feel a team would respond to a leader who fitted the metaphor you have selected?
- Which metaphors for leadership would best encourage active, motivated, self-reliant team members?

Activity **Your advice to the leaders?**

- If you want some ideas on how to motivate and lead others, give consideration to what it is like to be 'led'. What kind of behaviour, communication or strategy would motivate you to 'go the extra mile' that is often needed for successful project completion?
- Jot down a list of behaviours that you would associate with an effective team leader.
- Use your insights to formulate a list of 'Advice' points for team leaders.

When you have completed your list, compare it with the 'characteristics of an effective leader' given below.

Are you a leader?

Everyone has leadership potential, but not everyone recognises this in themselves. It takes courage to lead, and wisdom to see when somebody else might be a better leader in a situation. You can lead if:

- you see that somebody needs to take the lead
- you can see what needs to be done
- you can convince others of this, in your own way.

Reflection: Do I take the lead?

- How far do you envisage yourself as a leader?
- When somebody needs to take a lead, is that person you?
- If so, why? If not, why not?

Characteristics of an effective leader

Inspire others

A good leader will ensure that the vision is kept in view, and does not become lost amongst a forest of targets, deadlines, and problems.

Heerkens, 2002

A leader develops the vision and exudes a realistic confidence in that vision. They must also communicate it well to others, ensuring that everybody else can see what the benefits of achieving that vision would be.

A good leader can see ways that the overall goal can contribute to individual and personal goals. Typically, the vision of successful leaders is for the project or the team, rather than for their personal goals (Taylor and Humphrey, 2002).

Reflection: Leading towards a vision

- What kinds of vision would you feel most comfortable in encouraging other people to work towards?
- In what ways would your values assist you in developing an interest in leadership skills? (See Chapter 1)
- In what ways would your values help or hinder you as a leader?

Create a sense of commitment

Team members are more likely to contribute if they feel committed to the project. An effective team leader:

- offers a clear and motivating 'vision'
- ensures that the whole team is clear about the purpose and aims of the project
- identifies the significance or relevance of a successful outcome to the project
- clarifies how the work of each member is significant to the overall project
- leads by example.

Develop the strategy

One of the main tasks of the team or project leader is to develop the strategy. This will orchestrate the efforts and resources of the team towards the goal. A strategy may be simple or complex.

Reflection: Using strategy

- What experience of developing a strategy have you had so far?
- What skills have you developed in evolving a strategy for yourself or for a team? (See Chapter 6)
- What opportunities could you create for yourself to become more involved in strategy or policy formation (e.g. student clubs; political groups; charities; local government; being a student representative; starting a business; setting up a new group or project)?

Encourage contributions from others

Team members are more likely to contribute if they feel valued. An effective team leader:

- notices people's contributions
- thanks people for their contributions
- makes it clear to the whole team where everyone fits in – and draws attention to achievements that are less visible
- clarifies how the achievements of individuals contribute to the benefit of the overall project
- treats all of the team with fairness, courtesy and consideration.

Demonstrate the value of all team members

Team members are more likely to contribute if they feel their opinions are valued. An effective team leader:

- creates opportunities to ask the team for their opinions and encourages them to help evolve a solution
- creates opportunities for the team to contribute to the planning and setting of targets
- demonstrates how suggestions and comments from the team have been considered and adopted
- allows individuals opportunities to develop their own plans for achieving targets.

Clarify expectations

Team members are more likely to contribute if they know what is expected of them. An effective team leader:

- negotiates clear targets for each person
- clarifies how each person's work connects to the work of others
- negotiates clear ground rules for group behaviours
- makes it clear what a successful outcome would be for each person
- ensures that feelings of uncertainty are kept to a minimum.

Ensure the team works

Leaders ensure that the team works well, knowing what different people can contribute. Good leaders ensure their team is functioning smoothly, and intervene when it is not. They act as full members of their teams, and are readily available if things become difficult. (See 'Team work', above.)

Reflection: Leading a team

- For what aspect of team work would you find it easiest to take a lead?
- When or where do you do that now?
- If you lack experience in leading groups or sessions, what opportunities could you create to gain that experience?

Take responsibility

Leaders are the most prominent members of the team. They take the lion's share of the glory when things go well. They must also be prepared to take responsibility if things do not go well. This can be quite a daunting thought. However, taking responsibility for our actions is important in most contexts.

Demonstrate excellent 'people' skills

Leaders need to communicate well. Without good inter-personal skills, it would be almost impossible to bring a set of people to share a vision, pull together, commit to a project, meet deadlines and resolve their differences. Leaders may also have an ambassadorial function, speaking and negotiating on behalf of the team.

Reflection: Taking responsibility

Consider a situation where you had responsibility for the outcomes. If possible, select an occasion when it was difficult to take responsibility but where you did so.

- What happened?
- What was your role?
- What did it feel like to take responsibility then?
- What have you learnt from the experience that will be useful to you in other circumstances?

Activity Updated self-evaluation

Complete a new self-evaluation of your people skills (see p. 132).

Compare this with the initial self-evaluation you undertook. What differences do you notice?

- What are your current priorities for developing your people skills?
- What opportunities could you create to develop your people skills further?

Closing comments

Increasing numbers of graduate and non-graduate jobs will include leadership and management roles, with responsibility for managing other people and their relationships with each other. There are much higher expectations of most employees now for managing other people, whether colleagues, customers or clients.

Many roles require a wide range of people skills, from communicating clearly, negotiating and persuading, to being a good team member or leading a team.

On the other hand, academic work is often organised to emphasise individual effort and achievement. There are a number of reasons for this, including the need to secure academic standards and to ensure every student is performing well on an individual basis. However, many programmes now include group work, team work and work placements to ensure students have real opportunities to develop their people skills.

Whether inter-personal skills are provided through the curriculum or not, it is a good idea

to search out opportunities to develop them. Careers Services, the Students' Union, Schools Liaison Offices at the university, and voluntary agencies can provide such opportunities.

Inter-personal skills require, above all, good self-management. This chapter should be read alongside Chapter 4. Emotional intelligence is a key factor in being able to manage oneself in interactions with others and to understand the needs and requirements of other people. Some universities run additional programmes such as basic counselling skills and assertiveness to develop people skills.

Effective people skills are invaluable in all aspects of life, study and work. They provide the oil that enables your interactions with others to run smoothly. When you develop good people skills, you can see ahead to where difficulties may emerge, take steps to minimise these, and increase the harmony in everyday social interactions. This reduces stress, saves time and improves conditions for everybody. Everybody is happier – which is why people skills are becoming so valued.

Further reading

Belbin, M. R. (2010) *Team Roles at Work*, 2nd edn (London: Butterworth-Heinemann). (For more about using Belbin types for team work.)

Benson, J. F. (2009) *Working More Creatively with Groups*, 3rd edn (London: Tavistock). (Useful for dipping into; contains many ideas about making groups work effectively.)

Cottrell, S.M. (2013) *The Study Skills Handbook*, 4th edn (Basingstoke: Palgrave Macmillan). (An introduction to the skills of working with others, specifically in university contexts.)

Kozubska, J. (1997) *The 7 Keys of Charisma: The Secrets of Those Who Have It* (London: Kogan Page). (Particularly useful for those considering management, media and high-profile jobs.)

Luft, J. (1984) *Group Processes: An Introduction to Group Dynamics*, 3rd edn (Mayfield, CA: Mountain View). (For more advanced reading about group dynamics.)

McGill, I. and Beaty, L. (2001) *Action Learning: A Practitioner's Guide*, 2nd revised edn (London: Routledge), Chapters 2, 5 and 9. (For more detail specifically about action sets.)

Ribbens, G. and Thompson, R. (2002) *Understanding Body Language* (Abingdon: Gower). (Looks at body language in a range of everyday work settings.)

Taylor, R. and Humphrey, J. (2002) *Fast Track to the Top: Skills for Career Success* (London: Kogan Page). (The skills associated with successful chief executives, including inter-personal skills.)

Chapter 6
Successful problem-solving and task management

Learning outcomes

This chapter offers opportunities to:

- understand what is meant by problem-solving
- develop techniques and approaches associated with successful problem-solving
- develop the confidence to take on tasks, problems and projects
- become a 'good self-starter'
- understand the processes involved in basic project management
- audit your own 'competitiveness'.

Introduction

Problem-solving is highly valued by employers. They want graduates to 'hit the ground running', able to apply skills to new situations and deal with new tasks with minimum supervision. Almost every activity, task or problem will draw on the following set of processes and skills:

1 Strategy: tactics and an overall plan.
2 Techniques: methods to use.
3 People skills: working with others in appropriate ways to achieve the goal.
4 Self-management: managing your time, personal issues, feelings and performance.
5 Creativity: finding ideas that contribute towards a solution.

People who are very good at problem-solving usually bring people skills, self-management and creativity to the task. These three factors are so important that they each have chapters dedicated to them. This chapter introduces some basic problem-solving and task-management techniques.

Tasks and problems

'Task' covers a wide range of circumstances. In this chapter, 'task' is used flexibly to refer to any activity or part of a larger project. The term 'problem' is also used flexibly. It can be:

- any question that calls for an answer
- a puzzle waiting to be solved
- a situation requiring a response
- a challenge to be met.

It is important to separate the idea of 'problem-solving' from that of 'difficulty' or 'trouble'. Problem-solving is not necessarily difficult, although it can be applied to difficult situations. Any situation that presents a challenge or an opportunity for a new approach can be treated as a formal 'problem' that requires a solution.

Activity Selecting a focus

In order to provide a focus for this chapter, identify one problem, task, assignment or personal goal that is relevant to you. Refer to this as you work through each of the sections below.

For each of the following statements, rate your confidence on a score of 4 to zero.

Rating: *Very confident = 4   Confident = 3   Quite confident = 2   Not very confident = 1*
Not confident at all/don't know = 0

I am confident in:	Rating	See pp.
1 using basic approaches to problem-solving		165
2 knowing what is meant by 'elaborating' a problem		167
3 applying a similarity approach to problem-solving		167
4 applying a strategy to problem-solving		168
5 applying a multiple-solution approach to problem-solving		170
6 evaluating multiple solutions		172
7 setting criteria to evaluate a solution		172–4
8 identifying priorities		172–4
9 setting targets		175
10 drawing up an action plan		177
11 organising project time		178–80
12 my ability to get down to work on a task		181
13 my ability to be a good self-starter		182
14 my ability to stick with a task until it is completed		182
15 my ability to finish off a task		183
16 my understanding of what is meant by a 'project'		183
17 my understanding of the difference between student essays and student projects		183–4
18 managing a project		184–6
19 using performance indicators		186
20 using soft criteria to evaluate my performance		187
21 using benchmarks		187
22 my understanding of personal 'competitiveness'		188–9
23 my ability to lead a project		159–61
24 making best use of the strengths of project team members		137–42
25 my ability to find creative solutions to problems		204

Score [   ]

Interpreting your score

If your self-ratings were accurate, you have a score for your overall problem-solving skills. This is a rough indicator of how confident you are about these skills, which may, of course, be different from your actual ability. A score over 40 is reasonable, a score over 55 is quite good, a score over 70 is very good, and a score over 85 is excellent.

However, you should interpret how good your score is depending on:

- how long you have been on the programme
- how much experience you have in project work
- how much guidance you have already received in project work.

Compare your score now with the score you give yourself when you have completed the chapter or when you have undertaken some project work.

Basic approaches to problem solving

Activity **Your current approaches**

How would you go about solving the following problems? Spend a few minutes working them out, either on your own or with a second person. Jot down the processes you went through in order to arrive at a solution that satisfies you.

1   You want to go on holiday to a sunny place, within your budget. You do not know where to go yet, but do know that the options are all places where you do not speak the local language. What are the things you have to consider in order to ensure you will have a good time when you arrive?

2   You want to cook a meal for three friends to celebrate a birthday. One of them may be bringing a child. Another guest is allergic to nuts. You have three days to prepare this and want it to be something they would all really like. You also want to ensure that you have enough money to cover this. What will you cook? What else will you do to ensure that the meal is successful?

3   Your tutor has just pointed out that your essay must be in on Friday. You hadn't realised there were two essays to be completed this week. Both must be in on time. How will you go about meeting the deadlines?

Make a list of the approaches you considered. Then compare this with the 'basic approaches' list below.

Basic approaches

Your list probably included some or all of the following:

Talking to others

You would probably want to ask other people for ideas, their experience, what they know about the persons and places involved. People are a key resource in problem-solving. This is why successful companies value 'people skills'. Finding out what you need to know from others, or 'informal learning', is the dominant form of professional development for most American companies (Rossett and Sheldon, 2001).

 Lists

Many people organise their lives by lists. They are quick and easy tools to use and excellent starting points for any problem.

Finding out information

You may have included approaches such as browsing the Internet, checking catalogues and looking in books. Researching information, weighing it up and selecting what you need are all useful to problem-solving.

Calculating

Many problems include a number component, such as working out the budget and finances. Some problems are solved more easily by using a mathematical formula. You may have used calculations to work out how much time there would be for different aspects of each of the two essays, or how to meet the budget for the meal or holiday.

Item	£
glass	39
paint	24
glue	12
timber	53

Following the rules

Sometimes it is easier to follow procedures laid down for the activity. Mixing chemicals for a particular purpose requires very precise measurements of specific chemicals, for example. If you are not used to cooking, following a recipe step by step will be helpful. When you become more familiar with the process, you will know how and when to adapt rules in order to achieve the results you want.

Trial and error

You may prefer to jump in at the deep end, trying out various ideas until you hit the right one. This works well for some people, but is a very labour-intensive way of working unless there really are no options. You may find you are good at 'trial and error' for some areas (such as cooking) and less so in others (gardening). This is sometimes regarded as intuition, but may be the result of expertise built up over time.

Visualising

You may have pictured the problem in your 'mind's eye', checking off the places where you might go on such a holiday or what the meal might be like. You may have visualised yourself performing each of the activities. Successful sportspeople tend to use visualising techniques to see the exact details of how they will achieve victory. It can be applied to most areas of life.

Charting

You may have used a chart, flow diagram or other graphic device to draw out the problem, so that you could work it out visually.

Calling upon a similar experience

You may have thought about recent meals that you have cooked and whether you could adapt these to suit a child or the person with the allergy. If you have already completed an essay, you may have run through the processes involved, working out the time needed for each, based on your experience. You might even have been able to work out some ways of saving time in order to meet the deadlines.

Many problems are relatively simple like these. We can use different problem-solving strategies at once, moving back and forward between them as necessary. For example, to organise yourself to meet essay deadlines, you might:

- ask an academic adviser or tutor for advice
- negotiate with other people to arrange for cover for your work shift or cooking rota
- draw on a similar essay you completed for a previous programme
- calculate the time available for what you need to do
- chart in your diary the time available to you
- visualise where you left your notes
- draw a network or outline pattern of all the ideas you have on the essay
- research further information
- go for a walk to clear your mind.

Seven key tips for task management

1 Clarify the task: know exactly what you need to do and why.

2 Start where the energy is … all other things being equal.

3 Start much earlier than you think is necessary. This gives you more room for manoeuvre.

4 Think several steps ahead: plan out all the steps required to take you to the end point.

5 Always look for several solutions … it is easier than looking for THE one answer.

6 Give yourself tight time limits with early deadlines … otherwise tasks tend to expand to fill *all* the time available.

7 Find out the background to the project. Not only are you more likely to meet the project aims, things are also more interesting from the position of an 'expert'.

Problem-solving on the back of an envelope

Simplify

If you feel daunted by all the things there are to consider in working with a problem, begin by simplifying the problem down to essential features. See if you can summarise your strategy in ten steps on the back of an envelope.

Basic problem-solving

1. Define the problem — What is the real issue?
2. Desired outcome — What do I want?
3. Options — What outcomes are possible?
4. Feasibility — What is the best option I am likely to achieve?
5. Feelings — If I follow through on this option: how will I feel?
6. Decision — What is my decision?
7. Steps — What must I do, when, with whom, where?
8. Obstacles — What might get in the way? How will I deal with these?
9. Action — Do it!
10. Evaluation — Did it work?

Find the natural sequence

You may need to address stages of a task in a particular order, which may mean dealing with subsidiary issues before addressing the core problem.

When using a problem-solving model or framework, it is likely that you will move back and forth between stages, or between the kinds of questions identified on the envelope above, until you reach the decision-making and action stages. It is worth noticing how many of the ten stages above refer to thinking about the problem before any action is taken.

Problem elaboration

Research shows that people who spend more time at the beginning working out what a task really involves, perform much better. For example, successful mathematics students spend much longer reflecting on what category of mathematical problems they have been set. They look for similarities with problems they have worked on before. They consider various approaches and weigh these up before beginning calculations to solve the problem. Less successful students tend to launch into an assignment too quickly without defining clearly what the problem entails and what needs to be done.

The early planning stage is sometimes referred to as 'problem elaboration'. Elaboration involves analysing a task from all perspectives and defining what the task really involves. The similarity approach outlines one way of doing this.

The 'similarity approach' to problem-solving

Butterworth (1992) argues that we are more likely to succeed at new tasks if we can find similarities with ones we have accomplished already. If we cannot see those parallels, then we may believe ourselves incapable of tasks well within our actual competence. This suggests that it is worth giving time and thought to what we have achieved in any one context and its applicability to other contexts.

1 Clarify the core questions

State the core questions as simply as possible. Remove unnecessary wording so as to pare the problem down to the essential features. This makes it easier to see whether it is similar to one with which you are already familiar.

2 Identify an analogous problem

- What are the core features or components of the problem? What skills, methods or techniques are needed?
- What similarities are there between problems or activities have you undertaken before and the current task?
- How can previous problems help you to think through what is needed for this problem?
- How can you make use of previous skills and experience to solve this problem?

3 Identify the limitations of the analogy

List the differences between the current problem and previous tasks. The situations will not be identical so the same strategy may not work for the current problem. Identifying the difference is as important as identifying the similarity.

4 Establish significance

- Weigh up the significance of the similarities and differences.
- How will you adapt your strategy to take account of these differences?
- What else do you need to know or to do?

The OPAL strategy applied to task management

The OPAL strategy (Cottrell, 2010), shown in the diagram below, offers a set format to help analyse a problem and manage the tasks that lead to its solution. This is a cycle that can be applied both to project management and to tasks that form part of a project. Reflection is at the core of the cycle, undertaken as you work through a task (reflection in action); it is also a process taken outside of the cycle, standing back from it to gain a vantage point (reflection on action). OPAL stands for:

- Orientation
- Planning
- Action
- Learning

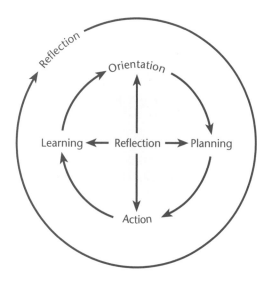

Orientation

The cycle begins with orientation, which includes problem elaboration and good advance planning. The orientation stage is rather like starting a journey. Before setting out, you would define your task and elaborate what needs to be done by considering such questions as the purpose of the journey, the starting point, the route, your mode of transport, and how you will know when you have arrived. Similarly, to solve a problem or manage a task, you need to consider the following:

- Define the task and identify the purpose of the task: what are you hoping to achieve? You may find it helpful to describe the problem in different words so that it is clear to you what needs to be done.
- What is the desired endpoint – what will indicate that you have accomplished what you set out to do?
- Where are you now – and what is the distance to that desired endpoint?
- Broadly speaking, how are you going to get from where you are to where you need to be?
- Is there another way of thinking about this? What might be an alternative way of achieving the desired endpoint? How many possible solutions can you generate in order to give yourself options on the way forward?
- What do you need to get the job done? Are these resources going to be available?
- What expertise can you bring to bear? You may find it helpful to use the activity on p. 61 to identify your expertise and consider its application to this problem.

Time spent productively in elaborating the problem in this way pays dividends later in the process.

Planning

Before launching into action, devise a strategy to achieve your goal and then plan out the various stages of what you need to do.

Strategy

What is the broad approach you will take to achieve your goal? Some of the following might be applicable in working out your strategy:

- Are you going to apply an approach you have used before, or try something new?
- Will you have a trial run, pilot or draft version first?
- Will you do this all at once or over a longer term?
- On your own or with others?
- Within current resources or do you need further resources? If so, will this involve fund-raising of some kind or securing a grant?
- Will you apply a particular model or theoretical framework?
- Are there key features to your strategy, such as a particular focus or emphasis?

Actions, targets, deadlines

Plan out what you will do, in what order, and by when:

- What are the main steps or stages?
- Set targets and time-scales for each stage?
- Set SMART-F targets (see p. 175)?
- How will you meet these targets?
- Draw these up into an action plan (see p. 177).

Draw up an action plan, identifying your mini-goals or targets as well as deadlines for these. Your action plan might be elaborate, or it may just be a list. It depends on how complex the problem is – and what suits you. (An outline is provided on p. 177.)

Priorities

- Identify priorities: what are all the things you need to do?
- What is essential? What can be left out?

Monitoring points

- Set specific times for monitoring your progress as you go along. Write these into your action plan.

At the end of the planning stage, you should feel that you have planned effectively, having thought through all possible angles. You should be clear about what action now needs to be taken.

Action

This is the 'doing' stage. Work through your action plan, observing your targets. This is the first real test of your planning and strategy.

Monitor and review your progress

Use your action plan to check that you are on target towards your goals.

- Do you need to amend your plan in any way so that it is more realistic?
- Are you meeting targets and deadlines? If not, do you need to revise these?
- Are you maintaining your motivation? If not, what can you do to improve this?
- Are you working within your budget and resources? If not, what action must you take?
- Do you need to revise your overall strategy?

Keep records

- Consider how you can demonstrate that you have worked to a strategy, reflected on your progress and revised your plan to increase your effectiveness. Gathering evidence as you go along will help you to do this.
- Keep a record of what you do and the outcome.

Learning

At the end of the task or project, before rushing on to your next project, or drawing a line under this one, pause to see what you can can learn from the experience. This stage consists of:

- Reflection (see Chapter 8)
- Evaluation
- Drawing out lessons for the future.

Reflection

Once you have completed the task overall, or specific actions that went either especially well or badly, stand back from it and take stock. You will find material and models for reflection in Chapter 8 that can be applied usefully here.

Evaluation

Evaluation is easier if clear targets have been set and, usually, is measured in terms of how well you have achieved those targets. However, it is useful to evaluate the overall strategy as well.

Achievement

Did you:

- Achieve your targets?
- Meet the deadlines for the overall project?
- Achieve the overall goal?
- Keep to budget?
- Maintain good working relationships?

Strategy effectiveness

- What worked well?
- What could be improved?
- What evidence is there of your performance, reflection and achievement?

A pro-forma of an Evaluation Sheet is provided as a resource below (p. 172–3).

Drawing out lessons for the future

Consider what you have learnt either from the project overall, or from specific aspects of it, such as:

- Whether the way you went about your advance planning was effective. Did it get you what you wanted in the way you wanted it?

- Are there aspects of the overall process in which you need training or more practice?

- Were there unforeseen consequences of the way you went about things?

- Were you over-ambitious? Or could you have been more ambitious?

- From what you have learnt, what would you do differently now? What went well that could be applied to future projects?

Activity **Solve that problem!**

Use the problem you identified in the activity on p. 163 as your 'target problem' for this activity. Apply the OPAL strategy by following the stages outlined above. Keep a record to help you evaluate the activity at the end and to learn from it. This can be completed electronically using the pro-forma provided in the electronic Resource Bank, and will also be of use for the activity on p. 171 below.

 Reflection: Using your experience

- How useful was your previous experience and expertise in finding and implementing a solution for this problem?
- What did you do well?
- What could you have done better?

The 'multiple solution approach' to problem-solving

You are more likely to arrive at the best option if you consider many solutions. The 'multiple solution approach' puts emphasis on generating several different solutions to the same problem. As you become more familiar with the OPAL model above, you can incorporate evaluation of multiple solutions into the Orientation Stage.

Propose an initial solution

You may arrive at your initial solution by using the similarity approach (p. 167) or the Expertise Metaphor approach (pp. 61–3). Your proposed initial solution does not need to be perfect as it is only one of many that you will consider. Jot down:

- the ways in which this already meets the needs of the situation

- weak points in the proposal or aspects that need to be considered further.

Brainstorm further ideas

- Jot down, quickly, as many ideas as possible. For this stage, put words such as 'realistic' and 'sensible' aside for a moment: release your imagination.

- Brainstorm solutions to the 'weak points' of the first solution you proposed.

Identify 'seed' ideas

For every idea, look for the seed of one positive aspect. The idea itself may be maverick ('relocate to the moon'; 'win the lottery'; 'kidnap the professor') but it may hint at a workable solution. For example:

- 'Relocating to the moon'. The idea of relocation might be useful. Would a change of room or building help? Have all options been considered?

- 'Winning the lottery'. There may be other sources of money. Would it be useful to look for financial backing from a local business or charity?

- 'Kidnapping the professor'. Would a tutor, student or local employer offer advice or mentorship?

Evaluate solutions

Weigh up factors for and against each solution, considering such criteria as:

- Cost: can it be afforded?
- Time: can it be completed in the time available?
- Expertise: is the necessary expertise available?
- Suitability: does it suit the circumstances and people involved?

- Value: which solution provides a good result with the least effort and cost?
- Risk: will it work? What are the risks?
- Goal: which best meets the project objectives?

Synthesise the best

- Select two or three solutions to consider in more detail.
- Identify the best aspects of each solution.
- Identify ways of synthesising the best features of each solution.
- Check whether the best features of each still work well when brought together into one strategy.

Identify the essential criteria

- Which criteria must be met (time, cost, design, etc.)?
- List these in order of priority. Which are the most important criteria to meet?
- Which solution do you want to go with? Does this meet the criteria you identified as priorities? If not, what can you change or do to ensure that those priorities are met?

Decision making

- Select one solution that best meets essential criteria.
- Fine-tune this option to meet the essential criteria.

Resource sheet

The resource sheet on the following page can be used to weigh up each solution.

Activity Multiple solutions: solve that problem again!

Using the problem you identified for 'Solve that problem!' (p. 170), reconsider the problem from a different perspective, to see whether there could have been a better solution.

Orientation

1 Define the task again, using different words.

Plan

2 Brainstorm as many other possible solutions to this problem as you can, without censoring too much at this stage whether they will work.

3 Identify the good ideas hidden within each solution.

4 Select two or three solutions to consider in more detail.

5 Evaluate each solution according to criteria relevant to you (cost, time, etc.).

6 Synthesise the best ideas from all the solutions.

7 Decide on a solution that best fits the priorities and adapt it to meet the criteria.

8 If there is the opportunity to test out the solution, draw up an action plan (see p. 177).

Action

9 If there is the opportunity, apply the solution to the problem, carrying out your action plan.

Learning

10 What have you learnt from this activity about how you might solve the problem you identified, and how you could improve your approach to problem-solving in general?

Evaluating Multiple Solutions

Complete this page on paper or electronically when considering a new problem or project. In addition, complete a separate copy of page 173 for each potential solution that you are considering.

Problem to be solved (*state briefly*):

Criteria for success

In evaluating your solution, consider such factors as those listed below. It may help to highlight or circle those you believe to be especially important. Then, identify those that are essential.

1 particular details that must be included in the solution

2 originality

3 maximum cost

4 likelihood of gaining funding/financial support

5 market

6 sustainability

7 time available

8 desired finish date/ deadlines

9 quality issues

10 design features

11 specific expertise needed and/or available

12 additional opportunities it creates

13 risks to be managed

14 assignment criteria

15 clients' criteria

16 health and safety issues

17 inclusiveness/ cultural issues

18 ethical issues

19 legal considerations

20 other

Essential criteria (in order of importance, drawing on the list above)

1		4	
2		5	
3		6	

© Stella Cottrell (2003, 2010, 2015), *Skills for Success*, Palgrave

Aspect	Solution number or name
Outline of this proposed solution	
Strengths of this solution	
Gaps, weaknesses or risks	
Seed ideas: interesting aspects of this solution	
Time considerations:	
Costs: good, bad, resolvable?	
How far does the solution meet your other essential criteria (page 172)?	
Parts of this solution to keep and build into the final solution?	

Problem-solving techniques

This section introduces some common problem-solving techniques. These include:

- setting goals
- setting criteria to evaluate a solution
- identifying priorities
- setting targets and drawing up an action plan
- planning project time
- getting down to it
- becoming a good 'self-starter'
- sticking with a task
- completing a task.

Setting goals

Setting goals is an important part of the orientation stage of your strategy. When considering your goal:

- Visualise what it would be like to achieve it (see p. 34, Chapter 1).
- Identify how you will know when you have achieved it: what will be different?
- Evaluate whether it is realistic.
- Identify what you will have to sacrifice in order to achieve it. Is it worth it?
- Think about your beliefs and values. Is it 'you'?

Setting criteria to evaluate a solution

Although evaluation takes place at the end of a task or project, you need to consider, at the beginning, the criteria by which you will evaluate success. Develop criteria that give you what you want but which are achievable.

Dream solution

Begin with the ideal. As Chapter 1 emphasises, it is important to work towards a 'vision'. However, use the vision to inform what you want, using it as a guide rather than a strait-jacket.

Realistic option

What would you accept as a reasonably good outcome that is both motivating and achievable? What are the main features of this option?

Identify relevant criteria for a solution

For each problem, consider the relative importance of issues such as those listed on the 'Evaluating Multiple Solutions' sheet on pages 172–3. Jot down details for each of those criteria that are most relevant for the task or problem on which you are working. Use these details to help you decide between solutions or to identify the best aspects to take on board from each of your potential solutions.

Identify priorities amongst the criteria

When you have a complete list, write these down in the order that is most important.

- Which criteria are essential and must be met?
- Which criteria are relatively flexible?
- Which criteria are very flexible?

Select only a few essential criteria and be prepared to be flexible on the others. The more essential criteria you set, the more difficult it will be to find a solution.

Identifying priorities

One common reason for not getting under way with a problem or project is that there are too many things competing for your attention. Emotions such as fear of not getting everything done, or guilt at letting someone down, make it hard to separate out what can be left and what must be addressed straight away.

To help set priorities, Neenan and Dryden (2002) suggest dividing tasks into one of four categories:

1. Urgent and important
2. Not urgent but important
3. Urgent but not important
4. Not urgent and not important

You may find it helpful to colour-code these using the resource sheet on p. 176 so that you can see urgent items most easily. For example:

1 Red – Category 1: urgent and important
Deadlines, crises, tasks timed for today, tasks which must come first in a sequence.

2 Yellow – Category 2: not urgent but important

Category 2 activities enable you to plan ahead. These should be addressed before they become urgent. Prioritise between these according to when they must take place in a sequence, or the consequences of leaving them for too long.

3 Orange – Category 3: Urgent but not important

If possible, leave these until category 1 tasks are completed. Category 3 items may not need to be undertaken at all, but can attract our attention unduly because they are 'urgent'. Emails are a good example of this. What other examples are typical of your own week?

4 Blue – Category 4: not urgent and not important

These are often good time-wasting activities. They can make us feel like we are busy, so that we do not get down to what is really needed. Reading junk mail, sorting out old papers, cleaning out cupboards may fall into this category.

Activity ○ **Identify priorities**

For the problem you are addressing at present:

- Brainstorm a list of all the things you need to do.
- Divide the items on your list into the four categories on the priority sheet on p. 176. Write the things that are most important and urgent in the top left-hand box. Use the top left of that box for the most urgent items.
- Use the bottom right of the page for the least important items.

When you have completed the priority sheet, use it to guide you in organising tasks into a logical order:

- Reorganise your original list of priorities into the order in which you will now complete tasks.
- Set targets for each priority (see 'SMART-F targets' below).

SMART-F target setting

Most tasks benefit from clear, achievable targets. SMART targets make it easier to see what must be done and then to evaluate success. SMART-F targets build in reasonable flexibility, so you can plan for unexpected contingencies. SMART-F stands for:

- *Specific*: 'I will complete the first section of my essay by this evening.'
- *Measurable*: 'I will produce the first three draft pages of my essay by this evening.'
- *Achievable*: 'This should be achievable because I have completed the research, organised my notes, and already produced the outline plan.'
- *Realistic*: 'I should be able to write three pages as I have written up to ten pages in a day before, and have done the preparatory work.'
- *Time-bound*: ' I will finish by 8:30 p.m.'
- *Flexible*: 'I could continue until 10:30 p.m. if necessary. If I find I have additional research to do for those pages, I can slot that in tomorrow between 9:00 and 11:00 a.m.'

Targets should provide clear guidelines for action and be built into an action plan (see p. 177). However, they are not written in stone: they should be monitored and reviewed as the project proceeds so that it can be completed on time.

Activity ○ **Evaluating Targets** (p. 178)

An example of a set of targets is provided for you to evaluate against SMART-F criteria and to check your responses. This will give you some insights into your own understanding of setting SMART-F targets.

Evaluating targets

Evaluate your own targets

Before launching out on a project, stand back for a moment and evaluate whether your targets are really helpful. An evaluation is provided on page 179 as a ready-made structure for your evaluations. You can copy this sheet for future use, or use it in the Electronic Resource Bank.

Priority Sheet

Divide your list of tasks into the four categories below. Then set targets for each priority (see 'Identifying priorities' on pp. 174–5).

1 RED *Urgent and important*	2 YELLOW *Not urgent but important*
3 ORANGE *Urgent but not important*	**4 BLUE** *Not urgent and not important*

Action plan

Goal:

Completion date:

Target	Milestones (steps to be taken)	By date	By whom	Evidence that milestone is completed	Done ✓
	1				
	2				
	3				
	4				
	1				
	2				
	3				
	4				
	1				
	2				
	3				
	4				
	1				
	2				
	3				
	4				

Successful problem-solving and task management   177

Evaluate each of the following targets and tick ✔ where appropriate. Which of these are well-formed targets? How far is each a SMART-F target? Look for key weaknesses in each.

Target	Specific	Measurable	Achievable	Realistic	Time-bound	Flexible
1 Everyone will like me.						
2 No mistakes in this essay.						
3 Give up smoking.						
4 Accomplish something by 6:00 p.m. tonight.						
5 Write a 250–300-word introduction by 3:00 p.m. today. (Essay to be handed in at 6:00 p.m. in two days' time.)						
6 Write a 1000-word report within the next 24 hours.						
7 Attend more lectures from October onwards.						
8 Increase my marks by 5% for all assignments during this semester.						
9 Find a 3-month work placement in a retail industry before the start of next semester.						
10 Gain a work placement in the BBC by September.						

In your journal, jot down any weaknesses you can identify in these targets. When you have completed your evaluation, check your responses with those on p. 188.

Planning project time

Project schedules

Good time management may require you to use several time-management tools simultaneously:

- Action plans: set targets and deadlines for each step. Action plans are organised according to theme.
- Schedules: organise all tasks and steps in the order they must be completed. For large projects, there is software available to organise the work schedule.
- Diaries: organise tasks more closely within a week or day.

Evaluate how far your own targets are well-formed, SMART-F targets by using the table below. Use one row per target. Consider whether each is specific, measurable, achievable, realistic, clearly time-bound, and flexible. Write 'yes' or 'no' in the boxes as appropriate. The final column provides space for some reflection.

Target (*write below*)	Specific	Measurable	Achievable	Realistic	Time-bound	Flexible	Comments
1							
2							
3							
4							
5							

Example of a work schedule

Item	Jan 1	Jan 2	Jan 3	Jan 4	Jan 5	Jan 6	Jan 7	Jan 8	Jan 9	Jan 10	Jan 11	Jan 12	Jan 13	Jan 14
Group meetings	✗			✗	✗		✗		✗	✗		✗	✗	✗
Elaborate the problem	✗	✗	✗	✗										
Allocate group tasks and roles	✗													
Allocate research tasks		✗		✗	✗				✗	✗				
Finalise strategy				✗										
Research			✗	✗	✗	✗	✗	✗	✗	✗				
Discuss research progress				✗			✗		✗					
Analyse and discuss data									✗	✗	✗			
Allocate writing tasks				✗					✗					
First draft to group											✗			
Responses to first draft												✗		
Etc.														

Work schedule and project diary

The time slots on the project schedule are very broad. Several days are allocated for some aspects of the project. So that every project team member knows what they are doing, the project diary organises time in detail on a daily basis. For your projects, you may find it helpful to map out in diary form more specific aspects of each task, indicating when each task will finish. An example of a project diary entry is given below.

Projects often go wrong because there is no flexibility to the time schedule, or no 'slack' time, built in. Final deadlines are usually strict, leaving little scope for changes at the last minute. It is useful, therefore, to schedule the early stages of a project very closely, in order to increase the incentive to work efficiently. Set interim deadlines so that there are early achievements and so you can check if the project is running to schedule. This will make it easier to meet the final deadlines.

Example of a project diary

Tuesday 2nd January	
9:00–10:00	Jane buys coach tickets.
11:00–12:00	Jane and Miko attend the primary school to discuss project with headteacher.
10:00–12:00	Paul undertakes literature search.
12:00	Jane and Miko catch the coach back to college.
12:00–2:00	Paul and Raphaela look for articles on similar projects.
2:30	Whole team meets to discuss findings.
4:00–6:00	Elaborate the problem and define the area of research.

a Getting down to it!

Do you delay beginning an activity because:

- you get easily distracted into irrelevant activities?
- the time isn't right?
- you need more experience?
- you work better at the last moment?
- tomorrow is better?
- you worry that the outcome won't be right?
- you think something will go wrong?
- everything else is more important?

If so, procrastination prevents you from following through on an action plan.

As the project deadline looms, Michael finds it ever more essential to ensure that his pencils are lined up parallel to the Greenwich Meridian.

Procrastination can be a chronic condition (Sapadin, 1997). If you always struggle to start a task, you may need professional help. However, if the problem is less serious, some of the following steps can help.

Identify the core issue
- Acknowledge that you are procrastinating.
- What sort of things are you better at getting down to?
- What kinds of activity do you keep putting off?
- Identify what characterises the things you put off: are there any themes?
- Do you procrastinate more over some tasks than others? Are some times worse than others?

Check your motivation, vision and targets
- Check your motivation. Give yourself more rewards for each stage you complete.
- Check your 'vision' (see Chapter 1). It may not be motivating you sufficiently. Link tasks more closely to your long-term vision.
- Break goals and targets into small chunks that could be completed in a short burst.

Identify the hindrance zone
- Identify what feelings (boredom, fear, irritation, anger, frustration) you associate with the activity. Can you commit yourself to putting up with the discomfort of these feelings until the task is done? What would help you tolerate these until the task is completed?
- Give yourself more encouraging messages about the task.
- Find a different way of describing the activity so that it becomes more interesting for you.
- Combine the task with something you enjoy, such as listening to music.
- Stay away from anyone who encourages your procrastination.
- Identify the 'level of inhibition' (p. 122).

Commandeer support
- Arrange to do tasks in pairs or a group. It is harder to avoid a task if others are involved.
- Ask a friend to check on you. Give them permission to tell you to get started.
- Join an action set (see p. 142).

Create unavoidable reminders
- Write yourself 20 'Post-its'™ giving yourself instructions to get started on a particular task today. Put these on surfaces where you cannot avoid them.
- Write 20 'Post-its'™ detailing what you will gain by completing the project.
- Write more precise details of what you have to do into your diary.

Becoming a good 'self-starter'

Many job specifications ask for 'good self-starters'. Some people are naturally motivated to launch into a project with minimum assistance. However, the characteristics of a good self-starter can be acquired by most people. Self-starters tend to be:

- highly motivated; they create a clear vision of the task and set themselves specific goals
- able to use strategies for 'getting going'
- open to the possibility of success
- solution-focused: they will search out information that will bring about a solution
- organised: they develop a strategy and they use their time well
- self-confident: they trust they can manage the task reasonably well
- good at finding support and asking for help when they need it
- good at people skills (this is necessary as, when starting a new task, they usually need information and assistance)
- aware of their own limitations: this is essential – a good self-starter will be open about what they do not know and what they cannot do. They either develop the skills themselves or find someone who can help.

Such characteristics are usually acquired in the process of other tasks, such as team working, leading groups, managing smaller projects, and working up to larger projects. However, each time you undertake any assignment, you can practise techniques that are relevant to being a good self-starter.

Sticking with a task

The characteristics of successful people, noted in Chapter 1, included a willingness to 'do what it takes', even if this means working very long hours, and developing patience. Thomas Edison, who is quoted in the activity below, is remembered today for inventions that contributed to the development of film and the light bulb. Edison is also famous for his adage that genius owes only 5 per cent to inspiration and 95 per cent to perspiration!

Completing a task

The following characteristics are usually needed to take tasks through to completion on a consistent basis:

- enthusiasm
- ability to see or conceptualise the 'end product'
- perseverance
- patience
- self-belief: belief that you can do it
- being willing to give the task sufficient time
- being prepared to practise
- being prepared to keep thinking of different solutions
- accepting constructive criticism
- searching out a point of interest
- keeping the goal and benefits in mind
- pride in a job well done.

Reflection: Finishing off

- Which of the above characteristics are your strongest?
- What examples can you give of where you used those characteristics?
- Which do you need to develop further?
- Do you have other qualities that help you to take a task through to completion?
- Think of five things you could do to develop your 'finishing' skills.
- How and when will you apply these to meet your current goals?

If you find it very difficult to develop these characteristics, you may find it helpful to speak to a student counsellor.

Projects

What is a project?

A project is:

> 'A temporary endeavour undertaken to create a unique product or service.'

Project management is:

> 'The application of knowledge, skills, tools and techniques to project activities to meet project requirements.'
>
> (Project Management Institute, 2000)

Characteristics of a project

Projects are characterised by:

- *A goal*   There is a purpose, a desired outcome.
- *A discrete focus*   The activity is 'set apart' in some way. It is not part of the usual course of day-to-day events.
- *Magnitude*   Projects are associated with setting aside time to focus on something special, important or that needs to be completed. It suggests a mustering of effort and resources.
- *Time limits*   Projects must be completed within a set time-frame. It should be clear when a project is complete. As the definition above indicates, a project is a temporary event.
- *Management*   Projects are managed, organised and planned events, leading to an outcome within a time-frame.
- *Individuality*   The nature of a project is that it is a one-off event, leading to something unique.

Scale of the project

The characteristics of a project could apply to activities of any scale. An essay, for example, has:

- *A goal*   To address the essay title; to gain a good grade.
- *Discrete focus*   Each essay is a separate assignment.
- *Magnitude*   Essay writing requires a 'mustering' of time and resources.
- *Time limits*   Deadlines are set for assignments.
- *Management*   Essay writing involves multiple processes of elaborating the question, research, information management, selection, organising ideas, drafting, editing, fine-tuning, proof-reading. These have to be orchestrated to achieve the final goal.
- *Individuality*   Although all students on a programme may be given the same assignment title, each student is expected to provide an individual answer.

Writing essays can develop some of the skills needed for project work.

Student projects

However, essays are usually distinguished from student 'projects'. For example:

- *Goal:* the purpose of a student project is to develop a more in-depth study than would be expected in an essay. The desired outcomes are usually both the results of the project itself and the development of the competences necessary to manage a project.
- *Discrete focus:* projects are usually one-off pieces of work, related to the overall programme but covering ground decided by the student.
- *Magnitude:* projects usually have greater word limits, but the magnitude is in the level of personal responsibility involved.
- *Individuality:* as you have more control over the content and processes, it is typical for student projects to be more individual and varied than student essays.
- *Time limits:* the time allocations for projects tend to be greater than for essays.
- *Management:* projects are usually more complex than essays, requiring more management of the various processes.

Employers' interests in student project skills

Employers are interested in:

- skills and qualities associated with project management
- experience of undertaking projects
- the scale of the largest project that you have taken part in
- the scale of the largest problem you have managed alone.

The scale of projects can be differentiated by such factors as:

- how many people were involved
- the time scale – how long it was planned to last and how long it did last
- who 'commissioned it' – whether it was yourself, a tutor, an employer, an agency
- the size of the budget
- how many beneficiaries there were (who benefited?)
- the significance of the outcomes. What was the impact of the project?

Student projects do not always give opportunities to develop all these skills or to work on a grand scale, but some work placements do. The student union and voluntary work are also good sources for gaining such experience.

Successful project management

The skills identified on p. 164 are applicable to most projects as well as to general task management. The following items also contribute to project success.

Problem-solving

Problem-solving techniques can be applied successfully to projects.

Elaboration

Problem-elaboration is especially important to project work as the wrong strategy wastes time and other resources. Heerkens (2002) warns against 'solution jumping': 'the tendency of people to talk about what to do before analysing the situation adequately, trying to develop a solution before thoroughly understanding a problem'.

Piloting the methods

Have a trial run or 'pilot' to test out your methods and materials on a small scale before embarking on the full-scale project. Identify what needs to be changed. This is easier to do after a pilot rather than when the project is well under way.

'Doing what it takes'

Make a commitment to achieve specific goals. You can decide that you will give 'whatever it takes' to make a relationship work, to get good grades for your course-work, to get to grips with a subject you do not understand, to get a job in a specific field, or to launch a business.

'Doing what it takes' may mean that the majority of your time, energies, thinking and even finances go towards the achievement of the goal. This is not necessarily a healthy approach. However, that might be the difference between fully achieving a goal and accepting a compromise. It is a personal decision how far you want to accept a reasonable compromise.

Because projects work to set deadlines and focus on new areas, they tend to demand more time and thought than is usually anticipated. The project leader, in particular, is likely to spend every waking moment on the project if it falls behind deadlines, or if new solutions are required.

'Doing what it takes' is difficult to apply to more than one goal at a time.

Reflection: Commitment

- How far do you think you are generally someone who is willing to 'do what it takes' to gets something done?
- What kinds of activity are more likely to prompt you to put in the most effort and commitment?
- What conditions encourage you to increase your level of commitment?
- What are your limits?

Clarity

Good problem elaboration and planning should mean that it is clear what needs to be done, by whom, where and when. When the plan is clear, the team can work more effectively. Confusion leads to additional work, puts deadlines at risk, puts the team under stress, and can put up the costs.

Decision making

When projects are under way, you may have to make decisions at speed. This is easier if you have already considered different solutions and planned for contingencies. Keep the main goal in sight and know which compromises are possible. You will also have to weigh up the relative importance of key criteria such as:

- costs
- deadlines
- effects on other people
- the availability of expertise
- aspects of quality
- which changes will be acceptable to the client or commissioning agent (or tutor).

Know the project 'inside out'

To make decisions under pressure, you need to know the project 'inside out'. You need a keen sense of what the 'client' (maybe the tutor in your case) will consider acceptable. Spend time finding out the background to the project. For example, why is it considered important? Are there ethical or political considerations which should be taken into account? What are the most similar projects that have been initiated in the past – and what were the outcomes of these? This information can help you with your own planning and decision making.

Keep the vision in mind

Whilst it is important to keep to deadlines and budgets, it is easy to lose sight of the main purpose of a project. A good leader will keep the team focused on the end-point as well as on interim targets.

The leader is the one who climbs the tallest tree, surveys the entire situation and yells "Wrong jungle!" But how do the busy, efficient producers and managers often respond? "Shut up! We're making progress." (Covey, 2004).

The whole team must be clear about the background to the project and understand the vision of the person who commissioned it (you, your tutor, a client). This makes each team member feel more involved. It also means that each person is better informed to make interim decisions in line with the overall 'vision'. All project decisions should be guided by the overall goal, not by the requirements of short-term targets.

Team work

Most projects in the workplace are team efforts. If the team does not pull together, the project becomes a 'sick' project: people are unhappy and less willing to put in the extra effort needed to bring the project to completion. Successful managers ascribe their achievements to good team work and to trusting their team.

Team work requires the ability both to be a good team member, and to be able to take the lead where relevant. This calls for a range of people skills. Hallows (1997), argues: 'Hard though it may be to admit, the people side of projects is more important than the technical side.' Because of the importance of people skills, a specific chapter has been dedicated to this (Chapter 5).

Performance indicators (PI)

How do you know whether what you are doing is successful? 'Performance indicators' are one way of monitoring and evaluating your performance. They 'indicate' where you are doing well or need to improve. Performance indicators should be 'measurable' so that you can compare performance either over time or against the performance of other people. Some examples are:

- 95 per cent of targets to be achieved by the deadline.
- The project to be completed within 5 per cent of the project budget.
- 75 per cent of the participants to indicate in a feedback questionnaire that they are 'very content' with the outcome.
- A mark of 60 per cent or more to be achieved for every assignment.
- Attendance levels to achieve at least 95 per cent.
- Punctuality to be at least 95 per cent.

Meeting the criteria

Performance indicators should be closely linked to the criteria for success identified earlier in the project (see p. 172). They are unlikely to be exactly the same because some criteria may not be measurable. You may meet the criteria of a project without feeling that you performed well in all respects. Your individual or team performance may be different from the criteria for individual projects.

Activity   **Meeting the criteria**

When you have completed a current project, return to the criteria you set near the beginning of the project (see p. 172). Consider:

- Did you meet the essential criteria (the 'bottom line') that you set?
- Were these criteria realistic?
- What criteria do you think could have been better, if any?

Work with performance indicators

Performance indicators you could use for study or project work include:

- how often you meet deadlines for assignments
- the number and percentage of the times that you complete a particular action successfully
- how long it takes to perform a specific activity
- how often you reach your targets
- feedback received from others
- how many of the milestones you set for yourself were achieved
- how much it cost compared to budget
- percentage improvement over previous performance
- grades and marks.

Soft criteria

Some project criteria cannot easily include a number or 'measurable' component. For example, it is hard to quantify:

- creativity
- innovation
- ethical approaches
- sensitivity
- flexibility
- emotional intelligence
- how well you manage a difficult situation
- responsiveness
- assertiveness.

Soft criteria require you to develop skills in being an objective evaluator of your own performance. You have to develop a 'feel' for whether something is going well or not. Wherever possible, this should still be evaluated against specific criteria and performance indicators to get a rounded picture of how you are doing. Compare your personal evaluations with feedback from others.

Benchmarks

A benchmark is a point of comparison. For example, a sportsperson might benchmark their speed or accuracy against the records of people at the top of their own sport. A programme on TV might benchmark itself against audience ratings for other programmes. Organisations and projects use benchmarks to measure their performance against other companies or projects.

Good benchmarks compare like with like. For example, if your project involves writing an information leaflet for the public, the benchmarks would need to relate to another project that aimed at producing a similar number of leaflets in a similar time-scale on a similar kind of issue. The performance indicators for such a project might include some of the following:

- how much it costs to produce each leaflet
- how many readers, when asked, rated the leaflet as useful
- the percentage of readers who, when asked, rated the leaflet as useful
- an independent mark (by an independent assessor or tutor)
- a measure of how far the leaflet changed opinion or behaviour.

A good benchmark enables you to evaluate your own outcomes against those of a comparable project or set of benchmarks.

For example, you may find that you wanted to achieve a 90 per cent return for a questionnaire and yet received only 35 per cent. This might feel like failure as it is far short of the target. If you compare this with similar questionnaires in comparable circumstances, you may find that a typical (or benchmark) response is only 20 per cent. This would mean that your target was unrealistic but your performance for the questionnaire was good.

- For an activity that you are involved in currently, what would be a useful benchmark? (Consider existing statistics and written records of performance.)
- How could you use this benchmark as a way of setting your own targets for improving your performance?

The drawback with benchmarks is that if all similar projects are mediocre, the benchmark will be low. You may need to set targets that ensure you exceed the benchmark in order for your project to be successful.

Competitiveness

Competitiveness is a concept used to promote and evaluate good practice in business and industry. A high percentage of business projects fail very early on. Employers are being encouraged to think about their businesses or spheres of work in terms of 'competitiveness'. Depending on the business, this will include such factors as:

- skills and experience of staff
- use of performance indicators
- using feedback from other people
- improvements in quality and efficiency
- awareness of developments in the field
- thinking and planning ahead of the competition.

As people are the most important resource of any project, the quality of the personnel is a key factor in the competitiveness and success of a business or project. When you apply for work, employers may be considering how you could contribute to the overall competitiveness of their business or project.

The activity on p. 189 is a personal 'competitiveness audit'. It will give you a score out of a hundred – or your 'percentage competitiveness'. This is only a rough estimate. However, it gives you an indication of how you may be viewed in competition with other people. If you score well, you can be more confident about what you have to offer in job interviews. If your score isn't high, you have an indicator of where you can focus your energies next in order to develop your skills and extend your experience.

- Target 1: This is too vague, has no time limits and is unlikely to be achievable or measurable. It isn't realistic.
- Target 2: This is unlikely to be achievable or measurable as it is hard to define a 'mistake' with respect to an essay. Very few essays are perfect. This is not a realistic target.
- Target 3: This may be realistic and achievable for the person. Success could be measured. No time-scales are set so the target isn't SMART.
- Target 4: This has a clear time-scale and is likely to be achievable and realistic. However, it is so vague that it is meaningless.
- Target 5: This is specific, measurable, and time-bound. It is likely to be realistic and achievable, and if not, there is sufficient time before the hand-in date to adjust the deadline.
- Target 6: This is specific, measurable and time-bound. You would need to know more about

the circumstances to see if the target was achievable, realistic and sufficiently flexible.
- Target 7: 'More' is too vague. 'From October' sets an initial time-scale but does not indicate how long this will continue.
- Target 8: This is specific and measurable. A 5 per cent improvement is likely to be achievable and reasonable, unless the mark was already very high. Setting a target for *all* assignments is challenging: it has little flexibility. This target would need to be accompanied by other targets which specify more clearly how the improved mark will be achieved.
- Target 9: This is likely to be a SMART-F target.
- Target 10: This is too precise and allows for little flexibility in choice of work placement. It is not likely to be realistic or achievable.

Competitiveness Audit

Rate each statement according to how typical it is of you.

Rating: *Very typical = 4   Typical = 3   Quite typical = 2   Hardly ever the case = 1
Never true/Don't know = 0*

		Score
1	I am aware of my skills, personal qualities and expertise	
2	I know how to apply these strengths to new situations	
3	I take active steps to learn new skills and expertise	
4	I ask for help when I need it	
5	I have a clear vision of what I want to achieve	
6	I set myself challenging targets	
7	I am keen to receive feedback on my performance	
8	I pay attention to feedback I receive and use it to improve my performance	
9	I am usually keen to better my past performance	
10	I take steps to discover and meet my personal development needs	
11	I know how to measure my performance	
12	I can set clear priorities	
13	I am good at planning ahead	
14	I pay attention to small details	
15	I can see quick ways of doing things, without impairing quality	
16	I can get going on a new task without much direction	
17	I can make decisions quickly about what needs to be done	
18	I am good at managing money and keeping to budget	
19	I am good at meeting deadlines	
20	I can co-ordinate my work with that of other people	
21	I can manage responsibility	
22	I can take direction from other people	
23	I am good at finding solutions to problems	
24	I can adapt and be flexible according to what is needed	
25	I am prepared to 'do what it takes' to get a job done	

Your 'competitiveness' score   Total out of 100_____

Closing comments

Problem-solving is essentially a way of getting things done, and therefore can be applied to a very wide range of circumstances. If you develop the skills associated with problem-solving, you will have a good starting place for taking on any task.

This chapter has looked at the skills and processes that contribute to successful problem-solving and task management. It addresses some of the generic skills that contribute to the success of any kind of 'project' such as writing an assignment, conducting a student project, undertaking projects at work, or taking on an undertaking in your personal life. This includes such processes as defining the task, elaborating the problem, setting priorities, developing an appropriate strategy, setting SMART-F targets, developing an action plan, monitoring performance against targets and indicators, and taking a task to completion. These processes are key to almost any project in any environment.

Problem-solving and task management tend to push us beyond our previous limits. At university, for example, assignments become increasingly more challenging as we move from one year or level to the next. At work, the problems and projects facing graduates will tend to contain new aspects that colleagues will not have covered before.

A good problem-solving strategy, along with developed people skills, will enable you to take on such new tasks with greater confidence.

Further reading

Davidson, J. (2000) *The Ten-Minute Guide to Project Management* (Indianapolis: Alpha Books). (A basic introduction to project management.)

Heerkens, G. R. (2002) *Project Management* (New York: McGraw-Hill). (A readable introduction that also covers the 'softer' aspects of project management, such as personal qualities.)

Mingus, N. (2002) *Alpha Teach Yourself Project Management in 24 Hours* (Indianapolis: Alpha Books). (An advanced text.)

Part 3
Extend your thinking

Academic study generally develops your thinking skills, especially if you bring an attitude of intellectual curiosity and active engagement with the debates in your subject.

Reading widely, making judgements about material to use in assignments, discussing academic questions, completing mathematical formulae, tackling lab-based research, and formulating ideas in writing – all help to develop your thinking skills. Such academic tasks stretch the mind so that you develop the mental capacity to take on complex and difficult tasks in a range of contexts. Typically, courses of higher education require, and develop, such skills as critical analysis and reflection, creativity and problem-solving, which can be applied fruitfully to most academic and work-related tasks.

However, skills do not necessarily transfer automatically from academic study to broader contexts. It takes further thought to identify how to transfer and apply skills, including 'thinking skills', effectively to new kinds of task.

This section looks at two aspects of such thinking, both of which can strengthen academic and professional abilities: creative and reflective thinking.

Chapter 7, 'Thinking outside the box', looks in general terms at how you can maximise your brain capacity. It helps you to reflect upon how you think, and provides tools to help you to develop creativity, synthesis, and adventurous thinking. As creativity can sound challenging to those who don't automatically think of themselves as 'creative', the chapter also looks at the risk-taking and self-management that creativity entails.

Thinking reflectively in structured and systematic ways about your performance is now typical of many academic and professional areas. Chapter 8 looks at what is meant by the 'reflective practitioner'. Reflective thinking sounds simple, but students tend to struggle to do well at this aspect of their course. It is all too easy to fall into superficial, descriptive, or blaming approaches rather than bringing the high levels of analysis, evaluation, critique, synthesis, personal responsibility, and metacognition that are expected.

Building on the thinking skills developed in Chapter 7, Chapter 8 outlines diverse approaches to reflection in order to help you to understand what is required, to develop your skills in reflection and to find an approach that works for you.

You don't need to be an expert in each method and mode presented. Rather, experiment with different approaches until you:

- find the combination that best helps you to generate, organise, synthesise and fine tune your thoughts in ways relevant to your circumstances, and
- can apply creative and reflective thinking flexibly to benefit your academic and professional work.

Chapters in this section
7 Thinking outside of the box
8 The art of reflection

Chapter 7
Thinking outside the box

Learning outcomes

This chapter offers opportunities to:

- understand how your brain works so you can use it more effectively
- develop your natural ability to learn new things
- develop confidence in your creativity
- use strategies to generate ideas
- use creative approaches to thinking.

Introduction

Born to learn

Learning is a natural process. Our brains are set up to learn – they consist of approximately a hundred billion neurons, which are linked in elaborate networks. These neural networks enable us to:

- transmit information from one part of the brain to another
- form associations between new information and what we already know
- make sense of what we experience
- encode information for memory.

We can envisage our brains as billions of trees laid out in all directions, and whose roots and branches are all in contact. For any one activity, several billion contacts may be made between those branches and roots – and this happens in milliseconds. A thought is like a bolt of lightning illuminating a vast forest of connections.

Our brains are also very flexible. They allow us to learn in innumerable ways, through:

- listening
- imitation
- taking small steps
- practice
- watching others
- day-dreaming
- taking an inspired leap
- linking different problems

and so on.

Learning can be easy. The most complex things our brains will ever have to learn were accomplished when we did not even know what 'learning' was, before the age of five. This chapter will look at how you can make best use of your brain's amazing capacities. The earlier part of the chapter looks at some characteristics of your brain, so that you can use its natural tendencies to best effect.

Inspiration is most difficult when we think in rigid, logical ways. This chapter looks at ways of stimulating the idea-generating capacities of the brain – which may mean thinking and acting in ways that are not typical of your usual study or work habits. To begin, do the activity below.

Activity **The 'box'**

In your reflective journal, jot down your response to the following question:

- What is the use of a shoebox?

We will return to this later in the chapter.

Limiting intelligence

Are cleverness and creativity the same thing? If you did well at school, does that mean you are automatically a creative thinker? De Bono (2006) argues that clever people are often hampered by their apparent intelligence in two keys ways:

1   They are very good at arguing and are usually better at defending their position. As they are more likely to win the argument, they are more likely to think they have the best solution. You may know people like this. If you think you are 'right', there is no reason to listen to other people or to look for a better solution.

> *As a result, many highly intelligent minds are trapped in poor ideas because they can defend them so well.*

(De Bono, 2006)

2   It is easier, quicker, and more dramatic to prove somebody else wrong than to devise constructive solutions. Negative criticism adds to your visible 'superiority'. Being constructive can take longer and can make other people look good rather than yourself. However, negative criticism doesn't promote creative thinking.

Our views of what is 'intelligent' can prevent us from developing our minds to their full potential. If we hold negative thoughts about our own intelligence, for example, those thoughts can also limit our ability to perform well (Cottrell, 2013). People who feel they are 'not very bright' or 'not very creative' probably will fulfil that estimation of themselves. On the other hand, positive thinking and constructive mental activity develop the mind.

Creativity is like a muscle: it gets stronger the more you exercise it.

Reflection: Limiting creativity

Note in your reflective journal:

- any ways that you currently put limits on your capacity to think
- any ways you prevent yourself from achieving your full potential as a creative, imaginative person.

Make two copies of this table. Complete one now and one when you have completed the chapter or later in your programme. Rate each statement as follows:

Rating: *Very often = 4*   *Often = 3*   *Sometimes/it depends = 2*   *Hardly ever = 1*   *Never/don't know = 0*

		Score
1	I experiment with many ideas before I make a decision	
2	When I am working on a project, I discuss 'work in progress' with others	
3	I like to find out a lot about things I do not understand	
4	I have a wide range of interests	
5	I enjoy talking to a wide range of people	
6	I take a different route home at least once a week	
7	I set myself new challenges, regularly, so I feel 'stretched'	
8	I like the challenge of difficult problems	
9	I actively look for patterns and trends	
10	I actively look for similarities between things	
11	I actively look for connections between things	
12	I enjoy looking for the reasons that underlie patterns and trends	
13	I like to think up new ways of doing things	
14	I try to break my routine	
15	I actively look for new sources of inspiration	
16	I try things out even if I am no good at them	
17	If I get something wrong, I look to see what I could have done better	
18	I like to imagine different ways of doing things	
19	I take calculated risks	
20	Even if I am good at something, I look for better ways of doing it	
21	I have strategies for generating ideas when I need to	
22	I look for solutions even when it looks as if something is impossible	
23	I look for more than one perspective on an issue	
24	I like to play about with different ideas	
25	I spend time thinking about how I think	

Add up your score   Total _____

Interpreting your creative thinking score

You now have an approximate score for creative thinking. This is not an exact science, but it gives you an idea of how confident you are about your own creativity. It also gives you an insight into how you could develop your creative thinking skills further.

75–100 This is an excellent score. If your ratings were accurate, you already use the kinds of strategies that contribute to creative thinking. This suggests an invaluable approach to problem-solving and to life in general. Consider how you could develop these further, especially in relation to your programme and to the career areas that interest you. It is also worth checking whether your logical, analytical skills are as well developed as your creative thinking skills. It is important to develop both kinds of thinking.

50–74 This is a good score. If your ratings were accurate, this suggests your creative thinking skills are already well developed. Look for themes in the statements to which you gave lower ratings. What else could you do to develop your thinking skills? This chapter may give you some ideas.

25–49 If your ratings were accurate, this suggests that you have started to develop creative thinking skills. There is probably a lot more you could do to build these further.

It is worth spending time considering what prevents you from developing your creativity at present. It is important not to try too hard at creative thinking: it may be that you worry too much about doing things the right way. Experiment with a more relaxed approach and make sure you leave plenty of time to try out new approaches as well as your usual methods. It can take time to build confidence in new approaches.

0–24 If your ratings were accurate, this suggests that you have identified that creative thinking skills are not currently a major area of strength for you. Check with people who know you well whether you have rated yourself too harshly. Identify what kinds of thinking skills are most critical for meeting the requirements of your programme and career interests. Read through the comments for the score 25–49 above. These may also apply to you. Most importantly, do not be discouraged. This is not a scientific test – and creative thinking skills can be developed.

A dozen really useful things to know about your brain

- The brain loves complexity and change
- the more you learn, the easier it is to learn
- it uses short cuts
- it loves organisation and patterns
- it is naturally playful
- it works when you are not looking
- you can send it on errands
- it likes to be fed
- you can take it for a walk
- it won't work well when it is upset or does not feel safe
- it works well when it is excited
- it likes to be refreshed.

The brain likes complexity and change

The mind loves complexity. Even babies get bored with simple patterns; they look at complex images for much longer. Choirs prefer more difficult tunes: these are harder to learn but retain their interest when rehearsed and delivered many times. Throughout history, people have been fascinated by riddles, puzzles, codes, mazes and labyrinths. In many ages, art has been heavily allegorical or symbolic, so that an apparently simple picture could be decoded or interpreted, item by item, to read out a hidden message.

Reflection: Complexity

- What kinds of complex, skilled, multi-layered or multi-sequenced activities do you enjoy?
- What kinds of complicated tasks do you avoid?
- What makes you seek out and enjoy one kind of complexity and avoid others?

Our brain can cope with very complex problems. It sets up connections between our new experiences and what we already know. It develops increasingly elaborate networks as we become more expert in an area. However, it can't do this all at once.

> What we are *able* to learn is partly the result of what we have *already* learnt.

The more you learn, the easier the next thing is to learn

When we encounter new situations, we draw upon and develop our existing knowledge. We then organise this into internal models called 'schema'.

If we have been on one picnic, for example, we do not know how typical that is of any other picnic. When we have been on ten picnics, we have an elaborated idea of a picnic. We know the variations that are possible, we can anticipate what to expect at future picnics, plan for such occasions, and develop criteria to evaluate whether they are 'good' or 'bad' picnics depending on our experience. At this stage, we have a well-developed schema.

As we go through the day, this process is going on all the time. According to Piaget (1952), our experiences reinforce or alter what we already know.

If we expose the brain to varied and complex problems at a reasonable pace, it will usually develop the neural networks we need. It isn't how

many neurons or brain cells we have that makes us capable of tasks, but the number of connections between them. We develop these connections through engagement with the environment, with activity, with stimulation.

If we try to be experts when we are still novices at a task, the brain may not have developed the right connections to solve the problems we encounter. It can leave us feeling that we are incapable of the task. This can seem like failure and encourage us to give up when we may simply need more practice. The longer we perform or practice an activity, the more we build up the mental connections that we need to do it well. There really is sense in the old saying, 'If at first you don't succeed, try, try, try again.'

We often find that the things we found hardest to do, and had to practise the most, are those for which we develop the best overall and long-term understanding.

Reflection: Stimulating your brain

- What kinds of new challenges do you give your brain to keep it 'stretched' and stimulated?
- For what kinds of activity do you tend to stick with the task, increasing your chances of succeeding in the long run?
- What kinds of activities do you 'give up on' early?

The brain uses short cuts

The brain likes short cuts. Professional magicians know this and trick the eye by encouraging such 'short cuts'.

If the brain thinks it knows what it is seeing, it stops looking for explanations. It matches what it thinks it is experiencing with the 'schema' or mental models it has already built up. If it finds a good enough match, it uses the stored information to make sense of the new experience. If not, it uses the new experience to adapt the mental models.

The brain likes organisation and patterns

The brain organises information in many different ways. A colour, a scent or a few bars of music can evoke very detailed memories. Similarly, we can generate information quickly on the basis of the first letter of a word, the end of the word, words that mean the same thing, or any number of other similarities or differences. It is easier to remember information if we:

● organise it into groups, clusters or categories
● organise it into hierarchies
● make links between pieces of information.

If we find links between one kind of activity and another, we are better able to perform the second activity. Looking for patterns or similarities enables us to transfer 'expertise' from one area to solve new problems (see Chapter 2).

Expert chess players

Experts are experts because of the power of the brain in recognising patterns. Expert chess players can recall how all the pieces were arranged on a chessboard even if given only five seconds to view it. This is not because they have superior memories. Expert chess players see the whole configuration as one meaningful whole. They see it as one 'chunk'. They can only do this if they recognise the pattern as one that they have seen and used before. In effect, they are remembering only one pattern, which is easy.

Novice players have to remember the positions of up to 32 items – but the short-term memory struggles with more than 5–7 items. Novices have to work harder in order to remember more items – and are less likely to get the answer right. However, expert chess players are no better at remembering the layout of the pieces than anyone else if they haven't seen the pattern before (Chase and Simon, 1973). The effect of spending time practising, seeing and learning significant patterns over and over again, is very evident here.

Significant patterns

Although the brain can get used to any pattern, it works more effectively if the pattern you look for has an underlying meaning. The brain likes significance and meaning. For example, it is easier to remember a set of names if they all belong to

Most of the time the brain's short cuts are useful. We often refer to these as 'generalisations'. Generalisations help us to make sense of what is going on from one moment to the next, without having to start from scratch each time. We are able to tell what are 'typical' experiences, what are variations and what is new. If we can see a connection between something we are good at and the problem in hand, then we may offer the brain a short cut to solving the problem (see Chapter 2).

We can also feed messages to the brain that encourage it to take short cuts. 'I have tried and cannot do this' is one such message. Alternatively, we could choose to feed it encouraging messages such as: 'There is a way to solve this', or 'Let's look at this again' or 'This is interesting', and the brain will respond differently.

Reflection: Spotting the short cuts

● Which short cuts does your brain take? In other words what kinds of things are you less likely to notice that other people seem better at spotting?
● Which messages do you give your brain that may encourage it to think it can't do things?
● How could you change those messages?

members of your family. Similarly, if expert technicians are asked to reconstruct a circuit board, they will do so on the basis of what each part does – its function or significance to the working of the board. Novices will try to assemble the board according to how it looks (Egan and Schwartz, 1979). This approach is superficial and recall is less effective. You can test this for yourself with the activity below.

Activity **Memory for patterns (1)**

- Write down the start time.
- Time how long it takes you to learn the following sequence, in order. You can learn this in any way you like, as long as you end up being able to recite it or write it without looking.

O h n s t d o w t e u   o r h

- Put the sequence and all copies where you cannot see them. Now write it down.
- Check for accuracy.
- If you have not got it right, keep going until you do. Then write down the time again.
- Write down how long it took you, altogether, to learn the sequence perfectly.
- When you have finished, time yourself learning the second sequence, found on p. 203.

You probably found it took less time to remember the second sequence, even though you may never have seen this written down before. This is because you are familiar with the chunks of meaning (the words) and a single bigger chunk (the meaning of the sentence). The knowledge of experts for any task is divided into meaningful chunks, similar to words and sentences.

As you become more expert in any subject, you will start to construct the 'meaningful chunks' of the subject, so that you can 'read it off' as quickly as you did the second sequence in the activity on p. 203.

Activity **Subject chunks**

Sometimes working from two or three books, seeing how the material is arranged in each, can help to develop a sense of how the information can be organised into different sets of meaningful chunks. You may find some texts organise information in ways that are easier for you to understand.

- Look at three different books for a topic you find difficult.
- Write down the headings and sub-headings used by each.
- Browse the material written under each.
- Which book organises the information in the way that suits you best?

If you work with material in this way, you may also find that seeing the same information from several different angles helps to build up your overall picture of the subject.

The brain is naturally playful

The brain makes odd, unusual and unexpected connections. This enables us to make jokes and puns, to invent, to find solutions. Children use play as their main tool for learning. They act out adult roles. They play with the world around them, and experiment in order to find out more about it. As adults, we may be self-conscious about using 'play' to develop our thinking. When we allow it to be playful, the brain can provide the answers we need.

However, the brain often presents information to us in unexpected ways. It may disguise the answers in riddles or give us clues to decipher. It encourages us to 'play' with information.

Our brain may spot a dinner fork on the table, make a connection with garden tools, and send us a signal about gardens. In the past, we may have associated gardening with hard work, and the brain has spotted the fork as a reminder to us to work on an essay. Sometimes we can catch hold of this odd train of connections, which is meaningful only to the person concerned. More often, the links are hidden. When the brain plays with us in this way, we can, if we play with the 'clues' it sends us, find the solutions to problems that are teasing us.

The brain works when you are not looking

The brain is working on our behalf all of the time. Most of what we do and learn, we do without even realising it. The brain does not respond well to being forced. For example, if a word or idea is 'on the tip of your tongue' you can try for hours to remember but without success. However, a few hours later, when you are focusing on something else, the answer will seem to 'pop into your head' from nowhere.

You can use the brain to work for you by focusing on a problem, analysing it as far as you can, generating as many solutions as possible – and then leaving it for a while. When you stop analysing and labouring over the problem, allowing the mind to relax, the brain will continue to work on the problem for you.

Indeed, if you change environment, and return to a problem, your brain may have drawn your attention to clues from your surroundings without you being aware of it. Experiments with children show that they used the shape of the light bulbs, clouds, even shadows on the ceiling or cracks in the wall to resolve problems they had been discussing before taking a rest break.

You can make use of this capacity of the brain if you:

● spend time elaborating the problem so the brain is absolutely clear what you are looking for; 'day-dreaming' alone is not enough

● give the brain some space to work on the problem

● enter a relaxed state of mind for a while

● return to the problem after a break.

You can send the brain on errands

As the brain will work on a problem when you are not consciously thinking about it, you can give it directions about what you want it to do. You need to be precise about what you want, and be prepared to wait. For example, if you know where the Buddha was born but can't remember and want to know, the brain will often deliver the answer a few minutes or hours later. Sometimes, it sends the message in code: you may find yourself thinking about an Indian film or Indian music or food, even though the only link with the Buddha is India. Be aware of this so you are ready to spot the clues.

Sleep on it
Work on a problem before you sleep. Identify the core questions as far as you can. List the things that are puzzling you. Write these as questions. Focus on one or two questions that are really key.

Whilst you sleep, your brain may continue to work on the problem. It may not. However, you increase the chances of your relaxed, unconscious mind working on the problem whilst you sleep. Keep paper and a pen by the bed as you may wake up with lots of ideas.

The brain likes to be fed and watered

Greenfield (2001) describes the brain as the greediest organ in the body. Although it is less than 2.5 per cent of our body weight, when the body is at rest the brain uses up 20 per cent of the body's fuel input. It consumes oxygen from the air we breathe and glucose from the carbohydrates we eat, burning these off at ten times the rate of any other body tissue. A good diet assists the brain. Over time, starving the body of carbohydrates will reduce the fuel that the brain needs in order to function.

Our bodies are mostly water. Water conducts electricity – and the messages our brain sends and co-ordinates are ultimately electrical impulses. These are affected by dehydration. When we are dehydrated, we reduce the efficiency of our brain as well as the general functioning of the body. Drinking water increases brain efficiency; other drinks do not have the same effect. We need about eight glasses of clear water a day, taken in gradually over the day.

The brain uses energy to process food and drink. After a large meal, you can become drowsy as the brain diverts its resources to deal with digestion. A big meal or drink is best avoided just before an exam or interview.

'The brain is fundamentally a chemical system' (Greenfield, 2001). The chemicals ultimately come from what we feed the body. Nicotine, for example, puts the body into survival mode, raising heart rate and blood pressure, whereas creative thinking is associated with more relaxed states.

Various oils have also been associated with the way the brain functions (Stordy, 2000). For most people, a varied diet provides the small amounts of a very wide range of chemicals that the body needs.

Reflection: Nourishing your brain

- How well do you feed and water your brain?
- How much water do you drink each day?
- Does your diet help or hinder your brain? If you are unsure, speak to somebody at your student health centre.

You can take your brain for a walk

Our brains first developed to manage movement and to respond to the environment whilst moving. The brain is stimulated by movement. It has been shown that mice learn better after a period of brisk exercise, as the supply of endorphins and other chemicals to the brain is increased.

In humans, a very large part of the motor cortex in the brain is devoted to the fine motor movements of the fingers and mouth (for using tools, writing, playing an instrument, speaking). If you want to stimulate your thinking, take a walk, play an instrument, draw, *do* something.

Activity Exercising the problem

When working on a problem, take a brisk walk for about 20 minutes before returning to study. What is the effect? Do you come up with any ideas about your study whilst walking?

If you are required to sit and listen, find ways of increasing your personal engagement. For example, in long presentations or lectures, it is natural for the mind to wander after a few minutes. You can manage this process by:

- deliberately diverting yourself from listening for a few seconds at regular intervals. You can time this to coincide with when the speaker pauses or changes a slide. Otherwise, the brain will automatically 'switch off' but at less well timed occasions, and without you noticing.
- Listening actively, in a questioning way, jotting down your questions and opinions.

- Making notes: this can be an act of 'translation' of ideas from someone else's speech into your own words and ideas. Your listening is more active if you are choosing what to note, considering how to summarise, turning the talk into a diagram, and looking at how different aspects link up.

The brain won't work well when it is upset

When we are anxious, our body releases chemicals, such as adrenalin, which put us on the alert for danger. It is a very ancient bodily response, to help us survive. Our eyes look for movement at the periphery of our vision, so that we can detect danger, and we become more alert to noise, ready to react. We are easily distracted by our environment. Resources are diverted to large muscles in the arms and legs so that we can fight or run.

If we are anxious about an essay or exam, we can have the same adrenalin and survival response. As the body is then ready for large movements, we confuse it if we simply sit still. When we read or write or use the computer, we focus our attention on a small central space whilst our eyes want to look around for danger. We give mixed messages to the brain.

When we are stressed, the brain is not interested in 'thinking' tasks: it wants us to move, to escape, to survive. The more distressed we become at not understanding something, the more the brain diverts energy away from the thinking brain to the survival brain. Some strenuous activity, such as exercise, a brisk walk, housework – anything which uses the arms and legs – uses up the excess adrenalin, leaving us more relaxed and able to concentrate.

Strategies for managing stress and thinking positively can 'trick' the survival brain into believing that everything is OK, even if we do not fully feel or believe that at first. This allows us to use the parts of the brain needed to work out a complex solution. If we get too stressed, it becomes necessary to get help from somebody who isn't – and who can think more clearly.

The brain works well when it is excited and engaged

The brain likes to be stimulated and engaged. When tasks are not challenging enough, the brain finds it hard to stay focused. If tasks are too difficult for its current level of experience, the brain may become stressed. To work well, the brain needs to find a task that is stimulating but not a threat at its current level of competence.

If you look for the interest in a task, you are more likely to find it manageable than if you dismiss the task as too difficult. When we are excited or frightened, similar sets of chemicals are released in the body. We can direct the brain on how to interpret those chemicals. If we approach complex thinking problems as 'difficult', we may feel ourselves 'freeze up'. On the other hand, if we choose to look for the interest and excitement in them, we are less likely to 'go blank' and more likely to use the expertise we already have.

The brain likes to be refreshed

Although the brain enjoys being stimulated, the mind can become too busy. It becomes cluttered with thought and benefits from being 'stilled' occasionally. This is one of the most difficult things to achieve. One way of practising this is outlined on page 203.

Activity 🔄 'Mindfulness: Being in the present moment

Read through the whole activity first. After that, all you have to do is be in the present moment whilst watching your breath.

- Sit so you are upright but comfortable. You may find the activity easier if you close your eyes.

- Watch the way that your breath enters and leaves your body. Notice whether it is cool or warm. Notice whether your breaths are long or short, easy or laboured. Avoid changing the way you are breathing – just notice the detail. The exception is if your breathing is noisy: breathe as quietly as possible.

- Your mind will wander. This is natural. Avoid forcing it. Just notice when it wanders and gently return your attention to your breath.

- As ideas enter your head, tell yourself to 'let go' of them. If you notice that you are getting uncomfortable, shift very slightly and slowly, and then focus on your breath again.

- You may find that really interesting ideas and thoughts enter your head, or that you have become lost in a dialogue about an event that happened that day, or that you remember how angry you are with someone. The brain finds it difficult to let you remain quiet with just

yourself in the present moment. Don't explore interesting ideas or try to remember them just now. Let them vaporise or fly away.

- You may think that your brain is too smart, clever, fast-moving, idea-filled, and imaginative for you to benefit from this exercise. The exact opposite is true.

- This task is almost impossible for most people. However, noting which justifications you find for not doing it tells you a great deal about yourself, if you can work it out. Simply acknowledge the frustration or other emotions, and again, just let go of them.

- Smiling relaxes the face muscles, making this activity easier. If you feel agitated, remind yourself that you have created the luxury of doing nothing but breathing and being with your own mind in the present moment.

- Each time you 'let go', you clear and energise your mind. You give it a break. You allow it to stop worrying and give it an opportunity to relax and do nothing.

At first you may not notice any difference. However, doing this for 20 minutes several times a week develops better mental and emotional awareness. Sometimes, the activity will leave you feeling clear-headed, relaxed and calm.

Activity 🔄 **Memory for patterns (2)**

This activity is the second part of the activity on p. 199. Time how long it takes you to memorise the following set of letters, so that you are able to reproduce them without looking.

S h u t   t h e   d o o r   n o w

Compare this result with the time it took you to do the original exercise above. Then return to that page.

Reflection: Creative potential

- What do you think creativity is?
- Where did you gain that understanding of what creativity is?
- How many marks out of ten would you give yourself for your current level of creativity?
- What marks out of ten do you think you are capable of achieving? On what do you base that estimation?

a Creativity

Most people equate creativity with a particular kind of person. You may have associated creativity with being an artist, designer, performer or inventor.

Most of us underestimate our capacity for creativity. We may compare ourselves with great artists, for example, ignoring all the occasions when we have used our minds and resources creatively to deal with the situation we are in. We all have our own spheres where our natural creativity shines. This might be, for example:

- knowing the right things to say
- seeing the funny side when things go wrong
- finding ways of avoiding work and inventing unusual but convincing excuses
- co-ordinating the activities of several children so that they are all entertained, occupied and safe
- making patients feel at ease before an operation
- cooking a special meal on a budget
- soothing the waters when people are arguing
- finding the perfect present for other people.

Reflection: Personal creativity

- If you think of creativity in the ways suggested in the list above, what kinds of creativity do you show in your life? For example, what things do you do that seem easier for you than for some other people that you know? Do you have your 'own ways of doing things' for certain tasks?
- In which areas of your life would you like to be more creative?
- Do you feel comfortable with the idea of yourself as a potentially creative person?

Creative problem-solving

Previous chapters looked at problem-solving when managing tasks, yourself and other people. The magic element in all these situations is coming up with something new when it is needed – the 'creative spark'. This is often the hardest part of problem-solving. It is easy to sit waiting for inspiration, expecting an answer to fall from the sky. This chapter looks at strategies you can employ to oil the brain and assist it in generating ideas when needed.

The 'many quickly' approach

If you have one solution, look for five, ten, twenty more

Those who feel they know the answer to a question rarely look for a better one. Also, looking for one solution can take longer than ten possible solutions. We can be so concerned about finding the one 'right' answer that we block our thinking. If we look for ten solutions, our thinking can be more relaxed: we will not use nine of the ideas so it is safer to have some bad ones. Even if we then only find six ideas, we still have lots to work from. The chances of finding the best idea first time round are quite remote. The more alternatives we consider, the more likelihood of finding the best solution.

Phrase brain-stimulating questions

In the activity on p. 194, you were asked to consider the use of a shoebox. This usually prompts one response, as the wording of the question suggests there is only one use. However, if asked, 'How many uses can you think of?' people usually generate many more responses. The way we phrase the question influences the way we approach a problem.

Reflection: Multiple solutions

Jot down your responses to the following:

- How many uses for a shoebox can you think of in three minutes?
- For one problem that faces you on a regular basis, how many possible approaches to solving this can you generate in five minutes?

You probably found many more uses for a shoebox this time round. Answers people give include: carrying shoes; storage; for making a doll's house or garage; a door stop; carrying things; hiding things; a sandwich box; stepping on when the floor is wet; cardboard; rattling things as a musical instrument; protection from the rain; holding CDs; a small bench or seat; for babies to tear up; holding pencils; a treasure box for children; to decorate as a gift box; sending something in the post; papier mâché; food for goats, etc.

Reflection: Multiple solutions

- How typical is it for you to push yourself to keep looking for more answers?
- For which activities would it be most useful for you to adopt this kind of approach?

Just a minute

It may seem paradoxical, but it is often more productive to give yourself a short time limit to generate ideas. The brain can leap into action better if it knows it has a time limit. This does not usually work well if you leave things to the last minute, as you need to be relaxed. Approach the task in a 'playful' way.

Try it. Give yourself just *one* minute to jot down everything you can think of to solve a problem you are working on. If you do not generate any useful ideas in that time, you have lost only a minute.

Play with time

If an activity is likely to take three hours, leave at least four hours to complete it, but aim to complete it in two. If you plan to allow more time than you need, you reduce the need to 'get it right' first time. Less stress can mean more creative thinking. You will also have more time to fine-tune your answer and deal with emergencies. The time challenge creates just enough excitement to generate adrenalin to help with the task and reduce 'sluggishness'. If you have too much time, it is easy to start too slowly or work at a slower pace. Set off at a good pace, aiming to finish at an earlier target time rather than your absolute deadline.

'What if questions ...'

'What if ...', Why not?' or 'Supposing ... ?' questions stimulate the imagination. The wording suggests an imaginary state that is safe to explore (it isn't real so it can't do any damage) but which might provide real answers. If you reach a point where your ideas feel stuck, use 'what if ...' questions. For example:

- 'What if ... we designed a model that worked on its side/upside down/in reverse ...'?

- 'Why not ... ask those residents what they want their town to be like?'
- 'Supposing ... we ate ten small meals a day rather than any big ones?'
- 'Supposing ... we drew our reasoning rather than using words and numbers?'
- 'What if ... witnesses were never visible to the accused?'

'What if' questions open up an area for exploration.

Activity   **What if ...**

Take one problem or issue that you are working on at present.

- How many 'what if...' questions can you generate in three minutes?
- Select three of these.
- How many responses can you brainstorm for each question in three minutes (each)?
- Jot down any leads that arise from this activity. If there were none, take a walk or a break and then repeat the activity.

Generative thinking

There are many techniques that can be used to generate ideas and they are not difficult. An attitude of mind is the most important factor. Many people censor ideas at a very early stage if the ideas do not immediately seem sensible or useful.

Suspend judgement

Negative attitudes strangle creativity. We often dismiss the embryo of a good idea because we will not risk appearing foolish. Creativity, however, involves risks, mistakes, and 'bad' ideas as well as good. Only one in ten or twenty ideas will lead anywhere. To be creative requires the capacity to suggest ideas without immediately worrying about whether they are 'right' or what other people will say.

Nolan (2000) cites research which shows that when people's ideas are judged or dismissed, the number of ideas that are put forward drops dramatically. We tend to become more cautious and anxious if our suggestions are not welcomed, adopting a 'survival' response to avoid being discounted again.

Suspending judgement means:

- encouraging others to suggest ideas
- avoiding negative self-judgements such as 'I am not a creative person'
- giving all ideas a chance to flow
- being willing to express 'bad' or 'silly' ideas
- noting all ideas in the early stages, without immediately evaluating them
- being willing to look at all ideas for hidden potential
- not assuming that a good idea holds all the answers
- avoiding self-criticism if good ideas do not emerge quickly.

Activity **Self-censoring**

- How far do you censor your ideas to avoid appearing foolish?
- What allows you to let your imagination work more freely?

Thinking with a 'light touch'

Usually, when we work on problems, we use logical, sequential, ordered thinking. Sometimes this is referred to as 'left brain' thinking, although thinking is not strictly compartmentalised in that way. Logical thinking is a necessary part of arriving at a solution to most tasks. However, such thinking tends to run along tramlines, following predictable routes. If you do not already know the answer, the tramlines may not lead anywhere.

Creative thinking takes a lighter touch. It does not respond well to being forced. It works well with direction and a clear goal, but not if the mind is too rigidly focused on a particular

Creative thinking requires a light touch

outcome. It works when you 'hover' over an idea, or play with it, teasing out possibilities. It is rather like holding a small bird in the palm of your hand: if you hold the intention or goal or idea too tightly, you crush or suffocate it.

You can see this when you know the answer to a question but cannot remember it. The harder you try to capture it, the more the answer seems to elude you. Sometimes, playing with the idea or letting it rest works better than forcing it.

Other generative thinking techniques

Chapter 8 describes a range of other generative thinking strategies. These are useful for developing open reflection, but can be used more generally. These include:

- Brainstorming
- Free association
- Day-dreaming
- Free-writing
- Drawing and doodling.

Synthesis

Synthesis is an important aspect of creativity. At a simple level, combining any two items creates a new entity.

Imagine …

Take any item from the Animal list below; and any item from the Machine list and imagine them combined into one new object. Choose as much or as little of each item as you like, as long as you 'borrow' at least one characteristic or feature from each side.

Animal	*Machine*
Giraffe	Car
Penguin	MP3 player
Dolphin	Radiator
Octopus	Motor bike
Monkey	Book shelves
Snake	Oven
Dragon	Garden hose
Ant-eater	Fridge
Zebra	Speed boat

Experiment

● Do this at least three more times with two different objects each time.

Draw it

● Make a diagram or sketch of one of your creations (even if you 'cannot draw'). What further ideas or details does this generate?

Describe it

● Describe your creation in words. What further ideas or details does this generate?

Apply it

● If you haven't done so already, think of at least three ways your creation could be of use in everyday life (these do not have to be sensible or 'real' applications).

How many ways can you apply this strategy to your academic work or job? Give yourself three minutes to generate a list.

Think of two activities where you use very different skills and personal characteristics (such as in seminars, at work, sport, dancing, music, travelling, being with a difficult family member, etc.).

Write a list of the skills and qualities for each in the columns below:

	List 1: activity:		List 2: activity:	
1				
2				
3				
4				
5				
6				
7				
8				
9				
10				

● Take any item from list 1 and consider a way that it could be of use in managing your second activity.
● Take any item from list 2 and consider a way that it could be of use in managing your first activity.
● Repeat this at least once more.

In your reflective journal, jot down:

● Which of these are the most practical to put into operation?
● What would be the benefits of transferring these skills and qualities to new situations?

Synthesis as play

The 'Creating from two' activity invites you to play with ideas. Most of the time, ideas do not lead to earth-shattering discoveries. However, even apparently strange and silly ideas can lay down connections in the brain that one day might help you find the solution to a problem you do not yet know exists.

When you have a problem to solve, you can organise your ideas in lists, chunks or diagrams and then chop these up and rearrange them in new combinations. You can write or draw each on a separate piece of paper and shuffle these around until you find the best combination.

Play is about:

- having a go
- finding out new things
- stimulating the mind
- suspending worry about getting it right
- allowing the mind to relax
- experimenting
- 'letting go'
- informality.

Play is unpredictable. You may be playing with one idea, looking for a solution, and find that you are suddenly struck by the answer to something completely different that has been puzzling you for a long time.

 Reflection: On being playful

- How comfortable do you feel about the idea of 'playing' with solutions to academic work?
- Where do you allow yourself to be most playful?

Making connections

Expertise connections

In the synthesis activities above, you were, in effect, looking for and making connections. As you saw in earlier chapters, whenever you are working on a problem, the early stages are best spent in looking for connections and patterns between the current problem and:

- any similar problems or situations you have encountered before
- other problems you are working on or subjects you are studying
- the skills needed and those you have already used elsewhere
- your areas of personal expertise, even if these seem far removed.

Unlikely connections

It is logical to look for expertise connections. However, creative thinking can benefit from almost any set of connections. As the brain likes to be entertained, it will pay particular attention to what it finds curious or unfamiliar. It can use any change in your surroundings or experience to find unexpected connections with a problem you have been grappling with.

You can assist the brain by searching out new perspectives in an active and interested way. Be prepared to let what you see, hear or experience change your views or inspire you. Some ways of doing this are listed below. Tick those that appeal to you most:

- ☐ walk a different way round the campus or town so that you are exposed to new patterns and layouts
- ☐ go into shops that you do not normally visit
- ☐ browse books that do not normally interest you
- ☐ speak to students from different subjects about themes in their study
- ☐ talk to people about their work and life experience
- ☐ make friends with people from different walks of life
- ☐ find opportunities to talk to or work with people of different ages
- ☐ take a bus journey; visit a new place
- ☐ do something you do not usually do: draw, dance, sing, act, run, yoga, learn a language
- ☐ look at an object from a new perspective: draw it upside down or with both hands at once
- ☐ listen to different music; draw or write with the hand you do not usually use
- ☐ use a different medium to describe a problem (paint, model clay, use graphics, sing it, dance it).

Reflection: Change perspective

Which of these will you try out? Which could you do today?

Activity
  Change perspective

Add at least five other items to the 'Unlikely connections' list on p. 208.

Choose at least three suggestions from that list above and apply these to a problem you are working on at present.

- Jot down your observations of any changes in your thinking.
- If there was no effect, choose three more suggestions and repeat the exercise.
- How can you build some of these opportunities for making alternative connections into your daily life?

Search for 'the missing links'

When breaking your routine with a new activity, act 'as if' the answers or the clues that you are looking for are in that book, object, music, conversation, journey, etc. Search out connections between the problem you are addressing and the new activity. Use language structures such as:

- 'This is similar to my problem because …' or
- 'My problem is like this journey/statue/house because they both …'

Do this 10 or 20 times. The least likely connection may prompt a useful solution. For example, doing a degree is like going for a walk because:

- you can plan a specific route
- you can select alternative routes
- they can both take you to unexpected places
- the end of both can seem a long way off
- they both require some effort
- they both stimulate the mind; etc.

Activity **Connections**

Complete the following phrase as in the example above. Compare personal planning to one or more of the items from the list below.

'Personal planning is like … because …'

Football
Climbing a mountain
Dancing
Painting a picture
Watching a film

Networks

Networks follow the natural habit of the brain to look for patterns. Making notes in patterns to explore a problem is usually much quicker than writing in full sentences and paragraphs. You can use single words, phrases, images, symbols, or colour to indicate an idea. If you prefer, you can create 'webs' of links using images rather than words. Networks can be very liberating as there are few rules to follow. You can:

- start anywhere on the paper
- move from that focus point to anywhere else on the paper
- generate other focus points where one set of ideas meets another set
- write as much or as little as you like at each point (a word or short phrase usually works best; however, if your creative flow is stimulated by the process, go with the energy. You can return to the rest of the pattern once you have captured your idea)
- take the ideas anywhere you like, developing new connections: it is not a 'map' of what already exists but a new structure that you are creating
- let your mind take you for a walk
- be focused and logical or 'day-dream' and 'play', depending on what suits.

Information contained in networks is easier to remember if you:

- write in 'joined-up writing' (cursive script). It is easier for the brain to recall a continuous movement. Avoid capitals as these are harder for the brain to process

- write so that you can read the writing without turning the page around
- avoid using words such as *no*, *never*, *isn't*, *won't*, etc. as these are harder for the brain to process
- use colour, symbols and shapes that make sections of the pattern stand out as interesting in their own right
- take pauses to look for connections you might have missed
- ask 'what if …?' questions about links that initially look unhelpful
- work on the same problem more than once, designing a different network for each; on the second or third time, you may make very different sets of connections
- for your last or working model, develop the pattern into an overall image or shape that you find easier to remember, such as a real object. Use a different shape for each topic. You then have only one 'item' for your short-term memory to recall (see the 'Expert chess players' section, p. 198).

There is an example of a network on p. 211.

 Networks

- Do something relaxing, such as going for a walk.
- Then take a large piece of paper and as many coloured pencils, pens, paints as you like.
- Make a network for a problem or issue that you are working on at present. (See p. 198 for an example.) Hold the idea quite lightly at first and let your pen play with ideas.
- Follow the networks guidelines above.
- When you are finished, look at the overall shape that your map makes. Look for a real object or recognisable shape (flower, house, wheelbarrow, table, castle, etc.) that you haven't used before for this exercise. Draw in a few lines to outline the shape.
- Alternatively, use a distinctive image or style within the network to help you remember it.
- Consider how else you could make this pattern more memorable so that you can recall the different sections easily.

Lateral thinking

Much of the ground-breaking work on 'thinking about thinking' was developed by Dr Edward de Bono, who created the term 'lateral thinking'. Dr de Bono encourages unconventional ways of looking at a problem, playing with the most unlikely solutions and then looking for an aspect that might actually work. Lateral thinking values humour, looking for opportunity in the 'accidental', a willingness to do things in new ways, and exploring all ideas.

For example, a De Bono statement might be that aeroplanes should land upside down, or that a car should have square wheels (De Bono, 2006). By working 'as if …' this were a serious proposition, this creates an opportunity for really examining all the taken-for-granted processes such as the tyre pressure, tyre threads, braking devices, puncture problems and so forth. In practice, real-life advances have been made through such forms of thinking.

Activity **Crazy questions**

- Generate as many apparently 'crazy' 'what if …' questions as you can for a problem or issue you are working with at present.
- Select one of these and work through what would need to be changed in order to make this work. If possible, do this in a group.
- What light were you able to throw upon your problem by looking at it in a different way?

As if … it were them

You can also brainstorm solutions to a problem from the perspective of different people. This can generate a different set of responses from those you make 'in your own voice'. Imagine yourself 'in the shoes' of somebody who you think would have sensible things to say about the problem.

Network: creative thinking

Activity As if ... they were solving the problem

- Put the 'sensible you' aside for a moment.
- Select at least three people who you think would have an interesting perspective on a problem or issue you are addressing at present. You could include your lecturer or employer or somebody who inspires you, or a character from history that you find inspiring, etc.
- Put yourself into their shoes. Imagine their voice talking about the issue. How would they move their hands, head and body? Would they smile or frown? How would they describe the problem?
- What advice would they give you?
- Jot down the ideas that emerge

Wear different hats

Dr de Bono (1996) devised a system of imaginary hats, each a different colour and representing a different approach to thinking. When you 'wear' each of these hats, you address an issue in a completely different way. In effect, you give your mind permission to let go of one way of thinking for a while, and explore a different approach.

Activity Design your creative thinking wardrobe

- Imagine at least six hats that represent different types of people, occupations or approaches. If you prefer, use shoes, coats, chairs, etc.
- Describe or draw these if it helps you to imagine them clearly.
- Which kind of hats (or shoes, etc.) do you associate with: reflecting, planning, relating to others, analysing, finding information, writing, evaluating? Try these on when you perform these tasks!

Although De Bono has a specific series of hats, you could devise whatever set of hats works for you: a practical hat, a dreamer's hat, a philosopher's hat, a mechanic's hat, a chef's hat, a poet's hat and so on. Alternatively, you could devise a set of coats or shoes that suggest different ways of working and thinking.

Thinking upside down: sabotage

It is usually easy to think catastrophically. Most of us are quite good at imagining all the things that could go wrong. Use this ability to good effect by playing with the idea of deliberately doing everything wrong. The more the wording is exaggerated, the more inviting this task can be.

For example:

- What 20 things could I do, deliberately, to waste my time at college and have zero to show after three or four years of effort?
- What can I do so I feel more pressurised, irritated, thoroughly miserable, and miss all deadlines?
- What are all the things I could do and say in the seminar group to really inflame the situation and make everything thoroughly explosive?
- How can I really work myself up into a stressful state so that I make the job interview as difficult as possible?

It is usually easy to generate a long list of items to answer such questions, attesting to our native wit in knowing what we should and should not do in most situations. Once the list is generated, create a second list alongside it, writing the positive solution to each potentially 'catastrophic' action. It can be remarkably easy to generate ground rules or an action plan using this technique.

Activity Sabotage

- Select one problem that you are working on at present or a forthcoming event that is important to you.
- Brainstorm all the ways you could make this a miserable flop. Pay attention to the details that could ensure it all goes horribly wrong.
- Then go through your list and identify the positive action that you can take to avert each method of sabotage.
- Your second list contains the basic ingredients of a constructive action plan.

Working with raw material

Most of the strategies discussed above are 'early-stage' techniques. They emphasise letting ideas flow. Structure, selection, criticism, censoring, and evaluation are not helpful to the process of generating early ideas.

However, creative thinking does not stop here. The first stage develops a mass of material, which is like undifferentiated dough or clay. The next stage is to shape this into something that works. This means playing and working with your ideas:

- *Analyse*: What are the interesting aspects of each idea or suggestion?
- *Evaluate*: What could each suggestion contribute to an understanding of the issue or to finding a solution?
- *Synthesise*: Which aspects of each idea would work well together?
- *Spot gaps*: What is missing? For what else do you need to generate ideas and solutions?
- *Elaborate*: Add details to fill gaps and clarify ideas.
- *Select*: Which ideas do you want to take forward, and which do you want to leave to one side for now?
- *Organise*: Structure your ideas into a relevant pattern. This may be a diagram, flow-chart, model or piece of writing.
- *Plan*: Draw up an action plan to put your ideas into effect.

Develop the narrative

Write down how the whole solution or plan will work from start to finish, in order to provide your initial narrative. If you prefer, record yourself talking through your ideas. Producing the narrative can, itself, allow a different set of ideas to flow. Focus on the aim (to develop a solution) rather than on the quality of the writing at this stage.

Creating the narrative may be a stop–start process. The halts are also part of the creative process. They usually indicate precisely where you need to dig deeper to ensure something will work well. Geologists, for example, look at the surface of the ground for signs of a break or a change or something that doesn't 'fit' or match. This 'glitch' or 'bump' is a sign that something is worth investigating below the surface. The same is true for the creative process. It is the bits that seem to be getting in the way of finding a solution, the tricky bits, that lead to creative and sound solutions.

When you hit a 'bump' or the narrative stops, it is important to return to the early-stage techniques again, brainstorming, free writing, discussing, developing networks of ideas. Focus on the area of difficulty. Then return to the narrative until you hit the next 'bump'.

Creativity and risk taking

Behold the turtle. He makes progress only when he sticks his neck out.

James Bryant Conant

Creative thinking requires risk taking. Most of us have been trained from a very early age to be logical, sensible, not to act the fool. It can be hard to work against that training and to remain confident in what we are doing. It is easy to feel embarrassed or anxious about what others will think.

Creativity and emotional self-management

Nolan (2000) argues that an education aimed at developing innovative, creative thinkers must begin at the emotional level. If we do not have the emotional stamina to deal with other people's opinions, then we divert our creative energies into protecting ourselves from being judged. We won't be able to risk other people's opinions of us.

Creativity carries an element of anxiety and stress. Goleman (1995) has described the physiological reasons for this. It is a natural part of our biology to resist negative feedback. However, we can develop our mental attitudes so that we are less affected by fear of criticism. Goleman's work suggests that the better we are able to manage our anxiety, the more we can think freely and creatively (see Chapter 4).

Calculated risks

The creative risks we take may not pay off. In the early stages of generating ideas, it is a good idea to take risks. At this point, ideas are only on paper.

As you move towards developing an idea, costs come into play. There may be costs in terms of time, money, resources, the environment, or personal prestige. It is then important to limit the risks, without necessarily dismissing the possibility of taking a risk. This means considering such issues as:

- The consequences of a course of action: who will be affected; what are the costs to all parties?
- What are the possible benefits? Who will gain? How significant are the advantages compared with the disadvantages?
- What are the chances of success?
- Can you really afford the solution?
- Is the risk worth it?
- Can you deal with the consequences if it does not work?

Not all risks are worth it. Some will pay off; others will not. You need to be sure that you and all the affected parties can cope emotionally and financially with the consequences if things do not work out as hoped.

Taking responsibility

Because creativity involves risk taking, it also involves taking responsibility for one's own actions. This means:

- thinking through the needs and interests of all parties, including yourself
- being able to accept the consequences of your own actions
- planning safety nets where necessary, so that other people do not get hurt
- being aware of legal and ethical responsibilities.

If you are being creative in the way you approach an essay or experiment, this may simply mean being prepared to accept a low mark if the tutor does not agree that your novel ideas meet the requirements of the assignment. Check what possibilities are open to you, especially if you really need to get a high mark. On the other hand, you may wish to push the boundaries, no matter what the cost. That is your decision.

If, on the other hand, you are designing products for the public or making decisions that affect people's livelihoods, you need to consider a wider range of issues that will become your responsibility, such as:

- health and safety requirements
- legal requirements
- financial issues
- ethical considerations.

Boost your creativity: Action planner

Consider how you will bring more creativity to your study or work. For each of the following means of boosting your creativity, indicate ☑ your level of interest for trying this out.

Item	Action	No interest	Low interest	Some interest	High interest
	Hold a question in mind over time: see what emerges				
	Change my daily routine				
	Put time aside each week just for thinking				
	Generate more options – so I have more to select from				
	Keep an ideas book or file on or near me				
	Be more playful in working with ideas				
	Be more open to new ideas – reject them less quickly				
	Set aside time not filled with activity, to let ideas emerge				
	Browse more widely online				
	Ask myself 'what if I ...?' questions				
	Set a creative project for myself				
	Join a new class, group or club				
	Spend more time with people who value creativity				
	Be more active looking for sources of inspiration				
	Cut out things that prevent me being creative				
Add your own ideas.					

Prioritise items for action
- Select a realistic number of items (3–5) which you consider you are most likely to carry out, taking on board your level of interest.
- Circle the numbers for those items on the list above.
- Then complete the activity below.

Plan. Do. Observe
- In your reflective journal or blog, outline when and how you will implement these.
- Put times into your planner or diary for undertaking these activities so that they are not forgotten.
- Consider how these actions could have a direct, or indirect, effect on your work. Look for signs that that is happening. If not, take a different approach.

Closing comments

This chapter emphasises that creativity is both a state of mind and a way of developing the mind. Creativity is accessible to everybody. Strategies which develop creativity require relaxation, playfulness, a light touch, and enjoyment in order to be most effective. Our level of creativity, and hence our ability to be a creative problem-solver, will be affected by our attitudes and beliefs, our sense of humour, our emotional self-management, our health and well-being. Creativity does remind us that mind and body function as an integrated whole.

Creative thinking strategies are unpredictable. They can be time-consuming. It is hard to say how long 'thinking' or creativity will take. When work is left until the day before a deadline, there is not time for the brain to tease out the connections between things, and for you to mull over possibilities. It is also harder to stay relaxed and open to creative possibilities when a deadline is looming.

On the other hand, creative thinking may lead to answers in a small fraction of the time taken by logical, analytical thinking. Time spent in play, musing, synthesis and making connections can lead to innovatory ways of seeing and thinking.

Further reading

De Bono, E. (1996) *Teach Yourself to Think* (London: Penguin).

De Bono, E. (2006) *De Bono's Thinking Course*, revised and updated (London: BBC Active).

Greenfield, S. (2001) *The Human Brain: A Guided Tour* (London: Phoenix).

McCormick, R. and Paechter, C. (1999) *Learning and Knowledge* (London: The Open University).

Van Oech, R. (2008) *A Whack on the Side of the Head: How to be More Creative*, revised and updated edn (New York: Grand Central Publishing).

Chapter 8
The art of reflection

Learning outcomes

This chapter offers opportunities to:

- understand what is meant by 'reflection'
- understand the importance of reflection to evaluating and improving personal performance
- identify different kinds of reflection for different purposes
- develop methods for improving your reflective skills
- devise your own model for reflection
- consider how to communicate the results of your reflection to other people.

Introduction

If you have a fleck of bright green paint between your eyes, or egg on your chin, you cannot see them as they are too close to your eyes to be visible to them. Without a mirror or a comment from other people, you could pretend there was nothing to see. This won't, of course, prevent others from seeing what you cannot.

Similarly, we are usually too close to ourselves to be aware of the things we most need to know. We can easily fail to recognise what may be very evident to other people. Fortunately, we can stand back occasionally and reflect about such things as our aims, responses, feelings and performance. Well-developed skills in reflection can help us to:

- gain a more in-depth and honest picture of ourselves
- become more aware of our hidden motivations, our thinking styles, and of how we appear to other people
- develop a better understanding of what affects our own performance and progress
- develop our insight and judgements
- gain more control over our own thoughts, emotions, responses and behaviour so that we are in a better position to achieve what we want to achieve.

Reflection in everyday life

Reflection is a natural activity. To a greater or lesser extent, we all spend time going back over what we have said or done, or what we wish we had said and done. Often, reflection accompanies hindsight: we realise long after an event how things might have been different, or how some small event was more significant than we realised.

This is reflected in everyday expressions:

- 'If only I had known then what I know now …'
- 'With hindsight, I realise …'
- 'I could never have imagined that doing X would result in Y …'
- 'Now I realise where this leads, I wouldn't do it again …'
- 'If I had the chance, I would do it all over again.'
- 'It was worth it/it wasn't worth it/it was worth the risk.'
- I wish I had …'

In other words, we review what was said or done, weighing up the consequences and considering what the alternatives might have been. We evaluate whether we would do things differently if given the chance again or whether we were right first time.

Reflection as challenge

The reflective process is challenging. We do not always like to discover the truth about ourselves: it can be embarrassing to find we have walked around for several hours with a dab of egg yolk on our chin. We would rather believe it wasn't there or that nobody could see it. The same is true of the reflective process. When it works well, we discover things that make us feel uncomfortable. Our natural reaction is to pretend they do not really matter, or to look for an excuse, or to blame someone else. The things we most need to know can be the hardest to hear.

It takes time and practice for people to develop good reflective skills. Don't be discouraged if you think reflection does not come naturally to you. This book structures reflection on a wide range of issues. If you have undertaken some of the reflections and activities, then you will already be developing a sense of what is involved.

In retrospect, Ulrika wished she had planned her landing location more carefully

Is reflection important?

At university level, you need to take responsibility for your own progress. Students are expected to develop into independent thinkers, capable of evaluating their own performance, drawing conclusions about what they did well and how to improve. Your success will depend, to a large extent, on yourself.

You need to be confident in your own judgements of your work. The feedback you receive from tutors and other students gives you a rare opportunity to compare your own evaluations with those of other people.

Your evaluations should be based upon sound criteria rather than a general feeling that you are right and others wrong. Consider the differences between your own evaluations and the feedback you receive from others: these may hold important clues about how to achieve better grades and to improve your performance generally.

Reflection and Personal Development Planning

All British universities are required to provide personal development planning (PDP) for students as a 'structured process of reflection'. By the time you leave university, you are expected to know how to use structured reflection to understand:

- yourself, your motivations, choices and behaviours
- what you want to achieve
- how to plan, follow through, review and evaluate a course of action
- how your responses and performance affect other people
- how to take action to improve your work or learning to the benefit of yourself and/or others.

The 'reflective practitioner'

Many occupations now require a 'reflective practitioner' approach. This is built into the work cycle in some way, such as through staff reviews or appraisal. Typically, this means taking personal responsibility for:

- your continuing professional development (CPD)
- evaluating your personal experience, strengths, qualities and skills
- identifying ways of using your strengths well, within your professional area
- identifying personal limitations and areas that could be improved through training, practice or informal learning
- recognising the effects of your own responses and behaviour and taking responsibility for these
- making useful contributions to team discussions
- improving individual and team performance
- identifying your own contribution to the results of a task, project or outcome.

Your current programme may include reflective activity. If not, the self-evaluation questionnaire on p. 221 can help you to decide where you need to work next.

What is 'reflection'?

Reflection is a type of thinking. It is associated with deep thought aimed at better understanding. It includes a mixture of elements, such as:

1 Making sense of experience

It is important to note the difference between 'experience' and 'learning'. Experience can be the basis for learning and development. However, just because we have been through an experience it does not mean we have learnt all there is to learn about it – or even that we have learnt anything at all. Reflection is an important part of the learning experience. It is where we analyse experience, actively attempting to 'make sense' or find the meaning in it.

2 'Standing back'

By 'standing back', we gain a better view or perspective of an experience, issue or action. It is not always easy to reflect when caught up in the midst of activity.

3 Repetition

Reflection involves 'going over' something, perhaps even several times, in order to look at it critically from several points of view or to check nothing has been missed.

4 Deeper honesty

Reflection is associated with a striving after the truth. It is through reflection that we can come to acknowledge things we find difficult to admit in the normal course of events.

5 'Weighing up'

Reflection involves a sense of even-handed judgement and critical evaluation – it usually involves 'weighing things in the balance', taking all things into account rather than just the most obvious.

6 Clarity

Reflection can bring greater clarity, as though seeing things reflected back in a mirror. This can be useful at any stage in the process of devising, carrying out or reviewing activities.

7 Understanding

Reflection is associated with opening up to learning and understanding at a deeper level, including gaining insight into theories and concepts that are difficult to access by other means.

8 Making judgements

Reflection involves an element of making judgements and drawing conclusions.

Circle as many of the following as are relevant and of benefit to you. Use the empty circles to add in any others of importance to you.

To think about how what I am learning all fits together

To consider how I could get better marks

To see how I could do things differently at work

To manage my emotions better

To put time aside to consider my life plans

To check I am on track with what I need to do to get a job

To check I am on track with what I need to do to gain promotion

To make sense of what I am learning

To check that I am taking things in on my course

To apply theories to my work

To be more efficient

To be more mindful of how I do things

To make me slow down and think

To become more self-aware

To think about how my actions affect others

To see how I change over time

To be more professional in my approach

To take on board feedback from other people

I need to do it for my course

I need to do it in my job

To gain a broader perspective

For staff appraisal

For better self-understanding

To consider what training I need

To avoid getting into a rut

To find out where I could introduce more variety to the way I do things

For space to think about what matters to me

To take on board new ideas

Highlight the one that is the most significant for you.

Self-evaluation on reflective practice

For each of the following statements, rate your responses as outlined below. Note that the rating for 'strongly disagree' carries no score.

Rating: *4 = strongly agree 3 = agree 2 = sort of agree 1 = disagree 0 = strongly disagree*

'I am very confident that I …'	Rating
1 know how to use logs or reflective journals	
2 understand myself very well	
3 challenge my own thinking sufficiently	
4 spend sufficient time looking for relevant links between different things	
5 spend sufficient time 'making sense' of what I learn and experience	
6 spend sufficient time thinking about the significance of what I learn	
7 spend sufficient time thinking about how to improve my academic performance	
8 spend enough time thinking about the effects of my actions and behaviour	
9 make an accurate evaluation of my own strengths	
10 know how to apply my experience and skills to novel situations	
11 am aware of my personal limitations	
12 am aware of my own personal development needs	
13 always consider all options before arriving at a decision	
14 am always aware of all the motivations underlying my behaviour	
15 always take full responsibility for my own part in events	
16 spend enough time thinking about how to improve my skills in dealing with other people	
17 spend enough time thinking about how I could make a better contribution to groups I am in	
18 spend sufficient time thinking about the significance of other people's actions	
19 spend sufficient time thinking about the significance of what other people say	
20 can reflect accurately about my emotional responses to events	
21 could draw upon my reflections well for assessment purposes	
22 spend sufficient time thinking about how to use the feedback I receive from others	
23 know how to use reflection effectively when applying for jobs	
24 am clear about the different kinds of reflection that are open to me	
25 do not need to develop my skills of reflection any further.	
Add up your score **Total**	

Interpreting your score

You have a score out of 100. This is a rough guide to your strengths as a 'reflective practitioner'. If the score is less than 100, then there is more work that you could do to develop your reflective skills.

- What are your priorities for improving reflection?
- Which *one* thing could you do this week in order to develop your reflective abilities?

Basic steps for reflection

If you are new to reflection, the following steps outline some basic features of reflection to help you get started.

- *Small regular bites*   Keep a regular journal, log or blog. Write something in this at regular intervals. Little and often is better at first, so that you develop the habit of reflection. Seven minutes every weekday evening is all that is needed. Alternatively, you may prefer to take half an hour once or twice a week.

- *Be specific*   Choose a particular incident or a feature of your day or week to focus on for each entry. This will develop your critical thinking better than writing on a superficial basis about your whole day.

- *Aim at improvement*   Choose something that was difficult or 'sticky' during your day. Think through what gave rise to the problem. Consider how you might achieve a better outcome next time. Alternatively, spot the things that went unexpectedly well, and consider why that might have been the case.

- *Focus on yourself*   Avoid using reflection as a way of blaming and taking out anger on others, even if you feel they deserve it. Focus on your own role, and how you can make a similar situation more manageable next time. This helps to take you forward.

- *Use prompts*   Select an activity from the book and use this to structure your reflection. See pages 235–8 on the 'Core Model for Reflection', for ideas for prompt questions.

- *Critical rather than descriptive writing*   Reflection involves critical, analytical thinking. Weigh up the strengths and weaknesses, costs and benefits, decisions and outcomes. These are thinking skills required for most academic work. Avoid descriptive writing that simply recites what happened, or who said what, unless there are particular reasons for doing this as part of your course. For more about critical thinking, see Cottrell (2011).

- *Have a purpose*   Reflection should be directed to a purpose. It is better to write a short entry that is meaningful than a long one which is simply pages of description. Find a topic that is useful to you. What do you most need to improve? What do you need to think through?

- *Find the right questions*   Consider the right questions for structuring your reflection. It is easier, when you start out, to answer questions that give shape to your thinking. See p. 223.

- *Review*   After a few weeks, read back over your entries. Look for the main themes in what you have written and consider the significance of these for you. Decide what action to take next.

Example

Brief critical entry aimed at improving performance

How good were my people skills today?

Today was useful as I realised I am still interrupting people when they are talking. I cut right across Mary today during the seminar break. I realise this was not very skilful or considerate. Mary looked annoyed. I just ignored this at the time because I was embarrassed. It would have been better to have apologised as soon as I realised. I will next session. I have to take more care not to burst in when other people are talking. Maybe I could ask Joe and Ali to point it out to me for a while so I notice it more.

Descriptive entry

The following is an example of poor reflection. It simply describes what happens and focuses on other people. The writer doesn't take personal responsibility for actions or plan to improve performance. It doesn't take the writer forward.

In the seminar break today, Mary was talking and I wanted to say something. She had been talking for a few minutes already and I hadn't said anything. I was interested in what she was saying but then just interrupted. It was a simple mistake. I didn't mean to upset her. Mary carried on talking for a moment and then decided to stop. She looked angry. Everybody just looked at me as if I was in the wrong. I didn't even talk for very long. Peter said I had an interesting point. Then we went back in the seminar and Mary avoided looking at me all the way through.

Approaches to structured reflection

There are many ways of approaching reflection and you are unlikely to need them all. Browse through the chapter and see which activities most appeal or are most useful to you at present. The types of reflection introduced below are:

- question-based reflection
- open reflection
- synthetic reflection
- developmental reflection
- evaluative reflection.

As you will see, there are overlaps and connections between these different types of reflection. Each type may be useful for a different task or for different stages of a task. As you develop your reflective ability, you will find that you begin to move quite easily between these different methods to suit the task in hand. Your tutors may also be able to guide you about the types of reflective activity that are most suitable for your subject.

Question-based reflection

Question-based reflection is a highly structured form of reflection; it is used extensively throughout this book. The method is relatively simple. Generally, a series of questions is given under a set of headings. Question-based reflection has a number of advantages:

- it prompts and guides you through the reflective process
- it helps ensure you don't miss out any essential elements
- it can give shape and direction to the subject of reflection, reducing vague discussion and 'waffle'
- it enables everyone in a group to reflect on the same set of issues in a particular way in order to make direct comparisons on specific issues
- questions increase motivation to produce a response and can sharpen thinking.

Who does it suit?

Question-based reflection is associated with analytical, serial thinking. It tends to suit people who like or need to work in a logical, ordered or controlled way, and who appreciate some external direction.

But why did I ... ?

Could I have ... ?

At what point did ... ?

What was the best ... ?

Did I ... ?

Which ... ?

Example

Question-based reflection

Question
How did I make use of feedback for my course-work?

Response
I read through it, I accepted most of it, I identified themes that need to be addressed.

Question
Did I make the best use of the feedback I received on my report?

Response
At the time I thought I had made good use of the feedback. I did read it and I set myself priorities for action. However, looking back, I don't think I took it seriously enough. I wondered if the tutor had been too harsh on me, so when I did my essay for the next tutor, I didn't really follow through on the advice I had been given. I then got some of the same feedback again. I realise I ignored my own priorities.

Question
How can I make more effective use of feedback?

Response
I need to set myself a realistic target. I tried to take on too many changes at once last time and then got discouraged. I need to speak to my tutor to work out one or two changes that would make the most impact. Basically, I need to be more focused and accept that I cannot change everything at once.

Select an activity that you engage in regularly or you wish to improve.

In your reflective journal, jot down a list of at least ten questions to structure your reflection about your performance.

● Answer your questions.

● What did you find out about your performance by questioning it in this way?

Open reflection

Open reflection methods encourage you to 'let go' of some concentration, and 'go with the flow' rather than trying to control the process too tightly. Open reflection can seem 'unstructured'. However, there is usually a structure of some kind to the method, such as working from prompts, working through several stages in a process or following semi-formal rules.

The benefits of open reflection are:

● it makes it easier to get started on a task as it helps you to generate thoughts and ideas

● it allows the imagination free rein so that a relatively uncensored set of associations can be formed

● unexpected ideas may emerge, which can be energising and exciting

● it can be more personally relevant than working through questions set by somebody else.

Open reflection is good for generating ideas, but not always for structuring and making sense of them. It can help to combine open reflection with other methods to structure your thoughts effectively and make meaning from experience.

This method of reflection suits people who like to work in organic ways, and who appreciate things evolving in new or original ways. Open reflection can be conducted in an orchestrated way (a tutor guides the process) or can be personally controlled.

The various methods of open reflection are discussed below.

Brainstorming

Brainstorming is a very simple and quick technique. Take a large piece of paper and a pen. Write the problem or question down somewhere on the paper – the centre is often a useful place but you can choose wherever suits you. Write down every idea or solution that comes into your head. At this stage, do not evaluate or judge what emerges – just let the ideas flow.

Brainstorming is one of the most widely used techniques for generating ideas quickly. You can use it to start the process of reflection, as well as for writing essays or other assignments.

Activity — Brainstorming

- Select a topic that you need to think about this week – or brainstorm ideas about an ideal birthday gift for someone you know.
- Write the topic somewhere on the paper.
- Give yourself five minutes to jot down as many ideas as you can.
- Avoid judging your ideas as you go along; just write down whatever comes into your mind.
- Once you have finished the brainstorm, consider each suggestion in turn. Cross out the least useful. If other ideas emerge as you do this, jot them down for consideration too.

Discussion

Discussion can be a very valuable form of reflection. It has the advantage of offering multiple perspectives. Paired or group discussions may raise challenging questions that you, as an individual, may wish to avoid. Such questions are often the ones we need most to address – so discussion-based reflection can keep you on your toes.

Discussion, unless strongly steered, can tend to drift in many directions. It is more creative if only a limited number of prompt questions or statements are used. This allows the discussion to wander broadly over the topic. For a more controlled discussion, set more questions and time limits for responses. If the discussion veers away from the agenda, don't dismiss the tangents straight away. The tangents may be giving you important clues about the target subject, or about how well the group is working together, or how you might approach a particular problem.

Day-dreaming

Without forcing the issue, let your mind drift over the target subject. Day-dreaming about the target subject is more likely to occur if we give the subject serious and detailed consideration, and then do something very different for a while. Day-dreaming is not something that can be forced, but it can be encouraged and nurtured. Keep pen and paper, a digital recorder or a lap-top computer nearby to capture ideas as they occur. Reflections that arise in this way are easy to forget. Sometimes, there

is a natural movement from this more relaxed reflection towards more analytical questioning, as you become aware of what you are discovering.

Networks

These are useful for letting your mind develop an idea in a visual way that follows the way the brain works. See page 211 for details.

Free-writing

Writing as a reflective tool is different from writing intended for an audience or tutors. Its aim is to stimulate thinking, not to communicate a message to others. This means that the writing may look, sound and flow differently from other writing that you do. Your method will be quite different from any other person's. You may just pick up the pen and write; you may write words and phrases rather than sentences; you may scribble and draw as you write; you may write in verse. In other words, you assess the value of this writing for yourself, in terms of whether it helps you to reflect and achieve your own aims.

Activity — Free-writing

Choose a subject that you want to think about this week. This may be the same as one you considered for a previous activity.

- Give yourself ten minutes to write down, as fast as you can, any thoughts that come into your mind on this subject.
- Unlike brainstorms, where you just jot down any phrase, for free-writing aim to link the thoughts to some extent. Consider how one idea connects to others. Monitor, lightly, where your thoughts are going. As in the example above, this does not have to be a very developed process.
- When you have finished, read through what you have written. Look for *one* key theme or idea. Highlight or underline this.
- Give yourself a few minutes to free-write on only that *one* theme.
- Then highlight a *second* theme and free-write on that.
- You will find that your ideas on the subject are starting to develop.

Reflective free-writing, like other free-writing, will probably take more than one draft:

- a draft that generates ideas
- a draft that explores some issues in more detail, going off at tangents and with more details
- later drafts with more structure, as you begin to draw conclusions from your reflection and write them for others to read.

Reflective free-writing

A good day. Enjoyed the session. Made contributions. Really liked it when we saw video and discussed the video. I got very involved in the debate, which surprised me. I hadn't thought I felt so strongly. Not sure why I do. Why do I? I don't like the design of the bridge. Ugly. Not that though. More … Reminds me of history lessons more than engineering. Hated history at school. Maybe not a good reason for me to respond to a design now. Or maybe it is. Maybe other people will feel the same way. What else influences my responses apart from history lessons? I like sculptured surfaces …

The above example may not make much sense to you, but it did to the person who wrote it. He knew the issue he was trying to explore and this was just his first step. Try for yourself the free-writing activity on page 225.

Drawing and doodling

Drawing and doodling can be used to distract you from controlling your thought processes too closely, allowing your mind to take you where it wishes. You may find that the drawing and the reflection have little in common. On the other hand, you may wish to analyse your drawings for clues about how your mind is working. You could need to check whether your interpretation made sense when weighed against other evidence.

Caricatures, cartoons, paintings or other graphic means may be your preferred methods for reflection, for exploring past actions or events and for getting a feel for their meaning.

Activity **Doodle**

- Select a new topic for reflection.
- Take a piece of paper and scribble in the middle.
- Either doodle as you think about the subject or draw a picture or diagram of it. The image does not have to be of good quality: it is simply a tool to distract you from concentrating too hard on the topic.
- If ideas emerge that you want to jot down or develop, then let yourself do so.
- After you have finished, consider how far you find this method suits your learning style.

Generative thinking

The strategies suggested above are associated with generative thinking styles. The strategies and approaches developed in Chapter 7, 'Thinking outside the box', can support the development of this way of working.

Synthetic reflection

Synthetic reflection involves a 'bringing together' or a 'synthesising' of different aspects and perspectives. It is useful for giving shape to a series of reflections or making sense of earlier stages of reflection. It helps you find the meaning behind your reflections, thoughts and actions. It also stimulates creative thinking.

Advantages of synthetic reflection

Synthetic reflection is useful for:

- seeing links and connections
- gaining a sense of the 'bigger picture'
- gaining a concrete overview from where to begin more detailed analysis
- giving shape or structure to the reflective process
- drawing reflections together into a coherent whole.

Synthetic reflection is associated with *gestalt*, holistic, or 'right-brain' thinking. It suits people who like to spot clues, solve puzzles or put things together into new forms. Artistic endeavour and synthetic processes are closely associated. Linking can be made in logical or creative ways, so synthetic reflection can suit those who like order and those who like to work organically. The importance of developing these modes of thinking is highlighted in Chapter 7, 'Thinking outside the box'.

As synthetic reflection helps to draw things together, it can be used to follow up reflection based on free writing or discussion.

Look for links and themes

Synthetic reflection is an active type of reflection. You are looking for links, connections and leads in material you have already produced. Use it to search out hidden themes that are there on the page but which you may not yet have noticed. Going over the material, re-writing it, colouring it, highlighting it, organising it, illustrating it, will help you to focus on each theme.

 Activity Synthesis

- Select one theme that you began to explore in a previous activity.
- Identify themes and links in your earlier reflections.
- Organise your thoughts so that the themes and links stand out clearly.

Developmental reflection

Whilst any method of reflection can assist the process of personal development, the following methods focus specifically on understanding and improving your performance and achievement.

 Activity Developmental reflection

- If you have not done so already, complete the activities on p. 221 to identify your developmental priorities.

 In your reflective journal, note down your thoughts about one of your priorities. For example, you may find it useful to consider some of the following questions:

- What made you select this as a priority? What is really the key issue for you?
- What is the goal? What do you hope to gain by developing this area?
- How does this contribute to achieving your long-term or short-term goals?
- What is the problem?
- What have you tried already? How successful was this?
- What will you do next?
- What would be a realistic time-scale to address this successfully?
- Who else would benefit if you addressed this priority?
- What might you do to sabotage your success in achieving this?
- What are your feelings about this priority? What emotions, if any, does it bring up for you?

Monitoring performance

You may be asked to keep a log, blog or journal as part of your course. Even if this is not a requirement, it is a useful practice. Many employers require logs to be kept of actions taken, along with the rationale and outcomes. These may be used in team meetings or staff reviews.

Example

Monitoring performance

Project Group: reflection

20th February

I chaired the project group meeting again today. This went better than last time. I was able to keep the group to the agenda. Unlike last time, this time I did not let people just bring up new topics as they felt like it. I was quite tough, for me. I summarised points well and the feedback on this was good.

Unfortunately, the meeting still ran over time. I did find it difficult to break in to interrupt the flow when Carla and Ian started arguing. I am not sure whether I should speak to them before the meeting, or whether I should just cut across them, which might seem rude. I am worried because they speak loudly and it would look bad if nobody could hear me when I try to interrupt. Because I didn't keep these two in check, we ran over time. Time-keeping looks like my big challenge, but really the issue is about knowing how to interrupt people. This is my next priority. I have arranged to speak about this to my tutor.

Transferable skills

Chapter 2 demonstrated that expertise can be used in diverse contexts. However, skills do not transfer automatically. Skills are likely to be 'transferable' only if we:

- identify the range of skills involved in an activity. It is easy to overlook the wide range of sub-skills that are integrated even into everyday experience
- make specific attempts to draw parallels between one activity and another, searching out the comparisons
- are able to see how one situation is similar to the other. If we cannot see those parallels, then we may believe ourselves incapable of dealing with situations that are well within our actual competence. (Butterworth, 1992)

Example

Transferring skills 1: communication

I have been working with children in a local school, helping them with their mathematics. The main developmental points for me were in taking responsibility for others and in using 'plain English'. However, I am also much better now at organising information so other people can use it.

The teacher pointed out that when I first started at the school, I launched straight in and tried to finish as much of the worksheet as I could. Now, I structure the work much better, so the children know what they are learning. This is partly good communication. However, I am also developing skills in structuring information. I look much more closely at how to break down instructions into small chunks that the children can take in at once. They don't like it if I have to repeat instructions.

I have found that this is useful when talking to adults too. In my part time job, I now do this when giving guidance on technical problems. I find I don't have to go over information so many times. This way of thinking seems to be helping me to plan and structure my written assignments. My tutor says I write more clearly.

It is worth giving time and thought to what we have achieved in any one situation and considering its applicability to other situations. The self-knowledge gained may help us later in new situations.

Example

Transferring skills 2: academic skills

I was very anxious about writing an essay as I hadn't written one before. My programme mainly uses report writing. Reports are very structured whereas I couldn't see how essays fitted together.

I spoke to a third-year student who talked me through the process. He pointed out that the discussion part of my reports is quite like an essay. If I take out the different sections of the report, such as the method and results sections, and remove all headings and tables, I have the core of an essay already.

I find it easier to write the main part of an essay as if I was writing a report. I use headings and write a paragraph under each of these. This helps me see the structure of my writing. I have noticed I need to check my paragraphs are linked because sections of essays flow into each other more than sections of reports. I then remove the headings when I am ready to hand in the essay.

Reflection: Spotting your skills

In your reflective journal, write for a few minutes about any one *new* activity that you have undertaken recently. Consider things such as:

- What skills did you already have that you used for the new activity?
- Were there any ways you adapted your usual ways of thinking or doing to help you with the new task?
- Did you discover anything about yourself by doing something new?

Reflecting on your academic development

Take time to stand back and look at the big picture regarding your academic development. Consider:

- Are you sufficiently motivated to achieve well academically? How could you increase your motivation?
- How coherent are the choices you are making for options or electives? How will these choices help you achieve your longer-term ambitions?
- Are your choices giving you a strong enough specialist base?
- Will your choices make you stand out as distinctive with interests and capabilities beyond your subject specialism?
- What are the most stimulating aspects of your current learning?
- What is blocking your progress in any area? Are your study strategies still relevant or do they need to be revised?

Example

Academic choices

I wanted to study nothing but chemistry as that interested me most but I am concerned that this will look boring when I go for jobs. I am also interested in travelling abroad. I couldn't see how the two could fit together as I imagined myself in a large British factory near where I grew up.

The Careers Service showed me some case studies of career paths that people from my programme had taken, and I was struck by the opportunities that are available through some big companies for working in international branches. I am not sure yet whether to take a language, which I could start from scratch. This would make it easier to get picked for a placement abroad in the future. However, a specialist IT option might be more useful.

I also need to look at the opportunities open to me if I take a subsidiary in a subject such as health science or nutrition. I have put some time aside next Thursday to look through materials in the Careers Service library.

You could reflect on differences in your performance from one topic or option to another. For example, you may experience a sudden drop or increase in your marks, or find you are more successful in some areas than others. You can begin to investigate this by techniques such as:

- listing how you approach each subject differently
- free writing about your attitudes or approaches to each subject
- brainstorming differences between the topics and how you will manage these.

Example

Reflection on assignments

I spent a long time on my last assignment and was disappointed with the marks. This time I spent less time and yet my mark was better. It seems to me the main difference is that I really thought a lot about what the question meant this time. All of my work was very focused on addressing the title. It felt like I really knew what I was doing – so it took less time. I spent more time, though, just working out my initial plans. I think I have made a breakthrough in the way I go about my assignments.

What I need now is to know how to work out what is needed for my land-surveying option. I can't really see how to work out the problems in the same way. I suppose I haven't actually tried applying my 'breakthrough' method to surveying yet, so I don't know if it will work or not.

Reflecting on your professional development

Take time occasionally to consider your short- and long-term professional development.

- What skills are you developing? Are there obvious gaps in your profile of skills and experience? Will these matter when you apply for jobs?
- Are your programme choices right for the type of career you have in mind?
- Are you focusing too much on study at the expense of other experience which would help your career?
- Are you making the best use of all that university has to offer to develop your skills, experience and CV?
- Is there some kind of work experience you could undertake to develop your people skills in the workplace?
- Are you making good (and early) use of the Careers Service and its resources?
- Would it be useful to have a mentor from the area you are considering for a career?

Example

Professional development

I have noticed that many job adverts require good team-building skills. There is not much opportunity on this programme to work in teams. I am worried that this will be a weak point when I come to apply for jobs. I have heard that there are volunteer activities being co-ordinated on campus and I will follow this up this week. Some of that might involve team work.

Another alternative might be to study an elective that includes team work in its skills profile. Unfortunately, I haven't found one that interests me. I might have to choose one that is not especially interesting. I would rather work in a team that was involved in real-life activities rather than study, as I think employers would prefer that …

Reflecting on your personal development

Reflection isn't useful only for academic or work-related contexts. You can use it to look hard at any area of your personal development. For example:

- Are your life ambitions changing in any way?
- Are your values and beliefs undergoing any changes? What is influencing such change?
- Are you giving sufficient time to friends and family?
- How are you taking care of your health?
- What are you doing to manage stress?
- What are you doing to ensure a good 'work/life balance'? Do you get time to enjoy yourself without undermining your work and study?

Example

Personal development

I have been working long hours at college and at work recently. I added this up to 65 hours last week. I was supposed to go to my brother's birthday party but in the end had to work an extra shift as it was double pay. This was good for the money, but my family was disappointed. I'm not getting the right balance.

I need clear breaks with no work or study. I have to start planning out my time so I get time to rest and enjoy myself occasionally. Just stop. I have noticed that I am not sleeping well. It would be better for me to start earlier and then finish off earlier in the evening. Studying late just keeps me awake at night, rattling it all round in my head.

I am also neglecting my interest in music. I would really like to spend more time listening to recent releases. I could do this by …

Evaluative reflection

Questionnaires and checklists

Self-evaluation questionnaires are useful starting points for self-evaluation:

- the questions help to define the field, indicating the areas that are important to consider further
- the questionnaire can be used in a 'before' and 'after' way, enabling more precise comparisons between answers given at different times
- it is often difficult to answer a questionnaire with a straight 'yes' or 'no'. Those questions that resist easy answers prompt longer answers, indicating what the real issues might be for you
- questionnaires are usually good starting points. They are not particularly useful if used in isolation from other reflective methods.

Critical event

One good way of finding out more about yourself is through an in-depth analysis of a single event. To begin with, select an occasion that was of some importance to you such as:

- the first time you …
- the last time you …
- a very difficult occasion
- a test of your values
- a test of your abilities
- a test of your will-power
- a test of character
- a turning point in your life
- a time you realised something unexpected about yourself or other people.

If you undertake this exercise several times you have valuable materials for reflecting on your performance. Consider:

- What themes emerge?
- What noticeable areas of improvement are there in your performance over time?
- What areas did you highlight for further action that you did not then attend to? What do you think is preventing you from doing so?

Example

Critical event

I undertook a student project for MMM Manufacturers, spending one afternoon a week working with their development team. I was responsible for designing paper-based materials that made their new software easy to use for short-contract workers. I worked alongside the IT-development team in Human Resources, and one of these acted as a 'line manager' . I piloted my materials with ten part-time workers, and used their feedback to make some major changes.

The paper-based materials I produced were used by the company. That was a success, but the work experience was an important event to me for very different reasons. First of all, I had no confidence that I could work in that kind of environment or work to deadlines. I proved to myself that I could be relied on to carry out a job well.

I had been very anxious about piloting the materials. I imagined that people would be very critical and that I would get upset if I was criticised. During the pilot, I was determined to listen to what the part-timers had to say, as I wanted my materials to work. They said some very positive things but they also pointed out a lot of aspects that needed to be changed. I surprised myself. I stayed very calm and encouraged them to say what they really felt. What they said was actually very sensible – I could see how most of it would improve the materials.

I learnt the value of feedback as I was able to put it to good use. I also learned how important it is to allow people to be critical. My main achievement, from my perspective, was in 'taking it on the chin'. I accepted what was said without being devastated that everything wasn't perfect in the first place. This is something I have not been able to do in the past so I feel this has been an important turning point.

This experience will help me in my seminar group. For example, I used to see all feedback as a kind of attack on me …

Reflection: Critical event

Select one event that is of key importance to you. Consider:

- What happened generally – the context?
- What did you do – your own role?
- What were the outcomes or consequences of your actions?
- What alternative actions could you have taken?
- How might you prepare differently for a similar occasion?
- How did your performance or action differ from your performance on other occasions? What were the reasons for this?
- How did you use or how could you use feedback from other people?
- What is the one main area where you need to focus to improve your performance? What do you need to do in order to take this forward?
- What did you gain and learn from the experience?

Reflection: Critical event *(continued)*

Write down your answers to each of the above questions so that you have a record to which you can refer on future occasions.

NB If anyone else will see these reflections, check first that you have not included names or other information that identify people, departments or organisations without their express permission.

See Resource Bank, page 345.

Using feedback

As a student, you will receive regular feedback on your work in ways you may never experience again. Such feedback, provided by experts who want you to succeed, is an extremely valuable resource. Be open to all feedback, irrespective of whether, in your opinion, it is fair and accurate or not.

Latifa could always find constructive use for her tutor's feedback.

You can use it as a basis for reflection on your development by:

- reading it! – and reading it again a few days later, as you probably will not be objective the first time you see it
- considering whether the comments are unexpected; if so, why is that?
- considering whether you agree with the comments. If not, what are the grounds for your disagreement?
- deciding if you want to see similar comments on future work. If so, consider what you can do next time in order to gain similar comments again. Bear in mind, that just doing the same

kinds of things may not draw the same positive feedback a second time – how will you build on your success so that you show you are developing from where you were before? If you disliked the feedback, what steps can you take to change or improve that area of your performance?

- considering sources of support available to you (books, web pages, tutors, support services) to address areas for improvement.

Put time aside at least two or three times a year to go over written feedback that you have received. Note any emergent themes as these may be losing or gaining you marks on a consistent basis. Jot down guidance for yourself on how you will address those points so that you really gain from having received this feedback, whether it pleased you or not.

Varieties of feedback

Bear in mind that much of the feedback that you will receive both as a student and in life more generally is not written out as individual comments at the end of an essay. If there are comments that apply to most of a class, it can make more sense for the tutor to avoid writing these out individually for each student, and to provide these to the whole class verbally or through a group handout or on the course website. This is still important feedback for you to consider.

Look out for feedback that may be available to you in a wide range of formats depending on your programme, such as:

- short or passing verbal feedback on your performance during lab work, on the wards, in the studio, etc.
- comments provided on your ideas or an early plan or draft for an assignment
- opportunities created for you to receive feedback from other students, employers, clients, patients, or other stakeholders
- comments during a taught session which provide insights into what is expected of you as a student or for that module of study
- feedback from supervisors on work-placement.

If feedback is not provided in written form, consider how you will capture this and record it in your own notes so that you will be able to make use of it later.

Models of reflection

Reflection is now a key component of many professions and courses of study. Various models of reflection have developed that provide structures for considering the rather abstract or 'fuzzy' concept of 'learning through reflection on your own experiences'. A summary of some key models is provided below, so that you can recognise these when you see or hear them referred to, and draw on them to develop your own model of reflection.

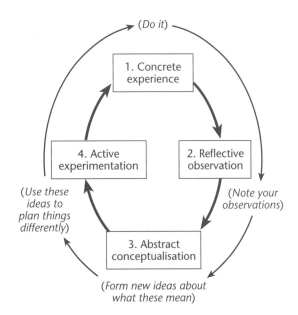

(*Do it*)

1. Concrete experience

2. Reflective observation

(*Note your observations*)

3. Abstract conceptualisation

(*Form new ideas about what these mean*)

4. Active experimentation

(*Use these ideas to plan things differently*)

The underlying concept

Reflective models, in summary, assume we can:

1 think about our experiences

2 understand them at a deeper level

3 learn from that thinking and understanding so as to effect change.

Staged models

Models of reflection often break down the various reflective processes into steps or stages. These stages are usually represented in the form of a cycle, the idea being that we can use what we have learnt from active reflection in order to bring greater understanding and better forward planning to similar experiences in the future. The reflective process may be conceived of in different ways, with a number of stages depending on the model.

Four stage Experiential Learning Cycle (*Kolb*)

Kolb's *Cycle* (1984) has been particularly influential on the developments in thinking about experiential learning.

Kolb's cycle consists of four stages:

1 Concrete experience: experience or action

2 Reflective observation: actively taking note of what you are observing about that experience

3 Abstract conceptualisation: forming ideas about what you have observed

4 Active experimentation: putting those new ideas into practice.

The third stage, *abstract conceptualisation*, gives significance to the act of drawing generalisations – an important cognitive step in identifying how one experience could relate to others.

Many-stage models

Other models have more and/or different stages, each focusing on particular components of the learning process such as:

● awareness of initial responses

● the impact of emotions on behaviour

● consideration of issues and theories

● etc.

A five-stage model, the core model for reflection (Cottrell, 2010), is provided below on page 207. Atkins and Murphy (1994) use a six-stage model incorporating stages for:

● *awareness* of thoughts and feelings

● *describing* these and the broader situation

● *analysing* them, challenging assumptions.

Reflection: Working with staged models

How useful do you think the concept of 'stages' would be for your own reflection?
Are you likely to work better with:

● a model that has few stages, and you elaborate the details and prompts yourself?

● a model with more stages, with prompts provided that you select from as needed?

Schön's model

Schön (1983) drew distinctions between reflecting:

- *in* action: reflecting on what you are doing whilst in the process of doing it, such as when experts call upon pre-existing knowledge as they work
- *on* action: making sense of an action or event once it is over, so as to learn from it for the future.

Many models refer back to this distinction. There is also a case for reflection:

- *before* action: drawing on knowledge (including theory), experience and input from others before you do something.

It is generally easier to reflect:

- Before action: as part of forward planning, putting aside time to find out useful information and examples of good practice, identifying relevant skills and learning or refreshing these; simulating difficult scenarios; practising what you are going to say or do, and giving thought to how this will all be put into action when needed.
- On action: putting time aside to think significant events through in detail, as outlined above.

Reflection: 'Before action' and 'in action'

Your response for the reflection above, 'Critical event' (page 231), was an example of reflection *on action* – so if you managed that, you know what that kind of reflection feels like. What kind of reflection do you think you could also undertake:

- *Before action*? (How would you plan differently in future for that kind of scenario?)
- *In action*: whilst you are actually in the midst of the scenario? What would you be able to call to mind and do differently whilst 'in action'?

Themes and focal points for reflection

There is a wide range of themes that could be used to provide a focus to reflection. For example, models could include broader contextual issues such as culture, society, politics, economics and media. These have an overarching influence on our experience – and our interpretations of that experience. Themes could include:

- Behaviours
- Interactions with or between others
- Feelings
- Knowledge
- Thoughts
- Theories
- Local practice
- Systems and structures
- Policies, procedures, rules
- Ideas
- Values
- Ethics
- Feedback from stakeholders
- Personal histories
- Language
- Broader issues (e.g. history, ideology, economics, politics, culture, media).

Activity **Focus points for reflection**

- Which of the points on the above list of focus points strike you as being of most relevance and interest to you when considering your experiences?

Example: focus on feelings

Boud, Keogh and Walker (1985) emphasised that experience, and reflections on experience, are both influenced by unconscious aspects such as emotions as well as conscious ones such as intent. Boud et al. argued that emotions tend to override our rational thinking without us being fully conscious of this, making us less aware of how and why we are acting as we do. If we re-evaluate an event, focusing on feelings and their impact, this helps us to identify how to manage similar events differently in the future.

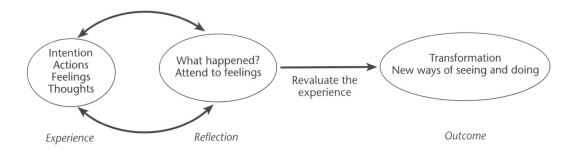

Intention	What happened?	Transformation
Actions	Attend to feelings	New ways of seeing and doing
Feelings		
Thoughts		

Revaluate the experience

Experience　　　　*Reflection*　　　　　　　*Outcome*

Adapted from Boud, Keogh and Walker (1985)

Developing your own model for reflection

Your current model?

Does your current model for action and reflection sound at all like the following?

I usually launch into action with a rough idea of what I think is needed. I work out my next steps as I go along, adapting to the evolving circumstances, using ideas that come into my head, or memories of doing something similar in the past, or other people's suggestions, or thinking on my feet as I read the situation and calculate what is needed. Often, I don't know why I did exactly what I did but it all works out pretty well anyway. Sometimes, if things go well, or someone compliments me, or if I feel things didn't go well, I find myself mulling over who did or said what, or what I should have said or done. I might remember this next time I am in that situation – but then again, I might not.

If you recognise this scenario, then you are in good company. Much of the time, this approach works well enough. Depending on the task, we form unconscious expertise in a variety of ways, such as training, practice, hearsay, reading, watching TV, or being around others who are experts. However, this model doesn't include setting time aside specifically to focus in a structured way on how things might be improved for the better.

Reflection: My current model

- Jot down a brief outline of how you approach your work and/or study or a particular kind of activity in which you engage.
- Is this generally true of you in most areas of life?

Why develop a better model for yourself?

We saw above that reflecting on your learning and experience is regarded as a means of deepening your understanding of how and why things work out the way they do for you. This can help you to make better decisions and exercise more control over the outcome of events. Reflection is a valuable tool.

Unless you are required by your work or course to use a particular model of reflection, then there is value in devising a model that:

- makes sense to you
- with (or without) prompt questions
- with as many stages as you find useful
- adapting existing models or starting from scratch.

The 'Core Model' below is suggested for you to adapt, drawing if you wish upon the models outlined above and selecting those focus points (page 234) that you feel pertinent to your experience.

Core Model for reflection

The Core Model below suggests 5 key components that you can draw from to help you formulate your own model.

1 Evaluate significance: is it worth reflection?
2 Reconstruct the experience: what happened?
3 Analyse: why did it happen that way?
4 Distil learning: draw out lessons for the future.
5 Apply: prepare for future situations.

Select those you find appropriate. Further details and prompts are provided below.

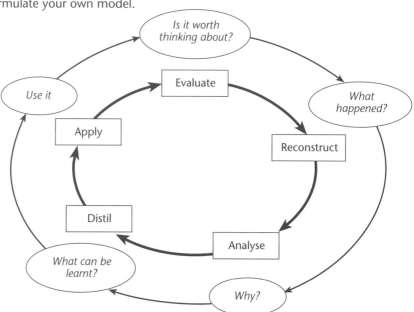

Core Model for Reflection (Cottrell, 2010)

1 Evaluate significance: Is it worth reflection?

Before launching into reflection, it is worth making an initial evaluation of the relative value of that experience as the focus of your reflective energies. Consider, for example, the following prompts:

- Will I encounter this kind of experience again?
- Could it provide lessons for the future?
- Does feedback from other people suggest I need to do this differently?
- Were there things I did really well that I could apply in the future?
- Would working this through help me understand niggles and concerns I have and how to deal with them?
- Is this a key aspect of my job that merits reflection from time to time?
- Would reflecting on this experience lead to positive outcomes for other people?
- Is there an aspect of my life, work or study that I take for granted but which could benefit from refreshed thinking?
- Does thinking about this experience arouse strong emotions suggesting it merits reflection?
- Is this the issue that most merits deeper reflection now?

2 Reconstructing the experience

This is the stage where you go through the surface aspects of the experience, from where you consider it 'starts' to where you consider it 'finishes'. Inevitably, this is an act of reconstruction, not an exact record. Draw out what you feel are the most salient points. You may find it helpful to consider the following prompts:

- *Events* Is it helpful to go through the storyline of the experience point by point, identifying who did what and when? Sometimes this helps to uncover details that might prove to be significant, sometimes not.
- *Intent* What was the purpose of your involvement? What were you aiming to achieve through your actions, words, silence or inaction?
- *Feelings* How did you feel during the experience? Do the feelings evoked in reconstructing the event throw any further light onto your own behaviour?

- *Your role*   What role did you think you were playing at the time? In retrospect, what role did you play? What was the impact of your involvement? What might have been different if you had not been present, or if someone else had taken the part you played?
- *Other people*   What part did others play? What could you have done to change the flow of interactions for the better?
- *Surface outcome*   What was the outcome? Did it end well? well enough? as a disaster?

3 Analysis: Why did it happen that way?

This is the analytical stage, where you go behind the surface events to examine why things unfolded in the way they did and arrive at a deeper understanding. Consider such questions as:

- What interpretations, explanations and theories help me to make sense of it?
- What was really going on for me? For others? On that day? In the place?
- Were the final outcomes as intended? If not, why not?
- Which actions, words, or omissions were most significant in the way events unfolded – or on the final outcomes?
- What made the situation better or worse?
- Did the scenario have roots in something that pre-dated that occasion?
- Is it really 'finished' or are there loose ends and bad feelings that could be addressed?

It was all her fault.

4 Distil: What lessons can be learnt?

What lessons do you draw from your reflection? For example:

- Positive features that are worth applying in the future?
- Trigger points that could be better managed?
- Skills you exercised and qualities you demonstrated that you could apply to similar situations?
- Specific actions that you, personally, could take or omit in similar situations so that things run more smoothly, harmoniously or with better consequences?
- Ways of tracking and managing your emotions and responses differently?
- Areas for training or practice?
- Awareness of other people's needs or issues and how these could be addressed differently?
- Would different preparation, planning, or timing produce better outcomes?
- Could different theoretical models apply?

5 Apply: Prepare for future situations

In this stage, give active consideration to how you will make use of your reflections so that they have an impact on future experiences. For example:

- *Identify your wish list*   What do you want to be different?
- *Identify potential scenarios*   What kinds of situations are suitable for applying what you have learnt?
- *Identify the consequences*   What will be different as a result of you changing the way you do things?
- *Who are the beneficiaries*   Who will gain as a result of these changes? What will be different for them?
- *Identify personal benefit that will motivate you to act*   What will you gain through these changes?
- *What will you do differently?*   (Focus on what *you personally* can do or say – as these are most under your control.)
- *Advance planning*   What preparation do you need to do now so as to respond differently in such situations in future?
- *Plan memory-joggers*   Once those situations arise, what will trigger your memory about what you wish to do?

Devise your own model for reflection

Jot down the steps or stages that you consider you would find it helpful to have in your model. In deciding this, give thought to the different steps you feel that you need to draw your attention to – so that you don't miss them out. Balance that against the number of steps that you feel will motivate you and be easy to remember.

Looking at the 'Core Model' above (page 236), decide whether you would wish to merge some of those stages into one or, alternatively, divide up further some of the stages of the Core Model.

Once you have decided on the number of steps, give each a name. Naming the stages may cause you to reconsider how many stages are really useful for you.

Once you have decided on your stages and the order that you want to place them in, use the pro-forma on page 239, to record these. If you find that you want to include more than six stages, copy the table and use two or more sheets.

- Use the first column to number your stages.
- Use the second column to record the name of each stage.
- Use the third column to devise a range of 'prompt questions' to structure your reflection. If you are not sure what to include, draw on those in the Core Model, on pages 236–7, as a starting place.

Activity   **Test your personal model for reflection**

- Identify one event – using step 1 of the 'Core Model for Reflection'.
- Using the model you have designed, work through your own stages and prompts.
- Consider, then, whether you wish to adapt your model.

Presenting your reflection to others

Raw reflection: first stage reflection

Most of us engage quite naturally in very deep reflection when we do it in our own time and way. It is important to capture such reflections in a way that suits our personal styles. However, such 'first stage' reflections are in raw form. They are not usually accessible to other people and are not necessarily in a form that is useful to you.

Worked reflection: second stage reflection

Second-stage reflection is characterised by:

Time   Leaving time between the initial reflection and the current stage of reflection.

Summary   Second-stage reflection seeks out and summarises key themes and salient points, noting down where more detailed evidence can be found in the portfolio.

Insight   Identifying what has been learnt – especially the less obvious learning. This will refer to broad themes rather than specific subject knowledge. It will bring out issues of relevance and significance rather than focus on data. During second-stage reflection you come to appreciate the deeper and subtler aspects of your learning.

Communication   It is at this point that you are ready to consider presenting the results of your reflection to others. The context will determine what it is appropriate to show to others. For most purposes, you will need to remove:

- material about your personal life you wish to keep private
- personal details about other people
- repetitive or irrelevant material
- unnecessary examples
- materials produced by other people, such as guideline materials, tutor notes, copies of background reading, lecture notes, etc.

Personal model for reflection

See page 238 for guidance on devising your model for reflection and using this pro-forma.

Stage number	Name of this stage	Prompt questions

Submitting reflections to tutors

You may be asked to submit your reflections to tutors either as part of assessment, or for more informal monitoring. If so, you may be asked to submit either raw or worked reflections, or both. For example, you may be asked to submit a journal, log or extracts from a blog as part of a portfolio of materials.

Alternatively you might be asked to draw on your reflections as the basis of work undertaken in class or to provide material within an assessment such as an essay, case study, position paper or observation, without there being a requirement to submit your journal.

Confidentiality

NB   If anyone else will see these reflections, check first that you have not included names or other information that identify people, departments or organisations without their express permission. The details you provide should not enable people to make a good guess at who is being referred to in your reflections or any other assignment.

Submitting selective portfolios

If your tutors are going to mark your portfolio, they will look for such factors as:

How well it meets the required learning outcomes. How well the portfolio overall meets the learning outcomes of the unit, module or course; make sure you know what these are before you start to put your portfolio together. These are usually provided in a handbook or on a website for the course.

How well you summarise your insights into your learning (or the subject of the portfolio). Most marks are likely to be given for the reflective essay, position paper or similar document, which draws together the main points, rather than for raw reflection and supporting documents, important though these are too.

How well you select and edit relevant information for inclusion in the portfolio. Large, unedited portfolios that contain all the information you could possibly gather on a subject are unlikely to impress. Bulk does not usually gain marks. The tutor is likely to give marks specifically for skills in selecting,

drawing out clearly what is relevant, good editing and cross-referencing.

How well the evidence and examples you refer to in the portfolio really do support the point you are making. If you say the evidence demonstrates a particular skill or insight, it must be a very clear example. You need to specify how skills or the application of theory were demonstrated, rather than assuming these are obvious to the tutor.

How well the portfolio is constructed. Clear contents; all documents labelled; the summary writing makes exact cross-references to the page where the evidence can be found. Use a highlighter pen or number the lines to indicate exactly where the tutor should look to find the evidence if these are submitted in paper form. If you are submitting this electronically, you can use editing and reviewing functions such as those for inserting comments, to provide a commentary on your text. If you make vague references to long free-ranging reflections, leaving the tutor to find what you are referring to, this is unlikely to be accepted.

How well you select one or two good pieces of evidence for each main point you make. More than one piece of evidence is usually not needed or wanted.

How well you draw on relevant theory as part of your reflections. If you are submitting work as part of an academic assessment, then it is generally assumed that you will demonstrate that you are aware of which theories are relevant and how these provide insights on the issue under consideration.

In other words, good guidance for portfolios is:

- include a contents page and a strong summary document (e.g. position paper or essay)
- label and signpost clearly
- back up your main points with good evidence
- cross-reference your argument clearly to evidence in the portfolio
- include only essential evidence
- keep it as succinct as possible.

A reflective essay

Purpose

Some programmes set reflective essays as marked assignments. The contents of the essay will vary depending on the focus of the programme and the purpose of the essay. For example, some programmes ask for a reflective piece of writing at the beginning of the programme in order to encourage students to focus on their goals and learning needs. Others set an essay at the end of a module for students to draw together their learning and identify next steps.

Usually, you will be given specific guidance on what is required. If not, the guidance below outlines features typical of reflective essays. The structure is not dissimilar to that of other essays. The content and style are distinct.

Structure

Like any other essay, a reflective essay will have:

- a specific title: you must structure your essay to respond to the question contained within the title

- an introduction that identifies your overall position and prepares the reader for what to expect from the essay

- a main body divided into paragraphs: this does not usually contain any headings or bullet points

- a conclusion that sums up the main points: this does not introduce any new material

- references to source materials within the text

- a list of all references at the end of the text.

Contents of a reflective PDP essay

Typically, a reflective essay will contain a selection of the following elements.

Personal aims and goals

- Why did you choose your programme: what were your aims and objectives?

- Have these changed since starting the programme? In what ways and for what reasons?

Expectations

- What were you expecting from the programme?

- What did you expect from yourself?

- What led you to form these expectations?

Programme learning outcomes

- What are the learning outcomes for modules you have taken so far?

- What skills development is linked to the modules you have taken?

- How do these outcomes and skills correspond to your own aims and goals?

Other activity

- What else do you do outside of your programme in order to achieve your personal goals or to supplement your learning for the programme?

Learning goals and targets

- What are your current areas of strength in relation to your programme, career or life ambitions?

- Which areas do you need to improve?

- What are the priority areas for improvement as 'learning goals'?

- What are your targets, milestones and time-scales for meeting these learning goals?

Personal reflection

- What methods have you used for reflection?

- How do you use reflection?

- A detailed example of how you developed and evaluated your performance in one area.

Use of feedback

- What kinds of feedback have you received from tutors, students, employers or other people?

- How do you feel about this feedback?

- How have you made use of this feedback?

Evaluation of personal choices

- In practice, how far does the programme meet personal goals and interests?

- Would any other programme or set of modules be more suitable for you?

- What other subject choices, additional modules or supplementary programmes would help you to meet your personal goals?

Evaluation of learning

- How well are you achieving the learning outcomes of your programme?

- What else have you learnt through the programme?
- What are you gaining, additionally, from your programme or from university that was not part of your original goals?

Evaluation of the programme

- How does each module or aspect of your programme contribute to your professional and personal development?

Evaluation of personal performance

- How well are you achieving your personal goals?

- How well have you engaged with your programme? (Attendance? Punctuality? Level of interest? Contributions made in class? Efforts to make personal meaning of the course material? Additional reading or work undertaken?)

- How far do you consider you have taken responsibility for improving your own learning?

Personal development

- How have your opinions, attitudes, beliefs or values changed since starting at university?

- In what ways have you changed as a person since starting at university?

Critical incident

- Identify an incident that illustrates your approach to your learning.

- What does this incident demonstrate about you?

- How does this incident relate to any theories of learning you have covered on your programme?

- What did you learn from this incident?

- See the Reflection on p. 231 above, and the Critical Incident Sheet in the Resource Bank, page 345.

Use of theory

A reflective essay is still an academic piece of work. You should draw on your background reading for the subject, relating your own experiences to the theoretical perspective relevant to your programme of study. Consider:

- Does your experience support or exemplify theories you have covered in class or through your background reading?

- Or does your experience run counter to those theories? If so, why might that be the case? What is different about your experience that might account for this?

Style

Reflective essays are about your own experience. This means that it is more acceptable for these to be written in the first person ('I', 'We').

Personal statement

Personal statements are important tools for making real use of on-going observation, reflection and evaluation. They are characterised by:

- being written in a more formal manner than reflection for personal purposes

- drawing together learning that has taken place

- identifying themes (from a portfolio or journal) and summarising these

- identifying the overall path that developmental work has taken over a period of time

- identifying the lessons that have been learnt

- evaluating current performance

- making recommendations for future improvement

- identifying action that needs to be taken.

The emphasis of a personal statement may differ depending on whether it is written:

- at the beginning of a programme

- as developmental work within a programme

- for assessment or submission at the end of a programme

- for a specific purpose such as a job application.

An example is provided on page 213.

Example

Personal statement

This semester, I took three modules in Business Studies. These covered project management, business communication and entrepreneurship. I was able to draw out several themes that ran across the three modules.

First of all, the communication skills were important in identifying ways of varying a message so that it comes across to very different audiences: client groups, bank managers, the buying public, products aimed at different age groups and at people who purchase for those client groups. We also focused on communication within teams.

Communication skills
Communication skills were important to my entrepreneurship project as I was part of a team that took a product (light-weight collapsible bikes) through from idea to design to market. We drew up a business plan that we presented to a funding panel. There was an accountant on the panel who gave us feedback on our presentations. Although our group did not win the funding, we were given valuable advice on what a business plan should look like and how to communicate its strengths when asking for funding.

The entrepreneurship students were not all from a business background: some were from product design, fine art, engineering, marketing and multi-media. One important lesson was in discovering that students from each discipline use very different ways of describing their work process and the product than we expect from a business perspective. Although we learnt that we have to find a common vocabulary, a shared way of communicating, we could have approached this is in a more organised way and avoided some misunderstandings. Communication for team work across disciplines is an area that I would like to investigate further.

Team work
The product designers and engineers, in particular, approached their work in ways that the business students found challenging. This meant that we had to establish ground rules for working together as a team. This took several attempts because our starting points were so different. We had not anticipated this and did not realise   n the beginning, each of us was unwilling to compromise on methods we had been trained in.

However, as the deadlines drew closer, we made a choice to develop a hybrid way of working that met the needs of the project rather than what we thought we should do as 'business students' or 'design students'. This felt like a risky strategy but we were encouraged by our tutors, who gave us some useful tips on how to negotiate a strategy ...

Position papers

A position paper is a 'snapshot' of where you are now, which draws together reflections on your personal development. Typically, its format follows a time-line from past to future. You are usually asked to:

- look back over past experience and identify what you have learned from your experience

- evaluate your current position

- project forward to where you wish to be

- decide a plan of action that takes you from where you are now to where you wish to be in the future, using your past experience

- identify how you will be able to recognise when you have achieved your goals.

To write a position paper, you can draw upon entries from your reflective journal, responses to activities in this book, self-evaluations and action plans. A possible structure is suggested below, organised through a series of questions. You can use these to guide you, selecting relevant questions. Where possible, include references to texts you have read in order to support your reasoning.

Orientation

Aspirations and motivation: where am I going?

- What are your aims for your future? Where would you like to see yourself in five or ten years' time? (Be imaginative and bold.)

- In what ways do you think your programme will help you to achieve those aims?

- What skills and attributes do you want to develop whilst at university?

Review

What do I bring from my past?

- What has led you to the present stage in your study or career?

- What has inspired you? (Give references where possible.)

- How has your past learning and life experience equipped you for this course and for being a student now? Evaluate the knowledge, qualifications, skills, attitudes and experiences that you bring with you and which are relevant to your study and goals.

Appraisal

Where am I now?

- What skills and abilities will be required of you as a student on this course?

- What are your main strengths and weaknesses as a student on this course?

- What will you need to improve in order to do well?

Planning

How will I achieve my aims?

- How do you plan to achieve your ambitions and study aims? What are you going to do, when and how?

- What targets have you set as milestones (to what time-scales)?

- What difficulties might you encounter?

- In what ways might you sabotage your own success? What steps will you take to prevent yourself or others from sabotaging your success?

- How will you keep yourself motivated?

- What other preparation and planning do you need to undertake?

Evaluating progress

What have I achieved?

- How will you be able to recognise that you have achieved your aims?

- What changes do you expect to see in yourself, your work, and in the attitudes of others when you have achieved your aims?

- How will you be able to demonstrate to others what you have achieved?

Extrapolation
What have I learned?

- What have you learned about yourself or your learning that was unexpected in some way?

- How might this learning help you more generally with your studies, life and work?

References

Include references to books, films, music or other sources that have inspired you on your journey to where you are today. Include references to all materials you have used in writing the position paper. Remember to use the correct referencing system, such as the Harvard or Vancouver system, as recommended by your tutors.

Closing comments

Reflection is not something that comes easily to everyone. However, there are many strategies and approaches that can be used to develop your skills in undertaking reflection. Reflective abilities develop over time and with practice.

- Put time aside on a regular basis to reflect upon your performance.

- Use a structured approach. Make use of activities in the book if you are not sure where to begin.

- Read back over your reflections on a regular basis. Look for themes.

- Consider regularly how far you have achieved personal goals.

- Find approaches that suit you and your programme.

- Look for changes in yourself, your actions, goals or values.

- Notice and celebrate your achievements.

- Be positive about the process: over time, you will see the benefits.

Further reading

Boud, D., Keogh, R. and Walker, D. (1985) *Reflection: Turning Experience into Learning* (London: Routledge).

Buzan, T. (2006) *The Mind Map Book* (London: BBC Active).

Cottrell, S. M. (2010) *Skills for Success*, 2nd edn (Basingstoke: Palgrave Macmillan).

Cottrell, S.M. (2011) *Critical Thinking Skills: Developing Effective Analysis and Argument* (Basingstoke: Palgrave Macmillan).

Cottrell, S.M. (2013) *The Study Skills Handbook*, 4th edn (Basingstoke: Palgrave Macmillan).

Mezirow, J. (ed.) (1990) *Fostering Critical Reflection in Adulthood: A Guide to Transformative and Emancipatory Learning* (San Francisco: Jossey-Bass).

Moon, J. (2004) *A Handbook of Reflective and Experiential Learning: Theory and Practice* (London: RoutledgeFalmer).

Thompson, S. and Thompson, N. (2008) *The Critically Reflective Practitioner* (Basingstoke: Palgrave Macmillan).

Part 4

Employability: enhancing your career prospects

Getting a good job is high on the list of priorities for most students.

Whilst some know exactly what kind of work and career they want, many have only vaguely formulated ideas or even no idea at all. Whether or not you know what you want to do, you can still start to prepare ahead now, so that, when the right job comes along, you are ready.

The likelihood is that, sooner or later, you will be competing with others for a job, placement or internship that you really want. At that point, you will want to feel confident that you understand what is required of you and that you are well-prepared both for the appointments process and for the requirements of your new role.

Whilst it is not impossible to gain a great job with minimum effort, it is unusual. It is much more likely that you will succeed in your application if you have put some time into preparation and into understanding the field. This means:

- Understanding the appointments process from the perspective of a recruiting employer
- Understanding what you really want from your next, or first, job
- Knowing how to manage the appointments process, from first contact through to acceptance, or rejection, and beyond.

This section looks at employability from the angle both of the employer and of you, the potential job applicant. It can help you to clarify such things as:

- What employers look for in job applicants
- What is meant by employability
- Whether you should apply for a particular job or placement
- How you can make a strong application
- The kinds of appointments processes that you may encounter and what employers look for when they use these
- How to keep records, prepare and practise so that you feel more confident and more in control during the appointments process
- How to make good use of placements and current work, in preparation for the future
- Whether you want to work for yourself rather than for anyone else and, if so, where to start.

Chapters in this section
9   What do employers want?
10 Getting the job you want
11 Maintaining good personal records

Chapter 9
What do employers really want?

Balanced consideration

It is natural, when looking for a job and reading job advertisements, to look at how each role would suit us. Matching the job to our own needs is, of course, important, at least where there is some choice, and this point is addressed in Chapter 10. However, you are more likely to be offered a job if you are also able to consider new roles from an employer's perspective. Aim to balance your interests with the business needs of the prospective employer.

Understanding employers

This chapter helps you to understand employers so that you are better placed to take on board their needs. It provides guidance on:

- What is meant by 'the labour market'
- Generic attributes, such as work-readiness, that employers look for
- The skills and other attributes most in demand by employers
- Continuities over time in what employers say they want from graduate appointments.

Translate your skills

You will have developed a wealth of skills through your course of study. That is a bonus, but is not necessarily sufficient in itself. Your job applications will be more powerful if you can articulate your skills in ways that make sense in terms of the workplace.

This chapter helps you to look at your skills from an employment perspective.

Yourself as employer

There is an alternative to working for someone else and that is working for yourself. It is worth considering whether you would prefer to run your own business, either now or at some time in the future. This is an exciting option and many new businesses and start-ups have been formed by students and new graduates. You will have a chance to consider some of the pros and cons of this option.

What is employability?

Employability

Employability is a concurrence of:

- capability
- preparedness for employment
- and the relevance of these to the current job market.

The term can be used:

1 in general terms, to mean that you have the abilities needed to gain a job and keep it, or

2 in a narrower sense, with reference to your readiness for a particular range of roles, such as graduate jobs, or specialist posts in a given field, or

3 in relative terms, to indicate how strong your chances are of gaining a job compared with the competition.

Capability

In this context, your *capability* is the sum of your skills, knowledge, experience, habits, understandings, attitudes, qualities and personal attributes. These are relevant to gaining a job, keeping it, and making it work for you.

Preparedness

Preparedness is the outcome of the time, thought and practice you have put into developing and nurturing your capability from the perspective of future employment and for the appointments process itself. It includes your readiness, and ability, to make use of the opportunities that present themselves and/ or to create opportunities for yourself.

Employability capabilities

For students, developing skills for employability involves the following.

1 *Career development*: Being proactive and self-directing in gaining a portfolio of qualifications, attributes and experiences either that enable you to pursue a given career path, or that open up a range of future career opportunities.

2 *Labour market awareness*: Knowing what kinds of work are likely to be available, and being able to match your strengths, qualities and interests to these.

3 *Articulation*: Being able to recognise, evidence and demonstrate your strengths to employers during job application processes.

4 *Self-awareness*: Developing insight so that you are able to recognise your own strengths and preferences, as well as the significance of these, when making choices and decisions that have an impact on your career path.

5 *Self-management*: Building the perseverance, resilience, confidence, beliefs, motivation and attitudes needed to manage the demands of applying for work, responding constructively to setbacks, and presenting yourself at your best.

> **Reflection: Employability capabilities**
>
> - Which of these capabilities are strengths for you already?
> - Which do you need to investigate further?

must develop leadership skills. Jason says I am a bit of a follower

Put yourself in the employers' shoes

The employer's WIIFT

You are much more likely to impress an employer if you come across as having the business's interests in mind. Bright and Earl (2000) recommend that when applying for jobs, candidates should always keep in mind 'an employer's WIIFT'. WIIFT stands for 'What's In It For Them'?

- *Use the information available:* if the employer has provided background information and a job description, look at this in detail.
- *Investigate:* find out about the company, such as from its website, Companies House, LinkedIn, or their presence in social media.
- *Use common sense and empathy:* give some thought to why the employer is likely to be advertising for this post. What do they really need done? What would make life easier for them in looking for the right candidate?

Minimum effort, minimum cost

When employers advertise a new post, clearly they have work that needs to be done. Naturally, they want to get that work done with minimum costs, training and lost time. They will want someone up to speed with the job as soon as possible in order to avoid additional work for existing staff and to reduce any delays or disruption to clients and other stakeholders.

Generally, that means they look for applicants who, as far as possible …

- already have the skills, knowledge, experience, qualities, and desired behaviours outlined in the person specification for the job
- demonstrate a good understanding of the role and the business
- inspire confidence that they can get on with the job straightaway, with minimum direction, supervision and training
- share the values of the business.

Do employers all want the same things?

Every employer is different. The requirements of the first few employers might not be the same as those of the next. Just because you were not a match for one employer it does not mean that you won't be exactly what the next employer is looking for. If one employer was impressed by your course or your skills, these might not be relevant to the next. Such differences mean it is essential to investigate the requirements of

- the occupational sector
- individual employers
- each job.

Do they all want experience?

- Some employers recruit only people with previous work experience and practical expertise in the field.
- Others are keen to recruit recent graduates that they can train into the culture of the organisation. They look for candidates who could learn quickly on the job and meet their essential criteria. Some offer training or graduate schemes; others do not.
- Some employers prefer to focus on attitude, values or behaviours.

You should be able to tell which approach an employer will take, such as by looking at their website and reading the material provided about the job.

What employers want: large employers and SMEs

Understanding the labour market

Undergraduates are often advised to make sure they understand the labour market. That can seem a rather daunting task: it may feel hard to know where to begin or even what that means. Below, there is some key information about the labour market that provides a starting place to focus your research and thinking.

Where are most jobs to be found?

Large employers

Large employers will recruit, at most, only 10% of the total number of students graduating in any year (Wilson, 2012). Despite this, much of the information about what employers want is drawn from a relatively small number of large employers; such employers also play a prominent role in graduate job fairs and in job news.

The largest recruiter of graduates in the UK in 2014 was Teach First (1550 vacancies). This was followed by PricewaterhouseCooper (PwC) with 1200 vacancies, and Deloitte with 1000 (High Fliers Research, 2014). In 2013, PwC received over 22,000 applications for graduate places, and Teach First had 1262 places and 7602 applicants. As competition for such jobs is fierce, consider whether your application is likely to be competitive for the field.

Small and Medium Enterprises (SMEs)

The majority of graduate jobs are in SMEs: you are more likely to get a job with an SME than with a large company. According to BIS (2014), there were 4.8 million SMEs in the UK in 2013. This accounted for 99.95% of the total number of UK enterprises in the private sector, and 59% of employment in the UK Private Sector. The sector is dominated by businesses with fewer than 50 employees. Three sectors account for 44% of employment in enterprises in all sectors, these being (a) Construction; (b) Professional, scientific and technical; and (c) Wholesale and retail (Sear et al., 2012).

The importance of work placements

In 2014, employers anticipated that 37% of their graduate entry level positions would be given to graduates who had worked with them already in a work placement, paid internship or vacation work (High Fliers Research, 2014). Such experience gives a head start in gaining work with a company. However, it may also be reassuring to note that if you didn't get a placement with your first choice of employer, the large majority of their job opportunities don't go to those who have worked for them already.

'Most wanted' characteristics

Based on a survey of over 200 employers, large and small, Pennington et al. (2013) found employers gave their highest ratings to the following four items (out of eleven possible items).

(a) Interest in role
(b) Organisational fit
(c) Skills
(d) Work experience.

These findings are not untypical of various surveys of employers. However, each employer will give a different weighting to such characteristics and to their own organisational needs, so must be researched separately.

Behaviours, values and attitudes

Different sectors and companies look for particular characteristics in their staff. Pharmaceutical giant GlaxoSmithKline (GSK) expects all employees, whether new graduates or top management, to demonstrate a small set of key behaviours, which are available via their website. This emphasis on 'behaviours' is not unusual in large companies.

On the other hand, charities tend to put their emphasis on values. Law companies tend to lay emphasis on 'passion' for working in the legal field, commercial awareness, and people skills (TARGETjobs Law, 2014).

Evidence of career planning

Pennington et al. (2013) found that employers place value on students' having engaged in extra-curricular activities – but that students did not always recognise this or take it seriously. Employers also expect students to have firm career ideas by their final year and to show evidence of career planning. It is probably worth noting that the majority of employers don't know about the Higher Education Achievement Record (HEAR) used in UK universities, so it is best not to assume that they know what this is. Instead, draw on this to answer their questions.

Importance of degree classification?

Many employers state that they want a 2.1 or first class degree for some or all of their graduate posts. However, overall, Pennington's research found that both large companies and SMEs rated a 2.1 degree only fifth in importance out of 11 selection criteria.

Importance of educational institution?

In a list of 11 selection criteria, employers rated 'university attended' 10th, just ahead of 'school attended'. Overall, 74% of employers stated that their decisions to offer a job were not influenced by a graduate's institution. However, this was more pronounced for large companies, 91% of which agreed they were not influenced by the institution, compared with only 64% of SMEs.

Despite this, because of the costs involved, over 40% of employers preferred to focus recruitment on a limited number of specific institutions. They targeted institutions with the right courses for their field, and those in their geographical area.

Mobility and flexibility

Geographical mobility: large employers seek graduates prepared to be mobile to take up work;

they find graduates, especially those from low income backgrounds, tend to prefer to return to their home region after university (Pennington et al., 2013).

Job mobility: employers also prefer graduates who are mobile in moving between sectors and job roles early on in their career. Docherty and Fernandez (2014) note that this may 'come as a surprise to graduates and HE providers, for whom advice has emphasised a focus on developing skills and experience in a particular subject or sector of employment'.

UCAS tariff points

A third of large employers stipulate a minimum UCAS tariff (large employers are three times as likely as SMEs to state this).

What do SMEs want from graduates?

SMEs are far more varied than large employers, not least because there are so many of them. It can be hard to find generic information about SMEs. You may need to check with occupational sectors, sector skills councils, professional organisations and trade magazines for information about SMEs in particular occupational areas.

Miller (2014) identified the top attributes of the employees of small businesses as the following:

1   Bringing a 'can do' attitude and willingness to work beyond the core job description
2   Welcoming new opportunities and looking for opportunities to develop their role
3   Holding ambitions for the company where they work, seeking entrepreneurial opportunities for it
4   Working well in small teams
5   Being innovative, coming up with new ideas and ways of doing things better.

Activity ↻ **Which characteristics?**

Browse a range of job adverts on-line for SMEs in occupational areas that interest you. What kinds of graduate attributes are they looking for, typically?

What employers want: work readiness

...ork readiness?

...y they want students to be wor... ...eady. Having any work, whether paid or voluntary, part-time or full-time, helps to develop an understanding of what this entails. 'Work readiness' is hard to define precisely, but includes the following attributes.

Attitude

Employers want to take on new staff who identify with the needs of their business. Generally, employers are more likely to employ you if you:

- **bring a 'can-do' attitude**, undertaking reasonable tasks when asked (rather than when you feel like it or finding excuses not to)
- **take pride in your work**, going the extra mile when needed and being professional in all you do
- **use time effectively**, being punctual for work and meetings, and getting work done efficiently
- **spend work time efficiently**, remaining focused on your job rather than texting and phoning family and friends, browsing the internet for personal use, running personal errands, sorting out relationship issues, day-dreaming, writing your novel, playing computer games, taking long breaks, etc.
- **are generally helpful and flexible**, taking on additional paid hours or changing work hours, or working in a new location, if needed.

Professionalism

In a professional role: this means having the abilities and skills to undertake the specialist work associated with the role, to the required professional standards and adhering to relevant codes of practice.

In general: for any role, this is about the way you approach your work at all times. It involves setting out to produce work of a consistently high standard, with attention to such things as accuracy, precision, timeliness, punctuality, courtesy, sensitivity, and respect for the dignity, safety and well-being of others.

Olive prided herself on being four pairs of safe hands for her employer

'Customer service' approach

Employers usually want staff who are able and willing to 'put the customer first', even when this might be inconvenient or difficult. The same is true if the 'customer' is a client, student, patient or member of the public making an enquiry. There are usually protocols to follow about what to do and what to say in difficult situations. This is also a question of attitude and professionalism.

A 'safe pair of hands'

Employers value staff who they can depend on to:

- get the job done as they would want
- make sensible, workable decisions that are suitable to the context
- meet deadlines and other given requirements
- avoid reckless, unprofessional or risky or unwanted behaviours.

What employers want: work readiness

Initiative

Using your initiative in the workplace means:

- **working independently** – getting on with your job with minimum direction
- **being resourceful** – using imagination and inventiveness to address a problem or issue in a practical way
- **being proactive** – rather than waiting to be asked to do something or responding to what emerges, take action or ask how you can help
- **looking for improvements and alternatives** – thinking beyond the immediate task to consider how the overall outcome or process could be improved, and then taking your idea forward through the correct channels for the organisation
- **knowing when to act** – developing a fine sense of when it is appropriate for you to come up with your own ideas and ways of getting things done, and when it is more important to follow protocols exactly
- **seizing opportunity** – being able to spot occasions for advancing the business interests in the moment, often in a small but appropriate way, and getting on with it.

Understand how organisations work

Although it is unlikely that you will need to answer direct questions about how businesses operate, employers will look to see your general commercial and business awareness. They will notice if you don't seem to understand the basics.

(a) Browse employers' websites and financial reports on-line to get a feel for how businesses are run and the kinds of things that concern them.

(b) Become familiar with concepts such as
  - 'end-users', shareholders, stakeholders
  - vision, mission, strategy and business plans
  - company values
  - financial sustainability; profit and loss;
  - company performance; performance indicators; targets
  - staff appraisal, performance management.

(c) The checklists 'Make effective use of your experience of work' (pp. 280–2) provide a structured way of thinking through some of the above issues.

Understanding why 'time = money'

'Time is money' is a well-known adage in business. Broadly speaking, employers have a range of costs such as salaries, pensions, accommodation, maintenance, insurance, utilities and investment, all of which they have to cover even if they have less money coming in because of time wasted. When taking on new staff, employers will be looking for people who can use time efficiently.

Commercial/business sense

Increasingly, employers are asking for 'business acumen' or commercial understanding, especially for graduate jobs and management or team leader roles. They look for some evidence of interest in the kinds of issues relevant to their business. This might be such matters as: whether there is a good market currently for its goods; how that market might be changing; customer demographics; likely new competition or opportunities at home or overseas; costs; logistics; technological changes or recent innovations and their impact. If you are interested in the company, then you should be able to give sensible answers based on some research, some thought, and common sense.

You can build your commercial awareness for the kinds of business that interest you by:

- taking optional modules in business, enterprise or entrepreneurship
- reading trade or professional magazines
- a relevant work-placement or internship
- browsing questions and answers on LinkedIn
- talking to your Careers Service about relevant sources of information and websites.

What employers want: specialists or generalists?

Subject specialists or 'generalists'?

Almost all employers have graduate jobs open to students of any discipline. This is true even in sectors that may appear specialist, such as finance, management, accounting, HR, law, marketing, communications and advertising: these have jobs open to graduates of any degree subject, especially for those who achieve a good degree grade/classification – not just for those with specialist degrees.

Some roles do require a particular degree subject and specialist knowledge and expertise. That is especially the case for professional and technical roles such as in medicine and health, engineering and languages.

Even when a specialism is required, this is used as an initial filter to cut down the field of applicants. After that, employers look at all the other attributes a candidate may bring. For specialist roles, an applicant with the right specialist degree, a rounded portfolio and who meets the person specification will have a good chance of being short-listed.

Rounded applicants

Not all employers value subject specialisation. Increasingly, and especially in the international labour market, value is being placed on graduates who can draw flexibly across a range of disciplines and experiences. This position was articulated in the report *An Avalanche is Coming*:

> *The trend in the academy towards specialisation, which is at least a century old, continues unabated, but citizens of the world now cry out for synthesis – synthesis now provided largely outside of the academy by organisations such as OECD.* (Barber et al., 2013, p. 17)

There is a growing interest in employees who demonstrate a breadth of knowledge and experiences, who can connect these up, contextualise them, and identify the opportunities that arise. Steve Jobs, founder of Apple, wrote that, for the field of design and technology, it was essential for employees to be able to draw on as wide a range of experiences as possible (Jobs, 2011).

Like many innovators, he saw the value of a broad education rather than a narrow focus on a particular specialism alone.

Ability to innovate and integrate skills

Employers look for people who demonstrate that they can come up with soundly based ideas and then carry these through. Shell (2014), for example, stated:

> *We're looking for people with the intellectual, analytical and creative ability to learn quickly, identify issues and propose solutions. Can you reach informed conclusions through broad thinking? Can you work with incomplete or conflicting data and take well-calculated risks? Have you ever identified new ways of doing things based on an analysis of current conditions, data and feedback?*

Shell also states that its ideal candidates should display an ability to work effectively as part of a diverse team and form mutually beneficial, long-term working relationships, as well as demonstrate characteristics and achievements which could identify them as future leaders.

You might like to consider how you would demonstrate such abilities – and how you could develop them.

Broad approach to development

Typically, employers will be interested in your broad personal development. That is why universities and colleges encourage students to take part in activities outside of the formal curriculum and to start to build their CV as early as possible.

Reflection: Being a strong generalist

As there are so many jobs available for graduates with good generic abilities, it is worth considering how you would demonstrate how you could draw on a wide range of experiences.

What could you do to broaden your knowledge, expertise base and abilities further to better match the descriptions outlined above?

What employers want: how does this change?

How stable are employers' requirements?

When studying for your qualification, it is reasonable to wonder whether the skills that you are developing now will still be those that employers will want in a few years' time. Broadly speaking, the list of 'most wanted skills' does not change significantly over time but the range of skills required is extended.

Activity — Continuities and changes in employers' requirements

Compare the themes that occur in the employer skills needs (identified on p. 258) and Miller's report (2014) (p. 253).

- Note which skills needs remain constant.
- Note the additional skills that have appeared recently.
- Where do your own strengths and skills gaps lie with respect to these?

1998 TMP Research

Research by TMP Worldwide Research (1998) found the top five skills most valued by employers were:

- oral communication
- team working
- listening
- written communication
- problem-solving.

1998 CVCP Report

In 1998, the Committee of University Vice-Chancellors (CVCP) commissioned research by Coopers and Lybrand to identify 'employability skills' for graduates. This outlined four categories of graduate attributes.

1 Traditional intellectual skills
The ability to: evaluate evidence critically; argue logically; apply theory to practice; model problems qualitatively and quantitatively; challenge taken-for-granted assumptions.

2 Core or key skills
Communication; application of number; working with others; information and communications technology; improving one's own performance.

3 Personal attributes
Self-reliance; adaptability; flexibility; 'nous'; creativity.

4 Knowledge about how organisations work
The report points out that it is important that employability skills include this fourth area.

2009 CBI report

Ten years later, employers continued to want such skills but new items were being added to the list, such as 'cultural awareness'. For example, in March 2009, the CBI (Confederation of British Industry) and Universities UK released the report 'Future fit – preparing graduates for the world of work', based on a survey of 581 employers.

Employers rated 'Employability skills' as the most important factor in recruiting graduates. They were keen to find self-management, team working and a 'can do' approach in applicants. They were broadly satisfied with graduates' IT and numeracy skills, but less than satisfied by how well graduates were able to demonstrate skills in communication and literacy, business and customer awareness, and self-management.

2011 Lowden report

A report by Lowden et al. (2011) of HEIs and 22 leading employer organisations such as the CBI, the Association of Graduate Recruiters and Council for Industry in Higher Education (CIHE) identified employers' 'most wanted' characteristics. The top five skills and attributes most sought in graduate employees were:

- team working
- problem-solving
- self-management
- knowledge of the business
- literacy and numeracy skills relevant to the post.

What employers want: most-wanted skills

Leadership and management

In practice, employers are often looking for graduates who can step up quickly into managerial roles. That is why they are keen to see evidence of the following:

- *'Academic' / intellectual skills*: strategic thinking, making good decisions, exercising good judgement, analysing information, finding solutions, bringing a creative or innovative approach.
- *People / interpersonal skills*: managing relationships in the work place, team work, communicating clearly, inspiring, encouraging and supporting to get things done well and efficiently, understanding customers, clients and competitors.
- *Task-management / operational skills*: organisational skills, managing projects, setting goals, developing systems and processes, monitoring performance, using resources efficiently, managing money, all with attention to detail.
- *Self-management / intrapersonal skills*: the ability to manage your own needs, emotions, motivation and development so that you are able to work well under pressure and focus on your responsibilities.

Reflection: Using employers' steer

The quotations from employers in this chapter, and the lists and other information provided, offer insights into what employers want.

- From these, what messages do you take away as relevant to you?
- How can you act upon those messages?

Skills for particular jobs

Advertisements usually list the most important features of the job, including skills requirements. Browsing through the job advertisements associated with career areas that interest you will help you form a picture of the relevant skills for you to develop.

Activity **Job advertisements**

- Find at least 20 advertisements for jobs in career areas that interest you. To find these, you can look in locations such as the Careers Service vacancy bulletin, main national newspapers and leading websites for graduate vacancies (see pp. 385–6).
- For the range of jobs that most interest you, which kinds of skills are referred to the most often?

How strong are your own skills in these areas?

- Complete competence sheets (pp. update 346–82) for the skills relevant to your career interests and place these in your personal records.

Skills in context: same words, different assumptions

Although employers and job adverts may use the same words as HEIs when speaking of skills, the terminology often means something different in a work context. Employers do value the skills developed by a university or college education, but do not always understand or value examples of these drawn from academic contexts. They like to see examples of those skills being used in work and 'real-life' contexts.

Pages 260–6 can help you to break down your skills into some of their component parts, and to identify how these might be articulated in ways that make more sense to employers.

What employers say

Disciplined ambition

I like to see someone with a lot of ambition, that doesn't flow into arrogance; somebody who is hungry to learn, but at the same time is disciplined to actually put it into practice and put the hard work in. (Juergen Maier, Chief Executive, Siemens Industry UK; in *The Guardian UK 300 – The UK's most popular graduate recruiters 2013/14*)

Leadership and responsibility

Less is more – we'd suggest you get very involved in one or two clubs and societies that you join and take a leadership role. Recruiters will be more impressed with a president's role at one society than being involved at a basic level in four societies. (Donna Miller, Enterprise Rent-A-Car – European HR Director, in Sharp (2012) *'What do employers look for in graduates?'*)

Coping flexibly with precise demands

We need people who can manage the realities of today's workplace, who can juggle many projects at once, delivering all to a deadline. In a new graduate, we would want to see that they have experience of working on complex projects, have a good eye for detail, can cope with stress, get along with others and be flexible as needs arise. They will need to take on responsibility straight away, so we need to know they can handle that. (Chief Executive, SME, creative and digital sector)

Attitude is key for us. We look for candidates that are hungry for a job within our company. By that, we mean that it is evident from the care they took to research our company, to consider what we are looking for, and provide us with strong evidence that they can deliver what we need. (General Manager, manufacturing and engineering)

Reflection: What employers say

How well would you match up to each of these employer demands?

● Which of the 6 skills identified by the UK Top 300 do you consider are your strongest?

● Which of those 6 skills do you need to develop most?

Do employers value graduates?

Each year, employers invest time and money in visiting HEIs to talk to students about job opportunities in their businesses, in creating placements, internships and graduate training schemes, advertising for graduates, setting up assessment centres for graduate recruitment, and interviewing students and new graduates. All this indicates that employers, especially large businesses, value graduates.

Translating academic skills for the workplace

Do employers value academic skills?

Although employers search out graduate employees, you may find that they have a more ambivalent approach to academic skills, or are uncertain what these might be. As academic skills are integral to gaining a degree, this might surprise you. However, whilst being sceptical about the value of academic study, some employers consider that a degree indicates that an applicant is bright and intelligent. It is up to you to find ways of demonstrating the value of academic skills to their business.

Which academic skills?

Most workplaces would gain from the application of academic skills such as:

- Research skills
- Information management
- Synthesising ideas and/or information
- Writing up and presenting reports
- Critical reflection on practice
- Analysis, criticism and evaluation.

You may find it helpful to break key academic skills into their component sub-skills, as in the self-evaluation opposite. It is generally easier to see how sub-skills could be applied to a workplace.

What employers say

More than anything, I value critical, analytic thinkers. I need to know staff can handle complex information, make sense of it for themselves, and present it in ways that make sense to me and my company. I need them to do the thinking, and be able to explain to me clearly why they are recommending a course of action. (CEO of a UK national charity)

We look for people who combine academic excellence with common sense. (Recruitment brochure; Travers Smith LLP)

How are your academic skills relevant?

I can ☑

☐ Undertake advanced searches for information

☐ Find relevant material at speed

☐ Make good judgements about which material is most relevant

☐ Synthesise information quickly from multiple sources to find what they have in common and where they differ

☐ Summarise relevant material succinctly

☐ Synthesise material to arrive at a new solution, position or approach

☐ Analyse numerical data to identify trends

☐ Analyse evidence well in order to derive accurate conclusions

☐ Make sensible judgements, using a range of data/information

☐ Undertake complex, multi-level tasks with little supervision

☐ Apply knowledge in order to solve problems

☐ Translate complex material into everyday language so that it can be understood by diverse audiences

☐ Present a well-evidenced argument in writing

☐ Present a well-evidenced argument at an informal meeting

☐ Identify relevant material to prepare management briefings

☐ Present a well-evidenced argument as a formal presentation, such as to funders and clients

☐ Reflect on my own work, identifying for myself how I can make improvements

Writing skills for the workplace

The value of academic writing skills

For most courses in higher education, writing tasks play an important part. Depending on the kind of tasks that you undertook for your course, it is likely that you will have developed written communication skills that are highly relevant to the workplace.

Writing skills – for work and study

Ideally, by your final year, you should be able to write accurately, at speed, to deadlines, selecting the most salient points, structuring these and clarifying their significance, drafting copy and proof-reading it, to produce a fluent, well-styled, relevant piece of writing for specific purposes and audiences. If you have developed such writing skills, then you are likely to do well in your studies. Such skills are real assets in employment. Conversely, if your written skills are weak, then it is worth fine-tuning them.

Note that, even if this is not specified, it will probably be assumed that you have perfect grammar, spelling and punctuation, and that all aspects of your application will be well proof-read and error-free.

What employers say

Communication, both written and verbal, is really important and I look for people who have an energy and spark about them. (Danella Bagnall, Vehicle Architecture Planning Director, Jaguar Landrover; *The Guardian UK 300 The UK's most popular graduate recruiters 2013/14*)

If I see silly mistakes in an application, even in a covering email, I bin it. I am not going to have time to correct their work if I appoint them. (Managing Director, SME)

Make opportunities

Experience of writing for audiences outside of your academic studies enhances your CV. Businesses, charities and community projects may appreciate help with tasks such as the following:

- **Summaries** of press clippings, position papers, government documents, research papers, and information about funding proposals
- **Informational literature**, such as posters, leaflets, web-materials, articles in a trade magazine or community newspaper
- **Promotional materials** such as fliers, webpages
- **Social media writing** – such as a community, twitter feeds in a professional context, team or manager's blog, Facebook or LinkedIn pages
- **Staff literature**, such as compiling or updating manuals, the staff handbook, a website, policy documents.

There may be good opportunities in your institution; workplace; place of worship; a student society or for a local community group. Some starting places would be:

- Your Student Union
- Careers and Employability Services
- Chaplaincy and student mentoring services
- Volunteering Services on campus or in the local community
- Community centres
- Enterprise and Innovation Centres.

Reflection: Written communication

- How could you gain experience of adapting and developing your writing skills for work and non-academic contexts?
- Complete an evaluation of your writing skills for the workplace on page 262 (the following page).
- Complete the written communication competence sheet on p. 376.

Communication skills for the workplace

1 Take at least seven different pieces of literature written for the public. Include two different types of newspaper, some leaflets on public information, advertisements, trade magazines, bank or building society information, or website marketing information. Browse through these, comparing the writing style with that used in higher education.

   ● What are the characteristics of such writing?

   ● What writing skills would it take to produce them?

2 Collect literature from occupational sectors or professional areas that interest you. Browse these, comparing their writing styles with that used in higher education. Consider the characteristics of such writing: how does it differ from academic writing?

I have made this letter longer only because I have not had time to make it shorter.

Blaise Pascale (1655)

Where do your writing skills lie?

I can ☑

☐ Spell, punctuate and use grammar correctly, proof-reading carefully for these aspects. (For a graduate job, these should be excellent in all your written communication.)

☐ Write clearly, making it easy for the reader to grasp the point

☐ Write with fluency, structuring my writing well so that it carries the reader through easily from one point to the next

☐ Produce good writing at speed, to deadlines

☐ Adapt my writing style to the needs of the task and to different audiences

☐ Summarise documents accurately, such as for briefing papers for management teams

☐ Use language precisely

☐ Present a strong, clear, reasoned argument

☐ Write balanced evaluations (and I am able to differentiate evaluation from description)

☐ Draft formal letters

☐ Draft or fine-tune papers for committees

☐ Take down and write up succinct, accurate minutes of meetings

☐ Produce web-based text, suitable for different audiences

☐ Write promotional material

☐ Write guides, handbooks or other informational literature for particular audiences

☐ Write concisely to a given brief

☐ Assist with writing a company blog

☐ Write Twitter feeds suitable to business needs

Oral communication skills for the workplace

Good verbal communication skills are real assets in the workplace. For most jobs, such skills are required continually in day-to-day work, whereas written communications may be used less frequently.

Evidencing your verbal skills

Students often cite 'presenting a seminar paper' as an example of 'oral communication'. Leading a seminar is a valuable experience and does develop public speaking skills. However, formal presentations are not typical of everyday working life.

It is probable, at work, that you will need verbal skills for meetings, formal and informal, to contribute as a team member to discussions, or to explain matters to clients, customers and colleagues. Employers will be interested to hear about how you have communicated with different kinds of people, fielded difficult questions or contributed to discussions in workshops, projects, on-line or in work contexts.

What employers say

I need my front line staff to be able to provide clear, accurate information to the public. They need to respond quickly to what they are hearing, adapting the message to suit the customer. Team leaders and managers must excel at communication in order to resolve difficult situations quickly and effectively. (General Manager, call centre for large, international utility company)

Where do your skills lie?

I can ☑

☐ Convey information accurately and clearly

☐ Give clear directions and instructions

☐ Speak confidently with colleagues

☐ Communicate well with colleagues at different levels within the organisation

☐ Make useful contributions to meetings

☐ Take turns when speaking, leaving gaps for others to contribute

☐ Get to the point quickly

☐ Present the essential information concisely

☐ Listen attentively to others, taking on board what they are saying

☐ Represent corporate views accurately through what I say

☐ Negotiate my own position and that of my team or organisation

☐ Offer verbal criticism constructively as and when appropriate

☐ Adapt my verbal communication style to suit different audiences and situations

☐ Communicate well with particular audiences, such as children, patients, trade unions, customers

☐ Make customers and clients feel their views are respected

☐ Inspire confidence through what I say

 Reflection: Oral communication skills

- Which oral comunication skills do you have that will be useful in work contexts?
- Where else could you develop verbal communication skills relevant to work contexts?
- Complete the oral communication competence sheet on p. 378.

People skills for the workplace

...n context

...y, because you are working towards ...qualification that is awarded on an individual basis, you are judged primarily on your individual effort. In the workplace, whilst individual input is still valued, the team and wider company goals are more important points of reference.

When employers refer to creativity, communication, problem-solving or any other skills, they tend to assume that you understand that it isn't just about whether you shine at these things alone. They want to know how well you can apply skills and draw on your knowledge and experience when working with colleagues, clients and other people.

They will also be looking to see that you understand that your development of such skills is not just about your personal satisfaction, but has relevance and adds value to the work of the team and the organisation.

What employers say

I need to feel confident that every member of my staff exhibits my charity's values in all of their interactions with our children and young people, their parents and carers and with their colleagues too. Valuing diversity and respect for all is at the heart of our work and I want to be able to see that through things such as taking the time to listen to what children and young people want, advocating on others' behalf and making sure that everyone who has contact with my organisation is treated in the way they would like to be treated themselves. The tougher the task, the more I need to know that they can stay connected with what really matters to us. (CEO, Charity for disabled children and young people)

Where do your skills lie?

I can ✓

- ☐ Establish rapport easily with work colleagues
- ☐ Make others feel included and respected
- ☐ Respect other people's dignity
- ☐ Respect other people's time
- ☐ Work well in a team, contributing appropriately
- ☐ Win people's trust and confidence easily
- ☐ Work collaboratively with other people
- ☐ Take on board other people's ideas
- ☐ Share well with others
- ☐ Recognise quickly what others need
- ☐ Explain things well to other people
- ☐ Deal well with difficult people
- ☐ Deal well with awkward situations
- ☐ Maintain professional boundaries
- ☐ Remain patient
- ☐ Demonstrate good customer service
- ☐ Encourage and support others to do well
- ☐ Develop or train colleagues
- ☐ Accept the leadership and authority of others
- ☐ Take the lead when appropriate

Reflection: People skills

- Which people skills have you gained that will be useful in work contexts?
- Where else could you develop people skills relevant to work contexts?
- Complete the competence sheets on pp. 352–7 and 362–5.

Task management skills for the workplace

Task Management skills

Good task management or 'operational' skills are essential at work. Employers tend to assume that graduate employees will have developed these skills.

Student life often involves a great deal of independent study, with most time left unscheduled. If you already manage your time well, working in a systematic way, with well-established routines, then you have a good basis on which to build further development of the operational skills needed for employment. If not, then start now to develop such skills:

- Establish a daily routine
- Develop systematic planned approaches to larger tasks and assignments
- Fine-tune underlying functional skills in literacy, numeracy and information technology
- Find projects where you can help with the management and organisation – or devise your own. (You may find it useful to use Cottrell, 2014.)

What employers say

As well as looking for graduates with potential, we want to recruit the technical leaders of tomorrow. These are individuals who can lead teams in designing and supporting the projects upon which we can continue to build the business. (RDS, the rig design and engineering specialist)

I want someone who is going to keep a sound grip on our projects. I want to feel reassured that the projects would be well managed, that I would be given early warnings of potential risks or problems, preferably with realistic proposals for resolving these. (CEO of UK national charity)

Where do your skills lie?

I can ☑

- ☐ Manage a project from start to finish
- ☐ Find solutions to work-related issues
- ☐ Manage a budget
- ☐ Identify resource requirements
- ☐ Manage resources well
- ☐ Undertake a health and safety assessment
- ☐ Work in a systematic way on work tasks
- ☐ Map processes
- ☐ Write instructions and/or procedures for others
- ☐ Identify which work tasks are priorities
- ☐ Scope tasks, identifying how long they will take
- ☐ Manage my work time to meet all deadlines
- ☐ Use work time effectively, avoiding distractions
- ☐ Draw up schedules for myself and others
- ☐ Maintain organised records and files, retrieving information quickly as needed
- ☐ Identify who needs to receive which kinds of communication, by when, making sure they receive it
- ☐ Identify my own training needs
- ☐ Pick up the IT skills I need to complete a task
- ☐ Use software to present data
- ☐ Use functional maths as needs arise
- ☐ Use grammar and punctuation accurately

Reflection: Task management skills

- Which task management skills have you gained as a student, either through your course, work placements or co-curricular activities?
- Where else could you develop such skills to broaden your skills base?
- Complete the competence sheets on pages 348–51, 358–61 and 366–7.

Self-management 'skills' for the workplace

Why are self-management skills valued?

Independence

It is an obvious advantage to an employer if an employee can work out quickly what is required of them at work and then just get on with the job without much guidance. If an employee is well-organised, responsible, and manages their time well, they are more productive. This saves on staff costs or opens up new opportunities for using that staff time.

Coping with change and challenge

The labour market is changing so quickly that it is a real advantage to be able to manage change and uncertainty well.

Change can be experienced as exciting, or stressful, or both. It requires you to move from known and safe terrain into the unknown. You may have to alter ingrained habits, adapt your preferred ways of working, learn new skills, adopt new working patterns, assimilate into a new team, move site and change your home or your travel plans. You may have to cope with disruption.

Employers value candidates who can demonstrate that they have encountered difficulty and challenge and managed these well, learning from experience.

What employers say

... so you won't expect to be spoon fed. You'll be eager to throw your ideas into the mix, shoulder your fair share of responsibility and prove you know how to put customers first. (Heinz, 2014)

Where do your skills lie?

I can ☑

- [ ] Take the initiative to make sure work gets done
- [ ] Motivate myself to produce high quality work
- [ ] Maintain motivation well even when things aren't going well
- [ ] Work out sensible solutions to problems
- [ ] Take care of my health and well-being so that I can perform well
- [ ] Cope well under pressure
- [ ] Manage stress effectively
- [ ] Respond well to challenge
- [ ] Raise difficult issues if need arises
- [ ] Ask for help when needed
- [ ] Work well independently, with little direction
- [ ] Juggle tasks flexibly to meet changing circumstances
- [ ] Be flexible in working hours and taking on new tasks to meet changing business needs
- [ ] Use direction and instruction constructively
- [ ] Balance independent working with team work
- [ ] Deal well with uncertainty
- [ ] Use feedback and criticism constructively
- [ ] Put my own needs aside when other people's requirements are more urgent
- [ ] Make good use of arising opportunities, to the benefit of the business
- [ ] Identify my training needs effectively and undertake professional updates and training

Being your own employer: pros and cons

So far we have considered what an employer might want when that employer is someone other than yourself. There is also the option of being your own employer, whether as a sole-trader or micro-business, freelance professional, small to medium-sized business owner, or growing a small business into a large company.

There are a number of professional areas such as in law, finance, accounting, psychology and architecture where, once you have experience and chartered status, you can set up your own practice.

If the idea of having your own business appeals, then it is essential to think this through in meticulous detail.

The benefits

If you have a good idea for a marketable service or product, and can sell it at a profit, then you can reap many benefits from self-employment.

- You can follow your own vision and take forward your own ideas with fewer restrictions.
- You have more control over your own destiny, more responsibility for success or failure.
- You can work to your own values: you have a larger say in the culture, ethos and lifestyle associated with your workplace.
- It suits those who want to work in creative, design, digital and performance industries, and also in retail, consultancy, coaching, counselling, therapies, translation, hospitality – and many other areas.
- You may be able to choose your own hours, so you can combine work flexibly with creative, leisure or family commitments.
- It can be really exciting and rewarding to take an idea to market and see it succeed.
- If the business is successful, you may take a larger share of the profits.

Realities

Working your own hours

In general, to make your business work, you have to be prepared to work very long hours, especially in the first few years. Most entrepreneurs are so passionate about their concept that they don't count the hours they work.

Being in charge

Being in charge does not mean that you get to do everything your own way. You have to listen carefully to your potential market and to anyone who invests, whether friends, family, partners, banks, or crowd-funders, taking their views on board. You may have to adapt your concept, product and plans to suit the market and investors.

Making a lot of money

It is possible to make a great amount of money if your business is a success. Some companies, especially some on-line start-ups, have been overnight successes. When starting out, and especially if borrowing money to invest, be realistic. Most businesses are small and remain small. You may make small profits – or a loss.

Self-employment allows you to work to your own values

Being your own employer: pros and cons

Responsibilities

Being an employer carries specific responsibilities, and these increase depending on the size of your workforce and your turnover.

- The first responsibility is finding out what are your responsibilities and liabilities – you are in charge, so you are expected to know.
- If you borrow money to get started or to invest in development, you are responsible for making sure your investors get their money back as well as agreed returns on their investment.
- For your goods and services, you have a responsibility to deliver on what you promise.
- You are responsible for the health and safety of employees, those visiting your work premises, and anyone using your goods and services.
- If you have employees, you have responsibilities to them, such as payment of pensions, employee national insurance, the minimum wage, and adhering to employment law, etc.
- It is up to you to ensure that you meet all legal and financial requirements, including those relating to taxes, the environment, equality, health and safety, data protection, charity and/or companies law, staff malpractice, goods and services, etc.
- You need to arrange insurance cover, to meet all your liabilities.

The risks

A high proportion of new enterprises fail. In some sectors, this is as high as 90%. Make sure you are aware of the likely pitfalls. Here are some reasons why businesses fail.

They spend too much on start-up costs, assuming that they will make bigger profits in the early years than is likely to be the case. For example, they invest heavily in refurbishing premises and in new plant rather than making do with serviceable and affordable options, such as recycled or second-hand plant.

> I want everything to look shiny and bright

> ... and then just a few other bits and pieces which shouldn't amount to much more money

They don't undertake a full cost analysis that covers all the incidentals such as insurance, energy, distribution costs, maintenance, wastage, slow markets, and myriad other things. All of the small items can add up to a significant amount, and total more than the obvious, larger items. They can eat into cash flow.

They don't watch cash flow. Without available cash to pay salaries, invest in stock, etc., even a large business can fold.

They don't understand the market. This may be because they don't conduct the right kind of market analysis, select the right kind of focus groups, or interpret their findings correctly. Generally, people love their own business idea, so they think others will too. They can assume a larger market for the product than is actually the case and/or underestimate competition.

> I think it is a great idea and my mum says so too. I really believe it will sell!

Being your own employer: eight essentials

1   **A concept.** Your starting place is having an idea for a product or service. This must be yours to sell, so check first whether anyone already holds the patent. If so, consider whether your concept could be adapted to be made sufficiently different for patenting in its own right. Find out about patents and intellectual property at the Intellectual Property Office at www.ipo.gov.uk.

> ### Great idea – will it really work?
> *Be enthusiastic for your idea, but also be hard-headed: can it really work?*

2   **A brand and selling point.** What makes your product or service stand out in the market? What does it have that would make customers choose that over others? How would people recognise your product and your promotional materials and messages as yours rather than a competitor's?

3   **A market.** However brilliant your concept looks to you and your friends, it has to be one that will sell. Your sales have to generate sufficient income to cover all costs, including your salary.

Investigate your market carefully and thoroughly. Have similar projects been tried already? If these were successful, have competitors captured most of the potential market already? If they failed, were there particular reasons? Think carefully about what lessons you can learn from the existing market, both looking at business ideas and those that haven't captured a market.

4   **A route to market.** Even if there is a potential market, you need to think through how potential customers would find out about your business and be able to purchase your goods and services. How would you promote your products? If on-line, how could customers check the product is right for them? Where are your products manufactured and/or the business located? How would you distribute your product and at what cost? What might restrict you in getting your product to market, or in scaling up your business? The answers would be different depending on whether you are trading in ice-cream, digital services, logistics or acupuncture.

5   **Finance and financial planning.** You will need to obtain finance to get started, though it is possible to start and keep businesses afloat with a good idea, a small initial outlay and plenty of hard work.
   ● Use any free financial advice available. See page 386.
   ● Consider taking an enterprise course.
   ● Produce a business plan, including a detailed financial plan. See www.startupdonut.co.uk.

6   **An exit strategy.** Take advice on how to manage the business finances so that, if the business does not succeed as planned, you can afford to pay your debts, cover any losses and not go bankrupt.

7   **Skills and mind-set.** You need the motivation, skills and drive to 'make it happen'. You have to be: prepared to work long hours; systematic in planning; disciplined in sticking to targets; willing to keep yourself and others focused and on task; able to negotiate with others and persuade people to believe in you and your product. If you can, find a good mentor as a sounding board, and partners or employees whose skills and qualities complement your own – then value what they offer and listen to what they say.

8   **A first step.** All businesses have to start somewhere. If the idea excites you, then speak to an expert adviser. There is a wealth of free advice and support available for entrepreneurs, including students. Visit the Employability/ Careers Service or see page 386.

Closing comments

In recent years, there has been a growing interest in 'employability' skills. Students say they want jobs, employers say they want employability skills, and higher education institutions have responded. Most HEIs now provide a broad range of opportunities for their students to develop such skills, whether through the curriculum, alongside it, or both.

It is up to you to make sure that you:

- *Understand the generic requirements* of today's employers, so that you can broaden the range of job opportunities open to you
- *Understand the specific attributes* required for graduate, specialist and management jobs in areas that particularly interest you, so that you are well-placed when applying for these
- *Make use of the opportunities on offer* to you through your institution, or external to it, so that you don't miss out and so that you come across to employers as well-motivated and forward-thinking
- *Are well informed about opportunities* on offer, so that you are in a position to apply for these and make effective use of them, as and when they arise.

You make yourself more 'employable' if you match what employers are looking for. There is a vast range of easily accessible information that can help you to develop for yourself a sense of what employers want. Your university or college careers service will also be keen to point you in the right direction.

In preparing for future work roles, whether for your first job, your first 'graduate job' or your next promotion, it is common sense to identify the kinds of qualifications, experience, skills and qualities that tend to be associated with that role and then to take steps to acquire these.

Your experience as a student will have developed your skills in all kinds of ways, often gradually over time, so that you may not be aware that this has occurred. Take time to stand back and reflect upon such things as:

- What kinds of activities you have undertaken repeatedly over your time as a student – continual practice is likely to fine-tune your abilities
- How, exactly, such abilities have developed – so that you can describe your strengths more precisely
- How these abilities would be relevant in work contexts – consider how you would persuade employers of this through examples that make sense in a work context.

This chapter has focused on employability from the perspective of the employer. Understanding the labour market and knowing what employers want from their new staff recruits are important aspects of gaining the job you want. The following chapter looks in more detail at employability from the perspective of you, the job applicant – what you want and what you can do to manage the job application process successfully.

Chapter 10
Getting the job you want

Learning outcomes

This chapter offers opportunities to:

- reflect on four key stages in career planning, identifying where to focus your energies
- decide what you want from your first, or next, job
- plan, and act, ahead in order to put yourself in the strongest possible position when applying for jobs
- extract the most value from work placements or current employment, to benefit your future job applications
- make a strong job application, managing the appointments process effectively from start to finish.

Introduction

Applying for jobs is an art in itself. It is no longer sufficient to send a CV to a host of employers and hope that one will notice you. The quality of your application is more important than applying in bulk: tailor your application to each employer and role.

For almost every job, you can expect strong competition – others will want that job just as much as you do. There are likely to be applicants who will have planned ahead for several years towards just such an application, building an excellent CV based on a range of experiences. You can do the same.

It pays to start the process of thinking about employability and careers planning in a systematic way from early in your first year of study. This includes being willing to do the following:

Aspire – aspire to the best possible jobs and career routes for yourself, whether short-term or longer-term.

Act – act now so as to improve your chances of getting the jobs you want.

Apply – apply for the right jobs for you in the most effective way possible.

Achieve – achieve the grades, skills, confidence and experiences that will, in turn, help you to achieve well both academically and in gaining a good job.

All this is not acquired overnight, so the sooner you start thinking and planning, the more successful you are likely to be.

What careers experts say ...

Getting the job you deserve

Remember, a degree on its own won't guarantee the job you have always wanted. The graduate labour market is very competitive: you need to make sure you are ready and able to compete with the very best.

Career Planning – When do I start?

It's never too early to start planning your career. We recommend you start this process from day one of your studies. The key element is deciding what you want to do with your degree and putting together a plan to ensure this happens.

(Femi Bola MBE, Director of Careers and Employability, University of East London)

What gives students the edge?

... in my experience, academic credentials *combined with* evidence of transferable skill such as problem solving, communication and team work, tend to form the real threshold level for serious consideration in graduate selection processes. The key differentiators (the "deal breakers") beyond this threshold are commercial awareness and career motivation.

Commercial awareness: this involves things like understanding why the organisation exists, its competitors, etc. The elements of the selection process which are designed to test this also test the applicants' career motivation. It would ... be very difficult to answer convincingly even a question such as "why have you applied for this role?" without a genuine understanding of the commercial issues relating to the business.

Be 'authentic': it might be helpful to think in terms of authenticity ... Are there industry sectors and/or job roles about which you could talk with enthusiasm and apparently little effort because they genuinely reflect your interests? If so, your answers about these will feel authentic rather than forced or contrived.

(Dr Bob Gilworth, Director of College Careers Services, University of London Careers Group)

Employability positioning

Having long-term career objectives is ideal but, realistically, not everyone is in a position to define their long-term objectives ... Apart from anything else, these objectives may change as more attractive ones emerge. Therefore, positioning oneself against an unknown future using education and training opportunities could be seen as a good investment.

What strategies can I adopt against an uncertain future?

- **Keep up to date with local labour market trends** – *local newspapers and local authority economic unit bulletins can reveal which sectors are recruiting, and skills and specialist qualification shortages*
- **Keep in touch with your skills** – *reflect and build on your skills on a regular basis*
- **Keep in touch with your aspirations** – *are there new things you may want to try?*
- **Keep an eye on your future** – *consider how things might change, personally, politically or technologically.*

(Mohammed Hussain, Academic Guidance Officer, University of Leeds)

Gaining success in the job market

In today's job market the key to success isn't just what you know. It's how you apply that knowledge, how you sell yourself, how you connect with people and, increasingly, it's also about having a global mind set.

Investing time in planning how you will develop your personal and professional profile and committing your efforts towards a particular career path or career sectors will enable you to identify and make the most of opportunities in today's job market.

(Joanne Beaumont, Head of Careers & Employability, University of Bradford)

Career planning: Aspire, Act, Apply, Achieve

Planning your career is like planning for a journey:

- Your planning can help to make the experience more enjoyable and, ultimately, successful.
- You can't plan for every eventuality, so you also have to be prepared for the unexpected.

What is 'Career planning'?

Career planning is mainly about thinking ahead so you don't miss out. It is about opening up possibilities rather than about precise outcomes.

It can appear rather off-putting, as it can sound as if you need to know your end point in order to plan towards it. Although that seems logical, it is not typical of career planning. Indeed, it is acknowledged that:

- career paths are hard to predict
- many students have little fixed idea about what they want to do when they graduate; those that do may change their minds along the way
- life circumstances pan out differently than expected and personal interests change, so particular career routes close down or open up
- the labour market changes, with old jobs disappearing and new jobs appearing.

Aspire, Act, Apply, Achieve

Broadly speaking, there are four stages to career planning; these could follow on from each other although, depending on when you start and when opportunities fall for you, they may run concurrently.

Aspire

- **Aim high.** Whilst it is sensible to aim for jobs within your reach, it is just as important to be ambitious, aspiring to the best possible jobs and career outcomes for you.
- **Consider leadership options.** For whatever field of work appeals to you, a leadership role may be open to you on graduation or in the future. Take steps to enable this possibility – even if you decide later that this is not for you. Consider the sections on leadership in this book.
- **Expand your options** rather than limit them.
- **Be proactive** in your aspiration, rather than just 'wishing and wanting' or thinking 'if only …'.

Act

Act now so as to improve your chances of getting the jobs you want. That includes:

- **Active self-reflection and self-evaluation**, so you know which strengths you can play to, and which areas to work on further.
- **Active planning**, so you know when you will fit in different aspects of careers development.
- **Active engagement** in activities and experiences that will build your CV.
- **Active decision-making**, to provide focus for your career development and job applications.

Apply

- **Use the available work opportunities** to build your experience; don't wait too long for the perfect job or placement to come along.
- **Gain practice** in applying for jobs, using workshops and mock interviews but also through real applications.
- **Tailor your application**: select carefully where to apply, then fit your application to the employer and job.

Achieve

- **Academically**: develop skills and habits that will enable you to gain the best possible grades, for their own sake and to improve your career options.
- **Professionally**: both short-term and long-term.
- **Personally**: develop in confidence and self-reliance; attain your own goals for success in life.

> ### Activity
>
> Use the Career Planning Journey evaluation on pp. 274–5 next to identify areas for action in your own career planning.

Career planning journey: Aspire, Act, Apply, Achieve

For the 4 stages below:

- Starting at the box nearest the star, check your progress on your career journey. (NB You may find that you skip some steps or complete some later steps ahead of earlier ones: that isn't usually an issue.)
- Identify which steps you have completed already, by filling in the circle. ○
- Identify which areas need your action now, by checking ☑ above the relevant box.

---

1 Aspire: Aim high, developing an ambitious vision for your longer-term future. Consider how current opportunities can serve as steps towards your goals. Don't restrict your options too early.

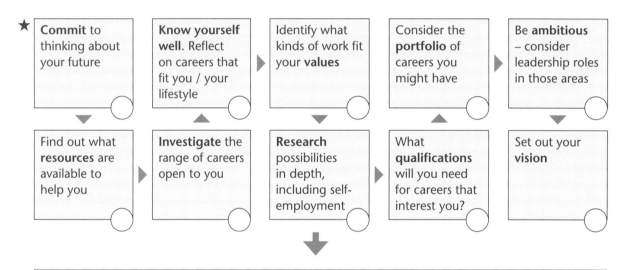

★ **Commit** to thinking about your future

Know yourself well. Reflect on careers that fit you / your lifestyle

Identify what kinds of work fit your **values**

Consider the **portfolio** of careers you might have

Be **ambitious** – consider leadership roles in those areas

Find out what **resources** are available to help you

Investigate the range of careers open to you

Research possibilities in depth, including self-employment

What **qualifications** will you need for careers that interest you?

Set out your **vision**

---

2 Act: Be proactive in investigating, planning, finding and using opportunities. Make decisions, so that you provide a focus to your career planning and action.

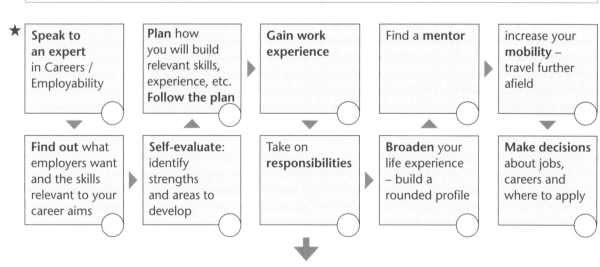

★ **Speak to an expert** in Careers / Employability

Plan how you will build relevant skills, experience, etc. **Follow the plan**

Gain work experience

Find a **mentor**

increase your **mobility** – travel further afield

Find out what employers want and the skills relevant to your career aims

Self-evaluate: identify strengths and areas to develop

Take on **responsibilities**

Broaden your life experience – build a rounded profile

Make decisions about jobs, careers and where to apply

---

3 Apply: Continue to research, prepare and practise thoroughly even once you start to apply for jobs. Be selective, tailoring your application as closely as possible to the best, most likely roles for you.

★ Familiarise yourself with the **graduate recruitment market**

Do **background research** on the company

Tailor your application to the person specification and company

Practise exercises for **assessment centres**

Make use of **workshops and mock interviews**

Investigate applications processes

Be **selective** in where you apply

Keep **well-organised records** of each application

Rehearse answers to possible **interview questions**

Present yourself well at interview

4 Achieve: Be aware of the close connection between academic achievement, accurate use of English and successful job applications. Be mindful, too, of your broader happiness and life–work balance.

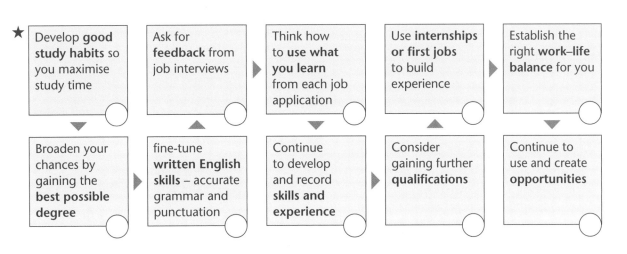

★ Develop **good study habits** so you maximise study time

Ask for **feedback** from job interviews

Think how to **use what you learn** from each job application

Use **internships or first jobs** to build experience

Establish the right **work–life balance** for you

Broaden your chances by gaining the **best possible degree**

fine-tune **written English skills** – accurate grammar and punctuation

Continue to develop and record **skills and experience**

Consider gaining further **qualifications**

Continue to use and create **opportunities**

Reflection: Career planning journey

- Are you giving sufficient time and attention to your career planning?
- Are you being proactive in gaining experience, work and skills that strengthen your job applications?
- What is the next step for you in planning for your career?

Models of career development

There are different models of what career development might look like ideally. You don't necessarily have to know about these, but understanding some of the theory can help to put your own endeavours into a broader context. It can be reassuring to compare these with your own activity. The previous pages outline one 'model' of career planning: Aspire, Act, Apply, Achieve (4 'A's). Two other models are offered below for you to consider.

The Career EDGE model

Formulated by Dacre Pool and Sewell (2007), this identifies specific components that promote employability. These are:

1 **Career** development learning, plus …
2 **Experience** (work and life)
3 **Degree** subject knowledge, understanding and skills
4 **Generic** skills
5 **Emotional** intelligence.

In the model, reflection and evaluation on these components build the self-confidence, self-efficacy and self-esteem that lead to employability. Interestingly, although the model includes experience of work, it does not specifically refer to employability skills.

Reflection: Experience of work

What would you find useful about this model?

The model refers to experience of work. Such experience on its own doesn't necessarily produce relevant knowledge and understanding. How do you think people could make use of such experience to make it most meaningful for their own career advancement? (See pages 280–2, 'Make effective use of your experience of work'.)

The Career Management model

Bridgstock (2009) argues that, as well as gaining skills that employers require, it is also important to gain and use career management skills. These are necessary to help you to direct your learning and skills development in ways that will prove meaningful.

This model recognises the importance of:

1 *career-building skills* (such as using labour market intelligence, developing the right networks and relationships for gaining work)
2 *self-management skills* (such as evaluating your skills, qualities and values)
3 *underlying 'traits and dispositions'* (such as being open to new experience, beliefs about your employability, your vocational interests, or willingness to develop career skills).

Such career management skills help you to direct your energies appropriately, so that you then make best use of the career-related opportunities available through your course and elsewhere. An important aspect of this model is the 'intentional management' of work, learning, and life. It calls for active reflection and evaluation.

Reflection: Career development model

- Does this model make sense to you?
- How focused are you on developing career management skills in a planned, intentional, reflective manner?

What students and graduates say

Make a start

What I have to say is probably what everyone says: 'I wish I hadn't waited so long before starting to think about planning my career.' So my advice is, just do it. Get on with it. You have to eventually, so it might as well be now. **Gloria, 3rd-year student**

Get experience

I am really glad that I joined lots of societies. Being president of one student society and treasurer of another made it much easier for me to answer questions at interview. I could talk easily about a long list of things – such as using my initiative, taking the lead to get things done, discussing things in meetings, making sure we had records of meetings and that we followed through on what we agreed, managing budgets, taking responsibility for making decisions, having to account for my actions, all the sorts of things you have to do in work all the time. I think this would be good for all students, taking on any roles where they can show they took some initiative and have some drive. **Imani, recent graduate**

I couldn't get an internship that I really wanted. I was very dejected at first. On the advice of the university careers service, I looked for other work instead. I did two part-time voluntary jobs, and then got some paid part-time hours at one of these. I then found another part-time job which I thought would be a dead-end. That employer asked if I had good writing skills and asked me to help out with some office work. After that, the manager asked if I would write material for their website. A partner company then offered me a job in their communications office, and now I am a trainee manager there. One thing can lead on to another, so if I hadn't taken what was available, I probably wouldn't have got this chance. **Basha, graduate**

Keep your options open

I left a job to start university and was convinced that when I got my degree I would go back to my old company. When I finished, I realised I didn't want to do that, and wished I had bothered to check out other businesses and what was required for management entry roles at these. I could have done much more to prepare my curriculum vitae, to be more interesting as an applicant. I don't look as if I have done anything except study in the last three years. **Raheem, final year student**

I didn't think I would work for an SME but the Careers Service was sent the option of a placement and asked me if I would be interested. I thought, 'why not?' and I am so glad because it has been amazingly helpful. There are only eleven people in the company and we all just pitch in as needed. I work with everyone and have a go at everything – almost everything. It has been good for me because I wasn't sure what it would be like working with colleagues at work and not just students. Because we work so closely as a team, I have learnt a lot very quickly, how to get on with people at work and how to handle clients too. **Shuang, 3rd year student**

Think of all options

I just assumed that I would work for a big company and that that is where the jobs were. That is all I heard about. I didn't even think about most being in smaller companies, although it is obvious when you think about it. I was disappointed not to get a job with a major corporate but it has been interesting joining a micro-company. Everyone knows who I am at work, and I feel like I really count. **Duncan, recent graduate**

Reflection: Applying for jobs

- What can you learn from these students' experiences that could help your own career planning?
- What advice would you give to others? Are you following this advice yourself, currently?

Gaining experience of work

'Must have experience'

product placement, customer service skills, brand awareness

Treat all placements seriously.

Job advertisements often state that experience is needed, but it can be tricky to find a job that provides this. If you are caught in this conundrum, don't despair. You *can* gain experience.

You can make any job work for you

Any employment experience is better than none. If the right placement does not come along, take the work that is available, even if not ideal.

Where to find work

Part-time work. If your university or college has a jobshop or recruitment agency, start there. Even while you are a student, you can apply for work at your institution or in the student union. Look in your local paper and register with on-line agencies. There will be recruitment agencies and jobshops in your region, and some shops, religious bodies and community organisations display job advertisements.

Work placements and internships. These come in various packages, paid or unpaid, short or long, part-time or full-time. Ask at your Careers or Employability Service. Look for a placement that provides you with the experience and skills that are most closely aligned to careers that interest you, but accept what is available.

Voluntary work. It may not seem ideal if this is unpaid, but it provides a starting place. Your student union or careers service is likely to offer volunteering roles and there may be some organised through your course. If you approach charities directly, be clear about what time, experience and skills you can offer.

Treat all placements seriously

It is likely that you will have to compete for placements and internships as well as for mainstream jobs. Approach the appointments process for every role seriously. This gives you practice in developing the skills you will need when you apply for graduate jobs.

Many placements and internships lead to a job within the company, so make a good impression from the outset. Even if you think, now, that this is not the company for you, you might find that you want to stay on once you have been there for a while and seen the potential for acquiring more experience.

Create opportunities: Ask

Let your work supervisor or manager know that you are keen to take on responsibilities. Such additional experience will be invaluable for your CV. Ask if you can have a meeting to talk through what you might be able to offer the company.

Create opportunities: Tell

Let your supervisor or manager know of any skills that you might have that could be useful. Look for occasions when you could apply your skills to help the company. These do not need to be related to your degree, though could be. For example, you might see ways that employers could use social media or student volunteers to help their business.

Create opportunities: References

When you apply for your next placement or job, you must provide details of all previous employers, including for work placements and internships. The employer will contact management for a reference. It is essential to present yourself well during all placements. Future employers will be interested to hear what employers have to say about you.

Work placements and internships: the benefits

If you haven't yet had a job or held a position with responsibility, then it is important to consider taking on either a placement or an internship, whether paid or unpaid. As Fanthome (2004) noted, 'work experience is becoming an essential component of an applicant's CV within the post-graduation employment market'.

What will I gain?

The key purpose of placements and internships is to gain experience and work readiness to support general employability. You can gain some, or all, of the following:

- Payment – some provide a wage or accommodation or other benefits; some don't
- Skills – either new skills or opportunities to fine-tune and apply existing ones in a new context
- Application of theory – the chance to test out, in practice, what you have learnt in class
- Work-readiness – practice in developing the attitudes, habits and life-skills needed to hold down a job
- Understanding – insights into how organisations work (see pages 280–2 regarding placements, etc.)
- Personal insights – greater clarity in what you want from your working life
- Experience and referees to help with future job applications.

Reading the work culture

Above all else, you can learn about how to read the work culture. Part of being a good employee is fitting in to the social and cultural life of the organisation, especially in your department or team. You can start to gain a sense of how workplace politics and conventions operate. These vary from one company to another, so being able to compare two or more workplaces is invaluable to building your general understanding.

Reflection: Experience of work

What do you think you could gain from a work placement or internship in the near future? What kind of placement or internship would you want?

What students say

I had become used to a student way of life. I worked hard as a student, very hard actually, but I could do this more or less on my own time schedule. It was a real shock to the system to have to work the same hours every day, Monday to Friday. After three days, I thought I would have to give up, that my system couldn't cope. I don't know how I got through the first week but I did. I got used to the routine and realised I could survive it! I am glad I found that out! *Hassan*

It was compulsory to do a work placement on my course. I was sent to a nursery 20 miles away. I had to get up at 6.30 a.m. to arrive for 8.30. I was not pleased about that! What I gained from the placement? It was all the organisational skills for managing my own life. I had to apply for financial support for the train fare, and then make sure I didn't spend it on anything else. And sort out my travel, smart clothes etc. It was hard getting myself organised to be in work on time, looking presentable. I even had to polish my shoes! I had to prepare what I would do all day with the different age groups in the nursery – and the legal requirements – there was a lot of responsibility involved. I really needed all that experience. *Jade*

I'd say get any experience and as much work experience as you can. If you can get a paid job in a relevant field, great! If not, just take any work and look at it through professional eyes. So, if you want to be an accountant or a lawyer, look at everything at the placement through the eyes of a legal or financial expert. Think about what they would notice, and the advice they would give, and the opportunities they would see. This helps you to think and speak like a professional. *Maisha*

Make effective use of your experience of work

Learning from experience

However good a match your current employment, internship or placement is to your preferred career, you can make more, or less, of the experience.

Senior staff find they can learn a great deal about their organisation by going 'back to the floor', including in the most junior roles, and seeing from there how things are operating currently at every level of the business.

If they can learn from 'the floor', then so can you. Even if your role is relatively junior, you can still make this into a rich opportunity to observe, reflect and learn about work environments and your developmental needs. You may even be able to draw on your insights to gain a job, or promotion.

Be systematic

Take a systematic and structured approach to reflecting critically and analytically about your workplace. Use your insights to help you to prepare for more senior roles. The following sets of questions can help to guide your thinking.

Jot down your observations. However, unless you have workplace permission for keeping notes about this, keep your personal records private.

1 Appointment process

1 What did the appointments process involve?
2 How typical is that likely to be of appointment processes more generally?
3 What did you do well? How do you know?
4 What could have gone better? What could you practise or prepare better for future applications?
5 If you were appointing a member of staff, would you do anything differently from those who interviewed you?

2 Induction

1 Did you receive an induction to your workplace? If so, what did this cover?
2 How much were you able to remember of your induction afterwards?
3 Do you have an information pack, staff handbook or website to follow up information?
4 Do you make use of the staff information that is available to you through such means?
5 How useful was your induction to you? What were the most useful aspects?
6 Were you introduced to your colleagues?
7 How well were you made to feel part of a team?
8 What do you think an induction process should cover?
9 What, if anything, would you do differently, if you were in charge, to induct new staff?

3 Organisational structures

1 How easy is it for employees to find out who everyone is and what their roles are?
2 Do you know to whom you are meant to report?
3 Do you know to whom other key people with whom you work report?
4 Is there an organisational chart that illustrates the line management structure to employees?
5 What difference does it make to your working day to know the people around you?
6 Why do you think the organisation is structured in this way?
7 In your opinion, do these structures help the business run effectively – at least in relation to work you can observe?

Make effective use of your experience of work

4 Health and safety

1 How were health and safety considerations communicated to you?
2 How thoroughly were health and safety matters covered?
3 Was this sufficient for understanding how to work safely in your own role?
4 Did your work colleagues take health and safety matters seriously? How aware were managers of employee attitudes and behaviours?

5 Understanding your role

1 Do you understand how your job contributes to the final product or outcome?
2 What difference does it make to your working day to know the people around you?
3 How clear is your job description? What does it say you must do?
4 How closely does the work you undertake match the job description?
5 Is the work what you expected from the information you had received in advance?
6 What initial training did you receive for the role? Was this pitched at the right level?
7 How effective was your employer in settling you into your role so that you used your time efficiently as soon as possible?

6 Management communication with employees

1 What methods are used for communicating with employees (such as general discussion, meetings, newsletters, blogs, etc.)?
2 From what you see, hear and experience, do these methods seem broadly effective?
3 If they seem to work reasonably well, why is that?
4 If they don't work well, why does that seem to be the case? What could be done more effectively?
5 Do employees get a chance to give their point of view on how things work?
6 If so, do they make sensible and well thought through suggestions?
7 If you were in charge, would you do anything differently to improve communications?

7 Training and development

1 What training and development opportunities are open to you at work?
2 How did you find out about these? Were these communicated to you clearly enough?
3 What training is compulsory? Why is that?
4 How effective is the training you receive? Does it do what it should?
5 Do employees seem to value the training they receive? If not, why is that?
6 Are there are other training needs that are not currently addressed? What difference do you think it would make if such training were provided?
7 Did you make good use of the training opportunities that were open to you?
8 If so, how could you present this training to best effect in future job applications and interviews?

8 Values

1 Does the company have a set of shared values?
2 How did you find out about these?
3 How are they communicated and promoted?
4 Are those values much in evidence in the day-to-day work of the company?
5 Do staff put the values into practice? If not, why do you think that might be the case?
6 Are the values interpreted differently within your team?
7 How do customers (or clients, patients, pupils, etc.) benefit from such values?
8 If you were in charge, what, if anything, would you change to embed company values effectively?

Make effective use of your experience of work

9 Organisation and culture

1 Is your workplace friendly?
2 Would you say staff morale is good?
3 Do people get on reasonably well?
4 Do they offer to help each other out as needed?
5 Is it professional in the way it conducts its business?
6 Would you want to use its services?
7 Would you recommend it to others as a place to work?
8 How would you describe the culture that you find around you at work?
9 Is the work culture one that you find motivating?
10 Does it encourage you to do your best?
11 If you were in charge, what would you do differently, if anything, to improve morale, motivation or professionalism?

10 Skills and Personal development

1 What skills have you developed that would be useful in a future role?
2 In general, what kinds of understanding of the workplace have you gained from your experience of work to date?
3 What have you learnt about work politics and culture that would affect your future approach to settling into a job?
4 What have you learnt about organising yourself for work?
5 What insights have you gained about the world of work that would help you in applying for jobs in the future?
6 What insights have you gained about the kind of jobs that would, or would not, suit you in future?
7 From your observations and experience as an employee, what have you learnt about leadership and management that could be of value to you in future management roles?

Relevance to your preferred career path

1 When observing in, and reflecting on, your workplace, what considerations tended to rise to the fore most often and easily? For example, did you find you were more interested in matters related to Human Resources (HR)? Finance? Legal issues? Management? Policy? Customer service? Design? Quality assurance? Operations? Other things? What does this suggest to you about future work that would most suit your interests?
2 What commercial awareness have you picked up through this work? How could you make this relevant if asked about your commercial understanding in a future job interview?
3 What have you learnt about your ability to get on with people in the workplace? How could you make this relevant if asked about your people skills in a future job interview?
4 Looking at the competency sheets on pages 346–82, which examples could you draw upon from your recent experience of work, to provide evidence of characteristics employers look for?

Reflection: Understanding personal preferences

Use the following prompts to make notes in your reflective journal or blog about your current preferences and the reasons that lie behind these.

Check off ☑ each item once you have considered it.

☐ Would I prefer to get a job on graduation – or take a break?

☐ Would I prefer to work in teams – or on my own?

☐ Would I prefer to work for a private company, the public sector, a charity, family business or for myself?

☐ Would I prefer to work for a large, medium, small or micro company – or no preference?

☐ Would I prefer full-time, part-time, or flexible work?

© Stella Cottrell (2003, 2010, 2015), *Skills for Success*, Palgrave

What do you want from your first 'graduate' job?

Developing your aims

In Chapter 1, you considered what your vision and values were for the next ten years. You may have changed your mind about these as you worked through the book.

Mature students and those in certain professional routes may have a good idea of the job they want when they leave university, although even they can change their minds when they find out about other options. Some students worry that they are not clear about what work they want.

It is easy to rush such decision-making. Although it is useful to make interim decisions that help provide focus, or at least a general direction, it is more important to gain experience, skills and insights when setting out on your career.

Career portfolio

Whatever job you choose, it is unlikely to be for life. It is more typical now to have a 'portfolio' of careers across a lifetime. Consider what there is to be gained from the opportunities available rather than panicking that the perfect career opening does not seem to be available to you straight away. Consider how particular opportunities or roles could advance your longer-term aims and career portfolio.

Jobs for graduates

Your first few jobs as a graduate may be traditional 'graduate' jobs. These offer reasonably good salaries and are often designed specifically for new graduates. They involve skilled work and recognise the value of a degree. Large companies offer graduate schemes but there are excellent opportunities in other companies too.

> *If you want a graduate job, then you need to apply early, preferably starting that process in your penultimate rather than final year.*

Waiting until after graduation to apply for jobs makes it more likely students will end up in non-graduate jobs.

Chris was delighted to discover that there really was such a job as 'professional sleeper'

More experience

Many graduates opt to enter the wider workforce with the aim of gaining experience and building their skills. This is especially true in creative professions, where it is expected that graduates will enter at a lower rung and plan for the longer term – or run their own business.

How can your next job help you?

Your first step is to think about what it is you want to gain from your first jobs after graduating, whether this is 'learning the ropes', personal projects, travel, trying out different occupational sectors, or developing expertise. You may prefer to work part-time on more than one job, or use agency work to build additional skills. If your plan is to walk straight into a particular job, make sure you have contingency plans in case this does not happen. Decide on other jobs that could carry your career or life plans forward.

Activity **What do I want from the job?**

Use the self-evaluation on page 284 to help you to identify what you want from your first job as a graduate.

Activity: What do I want from the job?

- On the table below, indicate with a tick ✓ if the item is something that you would like to gain or develop in the next (or first) job that you take. Put more than one tick if you feel this is very important.
- Then go through the items you have ticked and rate them in order of importance (1 for the most important, 2 for the next in importance, and so on).

From my next job, I want to . . .	Important to me?	Order of importance
1 Gain work experience in a new field		
2 Enhance career opportunities		
3 Earn more money		
4 Increase my job satisfaction		
5 Work in accordance with my values and ethics		
6 Work better hours		
7 Work in better surroundings		
8 Work near home		
9 Work with people who are like myself		
10 Take on more responsibility		
11 Broaden my mind		
12 Give myself more challenge		
13 Know myself better		
14 Develop technical skills		
15 Develop a wider range of skills		
16 Work with a wider range of people		
17 Develop problem-solving skills		
18 Develop inter-personal skills		
19 Develop a broader set of interests		
20 Make friends		
Other things:		
1		
2		
3		

Reflection

In your reflective journal, consider:

- What do I really want from my next job?
- What would most persuade me to apply for a particular job?

Employability: enhancing your career prospects © Stella Cottrell (2003, 2010, 2015), *Skills for Success*, Palgrave

Choosing a job

Know what is right for you

The Careers Service will have a wide range of paper and electronic resources, including psychometric tests, which will enable you to pinpoint the kinds of work that suit you. If you completed the activities in Chapters 1 and 2, you should have a good idea already of the general direction that you want to take in life.

When applying for jobs, consider:

- How could this job advance, in the short or long term, my professional aims?
- How could this job advance, in the short or long term, my life vision?
- Is it consistent with my values and beliefs? (It will be hard to come across well in interview if the job contravenes your basic beliefs and values.)

Consider the best route

Some jobs receive thousands of applications – they are very popular and the reality is that almost every applicant will be disappointed. That does not mean that it is impossible to find a job that suits you. The most obvious route isn't necessarily the only, or best, route to the profession that interests you.

Know all your options

Too many graduates select only the most obvious jobs.

- Talk to the Careers Service so that know the range of jobs open to you. More than two out of every five jobs are open to any graduate, whatever their degree subject.
- Find out about the labour market (see pp. 252–3).
- Identify which jobs have fewer applicants and whether any of these would suit you. They may provide easier entrance routes to the job you prefer over the longer term.

Plan long term

Consider alternative routes to your desired destination. Work experience, travel or gaining skills that are in short supply but relevant may all provide unexpected routes. Broaden your portfolio. Consider how you could network to meet potential employers in occupational sectors that interest you.

Starter posts

Companies tend to be loyal to their own personnel. It is worth thinking about entering at the bottom or in a less competitive post, and aim to work towards the job you want from inside the company. Consider interim jobs that you could fill for a few years and that would provide a sideways route into the job you want.

Choose jobs you can really do

Every employer receives a large number of applications from people who have not interpreted the job description correctly or have not addressed the person specification fully, generally because they are too inexperienced for the role. If you have very few of the qualifications, skills and experiences required, you will not be short-listed. You could have spent your time making a stronger application for a job that is within your competence.

Consider smaller companies

Many students consider only the kinds of large companies that are invited to careers fairs at universities. However, many small and medium-sized companies also recruit graduates (see pp. 252–3). These can provide very good opportunities to develop experience and to rise quickly within a company.

Reflection: Routes into work

In your reflective journal, consider:

- What kinds of jobs are you most interested in?
- Broadly speaking, what are the statistical chances of you gaining that job as a first job? Your Careers Service will give you details of what to expect.
- Brainstorm alternative routes into that job. Which of these would you consider? Which are you most likely to succeed in gaining as your first job?

What do you want from an employer?

For your first job as a graduate you may want to look for specific characteristics in an employer – or you may just want to get a foot on the employment ladder. Local and personal circumstances will affect what kind of choice is available to you. However, the following points are worth considering.

Investors in People

A number of companies have gained Investors in People (IiP) status. This means that the company has demonstrated a commitment to the training and development of its employees. If an employer has IiP status, they are more likely to welcome questions at interview about how they develop their staff. They are very likely to ask candidates about what steps they take to further their own professional development.

Equal opportunities

Equality legislation is aimed at protecting against unfair practices and discrimination, especially on grounds such as race, sex, disability, age, sexual orientation, and religion. Many employers will make a reference to being an 'equal opportunity employer'. This means, usually, that they are keen to be seen making efforts in equal opportunities. It does not necessarily mean that all aspects of work at the company will affect all workers equally, nor that discriminatory practices do not take place. However, if equal opportunities matter to you, you may feel more comfortable at a company that has an equal opportunities policy that extends beyond the basic legal requirements. For more information, see www.equalityhumanrights.com.

Career opportunities

Some companies expect their graduate employees to move very quickly from one post to another. This may mean travel, very varied work, and opportunities to gain a range of experience. Some provide opportunities to work or travel overseas. Larger companies will usually detail such opportunities in their graduate literature. It is reasonable to ask questions about this at interview. Smaller companies are not usually able to create such opportunities so this may affect the type of company that would suit you. However, a small company may be growing quickly and would offer a different kind of opportunity to employees who were with them from the beginning. For information about different kinds of companies, see:

- www.bloomberg.com (international and entrepreneur site)
- www.companieshouse.gov.uk (lists all UK public companies)
- www.bestcompaniesguide.co.uk (reports employee feedback on what it is like to work for named companies).

See also the websites on pages 385–6.

Graduate apprenticeships, internships and company schemes

Some companies offer programmes to bridge the time between university and work. Sometimes this is for an apprentice or intern, with training offered for a reasonable but relatively low salary (or no salary). These are useful for gaining experience of a new work context. Other companies offer outstanding opportunities to work on a particular project in a workplace but under supervision from the university. Your university or college Careers or Employability Service would have details of these.

Your 'bottom line'

A first job can offer experience and training that will be of use in future applications. You are well advised to accept less than the ideal employment in order to gain that first step. However, you should be clear in your own mind about what is and what is not acceptable to you. This may relate to the level of pay, working hours, location, behaviours, being the only person of your sex or colour, lack of reliable transport, or something personal to you. You should be clear where you will not compromise on issues such as:

- personal security
- health and safety
- disability access
- culture and values
- working hours
- travel requirements.

Plan ahead

Make opportunities

Career planning does not start with applying for jobs in your final year at university. Employers will want employees who know how to spot and use opportunities, think on a broad front, and can plan ahead for the good of the company.

They will look to see how you spotted, created and used opportunities on your own behalf. If you did not do this for yourself as a student, they will be less convinced that you could do this on behalf of their company. Ideally, your planning should start in your first year, so that you are in a strong position by the time you apply for jobs.

Develop a rounded portfolio

When people invest in stocks and shares, they are advised not to put all their money into one investment, but to develop a rounded portfolio that includes different kinds of investment. If one type of company fails, others may still provide returns on the investment.

Your time at university is a similar kind of investment. Your energy can be invested entirely in study or spread over a wider portfolio. Your degree is likely to be your most important investment at present, but it does not have to be your sole investment. Furthermore, there are 'smart' ways of putting a degree together so it counts for more.

A rounded student portfolio will contain 'investment' in at least three of the following:

- the degree subject
- complementary subjects
- a broad set of skills that could be transferred to the workplace
- unusual technical expertise
- work experience
- volunteer activity
- contributing to the community
- a position of responsibility
- general career awareness
- awareness of the professional field or the companies where you want a job
- evidence of taking responsibility for personal development needs or training.

When applying for a job, you need to consider:

- 'How have I used my time?'
- 'What have I done that makes my application stand out?'
- 'What will make this company consider me rather than somebody else?'
- 'What evidence have I got that I can deliver the skills they are asking for?'
- 'What experience can I offer?'

The subject and grade of degree are relevant, but are only a small part of the story for most jobs. You will not get a job simply because you have a 'first class' or '2.1' degree. That may be one of ten things the employer will consider, if at all, and is possibly the least important on their list.

Reflection: Developing your personal portfolio

In your reflective journal, consider:

- How are you currently planning ahead so that you have a better chance of gaining the job you want after you complete your degree?
- For jobs that interest you, what are employers likely to look for apart from your degree?
- Which aspects of the 'rounded portfolio' are you already working on?
- Which aspect will you work on next? How will you go about this? Who will you speak to first about this?

When to use the Careers Service

When to use the Careers Service

The Careers Service can give you excellent advice from your first year at university, so that you can plan the best possible route towards the jobs that will interest you later.

The Careers Service should be able to guide you to put together a rounded portfolio. They can advise you on how to spend your time as a student so that you:

- choose an interesting but relevant selection of subjects and options
- understand which skills are relevant to the field of work that interests you
- know how to make the best use of work experience
- plan and prepare well in advance for the areas of work that interest you
- are aware of the range of opportunities available to you through the university, locally and further afield.

Many also have 'job shops' or similar, to help you gain student jobs whilst studying. You may find it helpful to browse websites that give career guidance for graduates. For example, see:

- www.prospects.ac.uk
- www.gradunet.co.uk
- www.careerplayer.com
- www.insidecareers.co.uk

Activity ⟳ **The Careers Service**

- Visit the university Careers Service in person or via their website within the next three weeks.
- Find out what services are available.
- Find out how you can make best use of the service.

Plan to stand out

Employers see hundreds of similar people, all wanting the same job for similar reasons, and all holding similar certificates and qualifications. This is one reason why Careers Services ask to see undergraduates early, so that they can give advice about planning ahead towards the job-application stage. You can prepare to 'stand out' from other applicants by various means:

- *Choose unusual subject options as electives or subsidiary subjects*

Employers are likely to be interested in why you chose unusual options. They may appreciate that you have a broader outlook, or they may be able to use the subsidiary subject in some way. You should plan to choose companies that are likely to appreciate the subjects you selected. For example, you may choose to take a language as an option and look for companies that deal with overseas clients or have overseas branches. Be prepared to answer questions about what it was that interested you about the options you chose, and the links you can make between this, your subject and your career plans.

- *Choose smart combinations*

Consider combining different subjects. For example, lawyers, accountants or designers work for all kinds of businesses. A law student who has studied a module or two of sports science will look more appealing as a lawyer to the sports industry. Similarly, media industries or architectural firms might be more interested in business graduates who have undertaken some study in their own fields and therefore know something about these professions and their terms of reference.

- *Do something different*

An unusual interest, study abroad, travel, a curious combination of languages, success in a competition, holding an exhibition of your work, voluntary work and similar activities can spark an interest in employers. They are likely to ask you questions about these if they interview you.

Presenting yourself to employers

How should I 'stand out?'

Clarify to potential employers exactly what you can offer to them. This means:

- addressing directly and precisely what the employer has stated they want in the person specification, drawing on the job description
- drawing on your research of the business
- demonstrating the 'added value' you would bring.

Your 'value-added'

You may have skills or experience which bring value to employers and which would interest them even if they have not asked explicitly for them. Some areas worth mentioning are:

- additional languages, spoken and/or written
- work overseas, or possibly having lived abroad
- legal, HR, financial, technical and media expertise, especially if applied already in a business context
- experience of governance, such as being a school governor, or Board membership for a company or charity
- managerial or leadership experience
- work that directly supported a member of a senior team, such as PA, research tasks etc.
- undertaking a research project for a business
- having followed a non-traditional route into higher education or into the professional area.

How not to stand out

You can stand out in the wrong way. Avoid:

- *not* addressing the person specification, or leaving it unclear how *exactly* you match this
- inaccuracies in written English, in any part of your application, including emails, texts, covering letters, application forms, etc.
- cliches such as 'I would give 110%'
- focusing on how much you want the job (rather than what you can bring to the role)
- writing styles that are long-winded, pompous, apologetic or over-complicated.

Is it good to have a 'personal brand'?

Trought (2012) argues that you should develop a personal 'brand' to market yourself to employers. This is true to the extent that you need to consider how your application will compete against others.

However, bear in mind that employers are more interested in their own brand, company style and values, and will be looking to see how well you will

What makes you stand out from the rest?

'fit in'. Present your strengths in ways that make sense in terms of their brand and values. If you simply 'sell yourself' or your 'personal brand' you may come across as only interested in you.

Demonstrate your knowledge of them

Use company websites

Be well-informed about what a company says about its aims, plans, achievements, values and employee behaviours on its website. Look at what it requires of employees in general, not just from recent graduates or for this role. Read any company reports in the public domain.

Use LinkedIn

Many companies can now be found on LinkedIn. This is an easy way of doing initial research on:

- the company in general
- how it communicates to others, and what it chooses to communicate about
- key people who work for the company
- recent developments in the company.

Clicking 'see connections' will enable you to see who company personnel connect with professionally. This might also identify similar kinds of companies, opening up further possibilities for you to explore.

Making use of personal records

Chapter 11, 'Maintaining good personal records', provides a range of resources to assist you in recording the information you will need for applications and interviews. These cover most, if not all, of the material you need in order to apply for almost any job.

It is particularly important to focus on the section on personal competences and the competence sheets (see pp. 346–82). Some employers use competency-based approaches for recruitment. Most employers ask for, or welcome, answers rooted in your experience. These forms can help you to prepare well for a wide range of experience-based questions.

These resources are also provided electronically to help you build your electronic portfolio (see p. 23).

Reflection: Stand out from the crowd

Making use of the information in 'Presenting yourself to employers' (page 289), in your reflective journal, consider:

- What is it about you that would make you stand out on an *application form*, increasing your chances of gaining an interview?
- What is it about you that would make you stand out on in an *interview*, so you will be remembered out of a large number of interviewees?
- What can you do now or during the year to develop your profile in this respect?

All of the chapters in this book have been designed to assist you to plan towards your future, develop personal insights, devise strategies for improving personal performance, and understand the skills that are required in many occupations. If you have worked through the activities in this and earlier chapters, you will have developed a good picture of yourself, and the kind of career that might interest you.

When completing your application or preparing for an interview, you will find your 'personal statement' (Chapter 8, p. 243) is of particular value. In the context of applying for a job, a good personal statement will summarise your goals, achievements, and experiences in relation to the post you are considering. If you are not asked for a personal statement, then include similar information in your covering letter.

Activity Update personal records

- Put time aside to update your personal records this week. Which aspects need updating?
- Which three of the competence sheets on pp. 346–82 would you find most useful for the jobs that interest you? Your answers to competence-based questions need to be very brief and very specific.

Browse your personal records, progress file, Higher Education Achievement Record (HEAR) or equivalents, to help you prepare for the application process.

These will remind you of:

- what counts in your life
- what you aim to achieve
- what you have achieved and what you have to offer in a job.

Making the application

Making the application

Read the documentation

First read the documentation you are sent. You will usually receive one or more of the following items.

General information

This will tell you more about the company, work conditions, and sometimes includes information about matters such as pensions, holidays, bonuses, and so forth. Check the company website or contact their Human Resources or Personnel department for further information. Research the company: large companies expect you to know something about them. All employers expect you to know something about their general area of work, whether from personal experience, from having talked to others or from some basic research. Ensure that you are happy with the work ethos, the conditions on offer and the direction and ethics of the company.

The job description

This will outline the responsibilities of the post and what the post-holder is expected to do, building on information that was contained in the advertisement. Check that this does match what was said in the advertisement and that you are still interested. Tick all the responsibilities that you can manage successfully. It is unlikely that any candidates will be outstanding in all the areas that the employer requires, so do not be put off if there are one or two areas where you consider yourself to be weak. Consider what the essentials are and whether you could do these.

The 'Person specification'

The person specification will list the qualifications, experiences, skills and qualities that the employer is looking for. These may be divided into 'essential' and 'desirable'. If many candidates meet all the 'essential' specifications, employers will then look to the 'desirable' items and use these for making a short-list of people to interview. It is unlikely that many candidates will meet all the 'desirable' requirements; you need to make a judgement about your suitability for the job if you do not meet some of these. For example,

some qualifications are very specific, such as for a qualified engineer, or an educational psychologist to administer tests closed to the public. If you lack those qualifications, it is not usually worth applying. However, sometimes relevant experience and skills can be considered as alternatives.

Ensure that your overall application refers specifically to ALL of the items on the person specification, usually in the order they are listed. Typically, an employer will tick off each specification that has been addressed successfully, and then add up the 'ticks'. If you merge two or three characteristics into a single paragraph or example of your experience, some items may not stand out clearly enough to show you meet the specification and this may cost you the interview.

Person specifications usually include:

- *a requirement for qualifications*: 'educated to degree level', 'preferably a degree in a business subject', 'a degree in a care subject', 'preferably with a higher degree (MA)'

> You say here that you play a key role in managing national distribution of all Ace Supermarket's products. Tell us more about that.

> Yeah, that's right. On Saturdays I open the gates for the lorries to go out.

- *skills specific to the job*: 'experience and ability in managing a team', 'experience of working with the public', 'at least two years' experience of working in X'
- *general skills*: 'ability to work as an effective member of a team', 'excellent communication skills', 'ability to work independently', 'a good self-starter'
- *willingness to accept particular work conditions*: 'ability to work flexible hours', 'willingness to work across several sites', 'must be willing to travel'.

Information about how to apply

Read carefully to see whether the employer asks for a CV or other information to be sent in, and whether specific directions are given about completing the application form. Do exactly what is asked because if there are many applicants, the employer may choose to read only those applications that are completed correctly. Failure to follow instructions reflects poorly on applicants' ability to pay attention to details. If you are asked for a CV, send one; if you are asked not to, then don't.

Equal opportunities form

This form is usually for the personnel department and should not be available to the selection team. Large companies need to monitor that they are following equal opportunities policies, and to monitor for potential bias. If the form is not completed, it may make the company appear to be more successful at equal opportunities than they are, as the percentage of people they appoint from under-represented groups may appear to be a high percentage of those who actually apply.

An application form

Not all employers use these. If they do, you must complete it. If it has space for a long personal statement, you can usually provide this as a separate word-processed sheet, writing 'see attached' on the form. Forms are usually provided electronically now, but if they need to be hand-written, people with disabilities who cannot complete a form by hand can request other means of applying.

Complete the form

Complete the form, following the directions closely:

- Ensure the form is clearly written, proof-read and neatly presented: good impressions do count.
- Be honest and accurate: the company is likely to check on information you give them, either immediately or at a later date.
- Be complete: do not leave gaps in work or recent educational histories as this suggests you have something to hide. Include all relevant training and give reasons for work breaks. Complete all requests for information.
- Refer clearly to all skills, qualities, qualifications and experience.

Qualifications

Provide the names of qualifications *in full*, either in the space provided or in your CV or covering letter. The employer may not know what is meant by abbreviations so avoid using these. This is especially important if you are applying for a position overseas. Find out the local equivalent of your qualifications, and indicate these in the covering letter, so that the employer takes them into account.

If you have your degree results, you do not need to go into details about school history unless you are asked for this, or unless a particular school qualification is relevant to the job. However, if you have good A-level grades or equivalents, it is worth mentioning these. Also provide details of GCSE or equivalent in English, maths and, for jobs such as teaching, science.

Write the personal statement

This is an extremely important part of the application process and requires time and thoughtful consideration. Structure it well so the main points can be found easily. If you were asked to send only a CV or letter of application rather than an application form, it is a good idea to include a personal statement to accompany these.

Good personal statements

In good personal statements for job applications, it is clear to the employer:

✓ that you know what the job will entail

✓ that you understand what they are looking for in the new employee and can deliver this

✓ that you know something about the organisation or company

✓ why you want the job

- how your skills, qualities and experience match what they have asked for, in ways that are relevant to the job that you will be doing
- exactly where you are addressing each item in the person specification
- that you have tailored your application to this particular job rather than sending a standard response
- that you write well, clearly, and succinctly and can proof-read accurately (this is an example of your written communication so make sure it is perfectly presented)
- that, through the way you have laid out information so that key points are easy to find, you value the employer's time.

Refer to your personal records

If you maintain good records and competence sheets, such as those recommended in Chapter 11, it will be easier to select appropriate information to complete your personal statement. Read through your records to remind yourself of your strongest competences and the best examples of your experience.

Employers will want to know what you are capable of achieving, so it is important to identify which of your experiences and responsibilities can be described as achievements and successes. If you have held positions of responsibility, ensure that it is clear what your role was. If you held a post in a student society or have held down a job, identify your achievements during that time. For example, turn a sentence such as:

> As Social Secretary, I was responsible for organising social activities for the student body.

into a more detailed statement such as:

> As Social Secretary (2013–14), I was responsible for organising activities for a student body of 14,000 people. I successfully ran 10 events involving 3000 people. Satisfaction surveys were conducted and these received excellent feedback from 87% of respondents. I also increased income by six per cent over the previous year.

Write to the person specification

Go through the person specification and job specification in detail. Use each item in the person specification as a separate heading. Write a succinct paragraph to address each item, giving at least one good (but brief) example to illustrate each.

Example

Specification: 'ability to work as an effective member of a team'

As part of my current part-time job, I am a member of a team of ten people. This requires me to work towards common goals to strict deadlines. The employer has provided two training days in team-work skills. I have been asked to stand in as deputy team leader on several occasions, which attests to my team-management skills. I feel I am a good team member as I am ready to listen and act upon other people's ideas and am confident in making my own suggestions. I also have extensive experience of problem-solving in small groups as part of my degree. I completed a successful group project, which received good feedback from tutors. My main roles in that group were as meeting co-ordinator and data researcher.

Refer to the job

In the statement, include a few sentences in which you clarify why you are interested in the job and what you have to offer to the employer. Select three or four skills or qualities that you think are particularly relevant and list these as benefits that you can offer to the company. This will indicate to the employer that you are serious about this particular job. It will suggest you have thought about its needs and have selected it on the basis of your own suitability.

Writing a covering letter

If you have included a personal statement, your covering letter can be brief (see page 294). If not, your letter should cover the points addressed in the 'personal statement' section above. Your covering letter should:

- demonstrate real interest and passion for the job
- be clear, to the point and businesslike – avoid waffle and anecdote
- tailor the content to the job for which you are applying, including any reference number that was given
- state where you saw the job advertised
- be well-written and proof-read

Your name	Amit Evans
Your full address	1111 Apple Avenue Summertown, London
Your postcode	BB1 11B
Your contact details	Tel: 11111 0303030; Mobile phone: 22222 0303030 Email: agevans@freemail.happy
Date	31 August 2015
Employer contact name **Employer address**	Ms Samantha Browne Alpha Conferences 222–228 Olive Grove Berryfield BB1 XXX

Dear Ms Browne

State the name of the post, its reference, and where and when you saw it advertised

I am very interested in the post of Assistant Conference Manager (ref. AAP/223/01) advertised in the *Guardian* on 27/8/2015.

Give brief details of your experience and suitability. Look at your competence sheets for examples that support your claims

I have recently completed a degree in Business and Economics. As part of my degree, I undertook a project for an events company that mounted conferences for employers locally and nationally. As well as this providing me with experience of event planning, I thoroughly enjoyed the atmosphere and the opportunity to meet a wide range of people.

I have worked in sales and with the public for many years. I hope my ability to speak and write several languages including Welsh and Punjabi will be of additional benefit in the conference world.

Indicate that you know something about the company and why you feel it is the right appointment for you

I am particularly interested in working in a new and growing organisation with an international dimension such as *Alpha Conferences*. I would like to feel I had contributed to the development of a new company in its early stages. Your commitment to employee training is impressive and I would be keen to further my own professional development.

Indicate when you would be available for work

I live locally and would be ready to start work at short notice. I enclose my CV, as requested, and would appreciate the opportunity of an interview to discuss the post further. I look forward to hearing from you.

Use 'sincerely' when you address a named person

Yours sincerely

Sign the letter

[signature]

Type your name beneath

Amit Evans

- demonstrate with confidence how you meet the requirements of the job – or state that this is outlined in your personal statement.

If the employer's form offers very little space for details about your employment history, use the covering letter to detail the relevance of previous roles, responsibilities and training. Mention any other personal qualities, skills and experience that are relevant to the post.

Competence-based applications

Competence-based applications ask candidates to provide concrete examples of how they have demonstrated the skills and qualities needed for the role. This provides an opportunity to demonstrate transferable skills and how these can be applied to the role.

Such jobs are open to a wide range of people, rather than only those with experience of that line of work. This can be an advantage if you haven't had a previous job or if you wish to change your field of work. However, such jobs tend to attract many applicants, so care is needed in selecting the best examples of your experience for each competence and specifying their relevance to the demands of the new role.

Typically, competence-based applications use an application form and allow very small, specific amounts of space for you to complete details about each competence. You will probably be told not to send additional sheets or a CV. This means that you must be very precise and succinct in summarising your competences in order to include the maximum amount of information about yourself in the space available.

The competence sheets on pp. 346–82 will help you to identify the relevant information and to develop skills in writing brief summaries of key information. Competence-based applications are time-consuming, so it is useful to keep good and updated personal records that enable you to identify information quickly.

Curriculum vitae (CV)

This used to be the most common form of document required by employers. However, it is less in demand than it used to be. Agencies often request CVs, and some employers respond to CVs even when they do not have a job on offer. There is a wide variety of acceptable CV formats. However, as an employer may spend less than a minute reading your CV, whatever format you choose needs to be pleasing to the eye and contain a few key details that will make the selector choose you for interview (see the two examples on pp. 296–7).

Content

CVs must include:

- full name
- home address
- contact details (phone, email)
- educational history
- qualifications
- employment history
- complete interests and other information (relevant training, languages, certificates, driving licence).

Incorporate, in the relevant sections, a few key details that indicate levels and breadth of responsibility and experience.

Layout and style

Presentation
Presentation is extremely important to CVs. Employers may receive hundreds of CVs and may conduct the first selection on the basis of presentation skills. If so, they are more likely to eliminate CVs that are too long, which clearly omit essential sections, are handwritten or poorly typed.

Your CV should be:

- headed by your name (don't include 'CV' as a header)
- no more than 2 sides long
- divided into clear sections with headings
- laid out in legible lists or tables for educational history and employment
- easy to read and proof-read for errors
- brief and concise
- relevant to the job.

The whole document should be in the same font style. Use larger fonts and bold or underlining or italics for headings. Each main section should have the same level of heading (the same font size, style and format). Avoid colour, images, unusual or hard-to-read fonts. Avoid 'gimmicks' and special effects.

Amit Geraint Evans

Personal details

Address: 1111 Apple Avenue, Summertown, London   Postcode: BB1 11B
Tel: 11111 0303030; Mobile phone: 22222 0303030   Email: agevans@freemail.happy
Nationality: British

Educational history

2012–15	University College of England, Broad Street, Berryfield, BB1 22K
2004–2012	Albertina Sisulu School, Juniper Street, Hollyacre, YY1 22Y
1997–2004	Oak Primary School, Blethyn Avenue, Llanpwll, XX1 XX2

Qualifications

2015	BA Hons. Business and Economics	2.1
2012	A-level History	Grade A
2012	A-level Economics	Grade C
2012	A-level Business Studies	Grade D
2010	Seven GCSEs (five A*)	

Employment history

2010–2012	Phantom Books, College Street, Berryfield, BB1 33B	Part-time shop assistant	Two days a week; responsibilities for sales and dealing with the public; 2010 promoted to assistant supervisor.
2007–2012	Juniper Papers, Juniper Street, Hollyacre, YY1 22X	Newspaper round	Maintained the same job for five years.

Positions of responsibility

Dates	Position	Organisation	Achievement
2014–15	Student mentor	Holly FE College	Coached three pupils in maths. All successfully passed their GCSE Maths.
2013–14	Treasurer	University Rowing Club	Successfully managed accounts and increased profits by 15 per cent.

Skills and competences

As part of my degree, I undertook a team project for a local employer, Berryfield Employer Forum. We successfully set up a new processing system, which we devised to meet the employer specifications. This was adopted by the company. I took a lead in contacting the employers, encouraging them to take part and to attend launch events that I helped to organise. The project developed my team-building and negotiation skills, as well as familiarising me with events planning. I feel this experience will be of benefit to a post in your conferencing company.

Interests and achievements

I enjoy walking (British Isles; Germany) and rowing. I was a member of the rowing team that won the Community Shield (2014). I enjoyed working on a Mentoring Schools Programme organised by a local FE college, and felt a sense of achievement when pupils' number-skills improved.

Other information

I speak and write, fluently, in Punjabi and Welsh, have GCSE French, and communicate well with a wide range of people. I am used to dealing with the public. I am computer literate and familiar with most business and project software. I am a good self-starter, and enjoy working to tight deadlines. I am keen to develop my expertise in the conference and events business.

Anna Leroy

Personal details

Address: 1112 Apple Avenue, Summertown, London
Tel: 11111 0303031; Mobile phone: 22222 0303031
Nationality: British

Postcode: JJ1 11K
Email: aaleroy@freemail.happy

Educational history

2012–2015	University College of England, Broad Street, Berryfield, BB1 22B
2010–2012	Hilier College, Beckham Road, Oakfield OO2 1DD
1984–1992	Gotama School, Blossom Street, Oakfield, OO1 22Y
1979–1984	St Ann's Primary, Super Road, Ashby, AA1 2AA

Qualifications

2015	BA Hons. Psychology, Grade 2.2
2012	Access to Higher Education Diploma (Hilier College, Social Science Foundation Course)
2011	GCSE English, Grade B
1989	Maths GCSE grade B
1989	GCSE in Biology, Art, Chemistry, Business

Employment history

Dates	Employer	Post	Responsibilities
1998–present	Berry Lawyers, Sharpe Street, Berryfield, BB1 3BB	Part-time legal assistant	Assisting solicitor prepare cases for court; dealing with clients.
1992–1997	Accomb Solicitors, Tailor Road, Oakfield, OO1 22B	Part-time legal assistant	Assisting solicitor prepare cases for court; dealing with clients.
1986–1992	J. J. Field, Solicitors, Tailor Road, Oakfield, OO1 22X	Full-time Administrator/PA	Managing all aspects of a legal office; dealing with the public.
1985–1986	H. Smith Associates, Ash Road, Oakfield, OO1 22P	Administrative assistant	General office duties.

Positions of responsibility

Dates	Position	Organisation	Achievement
2008–2009	Volunteer tutor	University Volunteer Bureau	Tutored a deaf student on a local Access programme. Student has been offered a university place.
2008–2009	Chair	Mature Student Association	Worked with a team to organise 30 meetings and events.
2000–2002	Secretary	Oakfield Playgroup, Ash Road, Oakfield.	Established a thriving playgroup involving 40 families; it still exists. Co-organised meetings and events.
1995–1999	Chair	Oakfield Residents Association, Alder Street, Oakfield OO1 22A	Successful management of an association of 2000 residents; chaired over 50 meetings.

Skills and competences

My work and life history demonstrates that I am a natural organiser. I can see where there are opportunities and will take the lead in creating new groups. I am used to multi-tasking, and have managed to study and maintain family life without taking absences from work. I am very determined and highly motivated. My work in legal companies helped me to develop a wide range of analytical and people skills, which I have developed further through my programme and in the organisations that I have helped to run.

Interests and achievements

I enjoy playing an active part in community events and am generally good with people. I am keen to work in a profession related to the caring professions, where I can make use of the knowledge and skills gained through my Psychology degree.

Other information

I have a full driving licence and excellent technology skills. I am ready to start work at short notice. I am currently taking a course in basic counselling skills.

Language

Use words that emphasise action (verbs). Look for opportunities to include words such as:

> achieved, contributed, co-ordinated, organised, established, demonstrated, accomplished, applied, implemented, initiated, created, set up, developed.

Use words and phrases that demonstrate qualities that employers will value, such as:

> attention to detail, positive outcome, achievement, success, effectively, efficiently, care, creativity, team work, meeting deadlines, co-operation, value for money, time-saving, problem-solving, self-starter, coping strategies, negotiating, networking, flexibility, versatility, creativity, innovation, entrepreneurship, profits, leadership, decision making, priority setting, competitiveness, commercial awareness, communication skills.

CVs for different purposes

You may need more than one CV. The basic CV should be brief, and contain standard information. Academic CVs tend to be longer. If you are looking for an academic job, then include conferences and seminars to which you contributed a paper or workshop, all research projects with details of who funded these, and all your publications. When applying for a job, adapt your basic CV to fit what you know about the company and the requirements of the person specification.

Competence statements in CVs

Traditionally, a CV fits on 1–2 pages. If you have a large number of qualifications or jobs, the information may need to fit onto more than one page. In either case, use only a few words to list the responsibilities associated with each item.

Bright and Earl (2007) argue that candidates who include a brief competence statement within a CV have a good chance of being short-listed. They found that there was no particular place on the CV where it was better to position the competence statement. When you have elaborated your competences (see Chapter 11), you may wish to use short competence statements in your CV.

Sending uninvited CVs

Some employers do file and use CVs sent to them when they have not advertised for a post. Many will not, as those using equal opportunities practices usually will advertise all posts. If you have rare and marketable specialist skills, such as high-level IT skills, then the opportunistic CV can be particularly useful.

If you do send CVs on an opportunistic basis, include additional information relevant to the post, either in the CV or in a covering letter. The employer will need to know, for example:

- the kinds of job that interest you – using job titles if possible
- whether you wish to work full- or part-time
- an indication of the salary level you expect
- which parts of the country you are willing to work in
- the size and kind of company you are interested in working for
- what your ideal job would be.

These CVs may be slightly longer – but do aim to stay under two pages. Include more details about your skills, experience and what you can offer. Your enthusiasm and interest should radiate from the CV in order for it to be considered.

Using the Internet

A source of jobs and advice

Graduate jobs will normally be advertised through the Internet. There are several hundred job sites on the web. Good places to start your search with are www.monster.co.uk and www.gradunet.co.uk. In addition, there are career advice resources on the net, some aimed at students. Some employers will send job details and accept applications and CVs by email. A list of such resources is given in the 'Useful Websites' section at the end of this book.

Put your CV on-line

Large recruiters may provide their own facilities for you to create a CV using a 'wizard'. This is not simply a question of putting up the CV as you have already typed it as, if you do that, you can lose most of the presentational features such as font style and layout: it may look fine on your screen but look messy or bizarre when viewed on the employer's.

You will usually need to write in your details for each website. This takes time so it is worth researching the best recruitment sites for the jobs that interest you. Use a plain-text version to 'cut and paste', using the same font throughout and without using tables or formatting. This will save you time. Leave at least half an hour to do this for each site.

Some employers may simply ask you to send a CV as an attachment. If so, use a rich-text format so that you increase the chance of it printing with the desired layout and presentational features on the employer's printer.

Email cover letters

If you send an application by email, include a covering letter. This should follow the same general principles as any other cover letter. In other words, it should be brief, relevant, to the point, summarising your interest and what you have to offer to the company. Email responses can be signed off as 'Best wishes' rather than 'yours faithfully'.

Assessment centres

Employers state that many students do not do themselves justice at assessment centres and interviews, even after sending in excellent applications and CVs.

What is an assessment centre?

Assessment centres provide a series of extended selection procedures which are used by many companies during recruitment. Sessions typically last one or two days. They may be used either as an initial selection tool or for additional information in between first interviews and final selection.

What would I have to do?

Selection tasks vary. You may be asked to sit a set of written papers or you could spend time in a relatively small group of 6–8 people with 2–4 assessors. You can expect to be assessed through a combination of the following.

Group exercises
These are used to assess how effectively you can work in a team, and your communication and problem-solving skills.

In-Tray exercises
These assess your ability to manage complex information quickly, make decisions and manage your time. They are based on realistic work scenarios.

Presentations
These assess your ability to structure information and convey this to other people. You may receive details of the presentation topic in advance of the assessment centre or on the day itself.

Psychometric assessments

These are carried out by licensed professionals and provide a structured and standardised way of assessing how you might perform on a given task or within a given context. Assessments may be either ability tests or personality assessments.

1 *Ability Tests*
   These look at specific skills and knowledge within categories such as cognitive ability, e.g. memory, verbal reasoning, hand-eye co-ordination.

2 *Personality Assessment*

These are usually questionnaires that you fill in. There are two main types:

- Trait instruments: these focus on behaviour and what you are likely to do in a given context. Your scores are likely to change over time as your skills and experience change. A typical test is the OPQ32.
- Type instruments: these focus on our preferences for thinking, interacting, learning and working. These preferences tend to be more stable and less likely to change over time. A typical test is the Myers Briggs Type Indicator.

How to prepare for an assessment centre

Some aspects of assessment preparation are very similar to how you would prepare for a standard job interview. You can prepare by:

- researching the company website and taking note of any information on recruitment
- thinking about your strengths and potential areas for development
- planning your journey to the assessment centre to make sure that you get there on time.

You are not usually being assessed on what you know, so you do not need to learn specific information in advance. There are a number of websites that can help you prepare for specific aspects of the assessment centre by giving you more information about the types of task that may be given and opportunities to complete test questionnaires. Some of these are listed at the end of the chapter (page 310).

Assessment centres can be quite daunting but it is important to bear in mind:

- As a range of areas are being assessed, it is likely that you will find some assessments easier than others and that you will perform more effectively on some than on others. Try not to panic if you feel you have performed poorly on one task – you may perform well in other areas and it is your overall performance that is being assessed.
- Focus on your own performance and avoid becoming over-concerned about the performance of other candidates. You are being assessed against pre-determined criteria rather than your performance in relation to other people.

- Stay focused through the sessions. Even though assessment centres can be very tiring, your motivation levels are being assessed and you need to maintain these.

Referring to disabilities

Many students with disabilities are unsure whether they should mention a disability at interview or not. In Britain, legislation should protect your rights if you have a disability, but employers are still not always aware of what to do when faced with a candidate with a disability.

Should I tell the employer?

There is no easy answer to this. If you need particular help for the application process, the interview or the job, then you will need to disclose the disability. If you do not, then it may not be relevant and it would be an individual decision whether you say anything. You must ensure that you would not leave employers in a position where they could not meet their health and safety responsibilities to you or the public if you do not disclose.

How should I bring up the subject in interview?

If you have not needed to change the interview in any way because of the disability, then the employer may not be aware of the disability. Personnel usually keep this information confidential. It is probably best to assume that the employer may know little about what the disability means in terms of how you might do the job, and may even hold erroneous, very confused or exaggerated ideas about what different disabilities are.

Choose a positive way of introducing the disability. For example, identify the additional skills and qualities you have acquired because of the disability. It is likely that you will have developed additional skills and personal qualities to manage the disability alongside study, work and other people's attitudes. This may have become such a way of life that you underestimate how many skills you have developed in this respect. For example, you may have:

- IT skills (awareness of different ways of making electronic material accessible, which the company might need in order to meet disability legislation)
- people skills (familiarity in dealing with other people's discomfort, embarrassment or rudeness; familiarity with a wider range of people; awareness of how people respond to 'outsiders'; greater ease in dealing with people with disabilities, who form a large minority of the population)
- creativity and problem-solving skills (you will probably have had to find new ways of performing a range of tasks, some of which called for ingenuity)
- self-management skills (disabilities usually call for greater application, determination, self-motivation and endurance).

No two people are alike

Your disability and your strategies for dealing with it, as well as your individual characteristics, will mean that you are different from any other person with a disability that the employer has met. However, the employer may have had a bad experience employing a person with a similar disability. Even though it should be obvious, it is worth your mentioning that no two people with the disability respond in the same way, so that the employer starts with a cleaner slate in considering your application.

Be clear about your abilities

The employer may have very mistaken ideas about what a person with your disability can do. They may underestimate your capabilities. Outline, briefly, your achievements. For example:

I gained excellent feedback from my work placement, where I helped to design a new door operation system. I was able to call upon the design and IT skills that I had developed through my degree, and feel these would be very useful for this job too.

I worked as a volunteer technician for three years for a local theatre group. This brought me into contact with a wide range of people. Many community groups used the theatre. I feel this experience has developed my expertise in finding technical solutions at very short notice and on a tight budget. It also showed me that I enjoy working with older people. These skills and qualities should stand me in good stead for this post.

Outline briefly how the disability does affect you

If possible, present this in the context of what you can do, or the strategies you have developed in order to achieve a result. For example:

My writing skills are good when I use speech-to-text software. I am very familiar with X software. I work quickly and I have a clear writing style. I proof-read well but it is useful if someone else checks the final version.
I organise my time so that I change between tasks every few minutes if I can, so as to change the groups of muscles I am using. I tend to keep two or three different tasks on the go at any one time. This is usually very efficient because I do not get bored and it fills in the natural pauses that occur when you wait for responses from clients.

Mention ways that the disability will affect you at work and what your needs will be.

- 'I need to jot down verbal instructions and then I can work through them.'
- 'The wheel chair requires a width of X cm.'
- 'I am sensitive to light and will need to work in dimmed light or wear glasses with tinted lenses, which I will provide.'

ⓐ Preparing for the interview

Mental preparation

If you have made a sensible job choice, were able to meet the 'person specifications' and have thought through answers to likely questions, you should feel confident that you have a reasonable chance of being considered for the job. The majority of applicants do not receive an interview, so if you have been offered one, this is already a success. Focus on being calm, and on the questions you can answer. Remind yourself of your interest in the job and of what you have to offer the employer. Make sure you sound convincing to yourself. It is natural to feel anxious, but avoid feeding your anxiety by negative thinking.

Prepare for likely questions

Preparing for the more obvious questions will help you to feel confident about answering at least some questions well. This gives you more room for error on other questions. The section below gives an indication of the kinds of questions that you can expect.

Two-minute answers

When preparing your answers, aim to complete any answer in one to two minutes. The interviewer may wish to ask between six and ten questions, as well as using time to ask the question and make comments of their own. It is unlikely the employer will wish the question stage to last more than 20–30 minutes. If your answers are long, they may not be able to ask all their questions, which means you will be disadvantaged if they award points for each answer.

Identify your strong points for each question

Before the interview, identify what are the strongest points you can make for each likely question. A strong answer will refer to experience, achievement and success. It will also be specific: give at least one example, with reference to the scale or importance of the achievement, including one or two key pieces of data if relevant.

Prepare points to include in the interview

Use the interview to bring out your strongest points. Be very clear what these are in advance so that you bring them in when an opportunity arises. Before the interview:

- List your strongest five achievements, qualities or attributes
- sum these up in fewer than 20 words
- think of which questions you may be asked where you can bring in these five points
- be ready to bring them in elsewhere if they do not arise naturally.

Sense of time

Practise speaking aloud and timing yourself so that you develop a sense of what two to three minutes feels like. You should build up a sense of how much you can say within that time, without sounding rushed. You can cover a number of relevant details in two minutes if you are precise and to the point. The activity 'Speaking time', below, should help.

Activity 6 Speaking time

Look at the example below. How long do you think it would take to deliver? Read it aloud at a reasonable speed, with expression, and time yourself.

Q: 'Have you worked in a caring post before?' (The candidate has not done so.)

A: 'My most relevant work experience has been in acting as a student tutor to three young children in a local school. Those children were very vulnerable, and I had to develop skills which are typical of those needed in care posts. For example, I focused on building a rapport with the children, watching for non-verbal cues, and being sensitive to their feelings. I had to be prepared to wait and work at their speed. I also had to consider the wishes of the teacher and other parties. I feel I achieved a good relationship with the children and their teachers. I negotiated work schemes with the teacher and each child. The teacher said that they all made an improvement and I received very good feedback, so it seems to have worked well. I think that gives me a good foundation for this post, and I particularly look forward to working with children and parents.'

- What do you think are the strong points about this answer?

Presentation

Employers expect candidates to be smartly dressed and presentable: you may need to act as the public face of their company at some stage. Pay attention to details such as clean hands and fingernails, polished shoes, and a smart bag. This is true even if you will not be expected to dress smartly in the job.

In the interview

First impressions

Although the whole interview is important, you can make the interview run more smoothly if the first minute is well managed. This requires only a few simple actions.

- Look clean and smart.
- Be on time.

- Ensure your right hand is free in order to shake hands.
- No matter how you feel, smile and appear relaxed.
- Look pleased to meet the interviewers. Shake hands firmly, look them in the eye, and listen when they say their names.
- Move calmly so that you do not crash into furniture.
- Sit upright, alert and interested for the interview.

During the interview, avoid apologies and regrets. Work with the situation as it is, not with what might have gone better. Tell yourself that the interviewers' questions are interesting and manageable – keep considering what it is they are looking for in an employee and what examples you can give them to reassure them that you can meet their needs.

You do not need to be magical, a super-brain, or word-perfect. Everybody stumbles on some words and questions. Avoid gimmicks, 'hard sell' and theatrics. Be natural. If possible, imagine you are being interviewed by an interested relation of one of your friends or colleagues. Although this advice seems obvious, many candidates do not come across as genuinely interested in the job, easy to get on with, honest or natural.

Keep it simple

It is not unusual to ruin a potentially good interview by trying too hard to impress. If you demonstrate a reasonable degree of calm, interest and enthusiasm, you will already be well placed. Employers may take a number of approaches to selecting a candidate. They will usually look for a 'good fit' between what they want and what the candidates can offer. This is partly a question of skills and experience. However, the majority of candidates short-listed for interview will probably be well matched for skills and experience. Possibly, none may meet all the requirements. All will meet about 75–95 per cent, with different kinds of strengths. If the employer needs very specific skills which are in short supply, the person with the best skills will get the job.

However, the probability is that the choice will come down to inter-personal skills and behaviour demonstrated in the interview. The interview is about meeting you and seeing what you are like:

the employer already has information about your skills and experience. The employer or interview panel will want to choose someone who:

- can do the job with minimum training and supervision
- seems like a reasonable, sensible person, with common sense, whom colleagues could work with
- answers their questions, rather than delivers a sales pitch
- will 'fit' the post; who seems to suit the work temperamentally
- looks as though they will 'fit in' generally.

Team work and supportive working climates are important so it is understandable that interview panels will favour people who seem to have the right characteristics to suit their work environment. This is usually a question of apparent personality. Under equal opportunities legislation, interviews should not discriminate on the grounds of sex, race, disability, etc. However, personality and other characteristics can become confused in people's minds. If you suspect discrimination, you have legal rights.

It is important to project yourself as mature, reasonable and friendly. It may help to focus on this rather than struggling to make 'perfect answers'. Many people come across as very stilted, and even bizarre, in interview because they are nervous. Focus on the needs of the panel – what they are looking for – rather than on 'selling' yourself.

During the interview

Put yourself in the employers' position. They are likely to interview at least four people during a period of two to three hours. They may be interviewing dozens of people over several weeks. Even four interviews in a row can be tiring. It will be appreciated if you:

- provide brief answers which are to the point
- provide clear examples
- provide exactly the information you are asked for
- are ready for predictable questions so that you can answer promptly.

Avoid

- long, winding answers that go off the point

- 'interesting anecdotes'
- giving several examples if you are asked only for one
- giving a long background to your answers.

Opening questions

Employers tend to start interviews with one or two questions to settle the interviewee. Here are some typical questions.

'Have you had a good journey?'
This is politeness. Answer very briefly.

...traffic on Old St... dreadful... temporary lights on Windsor Road... and don't get me started on the contraflow!!

'Tell me a little about your programme'
Two or three sentences will suffice. Draw out unusual features as these may reflect well upon you.

'Why do you want this job now?'
Be as specific as you can. Include reference to something about the company that appeals to you. The employer wants to know why you want to work at this company, and that you have done some homework about the company, not that you are desperate for a job. Indicate what you think you can offer to the company.

'Where do you see yourself in 3/5/20 years' time?'
The employer is looking to see whether you are realistic and whether you are a good match for the job. They may be checking to see whether you are likely to leave within a few months or weeks of appointment. You may not know your plans five years into the future but give a strong answer that indicates you have an idea of what you want to achieve. Refer to the kind of experience you

hope to achieve from this job that will further your own aims in a few years' time. Your answer should suggest there is benefit to yourself as well as the employer in you being offered this post.

'What attracted you to this job?'
Candidates are unlikely to be interviewed and/ or appointed unless they show interest in the specific job and work context, unless they possess very highly valued skills in short supply. Find out about the occupational area or industry and the employer – at least enough to hold a conversation for a few minutes.

'Tell us about yourself'
This can be the most difficult question as there is so much to choose from. It is, therefore, a question for which you should prepare. Play safe by referring to your career ambitions and why you think these suit your personal characteristics and experience. Keep it very brief. The employer may be looking to see how aware of your audience and how concise you are, rather than being interested in your life.

Person specification and competency questions

Most questions will relate to the person specification. Although you will have given this information already when you applied, employers may ask similar questions to ones you believe you have answered. This may be for several reasons.

- The panel may not have been involved in the short-listing process and may have received your details at the last moment.
- The panel is seeing many people. They are likely to remember what they hear rather than what you have written.
- Do not assume that just because you have given the answer in the paperwork, the panel will have read it. Give a full answer in case they have not.
- The panel is looking at your people skills. They know you know the answers to most questions, but want to see how well you communicate information to other people.
- They are 'double-checking' to compare your verbal answers with those on paper.

Competence questions
For competence-based applications, most questions usually relate to the competences in the person specification. This means you can prepare for these with reasonable confidence. Think of

unusual angles for the question. A competence question may be phrased in very different ways. For example, a question on dealing with difficult people might be phrased as:

- 'From your life and work so far, give the best example of a time when you had to deal with a difficult member of the public.'
- 'Can you give us two or three examples of a time when you …'
- 'Think of an example when you dealt badly with a member of the public. What did you learn from that occasion and how has this affected the way you would approach a similar situation now?'
- 'What kind of advice would you give a new member of staff who had not dealt with the public before?'
- 'What professional development have you undertaken in recent years to improve your capability in dealing with members of the public?'
- 'What is the worst example of you dealing with a member of the public? What did you learn from this experience?'

Catch-all questions

A number of questions tend to appear in many job descriptions, and mean different things depending on the type of job.

'Team work' may be used to mean:

- good at people skills
- easy to get on with
- takes on board colleagues' needs
- has specific skills in negotiating with others
- has experience of working in project teams.

'Leadership' could be used to refer to:

- willingness to speak on behalf of the group
- a strong vision that carries other people – such as directing plays or setting up student groups
- a tendency to be the person chosen to act as group chair
- experience of running a project
- experience of running a major project.

'Good self-starter' may mean:

- enjoys working on their own
- will accept a job that offers little support
- works well independently
- can start a new job without supervision
- has good problem-solving skills

- can take on major projects in almost any area
- is a responsible worker.

'Flexibility' may mean willingness to:

- fit in
- work with a wide range of people
- work unusual or long hours
- change schedule at short notice
- respond quickly to crises
- work at different locations
- travel
- help out different departments in emergencies
- change department, role or workload
- find solutions to a wide variety of problems.

It is important to work out, from the level and nature of the job, what kind of interpretation to use. It is also important to gain a balance, so that you can show that you are able to work with and listen to others, but are also able to work alone, take responsibility, and give direction to your own and others' work.

Anticipating questions

For each element of the person specification, consider how you would respond to the following questions, bearing in mind the requirements of the job for which you are applying:

- Your best example. What is good about it? What worked well? What was your own contribution?
- Two or three brief examples. What do these suggest about the breadth of your experience?
- An example from which you learnt something that improved your current performance. If you are asked for your 'worst experience', this may be a useful example as you can emphasise what you learnt that benefits your current performance.
- How would you advise somebody else to perform this competence?
- What professional development have you undertaken in relation to this competence?
- What skills and personal qualities were involved in an example of this competence?
- How regularly do you demonstrate this competence? (This is to check whether your example is a 'one off' or represents your everyday experience.)
- At what level of responsibility do you demonstrate this competence? (This is to check your ability to take responsibility for tasks that involve this competence.)

Other typical questions

Other favourite questions are variations on the following themes.

An example of a highlight from your life or career so far

Be prepared to describe briefly what happened and why you consider this to be a highlight. For example, it may have developed particular skills that would be useful to the company. It may have been an occasion where you took on a challenge or worked at a higher level of responsibility than previously and proved your capability.

An example of your worst mistake

Use this as an opportunity to show how you are willing to learn from mistakes and to put that learning to good use. Avoid using an example that would make the employer worry about employing you. Select the kind of mistake that anybody could make. The employer will also want to see that you are willing to take responsibility for your own actions, rather than trying to lay the blame on others (even if it was someone else's fault, in your opinion). See the Competence Sheet on p. 374.

Examples of your commitment to personal development

You can expect this kind of question from employers who have 'Investors in People' status, professional organisations and posts related to public office.

What contribution do you think you can make? What have you got to offer?

Refer to specific experience and skills that you have gained and which are likely to be of benefit to the company. Relate your contribution to what has been described in the job specification and to what you have found out about the company. Include personal qualities. If possible, refer to feedback that you have received from employers or from colleagues or team members.

What personal qualities do you possess that would be of benefit in this work?

Select two or three qualities upon which you can focus. Give one or two sentences to sum up where you demonstrated this quality and why you consider it relevant to the current post. List briefly three to five other qualities that you also possess. Leave it to the interviewer to ask you more details

about these. Be prepared to give examples if questioned further. See pp. 319 and 346.

A critical event in your life or work that you have coped with

This may be another way of asking about 'worst mistakes' or 'highlights', depending on how it is phrased. You are unlikely to receive all three questions, so you should be able to use the same material to prepare for at least two of these questions. This question is looking for such features as evidence of levels of responsibility you have held, coping and problem-solving strategies, ability to reflect upon and learn from experience and apply learning to new areas. For caring professions, it may be used to explore your ability to describe and work with emotions and feelings; in creative fields, to see how you use experience as inspiration for your artwork; for management posts, to see how well you manage complex and difficult situations.

What you learned from …

You may be asked why you chose a particular study option or job, and what you learned from these. For example, you may have learnt to be flexible, to work with difficult people, to maintain high levels of concentration when working with numbers, to think analytically, to be a stronger person emotionally, to deal with the unexpected. Indicate how the subject or experience drew out your natural strengths and abilities. Focus on those aspects that are relevant to the job for which you are applying.

Closing questions

General interest questions

Sometimes employers ask about your general interests at the end of an interview. These usually seem to be easier, and so candidates may relax and let down their guard, revealing a different side to themselves. For example, the employer may ask:

> Q: 'I see you are keen on Mexico. What is the interest there?'

It is important to remember that you are still being interviewed. The employer is still looking to see what it is you have to offer the company. Your answer should reflect this. Keep your reply brief: this is not an opportunity to tell the employer all about your pet interests. Your answer might bring out personal qualities or an ability that is useful to the company. For example (depending on the circumstances):

A: 'I am keen to develop my Spanish.' (*Useful if the company has Spanish-speaking offices or customers.*)

A: 'I wanted to find out about a different culture and have always been interested in Mexican art.' (*This suggests you have a breadth of interests and the confidence to go and find things out for yourself.*)

Do you have any questions you would like to ask us?

You do not have to have a question, especially if the information is available in the literature that was sent to you, or is available from Personnel or on the Internet. Avoid unnecessary questions: they may suggest you have not done your homework. The employer will not want the interview to go on too long, so keep to one or two essential questions. Reasonable questions to ask are, for example:

- related to something that was reported recently in the trade papers about the company, especially if it allows them to make a positive response
- genuine questions that determine whether you want the job. Now is the time to ask these
- questions about training and professional development
- whether there is a mentoring scheme for new employees
- what would the employer consider to be a sign of your success after two years with the company? What are their expectations of you as a new employee?
- who you will be reporting to
- opportunities for travel, or for secondment
- what the next step will be. When are you likely to hear the outcome of the interview?

Questions to avoid

Avoid asking questions:

- where the information is provided already in the paperwork or on the company website
- that you could have checked with HR/Personnel before the interview
- that you should have checked before applying in order to make sure this was the right job

- about whether advertised terms and conditions can be changed just for you
- questions that start with 'Will I have to ...?' (Use: Will the job involve ...?)
- that your common sense should be able to answer.

Is there anything you feel we should know that you have not yet had a chance to tell us?

- Some employers are aware that candidates are anxious and may not have given their best answers. If you really feel that you have let yourself down on an answer, this is an opportunity to return to it, if you feel you can now give a better response.
- Before the interview, you may have rehearsed skills and qualities that you feel are important to this kind of job or company. If these have not been referred to in the interview, raise these now.

If we offered you the job, when would you be able to start?

Ensure you are clear about your personal arrangements so that you are in a position to answer this.

Activity **Sabotage the interview**

1 List all the things you can think of to really mess up an interview so that the employer is convinced you are unprepared and unsuitable. You may include comments related to:
   - your clothing
   - your punctuality
   - not knowing anything about the company
   - asking silly questions when given the opportunity.

2 Give yourself advice!

   What advice would you give to somebody else who said they sabotaged interviews in this way? The advice may seem obvious to you – but many people forget the basics. If you are uncertain about how to prevent the sabotage you suggest, speak to a careers adviser at the university.

3 Write a preparation list for yourself in order to ensure you are ready for your interview.

- Find one or preferably two other people with whom to practise your interview techniques. This may be embarrassing, but it is better to get feedback before the interview rather than after.

- Give details of the kind of job for which you are applying. The other person(s) can use and adapt the questions in this chapter to conduct an interview for your job.

- Give at least 15 minutes for each person's interview.

- Ask for (or give) feedback that is constructive. The feedback should give clear guidance on what is good about your interview performance already, as well as what could be even better.

- Note down the feedback you receive and decide what you will do to improve your performance.

After the interview

After the interview, you will probably remember all the things you wish you had said. It is not always easy to tell whether you were successful. Use the experience to learn more about your performance so that it was not a waste of time, no matter what the outcome is.

Analyse the questions

Jot down all the questions you were asked.

- Which ones were unexpected? Were any of these similar to questions that you had prepared, without you realising? Note the different ways that employers can word questions aiming at similar information.

- Note how many questions you were asked. How long was your interview supposed to last? Take ten minutes off that time and divide the remaining time by the number of questions. How long did the employer expect each answer to be?

- Were your answers too long? If so, practise punchier responses for the next interview.

- Were your answers too brief? If so, think of a good example of your experience that you could use to develop that answer more fully.

Analyse your performance

- Which examples did you use? Were these your best? Remind yourself of your best example so that this stays in your mind next time.

- Did you include all of your best points?

- What went well about the interview? Jot this down and read it before the next interview.

- What could have been better? How would you deal with this next time? Write this down and read it before the next interview.

Ask for feedback

Some companies will give brief feedback to unsuccessful candidates. It is worth asking for this. However, be prepared for very general comments such as 'the candidate we selected was the most successful in meeting the criteria'. Some companies refuse to give any feedback, in order to avoid legal repercussions.

Reflection: Learn from the job application

- Select one job interview that you attended, whether successful or not. If you have not applied for a job interview, now is a good time to practise with a friend.

- In your reflective journal, go through the 'After the interview' section above. Jot down ten things you did well.

- Jot down the three things which are most important to improving your performance at job interviews.

Closing comments

This chapter opened with an outline of the career planning journey: Aspire, Act, Apply, Achieve. The opening sections of the book encouraged you to consider what 'success' meant for you. This should help you to set life and career aspirations that are meaningful for you. Creating and taking the right opportunities for you will help you to achieve those aspirations.

This chapter helps you to put your career planning journey on a good footing, helping you with guidance on how to act, apply and achieve successfully. It guides you through the appointments processes for new jobs, placements or internships, so that these become more predictable, manageable and more likely to result in success. It also supports you in learning from work placements and employment, in order to help improve your future performance when applying for jobs.

This chapter has covered the basics of applying for work as a graduate student. There is a very wide range of materials available to help with specific aspects of the process. If you are very anxious about certain aspects, such as answering interview questions, or writing CVs for the Internet, then there are books to help with every detail.

However, in most cases, the basics are enough. If the employer wants someone with more experience or particular skills, they will employ on that basis, no matter how good your application. The important basic rules are:

- Apply a problem-solving strategy to finding a job. Good preparation is similar to the 'problem elaboration' referred to in Chapter 6.

- Research your options and look for opportunities that carry you towards your long-term goals.
- Choose well. Unrealistic and unsuitable applications may be a waste of your time.
- Rather than sending out hundreds of applications, select a few applications, research the companies and fine-tune the personal statement or competences so that they are precise, informative, clear and relevant to the job.
- Ensure you keep your personal records or progress file up to date so that you can make a good application at short notice. See Chapter 11.
- Prepare for the interview. Use the competence sheets in your progress file.

You will be a stronger job applicant if you can:

- demonstrate how a job matches your personal aims and values (see Chapter 1)
- talk knowledgeably about the business and role
- explain coherently how you gained relevant experience
- show how you made good use of opportunities
- articulate your skills in managing people, tasks and yourself, and demonstrate that you can think intelligently about the job.

Finally, aim to learn from the experience. You may pass the majority of courses or exams that you take in your life, but it is unlikely that you will be successful in gaining a job for each application. You will benefit enormously if you view each application and interview as a chance to gain experience, develop application skills, and learn something about employers or yourself. Reflect on the experiences and keep records so that you can benefit in the future.

Further reading

Bright, J. and Earl, J. (2007) *Brilliant CV: What Employers Want to See and How to Say It*, 3rd edn (London: Prentice Hall). (Useful if the jobs you apply for are mostly CV-based rather than form-based.)

Chapman, A. (2001) *The Monster Guide to Jobhunting* (London: Financial Times/Prentice Hall). (Detailed guidance on using the Internet. Useful if you are not already comfortable using the Internet.)

Hodgson, S. (2007) *Brilliant Answers to Tough Interview Questions*, 3rd edn (London: Prentice Hall). (One of a number of books that are useful to focus the mind when preparing for an interview.)

Jackson, T. and Jackson, E. (1997) *The Perfect CV: How to Get the Job You Really Want*, revised and updated edition (London: Piaktus).

Popovich, I. (2003) *Teach Yourself Winning at Job Interviews* (London: Hodder Education). (Traditional but sensible advice on job interviews.)

Rook, S. (2013) *The Graduate Career Guidebook* (London: Palgrave Macmillan).

Resources on assessment centres

www.prospects.ac.uk/links/AssessmentCntrs   General advice on exercises and how to prepare

http://targetjobs.co.uk/general-advice/assessment-centres.aspx   General advice

www.psychometric-success.com/assessment-centers/assessment-and-development-center.htm   Advice and practice tests

www.shl.com/TryATest/Pages/CandidateHelp.aspx   Practice tests

Chapter 11
Maintaining good personal records

Learning outcomes

This chapter offers opportunities to:

- create and build your personal records
- undertake a profile of current skills and qualities
- map your personal competencies in relation to the 'person specifications' frequently required for jobs, and to questions typically asked at job interviews
- record your education, training and other examples of professional development
- develop personal resources that you can draw upon to write a CV and personal statement when applying for work.

Introduction

It's never too early to start planning for life after university and you can save yourself a lot of time and effort if you record your achievements as you progress through your course. Chapters 1 and 2 focused on an analysis of yourself, and the vision and goals that should be informing and inspiring such advance planning, in order to assist your career development.

When you apply for a job or attend an interview, you will be required to identify, at speed, the best examples for a wide range of questions. Most of us have the information we need to make good responses – but accessing it at speed is not always easy.

This chapter provides resources for collating information about your experience and reflecting upon that experience so that you can identify your achievements easily.

It is important to bear in mind that employers will be looking to see not only what experience you have but also what you made of the opportunity: your successes, what you learned from the experience, its significance in your life, and how you can use the experience to benefit their company. They will want to see how you make use of experience and opportunity generally – so that they feel comfortable that you will make good use of opportunities on their behalf as well as your own. They will use the information you give them to form judgements about your coping strategies, your work ethic, your attitude to work and life, your character, and even the way you relate to others.

Paper or electronic personal records?

You are likely to need both paper-based and electronic personal records for different purposes. Many certificates, licences and similar records will be provided to you in paper format. It is useful to develop a system of records that holds these together. Moreover, you will be asked to send copies of these to employers, so keeping these together with your personal records will save you time. In addition, you may wish to include reflective notes, examples of your work, photographs, images, and hand-drawn records for your own personal use. These may be best stored in paper form.

On the other hand, some records (such as your CV, education and training history, personal statement, and competence sheets) will need to be updated regularly. This is accomplished most easily electronically. Hard copies of these can be useful for reminding you of things you need to do when browsing through your records.

a Developing your personal records

Organising your personal records

The contents of your personal records will be particular to you. Whatever you include, it is useful to:

- include a contents page or folder so that you can find records and evidence easily
- make electronic copies of data that need to be updated, such as records of your employment history, skills and competences
- number the items in each folder or section rather than from the front of the file. This will enable you to update sections with minimum effort
- for paper folders, invest in a large folder (as your records will grow as your work history develops) and section dividers.

An example of a *Contents* sheet is offered below (p. 317), as a guide to what you could include in your records.

Records for personal planning

The nature of these records will vary depending on the requirements of your programme. They will also vary according to the importance you place upon your own personal development and the role of reflection in your life.

The various chapters of this book have structured reflection along thematic lines and through a variety of activities and questionnaires. If you completed any of those activities, you will already have compiled a record of yourself, your thinking, your attitudes and your goals. You may find it useful to draw together some of those resources into a single electronic folder and supporting paper-based portfolio. In particular, you may wish to make a photocopy of responses you completed on paper to some of the following activities. If so, include copies of the blank pro-formas so that you can update your responses.

Include your responses to any of the following activities you choose to include: it is what is important to you that really counts.

Records for job applications

Chapter 10 looks at the process of applying for a job, and making best use of information about yourself. A good application will be tailored to the particular job and person specification, which takes time to put together well. Good interview answers may require you to reflect upon your experience from quite different angles.

It is extremely common for people to emerge from an interview saying. 'Why didn't I say that?' 'Why didn't I use this example rather than that?' Similarly, it is easy, once the envelope is in the post, to remember information that could have been included to strengthen the application.

The answer is usually in the preparation. Good preparation means that you have much more control over your responses, whether at the application or interview stage. Your memory is primed to call upon the examples you really want to use. Moreover, knowing that you are well prepared will increase your overall confidence, so that you come across as a much stronger candidate.

Records of reflection

Recording reflection

Keeping personal records of some kind is integral to personal development work. Your university may require you to keep a log, blog journal or portfolio and give you very precise directions about what to include and how to present it. Alternatively, you may be asked to devise your own records and presentation. Most of the resources associated with this chapter are provided in the Resource Bank for easy use, at the end of the book and electronically.

Logs, blogs and journals

In this section, the term 'reflective journal' is used to refer to all kinds of reflective logs, blogs, diaries, journals and notes. There are different ways of keeping reflective journals. You can:

1 Note down all aspects of a particular experience, such as the fine details of an observation or experiment or how you designed a product. Some subjects require you to note this objectively (without comment); others require you to reflect upon what you observe.
2 Keep a daily or weekly diary on a particular theme.
3 Keep together all the influences, inspirations, sketches and thought processes that led to a final product or outcome. This is particularly true of art, design and other creative programmes.

4 Share your thoughts with others through a blog.

5 Record all the information you consider significant about your learning. This could include items such as:

- the general topics covered
- exhibitions, placements, visits, field trips, etc.
- your feelings about the programme, teaching methods, students, and your responses to these
- contributions you make in class
- things you find difficult – and how you address those difficulties
- thoughts about your learning styles and habits, and the appropriateness of these for you and your learning goals
- ideas that arise from your study
- what you find most stimulating in your current study
- how your studies relate to real life
- how theory covered in class is relevant to practical or case work you are undertaking
- what you are learning about yourself through your interactions with others
- tips and strategies you are gathering
- what you are learning about how you manage your emotions
- sources of inspiration.

Maintaining a reflective journal

Keeping a reflective journal can be very challenging, especially staying motivated to make regular entries. It takes determination, good planning and a far-sighted approach. It also means having a strong sense of responsibility for your own development over time. Keeping a journal requires the 'stick-with-it-ness' Edison referred to above (p. 182). The benefits tend to arrive very gently and may not be noticeable for a long time. Even if you cannot detect them easily, the benefits are likely to be there.

Chapter 8 provides support and guidance on developing skills, methods and thought processes that underpin reflective practice.

Using your reflective journal

Reflective journals should be easy to use. This means:

- easy to carry around

- a notebook you like or electronic variant you enjoy using
- numbered or labelled so you can find previous entries easily and quickly. Use headings and dates for each entry.

A loose-leaf folder or electronic journal has the advantage that you can enter your responses to events out of sequence, when the idea strikes you. However, you may prefer to keep a notebook, diary or portfolio, depending on what is needed for your course and what suits your own style.

Format for a journal entry

As well as impromptu entries, such as those listed above, you may find it helpful to work to a format to explore your progress on current goals. One format is given on p. 336. Ideally, this should be used in conjunction with an action plan (see p. 177).

Portfolios

What is a portfolio?

Progress files were described in the Introduction. A portfolio or progress file of personal records is simply a file where you keep together relevant information about yourself. These assist the process of reflection. It is useful to keep and update a portfolio of information that you can call upon to:

- go over your reflections
- monitor your progress
- keep important documentation together
- keep feedback in one place
- use for sessions with tutors, careers advisers and support staff
- help staff write your references
- write your CV and job applications. See pages 295–9.

Contents of a portfolio

You may find it useful to include some or all of the following in your full portfolio.

A contents page

Divide the material in your portfolio into sections. Number and label these so that you can find material and update it easily: see p. 317. Use a detailed contents page to direct you to materials.

Summary

Include a personal statement or position paper (see pages 243–5). Aim to be selective and specific, identifying key themes and bringing out what you have learnt. The position paper should refer precisely, but very briefly, to evidence contained within the portfolio.

Formal documents

- certificates of any qualifications
- your academic transcript
- references and testimonials you have received
- an example of a recent piece of marked work is also useful when seeing support tutors.

Developmental documents

- completed, dated, self-evaluation questionnaires
- responses to any activities in this book or similar activities
- feedback from tutors and peers for past assignments and your commentary on these.

Planning documents

- documents you completed about your current goals and aspirations, such as what you want to achieve from the course, where you see yourself in five to ten years' time, who or what inspires you, what motivates you, and what you need to do to achieve your goals
- your updated action plan to achieve academic or other goals
- details of priorities you have set, including milestones, targets and deadlines, and how far you kept to these.

Documents relevant to future job applications

- a profile of vocational, technical, academic and other skills you have developed
- an updated summary of your education and training, including school, college, training courses and relevant short courses
- an updated list of all work experience, with the dates, addresses of employers, a brief job description, main responsibilities, skills or qualities demonstrated, and what you learned from doing that work which is of value to your current aspirations
- a curriculum vitae (CV) – a Careers Adviser can help with this, see pages 295–9
- examples of experiences that demonstrate typical job competences.

Personal papers

You may like to include personal material that you think relevant to your personal development, such as photographs, letters, school reports, poems, quotations, job descriptions or articles. These may relate to:

- sources of inspiration
- things that motivate you
- charts of your progress to date
- things that remind you of what you wish to achieve
- things that you find reassuring when stressed.

Maintaining records for job applications

Almost every job application will call for very basic information:

- education and training history
- employment history.

Although this should be a straightforward matter, information is usually scattered over many different pieces of paper from employers or across several CVs, depending on the nature of the job. It is useful to draw all of that information together in one place, so that you can access it at a moment's notice if the right job appears. Use one file or box to keep all such materials together. Keep a disk/memory stick of electronic records with your paper records.

Education and training history

At some point you could be asked for all or any of the following:

- Schools you attended (usually the schools where you took qualifications after the age of 15 will be all that is required). You will need the name and address of the school, the date you started and the date you left.
- Qualifications you took, the date, and the result. If you are asked for the awarding authority, that is usually printed on the certificate. If you are offered the job, you will be asked to bring in the original certificates, so it is important to be accurate when you give these details.
- If you took your qualifications in a different country from the one where you are now studying, or where you intend to work, ensure that you gather details of the local equivalent for

all your qualifications. Provide that information with your application, as well as details of where employers can check this equivalence for themselves.

- Training you undertook as part of a job. Give brief details of short courses and the dates of these.
- Much learning is informal – a colleague may have shown you how to use a piece of software, for example, or you may have trained yourself in using a piece of equipment. Include brief details of the outcomes of such informal learning (what you can actually do as a result).

You will find it useful to draw all your certificates together into one section of your progress file.

Employment history

Employers will look at your employment history to see:

- whether your work history suggests you have the type and level of experience necessary for the job they are advertising. It is important to check that you use similar wording to that in the job description. Slight differences in the wording of a job title may mean that your experience or response is not relevant

- if there are any gaps in your employment record. Employers are likely to ask you about any periods of a year or more where no work or education is indicated
- what your job history says about how often you change job, how likely you are to stay with the company, the kinds of work you have accepted in the past, and your career path. If there are unusual jumps from one job to another, employers may ask you the reasons for this at interview.

For mature students, the employer will probably want to see a period of continuity within the work history (at least two years). It is expected that younger applicants may have a number of short-contract jobs. This is also true for certain types of work that are organised in short contracts.

You will be required to give information such as:

- employer names
- employer addresses
- contact details for the employer (telephone, fax, email)
- dates you began and finished work for each employer
- your job title
- your chief responsibilities
- previous employers who can act as referees.

Contents of personal records file

Educational history

1 Record of education and training

2 Certificates for all qualifications

3 Degree transcript

4 Evidence of learning

Employment history

1 Record of employment history

2 Contract for current employment

3 Names, addresses, job titles and other contact details for at least three referees

4 References and testimonials (if any)

5 Your National Insurance number

6 P45 or P60

7 Pay slips

8 Pension details for all jobs

9 Analysis of learning through work

Other experience

1 Positions of responsibility in clubs, societies or organisations

2 Achievements (from sports, leisure, social life, etc.)

3 Travel

4 Languages

5 Voluntary and community work

6 Mentoring experience

7 Life experience that developed skills or personal qualities

8 Health and safety

9 Equal opportunities

Skills, competences and personal qualities

1 Personal profile (skills, experience, personal qualities)

2 Evidence of skills and personal qualities

3 Critical incident sheet(s)

4 Competence sheets for specific skills

5 Analysis of personal qualities

Personal development

1 Self-evaluation questionnaires

2 Reflective documents and activities

3 Extracts from reflective journal

4 Quotations that motivate or inspire

5 Drawings, photographs and personally relevant documents

Overview documents

1 Position statement

2 Personal action plan

3 Curriculum vitae (CV)

4 Analysis of knowledge and experience

Other materials

Anything else that you feel is relevant to you

Records of education and training

It is likely that every job you apply for, as well as any future courses, will ask about your education, qualifications and training. You may be asked to provide one or more of the following:

- your highest level of qualification (e.g. a degree, a master's degree)
- to confirm that you have particular qualifications required for the job and, if you are offered the job, to provide the certificates
- details of all your education from a certain age, such as from GCSE (or equivalent) onwards
- details of training you have undertaken, formal courses and informal learning such as on-the-job training
- evidence, either through your personal statement or at interview, of what you have learnt through your education, training and experiences, especially experiences of employment.

On the chart in the Resource Bank (page 338), record details of your educational history. Order these so that your most recent courses and qualifications are at the head of the list.

Record of your work history

You will need accurate records of your work history. This could be maintained as an up to date list within your CV. If you are not permitted to send in a CV, you can cut and paste these details either onto the form the employer sends or onto an attachment. If you do the latter, make sure that you include all the details that the employer requests. The information required varies from one job to another, and you may also need this for other purposes. For each job and period of employment keep a record of:

- the exact dates you start and finish
- the employer name and address
- the job title
- key responsibilities of your role
- the experience you acquired
- your reason for leaving
- details of anyone you may want to call on for a reference.

Employers tend to require details of the salary of your last job and any additional benefits provided by your employer. They may also ask you to account for any gaps in your work history.

Skills and personal qualities

It is likely that you will be asked to provide details of your skills and personal qualities on many different occasions such as:

- applying for jobs
- applying for promotions
- applying for voluntary work, roles in the community
- as part of annual review or appraisal
- for skills sets inventories drawn up by businesses, community organisations, Boards of Governors and Trustees.

In general, you can expect to do more than simply list these. You may be asked to describe how you applied those skills in particular situations. It is easy to forget occasions when we applied particular skills well, so updating your records of these occasionally can be useful.

- The 'Current skills and personal qualities' sheet in the electronic Resource Bank and on page 319 enables you to identify the range of skills and qualities you possess.
- The 'Evidence of Skills and Personal Qualities' sheet in the Resource Bank and on page 344 enables you to analyse one or more skills in more depth as preparation for when you need to call upon this information.

Current skills and personal qualities

People

- [ ] Ability to get on with people from different backgrounds
- [ ] Understanding other people's points of view
- [ ] Sensitivity to cultural differences
- [ ] Dealing with the general public
- [ ] Team work and collaboration
- [ ] Networking
- [ ] Managing or supervising others' work
- [ ] Teaching, training or mentoring others
- [ ] Negotiating and persuading
- [ ] Helping others to arrive at decisions

- [ ] Consideration of others' feelings
- [ ] Caring for others
- [ ] Supporting and motivating others
- [ ] Understanding others' body language
- [ ] Coping with 'difficult' people
- [ ] Speaking clearly and to the point
- [ ] Audience awareness
- [ ] Taking direction from others
- [ ] Giving constructive feedback
- [ ] Leadership skills
- [ ] Other:

Activities and tasks

- [ ] Creativity, design and layout
- [ ] Innovation and inventiveness
- [ ] Ability to see the 'whole picture'
- [ ] Argument and debate
- [ ] Seeing patterns and connections
- [ ] Attention to detail
- [ ] Searching for information
- [ ] Classifying and organising information
- [ ] Making decisions
- [ ] Managing change and transition
- [ ] Setting priorities
- [ ] Working out agendas
- [ ] Organising work to meet deadlines
- [ ] Facilitating meetings
- [ ] Reading complex texts
- [ ] Computer literacy

- [ ] Technological skills
- [ ] Using social networking tools
- [ ] Working with numbers
- [ ] Selling
- [ ] Problem-solving
- [ ] Quick thinking
- [ ] Practical skills
- [ ] Understanding quickly how things work
- [ ] Seeing practical applications
- [ ] Writing reports or official letters
- [ ] Languages
- [ ] Enterprise and entrepreneurship
- [ ] Business and financial skills
- [ ] Managing difficult situations, emergencies and crises
- [ ] Other:

Personal

- [ ] Setting my own goals
- [ ] Working independently
- [ ] Maintaining a high level of motivation
- [ ] Taking responsibility for my own actions
- [ ] Learning from my mistakes
- [ ] Willingness to take risks and experiment
- [ ] Assertiveness

- [ ] Determination and perseverance
- [ ] Self-reliance
- [ ] Recognising my own needs
- [ ] Taking care of my health and well-being
- [ ] Staying calm in a crisis
- [ ] Coping skills and managing stress
- [ ] Other:

Critical incident

During job applications, employers often ask if you can give details of an important event or experience that had a major impact upon your life or work. This is sometimes referred to as a 'critical incident'. In particular, they are looking to see what kinds of things you regard as important (your values), how you managed transition and change, or how well you learn from experience.

It is useful to be prepared for this question, and the 'Critical Incident Sheet' in the Resource Bank, p. 345, outlines some of the main themes that are worth considering. Even if you are not applying for work, this is a useful exercise to work through from time to time, either using the same incident, or comparing your responses to different incidents.

Responding to competence-based questions

When you apply for a graduate job, you will receive a 'person specification' that outlines the qualities required for the post. Increasingly, employers are introducing competence-based applications. These ask you to give specific evidence of your competence under a number of headings that they provide. Whether or not you are asked details about competences at the application stage, it is typical for some or all of a job interview to be competence-based.

Having a set of well-recorded competences can significantly boost your confidence in your performance during the application process. If you store these records electronically, you will find that you can save yourself a great deal of time in making each application.

What is a 'competence'?

To be competent means to be able to perform an activity reasonably well and on more than one occasion. To consider yourself competent at a task, you are likely to be able to do what is necessary to achieve a successful outcome without having to check continually what needs to be done, and without supervision. Competence is associated with the notion of repeated performance; simply doing something once is not usually a sign of competence. Competence is often associated with well-placed confidence. It requires proficiency in a set of relevant skills. If you can train or advise others in the area, this is usually a sign of competence.

Describing your competence

In interview, you may be asked to give evidence of your competence from one of a range of different perspectives (see Chapter 10). This can often catch people unawares so that they feel they have not done themselves justice. Similarly, when writing competence-based applications, it is easy to omit details for which the selection panel will be looking. This can make the difference between being selected or not.

The competences selected for analysis in the Resource Bank (pages 333–82) are those frequently asked of graduates and others when they apply for jobs. A set of competence sheets are provided. Select those that are relevant to your employment or the types of position that you are likely to apply for. Each sheet provides prompts to assist you to analyse your competence and identify details of your ability to meet the job requirements.

Your records should contain details of some or all of the following:

- the best example(s) of you demonstrating that competence
- brief contextual evidence of the occasion(s) when you best demonstrated that competence
- your level of responsibility (whether you were the manager with lead responsibility, or stepping in to cover in someone's absence, or part of a small or large team)
- your personal role or actions: what you did or said
- what was the outcome of your action?
- what would you do differently, if anything, in retrospect?
- what did you learn that you have been able to apply in other situations, or could in the position for which you are applying?

Selecting examples

For written applications, you are likely to be given a restricted word limit for listing skills or giving details of one example. In interviews, you may be given time only to describe one example in detail. It is not untypical to hear people say after an interview that the wrong example came to mind.

For instance, they may have prepared to answer a question giving a 'recent example' and be asked for the 'best example in relation to the current job' – or vice versa.

It is useful to update your records so that you are clear about:

- which is your *one* best example of the competence from your experience? Usually this will be a recent example but sometimes a significant event or achievement may not be recent
- details of all aspects of that best example
- two other good examples, in brief.
- what is the most relevant example for the job?
- what is a recent example?

Building your competence

If you find that you are not able to give good examples of competence in any area, you will need to decide:

- Is this a competence that is likely to be required for the kinds of jobs that interest you?
- What opportunities are open to you to develop that competence?

Most employers want to see that you have experience. It is a frequent complaint that people cannot gain experience because they cannot get a job and they cannot get a job they want because they cannot gain the experience. Students have many opportunities to develop experiences that are less easy to come by once student life is over. Again, this is often not appreciated until the chance has passed. See pages 278–9.

Seize the opportunity while you are still a student – and ensure you have a good portfolio of skills and experience by the time you leave.

Completing the 'evidence of competence' sheets

The competence sheets in the Resource Bank, pages 333–82, can assist you in elaborating your personal competences. You may consider that very little space is provided for each answer. This encourages you to summarise the most salient points: it is unlikely that, in applying for jobs, you will ever have as much space as is provided by one of these sheets, nor time at interview to give fuller

responses. You will be required to give very brief responses to each question, so your thinking must be clear, precise and succinct.

Employers are looking at your own personal involvement and the responsibility you take for your own actions. Anything which comes across as an excuse or appears to be blaming others for a poor outcome will sound unconvincing. Speak about your own role and take responsibility for what did not work. Identify what you have learnt about how you would do things differently in the future.

They will also be interested in knowing the level of operation: how high-profile was the work, how central were you to events, where did you stand in the hierarchy of people involved? Being able to contribute to projects led by others may be as important as being the leader, as both team work and leadership are prized qualities.

You may find it useful to copy the blank sheets before completing them, so that you can use them again in the future. Electronic copies are also available at www.palgrave.com/studyskills/pdp so that you can update them easily.

In completing the records, it is worth taking time to jot down all the occasions you can think of when you exemplified the competence in action. This will give you a full list from which to select your best examples. Make use of the responses you have made to activities in chapters earlier in this book or on your programme. It can help to have a friend or relation to prompt you if you struggle to find examples. You can call upon the same experience for more than one competence, but it is useful to refer to at least three separate experiences or examples overall.

Evidence of improvements in personal performance

When applying for a position, you may be asked questions about how you go about identifying areas for improvement, what you have done already to improve your performance and what the impact was of the action you took. It is likely that you will either be asked directly to provide one or more concrete examples of how you have drawn upon experience in order to improve performance, or that it will just be assumed that you will incorporate such examples in your applications and answers to interview questions. You may have to call upon such information as:

- A brief summary of the context.
- What needed to be done and why?
- What was your own role?
- How did you plan and prepare? (if relevant)
- How did you adapt your plan or strategy in the light of events?
- What was the effect of your action: what was different as a result of it? What could you have done even better?

- What did you learn about yourself and your own performance through this experience?
- What did you learn that has general applicability (such as to new skills, experience, insights, specialist knowledge) especially to the position for which you are applying?

The sheet in the Resource Bank on page 334 enables you to draw together your reflections of specific occasions where working on personal performance reaped rewards and provided insights that can be applied more generally.

Closing comments

This chapter provides guidance on developing personal resources that can assist in:

- making effective, well-evidenced, persuasive job applications
- structuring your reflection about your experience.

These resources are not for use on a single occasion. As you move through your programme and as you gain wider experiences

through life and work, you will find better examples to record. At the time, these experiences will appear very vivid in your mind but you will begin to lose the details over time. Write these down while they are still fresh.

Reflect back upon those same events in a year's time. Often, you will find that you see much more significance in the same events after time has elapsed.

Chapter 12
Drawing it together

Learning outcomes

This chapter offers opportunities to:

- recognise personal changes and achievements
- review your reflections on personal planning
- update your profile of skills and qualities
- identify your 'learning edge'
- identify emerging personal responsibilities
- plan your next steps.

Introduction

Personal planning is not simply about making a 'plan' and following it. It is a developmental process that each individual moulds to suit their own needs and interests over time. It is about getting to grips with issues such as:

- who you are and the kind of person you want to be
- the life you want to lead and what you want from life
- what matters to you and what you want to achieve
- the steps you will take to achieve your goals
- recognising changes in your interests and charting out a new plan in line with those changes.

Good planning involves taking steps to ensure you have the information you need at your fingertips when you need it. It involves thinking about possibilities, some of which may seem far-fetched, and starting to put the support and skills in place now that might be useful later.

This chapter offers structured opportunities to review your current position, referring back to activities undertaken in previous chapters, and looking forward to your next step. It looks at the process of managing personal development planning once you are already embarked on the journey of self-discovery and life planning.

Recognising personal changes

Goal inertia

Chapter 1 encouraged you to form a strong vision of what you aspire to be or to achieve. However, your views may already have changed. Each day, our experiences shape us anew. Over time, our aims and goals may become out of touch with who we have become: this is 'goal inertia'.

The 'newer you' is inspired by fresh ideas, moulded by experiences, changed by the knowledge you are acquiring, living in an environment that also changes each day. Is this 'newer you' still inspired by plans made one, three or five years ago?

Take ten minutes to brainstorm all the differences you can detect between yourself now and yourself three years ago.

	Me three years ago	Me now
Appearance		
Clothes		
Friends		
Interests		
Tastes in music		
Life aims or vision		
Attitudes		

	Me three years ago	Me now
Inspiration		
Personal qualities I want to develop		
People I admire		
People who support me		
Job taken		
Career interests		
Other significant changes		

Reflection: Change

In your reflective journal consider:

● What are the most important ways you or your life have changed over the last three years?
● What is the significance of the changes you identified above? What do they mean for the way you think, feel, act? Have they changed your attitudes to life, to people or to what you now find important?
● Have those changes influenced your personal goals and targets?

Review your goals

You may be inspired by the same vision or aims all of your life. However, if you feel that your goals are not inspiring you anymore, you have probably outgrown them. It is worth reviewing your goals from time to time. For example:

● Complete the 'Dream' or 'Long-term vision' activities again (pp. 34–6). Compare your current and previous responses.
● Talk to someone about your goals. Ask them to press you into really exploring what you want.
● Take a journey to somewhere you have never visited before. The change of scene can generate new ideas about what you really want.
● Speak to other people about their goals and interests. Broaden your perspective on the options open to you.

Success is a very personal thing. For you, success may mean reaching the stars or it may mean a particular source of happiness that other people would not appreciate.

Success is associated with happiness. Does your vision of your life leave you with a feeling of relative happiness? If the goals you set for yourself are unappealing, or make you feel that you are making more hurdles for yourself in life, or seem to be setting you off on paths towards places that you no longer find attractive, it is probably time for a rethink.

Reflection: Updating goals and targets

● Has your 'vision' changed since you completed the activity in Chapter 1?
● Is it likely to make you happy?
● How do your goals or targets need to change, if at all, to contribute to your sense of happiness?

Review your values

Your vision will be strongly influenced by your values – either in what you view as successful, or in the behaviours and lifestyle you find acceptable and desirable.

Reflection: Updating values

● In what ways, if any, have your values changed since you completed the activity on p. 31 in Chapter 1?
● Does this have any significance for your motivation in achieving your long-term goals?
● Do you need to review your inspiration, sources of motivation or your goals in the light of your current values?

Using the reflective process

Monitoring personal progress

Progress can be measured against your personal goals or against objective criteria such as exam marks. In the grand scheme of life, marks given by others count for much less than:

● the depth of your personal awareness
● your ability to monitor your own progress
● your ability and motivation to take action to improve performance without being told to do so.

In order to monitor performance and personal change, you need records. A reflective journal, maintained for your own purposes, is a key tool for monitoring change. If you haven't read through your reflective journal for a while, now is a good time to do so.

Reflection: Reviewing your reflective journal

Read through ten pages of your reflective journal, preferably from at least six months ago.

- What do you notice about your state of mind at the time? How does it differ from now?
- What things had you forgotten were in the journal that you are pleased to find?
- What things did you mean to do but have not yet got round to doing?
- What else strikes you as interesting from your journal?

Identifying change

Keeping a reflective journal provides material to help you monitor changes in yourself over time. The following activity invites you to look back over your reflection and identify themes and changes in your responses.

Activity Has your thinking changed?

- Select three activities from anywhere in this book. Include one you enjoyed and one that you found difficult or resisted.
- Do these again now.
- Compare your responses with those you made previously.
- How do you account for any differences in your responses?

Being a reflective practitioner

Reflective practice is very similar to making New Year resolutions. It is easy to start well, but by mid-year the resolutions are often long forgotten. Similarly, reflection on our goals, performance and personal development may start out well. However, reflection is often an early casualty when there is pressure on our time. You may find that this has been true of you. If so, just take up from wherever you left off. If you keep doing this, you will find that reflective practice becomes a habit.

Reflection: Developing skills in reflective practice

In your reflective journal, jot down your responses to the following.

- What did you gain from taking a reflective and self-evaluating approach to your academic, personal or professional development?
- How well do you feel you have developed and maintained a reflective approach?
- What steps could you take to improve your reflective practice?

Activity Building from personal expertise

In your reflective journal, jot down *one* skill or area of expertise which you feel is your strongest point. This could be a sub-skill such as organising space or drawing up timetables or planning a piece of writing.

- Take two minutes to brainstorm ways this skill or area of expertise might be helpful to your future study.
- Take two minutes to brainstorm ways this skill or area of expertise might help in work contexts.
- Take two minutes to brainstorm ways this skill or area of expertise might be helpful to your life more generally.

Once you have completed this for one skill, go through the same questions with at least two other personal strengths. You may find it useful to update your competence sheets once you have completed this activity.

Improving performance

Working with our strengths

One way of improving performance is to identify current strengths and to build upon these. Chapter 2, for example, identified ways of using expertise in one area to develop understanding in another area. Look back through the competence sheets and other evaluations of your skills and qualities in Chapter 11 to remind yourself of your current strengths. Look back over your learning goals and the areas that you have worked on to improve personal performance. Consider how well you drew on your personal strengths in order to achieve your learning goals.

Identifying 'transferable skills'

To transfer skills from one context to another, it is usually necessary to:

- be aware of the skills (and especially sub-skills) you already use
- identify which of those skills can be adapted to fit the new context.

The sub-skills are especially important as it is usually these that transfer to new contexts. For example, if you are good at working with numbers, the sub-skills might include paying attention to details, sequencing, seeing patterns, logical skills, seeing how numbers relate to words, having the patience to retest all the subsequent stages in a problem in order to identify an error, a good memory for formulas, etc.

If you are good at working with people, the sub-skills and personal qualities involved might include listening skills, coping with other people's anger, seeing things from another person's point of view, being very sensitive to your own feelings and the impact these have on others, taking responsibility for your own mistakes, being able to ask for what you need, etc.

 Activity — **Transferring skills**

- Select one of your skills or strengths.
- Where did you develop this skill?
- What are the sub-skills and qualities you have developed as part of the overall skill?

Now select one context or situation from the following list. Choose the context with which you are least familiar:

> Working with children
> Setting up an arts exhibition
> Designing an office
> Counselling others on a phone line
> Raising money for a charity
> Making a video
> Designing a Web page for a company
> Being the first on the scene of a serious accident
> Organising a conference
> Opening a restaurant.

- Take five minutes to brainstorm all the ways that the sub-skills you identified could be of any use at all in the new context you chose. There will be ways that are not immediately apparent.
- In what ways would you need to adapt those sub-skills so that they fit the new context?

Make the link!

Interconnections between areas of expertise

Very few skills are gained in isolation from others. Our development is usually a complex web of newly emerging strengths and relative weaknesses. When we develop one area of expertise, we usually enhance performance in others, even if this is not visible.

For example, people who sing in choirs develop their voices and their musicality. However, they also tend to acquire a good sense of timing in their 'response' to others, which can contribute to their people skills. A vast array of other skills can be linked to this one activity, such as developing confidence in performing in front of others, team work, taking direction, following a sequence, attention to detail, sensitivity to mood, etc. The same is true of most other areas of expertise.

The converse is also true. If we are weak in one skill or area of expertise, the ramifications of this will be felt in a wide range of contexts. For example, if we hate sport, this could impact upon our health, our stamina, our opportunities to mix with others, our ability to join in certain conversations, the number of connections we can make with other people, the range of metaphors we have to call upon, our understanding of other people's interest and motivations, etc.

Because of this, the root of difficulties we experience in one area of our lives may lie in a completely different area. For example, poor organisational skills may originate in one of a number of areas, such as poor time-management skills, low motivation, unhelpful attitudes, an inability to say 'No' to too many requests for help, or a lack of responsibility for our own actions. Unless we work on the root cause, the difficulties may not go away.

Raising the game

Recognising your achievements

It may be tempting to feel at times that your personal development could now 'come to an end'. That is usually a good signal for raising your game, setting new challenges, finding a new aspect to stimulate your interest.

One boost to motivation is reviewing your successes. Note what you have achieved so far with your own development and consider the benefits this has brought you.

Reflection: Linking skills and expertise

- What is the area where you have developed most expertise?
- What are the wider range of sub-skills and qualities that have developed as part of that expertise? List at least 20.
- Which one skill, personal quality or area of expertise do you feel you need to improve?
- How would improving this one area also lead to improvements in other skills, qualities, attitudes or areas of expertise?

What do you think is at the root of this area of weakness? What can you do to address this?

Activity   **Making the connections**

Make a list of 3–5 themes that you are working on at the moment. Then identify various sections of the book that can develop relevant skills for improving your performance. For example:

Your goals and how to achieve them: Chapter 1, 'The vision', and Chapter 6, 'Successful problem-solving and task management'.

Managing your responses when working with difficult people: Chapter 4, 'Successful self-management', and Chapter 5, 'People skills'.

Working on problems and looking for creative solutions: Chapter 6, 'Successful problem-solving and task management', and Chapter 7, 'Thinking outside the box'.

- Identify the ways that skills and insights developed in one aspect of your life can have an effect upon performance in other areas.

Reflection: Note success

Browse through your reflective journal for the last year – or since your last review. In your journal, note:

- What goals did you work on during that time?
- Which ones have you achieved?
- What are the benefits of having achieved these?

Consider what the effects of these achievements are. These may be changes in your life, successes in your study, the ability to manage a particular situation, or a feeling of accomplishment. Don't be modest. Make sure you include a list of all the sub-skills you developed and your minor achievements as well as the more noticeable ones.

Have you celebrated your achievements? If not: make sure you do!

Indicate how important each of the following is to you achieving well.

(a) I achieve best when I ...	Very important	Important	Quite important	Not very important	Not at all important
● can see some results quickly	☐	☐	☐	☐	☐
● have feedback from others so I know how well I am doing	☐	☐	☐	☐	☐
● receive guidance or suggestions from other people	☐	☐	☐	☐	☐
● know I am heading in the right direction	☐	☐	☐	☐	☐
● have planned out the whole process in advance	☐	☐	☐	☐	☐
● set short-term targets that I know are achievable	☐	☐	☐	☐	☐
● set goals that I am certain I can achieve	☐	☐	☐	☐	☐
● plan each step closely so as to avoid setbacks	☐	☐	☐	☐	☐
● have a clear vision of where I am going	☐	☐	☐	☐	☐
● have a safety net to fall back on if things do not work out.	☐	☐	☐	☐	☐

Indicate how far each statement below is typical of you.

(b) I am able to motivate myself to work towards a goal even if ...	Very typical	Typical	Sometimes the case	Not very typical	Not typical at all
● I have to wait a long time to see the results	☐	☐	☐	☐	☐
● it takes years to reach the ultimate goal	☐	☐	☐	☐	☐
● nobody else is available to tell me what to do	☐	☐	☐	☐	☐
● there is a really difficult challenge	☐	☐	☐	☐	☐
● it is not clear that the outcome will be successful	☐	☐	☐	☐	☐
● the eventual goal is rather vague	☐	☐	☐	☐	☐
● the plan has to evolve slowly over time	☐	☐	☐	☐	☐
● I have to work hard for something that I may not achieve	☐	☐	☐	☐	☐
● there are many setbacks	☐	☐	☐	☐	☐
● other people think I am aiming too high.	☐	☐	☐	☐	☐

Working at your 'edge'

Once you have built your confidence in your own success, you are ready to set yourself greater challenges. This can also mean looking at your approach to challenge itself. Do you welcome challenge? Are you prepared to take on goals that will stretch you?

Attitude to challenge

The greatest barriers to success are usually those that derive from our attitudes and fears. The challenge may simply be too great for us at that time. The challenges we set ourselves should be appropriate for our current coping skills, support networks, and emotional well-being. The activity on p. 330 gives an indication of the ways in which you currently cope with challenge.

Reflection: Using your responses for (a)

- Highlight all the answers to which you responded with a 'Very important' or 'Important'.
- Write these out in your reflective journal, starting: 'To cope with a new challenge, it is important for me that …'.
- As you write, add details or examples from your experience to illustrate how you know this is really true of you.

Reflection: Using your responses for (b)

- Highlight all the answers to which you responded with a 'Not very typical' or 'Not typical at all'.
- Write these out in your reflective journal, starting: 'I am unlikely to keep going with a new challenge if …'.
- As you write, add details or examples from your experience to illustrate how you know this is really true of you.

Interpreting your responses

Your answers to (a) provide you with a summary of the approaches that increase your chances of success with new challenges. For example, you may have indicated that you need support in order to achieve. If this is true of you, you are more likely to be successful if you remain open to guidance from others, plan carefully and set manageable targets. However, see 'The comfort zone' below.

Your answers to (b) provide you with a summary of how highly motivated you are likely to remain even in high-risk contexts. If you indicated many 'Very typical' and 'Typical' replies here, your responses suggest you are likely to respond well to challenge and risk. You appear to be highly motivated and able to manage your own path to success very well. However, see 'The comfort zone' below.

If your responses to (b) were mostly 'Not very typical' or 'Not typical at all', set yourself challenges that avoid most of those circumstances. Your 'edge' is likely to be working on developing your motivation so that you can achieve your goals even when conditions are not ideal.

The comfort zone and 'the working edge'

When we only work to our strengths and preferences, we run the risk of not setting sufficient challenges for ourselves. The 'comfort zone' is where we operate when we are running no risks, setting ourselves no challenges, ensuring we always have a very strong and wide safety net, ensuring we always have more than enough support. A good personal development plan will include areas for improvement that challenge us to work at our 'edge'.

'The edge' is the boundary between the comfort zone and unnecessary or inappropriate risks. It is different for everybody. For one person it might be learning to take advice from others; for another person it may be learning to work more independently of others. For people who avoid risk, the 'edge' might be in learning to set more adventurous challenges. This might entail developing related skills, qualities or attitudes such as managing change, seeing mistakes as opportunities to learn, developing emotional coping strategies, and so forth. For those who take high-risk strategies, the 'edge' might be in developing ways of coping with stress, or developing trust in other people, or in living without high excitement.

Reflection: Working at the 'edge'

- What do you feel is the 'edge' you need to work at next?
- What makes you feel that this is your 'edge'? Who could you speak to about this?
- How will you take on this new challenge?
- What support or guidance do you need?

Sometimes it is hard to acknowledge where the edge lies. For example, the kind of advice we dislike the most is often an indicator of where our personal 'edge' lies. We may need guidance on how to work at our edge. As with the 'edge' of a cliff or precipice, we should approach our personal limits with due caution and the right support. It is good to set challenges – but not to go over the edge without a rope.

Closing comments

Congratulations on reaching this stage of the book. If you worked through most of the chapters and activities, you will have a very strong sense of yourself, your strengths and what you need to do to achieve your goals.

It is likely that you used the book selectively, picking out activities that seemed most relevant or to which you were directed by your tutors. If there were aspects of this process that you at first resisted, found uncomfortable or absolutely hated but worked through, you have really achieved something. What exactly that 'something' is, is for you to judge.

We are always a 'work in progress':

- there is always more that we can understand about ourselves

- the range of our knowledge and expertise can always be extended
- there is always an area of our performance that can be improved.

Our personal development is as dynamic a process as we choose to make it. If we use a reflective approach on a regular basis, we will know ourselves more fully, be more aware of our needs and wants, and more able to achieve what we really desire.

> Seek out that particular mental attitude which makes you feel most deeply and vitally alive, along with which comes the inner voice which says, 'this is the real me', and when you have found that attitude, follow it.
>
> William James

Resource Bank
Full contents of the Resource Bank

Improving personal performance

Date:

Example of where I took action to improve my performance.

What needed to be done?

What were the issues?

What made this a priority or a good area to address?

The preparation and planning I undertook.

My strategy (plan) for improving my performance.

What I did. Any changes or adaptations that I made to the strategy.

What worked?

What changed?

What else could I have done or could I try on a future occasion?

What did I learn about my own performance through this experience?

The ways this knowledge is more generally applicable to my study, work or life.

Evaluating progress on learning goals

Current learning goals *(see Action Plan, p. 177)*	
Targets and milestones.	

Action taken to achieve the goal ('What have I done so far?')

Evaluation of performance so far ('How well am I meeting my targets? How sensible were the targets?

Do they need to be changed?')

What feedback have I received from others?

How have I made use of this feedback?

Things I have learnt about myself, other people or the task so far.

Strong points about my attitude, approach and performance.

Things I could improve about my attitude, approach and performance.

How have I changed?

Next steps?

Other comments

Signed _____   Date _____

2 Personal Records

Record of education and training

Education

On the chart below, record details of your educational history, excluding short courses.

Secondary school (ages 11–16; focus on qualifications after age 14)					
Dates (from … to …)	Name and address of institution or provider	Subjects studied	Qualification achieved (and grade where relevant)	Year of the qualification	Topics covered and skills acquired

Post-16 education (before degree level)					
Dates (from … to …)	Name and address of institution or provider	Subjects studied	Qualification achieved (and grade where relevant)	Year of the qualification	Topics covered and skills acquired

Copy and complete for additional qualifications

University education/Higher education					
Dates (from ... to ...)	Name and address of institution or provider	Name of course or programme	Qualification achieved (and grade where applicable)	Year qualification was awarded	Topics covered and skills acquired

Short courses, programmes and training

On the chart below, record details of other training you have undertaken at college, through work, or through private agencies.

Dates (from ... to ...)	Institution or provider	Name of course or programme	Qualification achieved, if relevant, and year	Topics covered	Skills acquired

Copy and complete for additional training and qualifications

Informal learning

Other learning developed through work experience, informal training by peers and 'away-days', etc.

Year	Where learning took place	Other people involved	Reason for undertaking the learning	What was learnt? Topics covered and skills acquired

Other qualifications, experience and assets

Driving licence, additional languages, familiarity with other countries or cultures.

1
2
3
4
5

Copy and complete for additional training and qualifications

Evidence of learning

Qualifications are one way of providing evidence of learning. However, employers are often interested in seeing what you have valued about your learning, or hearing what you think you have learnt, in order to find out how you demonstrate and apply your skills and intelligence. It is useful to be prepared for such questions.

What has interested you most about your programme?

What do you feel has been the most important thing you have learnt from your programme?

What do you think you have learnt on your programme that could benefit you in the world of work?

In what way is your subject relevant to the world outside of university/higher education?

What advice would you give to other students embarking upon your programme?

Record of work history

Starting with your earliest work experience after the age of 16, give details of all work that you have undertaken. You will then have a complete record of the essential information most commonly required when completing application forms.

Dates (from ... to ...)	Employer and employer address	Job title	Responsibilities	Experience acquired	Reason for leaving

The most important things I have learnt through my work history that are of benefit to me in other jobs (or in life more generally) are:

1

2

3

4

5

Copy and update

Learning through work

Place and date

Incident (*basic details*).

What I did.

Responsibility involved.

What others did.

What I learned.

Skills I acquired.

Feedback from employer.

Feedback from clients.

Feedback from others.

How I made use of feedback.

Evidence of Skills and Personal Qualities

Skill, quality or attribute	
1 How and when I developed this skill or quality.	
2 Examples of occasions when I demonstrate this skill.	At university/in higher education At work In life
3 Evidence that I possess this quality or skill (e.g. reliable feedback from others; qualifications, testimonials, etc.).	At university/in higher education At work In life

Copy and complete for other skills and personal qualities

© Stella Cottrell (2003, 2010, 2015), *Skills for Success*, Palgrave

Critical incident sheet

1	Context: brief details of the critical incident. What happened, where, and when?	
2	My role in the incident. What I did.	
3	My immediate response to the incident. How I coped.	
4	How I made use of advice and feedback from other people.	
5	The longer-term impact of the incident upon my life or work. How important this incident was in the grand scheme of my life. What changed?	
6	Positive outcomes for me or for other people.	
7	What lessons I learned from this occasion.	
8	How I applied what I learned to new situations.	
9	The impact of the incident upon my values, beliefs, attitudes and motivation.	
10	Personal considerations and comments.	

3 Competence Sheets

(1) Evidence of Team work

1 The best example.	
2 The purpose of the team, the nature of the team activities and membership.	
3 Context: brief details of the circumstances, event or activity when I showed good team skills.	
4 Level of responsibility in this team. The scale and scope of the work or event.	
5 Personal contribution: what I did; the role(s) I played in the team.	
6 Example of leadership: (e.g. planning, negotiating, persuading).	
7 Example of ability to work with others (e.g. accepting others' views, following directions, working out a compromise, etc.).	

8	What worked well on this occasion?	
9	The lessons I learned from this occasion.	
10	What would I do differently on another occasion?	
11	How typical is this example for me (a daily occurrence/weekly/ occasionally/rarely)?	
12	Brief details of a recent (or second) example.	
13	Brief details of a third, preferably contrasting, example.	
14	How do I measure my success for this competence?	
15	How could this competence be applied to other situations?	

(2) Evidence of competence in working independently

1	The best example.	
2	Context: brief details of the work undertaken, for whom and where it was undertaken.	
3	Level of responsibility for the work in question. The scale and scope of the work.	
4	Size or scope of the work undertaken.	
5	Outcomes: what I achieved.	
6	Contribution of this work to any larger project or team work. How this work linked to the work undertaken by other people.	
7	How I organised my work in order to motivate myself and meet targets.	

8	What worked well for this example of independent work?	
9	What lessons did I learn from this example of independent work?	
10	How would I manage independent work differently on another occasion?	
11	How typical is this example for me (a daily occurrence/weekly/ occasionally/rarely)?	
12	Brief details of a recent (or second) example.	
13	Brief details of a third, preferably contrasting, example.	
14	How could this competence be applied to other situations?	
15	How do I measure my success for this competence?	

(3) Evidence of competence in exercising responsibility

1 The best example.	
2 Context: brief details of the circumstances, event or activity.	
3 Level of responsibility on this occasion. The scale and scope of the work or event.	
4 Personal contribution: what I did.	
5 Who else was involved – and what they did.	
6 Skills I exercised.	
7 What worked well on this occasion?	

8 What lessons did I learn from this occasion?	
9 What would I do differently on another occasion?	
10 How typical is this example for me (a daily occurrence/weekly/ occasionally/rarely)?	
11 Brief details of a recent (or second) example.	
12 Brief details of a third, preferably contrasting, example.	
13 How could this competence be applied to other situations?	
14 How do I measure my success for this competence?	

(4) Evidence of competence in leadership

1 The best example.	
2 What I believe is meant by 'leadership'.	
3 Context: brief details of the circumstances, event or activity when I gave leadership to others.	
4 Level of responsibility on this occasion. The scale and scope of the work or event.	
5 Personal contribution: what I did.	
6 Who else was involved – and what they did. How I involved other people, such as delegating authority, or seeking opinions.	
7 Example of leadership skills I exercised.	
8 How I took on board the opinions and feelings of other people.	

9	The outcomes. What happened.	
10	What worked well on this occasion?	
11	What lessons did I learn from this occasion?	
12	What would I do differently on another occasion?	
13	How typical is this example for me (a daily occurrence/weekly/ occasionally/rarely)?	
14	Brief details of a recent (or second) example.	
15	Brief details of a third, preferably contrasting, example.	
16	How could this competence be applied to other situations?	
17	How do I measure my success for this competence?	

(5) Evidence of competence in persuading others

1 The best example.	
2 Context: brief details of the circumstances, event or activity. Why was it necessary to exercise persuasion?	
3 Level of responsibility on this occasion. The scale and scope of the work or event.	
4 Personal contribution: what I did.	
5 Example of leadership skills involved on this occasion.	
6 Who else was involved – and what they did. How I involved or worked with others on this occasion.	
7 Skills I exercised and qualities I demonstrated.	
8 The outcomes.	

9	What worked well on this occasion?	
10	What lessons did I learn from this occasion?	
11	What would I do differently on another occasion?	
12	How typical is this example for me (a daily occurrence/weekly/ occasionally/rarely)?	
13	Brief details of a recent (or second) example.	
14	Brief details of a third, preferably contrasting, example.	
15	How could this competence be applied to other situations?	
16	How do I measure my success for this competence?	

(6) Evidence of competence in negotiating a compromise

1 The best example.	
2 Context: brief details of the circumstances, event or activity. Why was it necessary to negotiate a compromise?	
3 Level of responsibility on this occasion. The scale and scope of the work or event.	
4 Personal contribution: what I did.	
5 Example of leadership skills involved on this occasion.	
6 Who else was involved – and what they did. How I involved or worked with others on this occasion.	
7 Skills I exercised and qualities I demonstrated.	
8 The outcomes.	

9	What worked well on this occasion?	
10	What lessons did I learn from this occasion?	
11	What would I do differently on another occasion?	
12	How typical is this example for me (a daily occurrence/weekly/ occasionally/rarely)?	
13	Brief details of a recent (or second) example.	
14	Brief details of a third, preferably contrasting, example.	
15	How could this competence be applied to other situations?	
16	How do I measure my success for this competence?	

(7) Evidence of competence in problem-solving

1 The best example.	
2 Context: brief details of the circumstances and the problem to be solved.	
3 Level of responsibility on this occasion. The scale and scope of the work or event.	
4 Personal contribution: what I did.	
5 The problem-solving approach I took – my strategy, the alternatives I considered.	
6 Who else was involved – and what they did. How I involved or worked with others on this occasion.	
7 The outcomes. What was achieved?	

8	What worked well on this occasion?	
9	What lessons did I learn from this occasion?	
10	What would I do differently on another occasion?	
11	How typical is this example for me (a daily occurrence/weekly/ occasionally/rarely)?	
12	Brief details of a recent (or second) example.	
13	Brief details of a third, preferably contrasting, example.	
14	How could this competence be applied to other situations?	
15	How do I measure my success for this competence?	

(8) Evidence of competence in project or task management

1 The best example.	
2 Context: brief details of the circumstances, project or task selected.	
3 Level of responsibility on this occasion. The scale and scope of the work or event.	
4 Personal contribution: what I did.	
5 The approach I took – my strategy, the alternatives I considered.	
6 Who else was involved – and what they did. How I involved or worked with others on this occasion.	
7 The outcomes. What was achieved?	

8	What worked well on this occasion?	
9	What lessons did I learn from this occasion?	
10	What would I do differently on another occasion?	
11	How typical is this example for me (a daily occurrence/weekly/ occasionally/rarely)?	
12	Brief details of a recent (or second) example.	
13	Brief details of a third, preferably contrasting, example.	
14	How could this competence be applied to other situations?	
15	How do I measure my success for this competence?	

(9) Evidence of competence in commercial awareness

1 What I understand by 'commercial awareness'.	
2 Where I have gained experience of commercial awareness, in general.	
3 Brief details of the context of one occasion where I demonstrated my understanding of commercial awareness.	
4 What I did.	
5 My reasons for doing this.	
6 What the consequences were of my doing this.	

7	What the consequences might have been if I had acted differently.	
8	What I would do differently on another occasion.	
9	Brief details of a recent (or second) example of where I acted in a way that demonstrated a good understanding of business interests.	
10	Brief details of a third example of where I acted in a way that demonstrated a good understanding of business interests.	

(10) Evidence of competence in managing a difficult situation

1 The best example.	
2 Context: brief details of the difficult situation: where it took place, and why it arose.	
3 Level of responsibility on this occasion. The scale and scope of the work or event.	
4 Personal contribution: what I did to manage the situation and resolve the difficulty.	
5 The approach I took – why I adopted the techniques or strategy that I did.	
6 Who else was involved – and what they did. How I involved or worked with others on this occasion.	
7 The outcomes. How far the conflict was resolved for the short or long term.	

8	What worked well on this occasion?	
9	What lessons did I learn from this occasion?	
10	What would I do differently on another occasion?	
11	How typical is this example for me (a daily occurrence/weekly/ occasionally/rarely)?	
12	Brief details of a recent (or second) example.	
13	Brief details of a third, preferably contrasting, example.	
14	How could this competence be applied to other situations?	
15	How do I measure my success for this competence?	

(11) Evidence of competence in working under pressure or to tight deadlines

1 The best example.	
2 Context: brief details of the circumstances that created the pressure or tight deadlines.	
3 Level of responsibility on this occasion. The scale and scope of the work or event.	
4 Personal contribution: what I did.	
5 What action I took to help me cope with the pressure and stress.	
6 Who else was involved – and what they did. How I involved or worked with others on this occasion.	
7 Evidence of ability to work with others under pressure.	
8 The outcomes. The extent to which deadlines were met or the work completed.	

9	What worked well on this occasion?	
10	What lessons did I learn from this occasion?	
11	What would I do differently on another occasion?	
12	How typical is this example for me (a daily occurrence/weekly/ occasionally/rarely)?	
13	Brief details of a recent (or second) example.	
14	Brief details of a third, preferably contrasting, example.	
15	How could this competence be applied to other situations?	
16	How do I measure my success for this competence?	

(12) Evidence of competence in equal opportunities

1 The best example.	
2 What I understand by the term 'equal opportunities'.	
3 Context: brief details of the circumstances and issues involved.	
4 Level of responsibility on this occasion. The scale and scope of the issue.	
5 Personal contribution: what I did.	
6 Who else was involved on this occasion – and what they did. How I involved or worked with others.	
7 The outcomes (long term or short term).	
8 What worked well on this occasion?	

9	What lessons did I learn from this occasion?	
10	What would I do differently on another occasion?	
11	How typical is this example for me (a daily occurrence/weekly/ occasionally/rarely)?	
12	General awareness of equal opportunities issues and legislation. Experience of working with people from a wide variety of backgrounds.	
13	Brief details of a recent (or second) example.	
14	Brief details of a third, preferably contrasting, example.	
15	How could this competence be applied to other situations?	
16	How do I measure my success for this competence?	

(13) Evidence of competence in managing change

1 The best example.	
2 Context: brief details of the circumstances where change was introduced and why it was needed.	
3 Level of responsibility on this occasion. The scale and scope of the issue.	
4 Personal contribution: what I did. How far I initiated the change, or managed my own or others' response to change.	
5 Who else was involved on this occasion – and what they did. How I involved or worked with others. How I supported others through a time of change.	
6 The outcomes of my actions or involvement.	
7 What worked well on this occasion?	

8	What lessons did I learn from this occasion?	
9	What would I do differently on another occasion?	
10	How typical is this example of my life or work experience?	
11	Brief details of a recent (or second) example.	
12	Brief details of a third, preferably contrasting, example.	
13	How could this competence be applied to other situations?	
14	How do I measure my success for this competence?	

(14) Evidence of competence in taking calculated risks

1 The best example.	
2 Context: brief details of the circumstances.	
3 The nature of the risk involved; the factors that needed to be weighed in the balance.	
4 Level of responsibility on this occasion. The scale and scope of the issue.	
5 Personal contribution: what I did.	
6 Who else was involved on this occasion – and what they did. How I involved or worked with others.	
7 What I did to manage the pressure and stress for myself and others.	
8 The outcomes of my actions or involvement.	

9	What worked well on this occasion?	
10	What lessons did I learn from this occasion?	
11	What would I do differently on another occasion?	
12	How typical is this example of my life or work experience?	
13	Brief details of a recent (or second) example.	
14	Brief details of a third, preferably contrasting, example.	
15	How could this competence be applied to other situations?	
16	How do I measure my success for this competence?	

(15) Evidence of competence in learning from my own mistakes

1 The best example.	
2 Context: brief details of the circumstances.	
3 The mistake(s) that I made on this occasion. What circumstances led to the mistake/error of judgement? How I discovered the mistake.	
4 Level of responsibility on this occasion. The scale and scope of the issue.	
5 Personal contribution: what I did.	
6 Who else was involved on this occasion – and what they did. How I involved or worked with others.	
7 What I did to manage the pressure and stress for myself and others.	

8	The outcomes of my actions or involvement. How I took responsibility for my own actions.	
9	What, if anything, was positive about my contribution?	
10	What lessons did I learn from this occasion?	
11	What would I do differently on another occasion? How I acted differently on a second occasion.	
12	How typical is it for me to use a reflective approach to improve my performance?	
13	Brief details of a recent (or second) example.	
14	Brief details of a third, preferably contrasting, example.	
15	How could this competence be applied to other situations?	
16	How do I measure my success for this competence?	

(16) Evidence of competence in written communication skills

1 The best example.	
2 Context: brief details of the circumstances.	
3 Level of responsibility on this occasion. The time-scale, word limits and importance of the task.	
4 The nature of the audience.	
5 Personal contribution: what I did, including how the writing was suited to the audience.	
6 Who else was involved on this occasion – and what they did. How I involved or worked with others on this occasion.	
7 Outcomes. The extent to which deadlines were met or the work completed. What feedback I received.	

8	What lessons did I learn from this occasion? How I used feedback.	
9	What would I do differently on another occasion?	
10	What skills have I acquired through academic writing?	
11	Awareness of differences between academic writing and that for the career area which interests me.	
12	How typical is this example for me (a daily occurrence/weekly/ occasionally/rarely)?	
13	Brief details of a recent (or second) example.	
14	Brief details of a third, preferably contrasting, example.	
15	How could this competence be applied to other situations?	
16	How do I measure my success for this competence?	

(17) Evidence of competence in oral communication skills

1 The best example.	
2 Context: brief details of the circumstances.	
3 Level of responsibility on this occasion. The time limit, scale and scope of the work or event.	
4 The nature of the audience and how I took this into consideration.	
5 Personal contribution: what I did.	
6 Who else was involved on this occasion – and what they did. How I involved or worked with others on this occasion.	
7 Outcomes. The extent to which deadlines were met or the work completed. Feedback I received.	

8	What worked well on this occasion?	
9	What lessons did I learn from this occasion?	
10	What would I do differently on another occasion?	
11	How typical is this example for me (a daily occurrence/weekly/ occasionally/rarely)?	
12	Brief details of a recent (or second) example.	
13	Brief details of a third, preferably contrasting, example.	
14	How could this competence be applied to other situations?	
15	How do I measure my success for this competence?	

Pro-forma for mapping other competences

(18) Evidence of competence in: _____

1 The best example.	
2 Context: brief details of the circumstances.	
3 Level of responsibility on this occasion. The scale and scope of the issue.	
4 Personal contribution: what I did.	
5 Who else was involved on this occasion – and what they did. How I involved or worked with others.	
6 The outcomes of my actions or involvement.	
7 What worked well on this occasion?	

8	What lessons did I learn from this occasion?	
9	What would I do differently on another occasion?	
10	How typical is this example of my life or work experience?	
11	Brief details of a recent (or second) example.	
12	Brief details of a third, preferably contrasting, example.	
13	How could this competence be applied to other situations?	
14	How do I measure my success for this competence?	

(19) Health and safety

Date:

My general understanding of health and safety issues and legislation.

Examples of specific health and safety issues that I needed to be aware of in one place I have worked or studied.

Health and safety training I have received.

An incident that demonstrates my management of health and safety issues.

Copy and update

Appendix 1: Applications for success

All of the apps listed below were accurate as of April 2014 and, at the point of publication, were free to download. Some apps may require payment to access all of the features available.

Creating your life story

Sociidot (Apple; Android in development) – Sociidot allows you to create both a life vision for yourself and goals and steps within these. It can help you with this by suggesting steps and offering advice on how to reach your goals.

Setting and managing personal goals

Everest (Apple only) – Everest is an app that allows you to set a personal goal or challenge and break this down into manageable steps. It then allows you to track each step you take. You can share your goals with others, who can help to motivate you and reward your achievements.

Lift (Apple and Android) – Lift allows you to set goals and monitor progress. It will store information on how long you have spent on specific tasks or behaviours. This is useful if you are trying to develop habits such as reading for 20 minutes a day.

Productivity Wizard (Apple only) – this app allows you to set both long- and short-term goals. It also has journal and reflections facilities to allow you to record your thoughts and actions as you progress towards your goals.

Developing and maintaining good habits

Habit Streak (Android only) – Habit Streak is a simple app that allows you to monitor progress as you establish new habits. Progress is shown as a chain that lengthens with each day that you perform the new habit.

EasyHabits (Apple only) – a basic app which allows you to set and track habits you wish to develop.

Task and time-management

MyLifeOrganised 2 (Apple and Android) – this app helps you manage tasks across different aspects of your life, such as study, work and home. It helps you prioritise tasks and measure your progress towards completing these.

Wunderlist (Apple and Android) – helps you create, organise and manage 'To do' lists. The app synchs across your mobile devices and computer.

Toggl (Apple and Android) – the basic version of this app is free and allows you to time how long you spend on different activities. This can be very useful if you suspect you may be spending too long on activities such as social networking.

Rescue Time (Apple, Android and Windows) – the basic version of this app is free. It runs in the background of your phone or computer and produces a report on how you have used your time. If you subscribe to the full version it allows you to track time away from the computer, and can send you alerts if it thinks you are spending too long on an activity.

focus@will – this app selects background music, which, it suggests, can improve your ability to focus by up to 400%.

Motivational apps

Unstuck (Apple and Android) – as the name suggests, Unstuck helps you at moments when you feel blocked in addressing a task or issue. The app helps you 'diagnose' why you are stuck, and makes suggestions to help you move forwards.

Tiny Guru (Apple only) – if you are inspired by the words of others to find your own motivation, this app provides a good supply of quotes, thoughts and suggestions to give you a nudge.

Forismatic (Apple and Android) – this app provides a collection of inspirational quotes from others on a wide range of topics.

Creativity

Thoughtback (Apple and Android) – this app makes use of notes and ideas you input, to email you suggestions of where to go next and inspirational quotes to motivate you.

Mindix (Apple only) – a simple app for brainstorming ideas and creating pattern notes and maps from these.

Idea Growr (Android only) – this app allows you to capture thoughts and ideas. It then poses questions to you to help you develop these further.

Mindfulness and stress management

Stop, Breathe and Think (Apple only) – this app will teach you meditation and help you develop a more mindful approach to life.

Mindfulness Daily (Apple only) – build your mindfulness and meditation practice day by day with this app.

Mindfulness Bell (Apple and Android) – this app rings a 'mindfulness bell' at several points during the day. The sound of the bell is a prompt for you to stop, and focus in on what you are doing at that point.

Record keeping

Microsoft OneNote (Apple, Android and Windows) – this app allows you to gather together thoughts, notes, documents, photographs and other media in a single place.

Evernote (Apple and Android) – create notebooks in which you can store and search all your ideas, photos, documents. Your notebooks can be accessed across all your computers and mobile devices.

Job applications and interviews

Career Builder (Apple and Android) – this app allows you to search for jobs and upload your CV on the go. You can tailor it to receive job notifications from specific types of employers or in specific locations.

Indeed (Apple and Android) – this app allows you to search for jobs, upload your CV and apply for jobs directly from your mobile device.

LinkedIn (Apple, Android and Windows) – LinkedIn acts as an employment-related social network. In addition to getting information about jobs and uploading your own details you can join discussion groups and track the activities of companies or individuals you are interested in working with.

Interview Prep Questions (Apple and Android) – this app generates practice questions for a wide range of possible job interviews. You can create sets of 'flash cards' relevant to your specific area.

Appendix 2: Useful websites

Assessment centres

www.prospects.ac.uk/interview_tips_assessment_centres.htm	General advice on exercises and how to prepare
http://targetjobs.co.uk/careers-advice/assessment-centres	General advice
www.assessmentday.co.uk/index.htm	Practice tests
www.shldirect.com/en/practice-tests	Practice tests

Career guidance

www.prospects.ac.uk	Advice and jobs for graduates
www.targetjobs.co.uk	Advice and jobs for graduates
www.gradunet.com	Advice and jobs for graduates
www.agcas.org.uk	Advice and information for graduates
www.hobsons.com	Guidance and jobs for school-leavers, young people and graduates
www.insidecareers.co.uk	Advice and jobs for graduates

Employment: companies

www.greatplacetowork.co.uk	Information about, and ratings of, named companies in the UK and worldwide
www.ratemyplacement.co.uk	Search for work placements and jobs, based on the reviews and recommendations of other students
www.vault.com	What it is like to work for named companies
www.companieshouse.gov.uk	Lists details of all UK public companies
https://uk.linkedin.com	Information about companies, job opportunities and professional networking
www.bloomberg.com	International and entrepreneur site
www.bestcompaniesguide.co.uk	Employee feedback site for named companies

Employment: job hunting

www.giveagradago.com	Graduate recruitment site with a focus on established businesses, Small and Medium Enterprises, and Start-ups
www.graduate-jobs.com	Graduate recruitment site

www.milkround.com	Graduate recruitment site
http://jobs.theguardian.com/jobs/graduate	Graduate section of a wider recruitment site
www.careerplayer.com	Graduate recruitment site
www.gradvert.com	Graduate recruitment site
www.grb.uk.com	Graduate recruitment site

Employment rights

www.equalityhumanrights.com	Equality and Human Rights Commission
www.adviceguide.org.uk	Citizens Advice Bureau
www.acas.org.uk	ACAS – advice on employment law
www.hse.gov.uk	Health and Safety Executive
www.i-resign.com/uk/home	Advice on leaving your job

Starting your own business / Working for a start-up

www.nacue.com	National Association of College and University Entrepreneurs – support for student entrepreneurs, including access to events such as Start-Up Career Launchpad
www.workinstartups.com	Job adverts and information for those seeking work in start-up companies
www.startupdonut.co.uk	Advice on setting up your own business
www.ipo.gov.uk	Information about intellectual property rights and patents

References

Atkins, S. and Murphy, K. (1994) 'Reflective Practice', *Nursing Standard*, **8** (39), pp. 49–54.

Bachelor, L. (2012) 'Graduate careers: the importance of employability skills', *The Guardian*, 8 June 2012, at: www.theguardian.com/money/2012/jun/08/graduate-careers-employability-skills (accessed 21/4/14).

Barber, M., Donnelly, K. and Rizvi, S. (2013) *An Avalanche is Coming: Higher Education and the Revolution Ahead* (London: Institute for Public Policy Research).

Beaver, D. (1998) *NLP for Lazy Learning* (Shaftesbury, Dorset, and Boston, MA: Element).

Belbin, M. R. (1996) *Management Teams: Why they Succeed or Fail* (London: Butterworth-Heinemann).

Belbin, M. R. (2010) *Team Roles at Work*, 2nd edn (London: Butterworth-Heinemann).

BIS (Department for Business Innovation and Skills) (2014) *Graduate Recruitment to SMEs – Final Report*, at: www.gov.uk/government/uploads/system/uploads/attachment_data/file/68936/bis-13-546-graduate-recruitment-to-smes.pdf (accessed 20/4/14).

Bridgstock, R. (2009) 'The graduate attributes we've overlooked: enhancing graduate employability through career management skills', *Higher Education Research & Development*, **28** (1), 31–44.

Bright, J. and Earl, J. (2007) *Brilliant CV: What Employers Want to See and How to Say It*, 3rd edn (London: Prentice Hall).

Butterworth, G. (1992) 'Context and Cognition in Models of Cognitive Growth', in P. Light and G. Butterworth (eds), *Context and Cognition* (London: Harvester).

CBI and Universities UK (March 2009) *Future Fit: Preparing Graduates for the World of Work* (London: CBI), at: www.cbi.org.uk/pdf/20090326-CBI-FutureFit-Preparing-graduates-for-the-world-of-work.pdf.

Chapman, A. (2001) *The Monster Guide to Jobhunting* (London: Financial Times/Prentice Hall).

Chase, W. G. and Simon, H. A. (1973) 'Perception in Chess', *Cognitive Science*, 13, 145–82.

Cottrell, S. M. (2010) *Skills for Success: The Personal Development Planning Handbook*, 2nd edn (Basingstoke: Palgrave Macmillan).

Cottrell, S. M. (2011) *Critical Thinking Skills: Developing Effective Analysis and Argument* (Basingstoke: Palgrave Macmillan).

Cottrell, S. M. (2012) *The Exam Skills Handbook: Achieving Peak Performance*, 2nd edn (Basingstoke: Palgrave Macmillan).

Cottrell, S. M. (2013) *The Study Skills Handbook*, 4th edn (Basingstoke: Palgrave Macmillan).

Cottrell, S. M. (2014) *Dissertations and Project Reports: A Step by Step Guide* (Basingstoke: Palgrave Macmillan).

Covey, S. R. (2004) *The Seven Habits of Highly Effective People: Powerful Lessons in Personal Change*, 15th Anniversary edn (London: Free Press).

Dacre Pool, L. and Sewell, P. (2007) 'The Key to Employability: Developing a Practical Model of Graduate Employability', *Education and Training*, **49** (4), 277–89.

De Bono, E. (1996) *Teach Yourself to Think* (London: Penguin Books).

De Bono, E. (2006) *De Bono's Thinking Course,* revised and updated (London: BBC Active).

Dilts, R., Hallbom, T. and Smith, S. (1990) *Beliefs: Pathways to Health and Well-being* (Portland, OR: Metamorphous Press).

Docherty, D. and Fernandez, R. (2014) *Career Portfolios and the Labour Market for Graduates and Postgraduates in the UK,* National Centre for Universities and Business, at: www.ncub.co.uk/reports/career-portfolios.html (accessed 19/4/14).

Donaldson, M. (1978) *Children's Minds* (London: Fontana).

Dryden, W. and Gordon, J. (1993) *Peak Performance: Become More Effective at Work* (Didcot, Oxon: Mercury Business Books).

Dunn, R., Griggs, S., Olson, J., Beasley, M. and Gorman, B. (1995) 'A Meta-analytic Validation of the Dunn and Dunn Model of Learning Style Preferences', *Journal of Educational Research,* **88** (6), 353–62.

Egan, D. and Schwartz, B. (1979) 'Chunking in Recall of Symbolic Drawings', *Memory and Cognition,* 7, 149–58.

Ellis, A. (1994) *Reason and Emotion in Psychotherapy,* revised and updated (New York: Birch Lane Press).

Fanthome, C. (2004) *Work Placements – A Survival Guide for Students* (Basingstoke: Palgrave Macmillan).

Goleman, D. (1995) *Emotional Intelligence* (London: Sage Publications).

Greenfield, S. (2001) *The Human Brain: A Guided Tour* (London: Phoenix).

The Guardian (2013) *The Guardian UK 300. The UK's most popular graduate recruiters 2013/14* (Wallingford: GTI media).

Hallows, J. (1997) *Information Systems Project Management* (New York: Amacom).

Heerkens, G. R. (2002) *Project Management* (New York: McGraw-Hill).

Heinz (2014) at: www.heinzcareers.co.uk/graduates-and-mba/what-we-look-for.

High Fliers Research Ltd (2014) *The Graduate Market in 2014 – An Annual Review of Graduate Vacancies and Starting Salaries at Britain's Leading Employers,* at: www.highfliers.co.uk/download/GMReport14.pdf (accessed 20/4/14).

Honey, P. and Mumford, A. (1992) *The Manual of Learning Styles Questionnaire* (Maidenhead, Berks: Peter Honey Publications).

Lazarus, R. S. (1999) *Stress and Emotion* (London: Free Association Books).

Lowden, K., Hall, S., Elliot, D. and Lewin, J. (2011) *Employers' Perceptions of the Employability Skills of New Graduates* (SCRE Centre, University of Glasgow, for the Edge Foundation), at: www.edge.co.uk/media/63412/employability_skills_as_pdf_-_final_online_version.pdf (accessed 20/4/14).

McGill, I. and Beaty, L. (2001) *Action Learning Sets: A Practitioner's Guide,* 2nd revised edn (London: Routledge).

Miller, R. (2014) *What Makes a Great Small Business Employee?* at: www.startupdonut.co.uk/startup/employees/hiring-employees/what-makes-a-great-small-business-employee (accessed 20/4/14).

Neenan, M. and Dryden, W. (2002) *Life Coaching: A Cognitive-Behavioural Approach* (New York: Brunner-Routledge).

Nolan, V. (ed.) (2000) *Creative Education: Educating a Nation of Innovators. Papers by Members of the Synectics Education Initiative* (Stoke Mandeville, Bucks: Synectics Education Initiative).

Palmer, S. and Dryden, W. (1995) *Counselling for Stress Problems* (London: Sage).

Pennington, M., Moseley, E. and Sinclair, R. (2013) *AGCAS/AGR Graduate Success Project: An Investigation of Graduate Transitions, Social Mobility and the HEAR,* at: www.agcas.org.uk (accessed 19/4/14).

Perry, W. G. (1970) *Forms of Intellectual and Ethical Development in the College Years: A Scheme* (New York: Holt, Rinehart & Winston).